3703887106

D1766190

...shire GL...
Telephone: 01242 71460...

GLOU
...at Cheltenham ...

3 DAY LO
FINES FOR LATE ...

Language in Late Modernity

The study of teenagers in the classroom, and how they interact with one another and their teachers, can tell us a great deal about late modern (contemporary) society. In this revealing account, Ben Rampton presents the extensive sociolinguistic research he carried out in an inner-city high school. Through his vivid analysis of classroom talk, he offers answers to some important contemporary questions: does social class still count for young people, or is it in demise? Are traditional authority relationships in schools being undermined? How is this affected by popular media culture? His study, which provides numerous transcripts and three extensive case studies, introduces new ways of perceiving established ideas in sociolinguistics, such as identity, insecurity, the orderliness of classroom talk, and the experience of learning at school. In doing so, Rampton shows how work in sociolinguistics can contribute to some major current debates in sociology, anthropology, cultural studies and education.

BEN RAMPTON is Professor of Applied and Sociolinguistics at King's College London. His previous publications include *Crossing: Language and Ethnicity among Adolescents* (2005), and he is a co-author of *Researching Language: Issues of Power and Method* (1992).

Studies in Interactional Sociolinguistics

EDITORS
Paul Drew, Marjorie Harness Goodwin, John J. Gumperz, Deborah Schiffrin

Language in Late Modernity

Interaction in an Urban School

BEN RAMPTON

King's College London

FRANCIS CLOSE HALL
LEARNING CENTRE
UNIVERSITY OF GLOUCESTERSHIRE
Swindon Road, Cheltenham, GL50 4AZ
Tel: (01242) 532913

CAMBRIDGE
UNIVERSITY PRESS

CAMBRIDGE UNIVERSITY PRESS
Cambridge, New York, Melbourne, Madrid, Cape Town, Singapore, São Paulo

CAMBRIDGE UNIVERSITY PRESS
The Edinburgh Building, Cambridge CB2 2RU, UK

Published in the United States of America by Cambridge University Press, New York

www.cambridge.org
Information on this title: www.cambridge.org/9780521812634

© Ben Rampton 2006

This book is in copyright. Subject to statutory exception
and to the provisions of relevant collective licensing agreements,
no reproduction of any part may take place without
the written permission of Cambridge University Press.

First published 2006

Printed in the United Kingdom at the University Press, Cambridge

A catalogue record for this book is available from the British Library

ISBN-13 978-0-521-81263-4 hardback
ISBN-10 0-521-81263-1 hardback

Cambridge University Press has no responsibility for the persistence or accuracy of
URLs for external or third-party internet websites referred to in this book, and does
not guarantee that any content on such websites is, or will remain, accurate or
appropriate.

For
Amelia
Robert and Silvia

Contents

9.6 The dynamics of classed speech   360
9.7 Interaction, subjectivity and social class:
      sociolinguistics and cultural studies   369
9.8 Language and class in late modernity   377

Part V *Methodological reflections*   383

10 Reflections on generalisation, theory and knowledge
     construction   385
     10.1 Case studies, contextualisation and relevance   386
     10.2 Underpinnings   389
           10.2.1 Ontological assumptions about social
                    reality   389
           10.2.2 Ethnographic and linguistic
                    epistemologies   391
           10.2.3 Tools and procedures for data analysis   395
     10.3 Knowledge production   398
           10.3.1 Descriptive generalisations about
                    particular types of practice   398
           10.3.2 Modelling structural systems   399
           10.3.3 Ecological descriptions   401
           10.3.4 General interpretations sanctioned by a
                    theoretical literature   403
           10.3.5 Claiming cross-disciplinary relevance   407

     References   410
     Index of names   435
     Subject index   440

Tables

Figures

Acknowledgements

First, I would like to thank the students and teachers who acted as the informants in this research. This book can only report on a very small part of their lives during the period I was doing my fieldwork, but I hope that the emerging portrait makes some sense. Second, I would like to record my debt to the funding bodies who made this research possible: the Economic and Social Research Council, which supported the fieldwork and the first round of data-analysis in 1997–99 (Project R 000 23 6602); the Spencer Foundation, which awarded a small grant for secondary analysis of popular media cultural influences in the dataset (2001–02); the Leverhulme Trust, for a Research Fellowship to write the research up in a book (2003–04); and the Belgian Science Foundation – Flanders (FWO), for funding the Research Group on Language, Power and Identity, in which a lot of the central elements in my thinking took shape. Third, I would like to thank a number of scholars and colleagues for their support and interest. The work reported in this book has been discussed with a lot of people over the last eight years or so, and it would be very cumbersome to itemise the different kinds of stimulation and benefit that I have drawn from these interactions. But that doesn't diminish my debts to Janis Androutsopoulos, Peter Auer, Allan Bell, Mary Bucholtz, Simon Coffey, Nik Coupland, Zoltan Dörnyei, Caroline Dover, Sandro Duranti, Julia Eksner, Kirsten Ellenbogen, Sue Gal, Alexandra Georgakopoulou, Annie Gillett, Candy Goodwin, John Gumperz, Monica Heller, Jane Hill, Dell Hymes, Jens Normann Jørgensen, Lanita Jacobs-Huey, Jeff Joseph, Helga Kotthoff, Claire Kramsch, Lars Anders Kulbrandstad, Don Kulick, James Lantolf, Adam Lefstein, Constant Leung, Theo van Leeuwen, Helen Lucey, Janet Maybin, Richard Nettell,

Diane Reay, Celia Roberts, Alissa Shethar, Michael Silverstein, Stef Slembrouck, Brian Street, Steve Thorne, Jef Verschueren, Kit Woolard, Ming-Bao Yue, Jane Zuengler. Needless to say, the misapprehensions are mine. Fourth, and with the same caveat, I am especially indebted to Jan Blommaert, Jim Collins and Roxy Harris, not just for careful critical discussion of a lot of specific issues, but also for crucial guidance as to what the book was actually about. Last, my appreciation of Amelia, Robert and Silvia's contribution lies beyond description.

Transcription conventions

Segmental phonetics

[ ] IPA phonetic transcription (revised to 1979)

The sounds of the phonetic symbols used in transcription can be roughly glossed as follows:

Vowels

[ɪ] as in 'kit' [kɪt]
[i] as in 'fleece' (but shorter) [fliːs]
[e] as in 'dress' [dɹes]
[ɛ] as in French 'père'
[æ] as in 'trap' [tɹæp]
[a] as in French 'patte' [pat]
[ɑ] as in 'start' (but shorter) [stɑːt]
[ʌ] as in 'strut' [stɹʌt]
[ɒ] as in 'lot' [lɒt]
[ɔ] as in 'north' (but shorter) [nɔːθ]
[o] as in French 'eau'
[ʊ] as in 'foot' [fʊt]
[u] as in 'goose' (but shorter) [guːs]
[ə] as in '*a*bout', 'upp*er*' [əbaʊt]
[ɜ] as in 'nurse' (but shorter) [nɜːs]
[eɪ] as in 'face' [feɪs]
[aɪ] as in 'price' [pɹaɪs]
[ɔɪ] as in 'choice' [tʃɔɪs]
[ɪə] as in 'near' [nɪə]
[ɛə] as in 'square' [skwɛə]

Transcription conventions

[ʊə]   as in 'cure' [kjʊə]
[əʊ]   as in 'goat' [gəʊt]
[aʊ]   as in 'mouth' [maʊθ]
[˜]   nasalisation of a vowel

Consonants

[p]   as in 'pea' [pi:]
[b]   as in 'bee' [bi:]
[t]   as in 'toe' [təʊ]
[d]   as in 'doe' [dəʊ]
[ɖ]   like [d], but with the tip of the tongue retroflexed
[k]   as in 'cap' [kæp]
[g]   as in 'gap' [gæp]
[x]   as in Scottish 'loch' [lɒx]
[f]   as in 'fat' [fæt]
[v]   as in 'vat' [væt]
[θ]   as in 'thing' [θɪŋ]
[ð]   as in 'this' [ðɪs]
[s]   as in 'sip' [sɪp]
[z]   as in 'zip' [zɪp]
[ʃ]   as in 'ship' [ʃɪp]
[ʒ]   as in 'measure' [meʒə]
[h]   as in 'hat' [hæt]
[ʔ]   glottal stop, as in Cockney 'butter' [bʌʔə]
[m]   as in 'map' [mæp]
[n]   as in 'nap' [næp]
[ɳ]   like [n], but with the tip of the tongue retroflexed
[ŋ]   as in 'hang' [hæŋ]
[l]   as in 'led' [led]
[ɭ]   like [l], but with the tip of the tongue retroflexed
[ɫ]   as in 'table' [teɪbɫ]
[ɹ]   as in 'red' [ɹed]
[ɾ]   like [ɹ], but with the tongue tip tapping once against the teeth ridge (sometimes used in English 'very')
[ʁ]   'r' pronounced with a German accent
[j]   as in 'yet' [jet]
[w]   as in 'wet' [wet]

[tʃ]   as in 'chin' [tʃɪn]
[dʒ]   as in 'gin' [dʒɪn]

Prosody

\   low fall
/   low rise
ˋ   high fall
ˊ   high rise
˅   fall rise
ˆ   rise fall
ˈ   high stress
ˈˈ   very high stress
ˌ   low stress
ˌˌ   very low stress

Conversational features

(.)	pause of less than a second
(1.5)	approximate length of pause in seconds
[	overlapping turns
/	place in the current turn where the next speaker begins to overlap
CAPITALS	loud
> text <	more rapid speech
( )	speech inaudible
(text)	speech hard to discern, analyst's guess
((text:))	'stage directions'
bold	words and utterances of particular interest to the analysis
<u>text</u>	words and utterances subsequently repeated by someone else in an utterance (in **bold**) that is of particular analytic interest

PART I

Introduction

1

Late modern language, interaction and schooling

Outside education, research on classrooms is often seen as rather dull:

it takes a tremendous effort of will and imagination to stop seeing only the things that are conventionally 'there' to be seen … [I]t is like pulling teeth to get [researchers] to see or write anything beyond what 'everyone' knows. (Becker 1971:10, cited in Delamont and Atkinson 1995:1)

Delamont and Atkinson go further:

Becker's diagnosis is still a valid one in 1994 … [T]his is because the researchers have failed to read widely enough, have consequently lacked vision and imagination, and have thus failed to make any substantial contribution to sociology. (1995:1–2)

These are controversial claims, and this book does not offer an assessment of whether they are fair or not. But it does argue that if you get students to wear radio-microphones, if you adopt the methods of ethnographic and interactional sociolinguistics and readjust some of the working assumptions of descriptive analysis (accepting, *contra* Delamont and Atkinson, that part of the 'blame' lies with the feeder disciplines), then classroom proceedings take on a very different character. Instead of recapitulating what everyone outside thinks they know, you move closer to what a lot of teachers and students actually experience, and classrooms emerge as sites where day-in-day-out, participants struggle to reconcile themselves to each other, to their futures, to political edicts and to the movements of history, where vernacular aesthetics often provide as much of the momentum as the transmission of knowledge, where the curriculum cohabits with popular music and media culture, where students make hay with the most unrewarding subjects, and where

participants wrestle with the meaning of class stratification, their
efforts inflected with social ambivalence (and sexual desire). Or at
least these are the issues in the classroom studies that comprise most
of this book.

Intimating both the rather grandiose and the fairly local, the book's
title, *Language in Late Modernity: Interaction in an Urban School*, is
intended to reflect the scope of these headline claims, and it contains
four key elements – late modernity, urban schooling, language and
interaction. This introduction explains my approach to these terms
and my understanding of the connections between them. I begin with a
macroscopic account of late modernity and urban schooling
(Chapter 1.1), and then move to an overview of the emergence of
'post-structuralism' as a general perspective in the humanities and
social sciences (Chapter 1.2). After that, I introduce my main methodological affiliation, interactional sociolinguistics, and point to its
relevance to late modern thinking and experience (Chapter 1.3).
Chapter 1.4 provides a sketch of the book's substantive content, also
pointing to some of the central sociolinguistic concepts, and the chapter closes with an account emphasising the crucial role that radio-
microphones have played in my data-collection (Chapter 1.5).

1.1   Late modernity and urban schooling[1]

It is very difficult putting precise dates on the emergence of 'late' – or
'high' or 'post' – modernity, and this is made harder by the fact that
late modernity can be associated both with the major changes in
the real world linked to globalisation, and with a slow, uneven
but nevertheless very consequential reworking of basic assumptions
in the humanities and social sciences, often characterised as post-
structuralism. Nevertheless, both kinds of shift – real-world and
philosophical – are important in this book, and to first get an idea
of the radical changes in schooling that form a backdrop to much of
the data that I shall analyse, it is worth looking back at education in
the period leading up to the mid to late 1980s, before 'globalisation'
gained widespread currency as a term in everyday and academic
discourse.

As an illustration of the discourses and political arrangements
that up until then had been central to education policy in England,
it is useful to briefly consider the 'Swann Report', the last major

government report on one of the defining characteristics of the urban educational landscape in Britain, linguistic and ethnic diversity. When *Education for All: The Report of the Committee of Inquiry into the Education of Children from Ethnic Minority Groups* was published in 1985, power in educational policy making was distributed very differently from how it is today. Central government had no direct powers over the curriculum, and curriculum decision-making lay in the hands of teachers and individual schools, who were usually provided with guidance by their local education authorities (LEAs) (DES 1985:221, 334). For the most part, control over education spending was delegated from central government to LEAs,[2] and LEA services came under the auspices of local government. Accountability to the local electorate made education policy development a matter of local persuasion and dispute, and one of the Swann Report's central objectives was to generate a view of ethnic pluralism with which central and local government, teaching unions, minority communities, other interested parties and the general public could all concur.

What kind of view was this? Swann offered a vision of nested communities within the framework of the nation-state: Britain as a community of communities, engaged in the process of reconciling itself to the legacy of its imperial past. For the most part, the Report conceptualised its ethnic minorities as well-known, well-defined, settled, and stable, and it made light of any connections that they might seek to maintain with other parts of the world. It focused primarily on people of Caribbean and South Asian descent (DES 1985:649); it dismissed a European Directive on the teaching of minority languages on the grounds that these groups were British and here-to-stay; it described their thoughts of living in other countries as the "*myth* of an alternative" and the "*myth* of return" (DES 1985:20–21); and it was in local social services rather than in world markets that minority language proficiency was envisaged as being useful (DES 1985:409–410). Similarly, the Report's discussion of the mass media, TV and press looked no further than the British nation-state (DES 1985: 16ff. and 38–44).

The educational strategy that the Committee proposed consisted of three basic elements. First, any linguistic and cultural disadvantage that minorities were suffering should be overcome, e.g. through the teaching of English as a second language (ESL). Second, *all*

children, minority *and* majority, should be encouraged to respect the
richness of minority cultures. Third, there should be no ethnic
segregation within the public schooling system: ESL teaching should
take place in the mainstream, instruction in minority languages
should be open to all, bilingual support staff should help everyone
(DES 1985: Chapter 7). The role of state schools was to eliminate
segregation and disadvantage, and to ensure that everyone shared in
whatever benefits minority students brought with them. Rather than
cultivating any specialised cultural or linguistic resources that ethnic
minorities might have, the Swann Report sought in effect to *nation-
alise* them ("Education for *All*").

The Swann Report, then, serves as a useful example of discourses
and institutional arrangements in education prior to the period that
I am calling 'late modernity'. But since 1985, the landscape that it
was embedded in has been radically transformed by globalisation
and neo-liberal market capitalism. For Swann, the nation-state was
the supreme political entity, but since then, a major growth in the
flow of people, finance, technologies and communications media
that criss-cross national borders have made it increasingly hard for
the nation-state to exercise effective authority within its traditional
territory (Appadurai 1990; Abercrombie and Warde et al. 2000:15).
Instead, it comes under increasing pressure to act as a hopeful host to
transnational business, seeking to attract inward investment by
offering a secure and stable environment, an abundance of skilled
low-wage labour, and limited state regulation (Bauman 1998).

There have also been major changes in the nature of migrant
labour. Particularly in the 1950s, 60s and 70s, Britain encouraged
the inward flow and settlement of new peoples who were needed to
work in the manufacturing, transport and health sectors where the
recruitment of indigenous labour was proving difficult (Rose et al.
1969), and this led to the emergence of the relatively stable, vocal,
working-class ethnic communities that Swann was primarily concerned with.[3] More recently in the 1990s, however, massive political
upheavals, including the collapse of the Soviet Union and the
'Eastern Bloc', have produced a dramatic growth of unofficial immigration, both in Britain and across Europe and Asia (Papastergiadis
2000:48). In the UK, there has been a very large increase in people
seeking asylum,[4] and there are also very substantial numbers without work and residence permits: "in practice, such people either

exist in limbo, outside state benefits and employment, or else are eventually granted some status due to the passage of time" (Fiddick 1999:13).[5] At the same time, global capitalism has altered the conditions for more established minority ethnic groups. For people who migrated during the 1950s, 60s and 70s, jobs in the UK might have been low paid, but initially anyway, they were reasonably secure, and the prohibitive costs of international travel encouraged them to build a congenial milieu in their local vicinities. In recent years, however, global market capitalism has changed this, so that "after transferring location, people are able to maintain instantaneous links with their point of origin through media and communications systems, strengthening the capacity of migrants to manage their own diasporic identities while resisting full assimilation into the new nation" (Marginson 1999:2).

In Swann's conception, 'minority' status was historically linked, either in actuality or in public perception, to forms of disadvantage that could be best remedied by their full participation in the nation-state. But as Cohen notes of members of diaspora in an age of global flows, "their language skills, familiarity with other cultures and contacts in other countries make many [of them] highly competitive in the international labour, service and capital markets" (1997:16–19), and he goes on to note that "[w]hat nineteenth-century nationalists wanted was a 'space' for each 'race', a territorialising of each social identity. What they have got instead is a chain of cosmopolitan cities and an increasing proliferation of subnational and transnational identities that cannot easily be contained in the nation-state system" (1997:175).

These cosmopolitan or 'global' cities serve as centres of finance, transport and communications, and as such, they are inhabited by populations that are both highly diverse and highly stratified. In London, ethnic diversity is particularly pronounced,[6] and wealth and income differentials are also sharper than anywhere else in the UK (Abercrombie, Warde et al. 2000:126). On the one hand, it is a home for cosmopolitan elites, professionals and business people, while on the other, there are large numbers of people working in low-skilled, low paid jobs, often in a substantial hidden economy (see also Hannerz 1996:129–131; Cohen 1997:167–169).

World cities of this kind are not merely 'nodes in networks' however. They are also places in themselves, settings for the juxtaposition and mixing of different cultural traditions in a range of different and distinctive combinations. Ethnic and cultural difference are highly salient, and subculturally specific resources – food, dress, music, speech – can be aestheticised and/or commodified, used in artistic production or sold commercially to a wide range of different consumers and not just to tourists and the transnational elite. As a point where a plurality of different transnational and diaspora flows intersect, this is an environment that generates high levels of local meta-cultural learning and awareness (cf. Hannerz 1996:135–137; Portes 1997), and although there will be different combinations and processes in different locations, this produces a post-colonial experience "defined, not by essence or purity, but by the recognition of a necessary heterogeneity and diversity; by a conception of 'identity' which lives with and through, not despite, difference; by *hybridity*" (Hall 1990:235–236).[7]

I shall point to the links between these developments and my own analyses at the end of this section, amplifying them in the chapters that follow, but before then, it is necessary to describe the transformation of schooling since 1985. In the 1988 Education Reform Act (ERA) three years after the publication of Swann, the Conservative Government embarked on a major programme of educational reform, bringing in a policy that introduced neo-liberal market economics to the structures of provision, combined with cultural authoritarianism in the curriculum.

One of the cornerstones of the new policy was the 'Local Management of Schools' (LMS), and it paved the way for a major shift of power away from LEAs to individual schools.[8] This was part of a move to introduce market principles to the education system, and rather than being able to call on LEAs to provide specialist support services free-of-charge, schools had to plan for special needs in their own budgets and to pay the LEA to provide them with specialist teachers. But at the same time as seeking to create a competitive 'internal market' among schools and LEAs within state education, government also centralised responsibility for the design and specification of the curriculum for 5 to 16 year olds. Individual teachers and schools were no longer the principal curriculum decision-makers, and the processes of persuasion and debate that the Swann Report had been tuned to were replaced by legislative coercion. A series of national working parties were set up for the 'core' curriculum areas of English, Maths and Science, as well as for a range of other subjects, and by the mid 1990s, a legally binding National Curriculum for 80% or more of the school day had been established, together with a system of national tests for 7, 11 and 14 year olds. These tests meant that the performance of children at different schools could be compared, and their publication in league tables was initiated and justified on the grounds that this was essential 'consumer information' for another new element in education policy, 'parental choice'. Prior to the 1988 ERA, children in the public education system had been allocated to a particular school by their LEA, but parental choice now gave parents the right to choose which school their child went to, with state funding following the child. In this way, a complex combination of marketisation and central control was developed. In order to survive, schools needed to attract parents, and they could vary their spending priorities in order to increase their competitiveness. But at the same time, central government dictated curriculum input and standardised the measurement of output (see Henry et al. 1999:89; Bernstein 1999:252).

These processes had an inevitable effect on schools' attitudes to social, ethnic and linguistic diversity among pupils. The league tables on school performance published raw data, and made no allowance for major differences between schools in their student intake. In this context, pupils from homes where English speaking was limited were increasingly seen as a threat to a school's public performance profile, depressing its published test scores, undermining its appeal to parents, and ultimately endangering its funding base. Whereas the Swann Report had called for inclusiveness, with the new market principles it was no longer in a school's interest to welcome refugee children and other newcomers to England.

These structural changes undermined the position articulated by Swann and they were accompanied by a number of major changes in the terms of debate. One of the factors widely judged to have helped the Conservatives win the 1987 general election was the so-called 'loony London effect', a perception that the Labour Party was dominated by London-based radicals who were committed to a dogmatic multi-culturalism and who were antipathetic to the traditional values of Englishness. In other words, (what others later came to call) the 'global city' was deemed a political liability, and in its place, the hearts and minds of 'Middle England' became the main target of competition between the major political parties. At the same time, as the replacement of the phrase 'middle class' with 'Middle England' itself reflects, social class also became less and less of a reference point in public discourse.

This decline in the usability and salience of traditional notions of social class was partly the product of the economic restructuring attendant on globalisation.[9] But the retreat from class in public discourse also fitted with the ascendance of two newer ideologies. On the one hand, the traditional association of class with collective solidarity, worker identities and the critique of capitalism was ill-suited to the new emphasis on individualism, consumer culture, and the market. On the other, notions of long-standing class conflict and division were at odds with an increasingly influential strand of opinion which emphasised (high) national culture as a central unifying element in the new national curriculum (e.g. Tate 1996). In practical terms, this meant that when particular groups continued to underachieve at school, the blame was shifted away from political economy – in which everyone was implicated, including the government – to culture, which laid responsibility with the underachievers themselves. In this way, the relatively poor performance of working-class boys became a problem of masculinity, while the disaffection of working-class boys of Caribbean descent was put down to ethnicity. Whereas the Swann Report made an effort to address the ways in which school achievement was influenced by both class and ethnicity together (DES 1985:71–76), Gillborn and Gipps' review of research noted in 1996 that "data on social class is often absent from research ... [and] it is exceptional to find studies of achievement by ethnic minority pupils that give full attention to *both* these factors" (1996:16; Gillborn 1997:377–380; Gillborn and Mirza 2000).

In 1997, the Conservative Government finally lost power after seventeen years in which free-market economics had been extended progressively further into the public sector. They were replaced by a 'New Labour' party that came to office determined to tackle social exclusion and to eradicate the "long 'tail' of underachievement in Britain, and [the] relatively poor performance from lower ability students" (Barber 1997:10). For the most part, however, this was not a return to class analysis,[10] and free-market philosophies continued to dominate education policy. The state school system, it was said, had much to learn from private schools,[11] the 'discipline of the market' still played a major part in the relationship between LEAs, schools and parents, and indeed schools and LEAs deemed 'failing' were privatised and taken over by educational and other management companies.

The technological dimensions of globalisation were given some recognition by the New Labour government, but at the same time, a National Literacy Strategy (NLS) was instituted first in primary and then in secondary schools, and in many ways this seemed to intensify their predecessors' rejection of the cultural dynamics of globalisation. The new digital communications systems embrace a plurality of expressive forms, values, interests and imaginings, and many commentators – including the Prime Minister (Blair 1999) – have suggested that this new power presents a considerable challenge to the traditional authority of parents and teachers (see e.g. Castells 1996:374–375; Sefton-Green 1998b:12; Holmes and Russell 1999). The NLS looked designed to reassert the kinds of authority that now felt threatened. The centre piece of the NLS was the 'Literacy Hour' – an hour a day that all primary schools in England were pressured to dedicate to reading and writing (DfEE 1998) – and this not only dictated what to teach but also how, prescribing a minute-by-minute programme in which whole class teaching – with pupils' eyes and ears tuned to the teacher – formed the main part (two thirds). In terms of content, the Literacy Hour assumed native English speaker knowledge of spoken language and cultural meaning. Pupils' attention was focused on the basics of print literacy and standard English grammar, and the multi-modality of integrated communications systems, consumer culture and the heteroglossia and multilingualism of the global city were overwhelmingly ignored.

Given the fact that face-to-face interaction is my principal point of entry into empirical analysis, this overview of 'late modernity and urban schooling' encompasses much more than I can actually cover in any detail in this book. Nevertheless,

a) it provides an essential background for understanding the field-site where I collected my data in 1997–98 – an inner London school experiencing high levels of mobility among its students, struggling with a national curriculum in the 'education market', more closely tuned in many ways to the discourse of Swann;

b) it includes a number of claims with widespread contemporary currency that I try to interrogate by taking a close look at everyday interaction in urban classrooms: Just how realistic are policy efforts to re-establish traditional authority relations in class (Chapter 2)? Just how far is young people's attraction to popular media culture at odds with education (Chapter 3)? And to what extent can anyone really claim that at school, social class no longer matters (Part III)?

In part, then, 'late modernity' stands for a number of very substantial material and ideological shifts which provide both topics and a context for the analyses that follow. But late modernity is also often associated with quite a profound reorientation in the philosophical assumptions guiding academic enquiry in the humanities and social sciences, and I would now like to describe the way this impacts on the assumptions I draw on in the investigation of contemporary classroom processes.

1.2   Late modernity in social and linguistic theory

In a 1992 paper entitled "A sociological theory of postmodernity", Zygmunt Bauman summarises a number of major differences between classical sociology and the late modern perspectives that became increasingly influential towards the end of the twentieth century, and Table 1.1 contains a summary of (my understanding of) Bauman's account of the main points of disagreement. For example, whereas modernist sociology saw 'society' and other collective entities as unified and integrated totalities, from a post-modern viewpoint this idea seems rather uncomfortably based on an idealisation of the nation state, and instead, "the reality to be modelled is ... much more fluid, heterogeneous and under-patterned than anything sociologists have tried to grasp intellectually in the past" (1992:65). In terms of human behaviour and development, classical ideas about our actions gaining significance from their function in the social system are challenged by the view that what we do plays a major role in shaping the habitats we live in, and it is argued that rather than simply being socialised into the norms of a social group whose monitoring subsequently keeps us morally in line, we 'assemble' ourselves from a plethora of changing options, deciding what is right and wrong for ourselves.

Table 1.1: Zygmunt Bauman on modernist ideas and assumptions
(plain font), *set against post-modern alternatives (in italics)*

1. Modernity (M): Priority is given to universality, homogeneity, monotony and clarity, and there is a belief in planned social progress [p. 188].
   Post-modernity (Pm): Plurality, variety, contingency and ambivalence aren't just deviant – they're fundamental to our social condition [p. 187].

2. M: 'Society' (and other collective entities) is a unified, integrated totality ('system', 'organism') [189].
   Pm: Our social condition is kaleidoscopic, and is the outcome of lots of very varied and momentary interactions. There are only 'randomly emerging, shifting and evanescent islands of order'[189].

3. M: People and actions gain their significance from the part they play (their function) in these totalities.
   Pm: Our social and cultural environment – or 'habitat'– is created by what we do, as well as providing the resources that we draw on to formulate and carry out our actions [190–191].

4. M: The state is the main institution in society.
   Pm: The post-modern habitat is made up of a kaleidoscopic array of different institutions (agencies), and there's no single institution that dominates. This means that what we do is only partly constrained by institutional regulations [192–193].

5. M: Our actions obey the norms of the social groups we belong to [203].
   Pm: In everyday life, there's a chaotic range of options open to us, and our actions involve improvisation rather than rule following [193].

6. M: We're socialised into the norms of our social group, and our lives pursue a relatively clear path (or 'life project') [193–194].
   Pm: We assemble ourselves, there's no clear development because the targets are shifting, and there's as much disowning and forgetting as cumulative 'growth' [194].

7. M: Social groups monitor our behaviour and keep us in line.
   Pm: We're desperate for reassurance that we've made the right choices, and in shaping and showing who we are, we rely a lot on both expert and popular opinion. Information is especially important, and there's inequality in access to it [195–196]. People affiliate with temporary and shallow consumer lifestyle communities [198–199].

8. M: Our bodies are externally regulated, drilled and disciplined at school, in factories, etc. [194].
   Pm: We devote a lot of time to cultivating our bodies as showcases for the identities we desire [194].

9. M: Social theory looks at abstract social systems, politics is about practical action, and so the two can be separated [196]. When it intervenes in practical affairs, sociology dreams of being a 'healer of prejudices', an 'umpire of truth' and an objective legislator [204].
   Pm: There's no such thing as a higher entity called 'society' which is unaffected by what we do on a daily basis. Our habitats and our social lives are shaped by practical actions, and so social theory and politics are connected [196]. Sociology is part of the social and political world, and so rather than trying to operate as an objective judge, it can only serve as a practical interpreter [204].

Table 1.1: *(Cont.)*

---

10. M: Politics is a matter for the state, and inequalities of wealth are the major concern [197].
     Pm: The role of the state is diminishing, and single-issue social movements operate outside official political channels. The big issues are human rights and freedom from discrimination [197–198].

11. M: The law decides right and wrong [201].
     Pm: We have to decide what's right and wrong ourselves. We're surrounded by a plethora of institutions operating with different norms, and we're continually reflecting on the rights and wrongs of our own choices [201–203].

Source: Based on Z. Bauman 1992 'A sociological theory of postmodernity'. In *Intimations of Post-modernity*. London: Routledge. 187–204.

This divergence of 'modernist' and 'post-modern' perspectives in sociology finds parallels in relatively recent work on language and society.[12] Historically, much of twentieth-century linguistics has been dominated by the view (a) that language study is centrally concerned with regularity in grammar and coherence in discourse, and (b) that these properties derive from community membership, that people learn to talk grammatically and coherently from extensive early experience of living in families and fairly stable local social networks.[13] This has been called the 'linguistics of community' (Pratt 1987), and the reassessment of these assumptions about both community and language have taken on several forms.

For a long time, linguists considered speech communities to be objective entities. A speech community could be empirically identified as a body of people who interacted regularly, who had attitudes and/or rules of language use in common, and it would be the largest social unit that the study of a given language variety could seek to generalise about (see Rampton 1998b). This linguistic view of community actually corresponded quite closely with the educational policy discourse exemplified in the Swann Report, but in the last fifteen years or so in sociolinguistics, it has broken down, and instead, the notion of 'community' has gone two ways.

In one direction, 'speech community' has been funnelled down into research on 'communities of practice', where there is close-up analysis of face-to-face interaction in a number of rather well-established settings and social relationships like workshops, classrooms and professional groups of one kind or another (see Eckert and McConnell-Ginet 1992; Lave and Wenger 1991). Research on communities of practice tends to focus on quite small groups, and predefined social categories like age, gender and occupational status are criticised for telling little of the way in which people develop, maintain and change community traditions and identities in social activity (Eckert and McConnell-Ginet 1992:471; Hymes 1996:9). Instead there is a commitment to ethnography and to micro description of the lived texture of situated experience, and this sometimes focuses on a range of expressive media and material artifacts in addition to language. This approach synchronises well with post-modern uncertainty about grand theoretical totalisations, and if social totality has been "dissipated into a series of randomly emerging, shifting and evanescent islands of order" (Z. Bauman 1992:189), then research on communities of practice seems particularly well-pitched.

In the other direction, 'community' expands outwards when it is analysed as a representation in ideological discourses that construct and naturalise very large groupings (e.g. Anderson 1983). Particularly in the work on language ideologies, there is a great deal of interest in how a spread of people gets constituted as a 'community' in the first place, how "linguistic units come to be linked with social units", languages with peoples (Gal and Irvine:1995:970; Gal and Woolard 2001; Joseph and Taylor 1990; also e.g. LePage 1988). A substantial part of this work is historical, and its critical angle on modernist assumptions differs from the one in the research on communities of practice. In communities-of-practice research, presuppositions about the larger systems embracing particular forms and practices are treated as a source of contamination to be avoided in any empirical account, but in the work on language ideologies, totalising ideas are actually treated as focal objects of analysis themselves, and there are accounts of the social, political and discursive processes involved in the institutionalisation of entities like nation-states and autonomous languages.

'Community', then, has been quite profoundly problematised in relatively recent sociolinguistics. So has 'language'.

Research on language ideologies makes it hard for linguists to treat particular languages like English, German or Bengali as natural entities. Rather than taking particular words and grammatical patterns as straightforward instantiations of English, German or Bengali, language forms are analytically separated from their social (including national) connotations, and the spotlight falls on the processes and situations that make certain socio-linguistic equations more automatic than others (making 'my pen' first and foremost an 'English' phrase, rather than a 'Scottish', 'Yorkshire' or 'family' one, even though it is used in these other settings as well). There has been a good deal of reflexive work analysing the political role that linguistics and philology have themselves played (and continue to play) in the construction and maintenance of the named languages that people take to be coterminous with particular ethnic groups and nation-states. But the capacity to step back for a critical look at what language forms are routinely taken to represent is not seen only as enterprise for academics. Ordinary speakers are also perceived as evaluating and reflecting on the cultural images of people and activities conjured by particular forms of speech, and there has been a very substantial growth of sociolinguistic interest in the artful use of speech in expressive performance, in which there is "heightened [evaluative] awareness of both the act of expression and the performer" (Bauman 1986:3; Bauman and Briggs 1990; Silverstein 1979, 1985). All this constitutes a substantial break with orthodoxy in modernist/structuralist linguistics, where novices are instructed from the first that "linguistics is descriptive, not prescriptive", and where opinions about what's linguistically good or bad are treated as a source of contamination for research, interfering in accurate observation of the (structural) facts (cf. Kroskrity 2004:499). In line with this, empirical work in traditional sociolinguistics has often placed a premium on tacit, unself-conscious language use, arguing that it is in unself-conscious speech that linguists can find the regularity, system and consistency that defines their professional interest (Labov 1972a; contrast Silverstein 1981; Lucy 1993; Cameron 1995).

In fact, this commitment to system-in-language has also been challenged by a "linguistics of communicative practice", which gives priority to situated action in the relationship between language and language use (Hanks 1996; Verschueren 1999). In a great deal of traditional linguistics, it has been the structure of language that gets privileged, language use being seen as little more than a product/output generated by semantic, grammatical and phonological systems, which are themselves regarded either as mental structures or as sets of social conventions. But in the 'practice' perspective, these conventions or structures are reduced to being just one among a

number of semiotic resources available to participants in the process
of local speech production and interpretation, and instead of the
linguistic systems being viewed as the main carriers of meaning,
meaning is analysed as an active process of here-and-now inferencing, ranging across all kinds of percept, sign and knowledge. This
meshes well with the empirical horizons of research on 'communities of practice', and it also provides a framework for engaging
with artful speech performances that depart from routine unself-
conscious language use. Such performances are difficult to deal with
in a linguistics of systems, but their disruption of regularity is much
less problematic for the linguistics of practice, since plugging holes
with whatever can be gathered from the contingent links between
different semiotic modes and levels is seen as a normal part of speech
processing.

These shifts in sociolinguistic theory impact on empirical description, and this is captured, for example, in Nik Coupland's 1997
reflections on ten to fifteen years of sociolinguistic work on language
and ageing. Coupland originally conceptualised his research as a
description of discrete age-groups, but over time, he came to see this
as an analysis of how people construct their own and other people's
age identities in interaction, so that when he and his colleagues
"needed to account for particular interactional data, it was the
strategic complexity and creativity of speakers that was most striking, rather than how they played out or reflected supposedly stable
beliefs about ageing or attitudes to old age" (1997:33). If I turn to
earlier work of my own, there have been some broadly comparable
shifts in the view of ethnicity, where it is no longer enough to see
ethnicity as either cultural inheritance, or as the strategic/political
accentuation of inheritance. It is also necessary to reckon with the
ways in which language can be used to extend ethnic co-membership
across the lines of ethnic–genetic descent in close friendship, as well
as the ways in which ethnic forms, products and symbols are mar-
ketised, disseminated and appropriated as desirable commodities,
life-style options and aesthetic objects (see Rampton 1995a). All in
all, whether it is age- or ethnicity-based, belonging to a group now
seems a great deal less clear, less permanent and less omni-relevant
than it did twenty-five years ago, and this makes it much harder to
produce to an account of 'the language of such-and-such a social
group', or 'language use among the ___', than it used to be. The

critical reflexivity associated with, for example, the language ideologies perspective interrogates the stereotyping involved in claims of
this kind; it asks where these claims are 'coming from' and where they
fit in ongoing processes of political argument and policy formation;
and it scrutinises them for what they leave out, why and with what
consequences. Along with other approaches, it wants to know more
about the social life of the language forms clustered under the label
'Asian', 'youth' or 'such-and-such a locality': under precisely what
conditions are these forms produced, doing what, when, where, in
relation to who else doing what in the vicinity, within what interactional and institutional histories? And so instead of investigating how
old people, or African Caribbeans, or Yorkshire folk, use language,
analysis turns to the role that language plays when humans interact
together in situations where (a) discourses of language group membership, age, ethnicity, region, etc., have currency (impacting heavily
on the distribution of material and symbolic resources circulating in
local, national and global networks), where (b) these categorisations
are relevant to the participants (classifying and rating them differently), where (c) the participants may need, want or happen to orient
actively to these categories and their associations, but where (d) they
might also have other things on their minds, or have come to an
understanding that temporarily neutralises the personal impact that
these discourses can have.

   These post-structuralist shifts also have major implications for
our conceptualisation of the politics of language and culture. For
much of the twentieth century, three very general perspectives have
been highly influential in attempts to account for inequalities in the
distribution of knowledge, influence and resources within stratified
societies. The first perspective, 'the *deficit* position', has stressed the
inadequacies of subordinate (out)groups and the importance of their
being socialised into dominant (in)group norms. The second, with
difference as its key word, has emphasised the integrity and autonomy of the subordinate group's language and culture and the need
for institutions to be hospitable to diversity. In the third, the focus
has shifted to larger structures of *domination*, and the need for
institutions to combat the institutional processes and ideologies
that reproduce the oppression of subordinate groups is stressed.[14]
There has obviously been a great deal of conflict between these
interpretations of the basic character of inequality, and different

perspectives have gained ascendancy at different times in different places. But they are all similar in treating the conflict as a relationship between groups and communities conceived as separate social, cultural and/or linguistic blocs.

More recently, however, they have been joined by a fourth very general perspective which challenges the assumption that people can be allocated unambiguously to one group or another. This view accepts the role that larger social, economic and political systems play in structuring dominant–subordinate, majority–minority relations, but argues that their impact on everyday experience cannot easily be predicted. Instead, the emphasis is on looking closely at how people make sense of inequality and difference in their local situations, and at how they interpret them in the context of a range of social relationships (gender, class, region, generation, etc.). This perspective is wary of seeing culture exclusively *either* as an elite canon, *or* as a set of static ethnic essences *or* as a simple reflection of economic and political processes; it takes the view that the reality of people's circumstances is actively shaped by the ways in which they interpret and respond to them; and in line with this, it lays a good deal of emphasis on the cultural politics of imagery and representation. Overall, it is a perspective which tunes well with late modernity, and preserving the alliteration, it has been summarised as '*discourse*'. These four positions are mapped out schematically in Table 1.2 (see also McDermott and Varenne 1996).

Such, then, is the cluster of ideas that I associate with poststructuralism and late modernity as a perspective, and in concluding this section, three points are worth emphasising.

First, in terms of 'periodisation', an engagement with late modern perspectives should not be interpreted as a belief that modernist beliefs and values are all now irrelevant. Zygmunt Bauman's discussion of a sociological theory of post-modernity is formulated as a series of ongoing tensions and disputes, and the cultural politics of 'deficit', 'difference', and 'domination' have certainly not been superseded by 'discourse' – to different degrees in different quarters, all four perspectives are alive and well. In fact, because these and other differences of view are still unresolved, it makes most sense to speak of the *intersections* and *junctures* of tradition-and-modernity and modernity-and-late modernity (see also Rampton 1998b, 2000, Harris and Rampton 2003:1–14).[15]

Table 1.2: *Four orientations to linguistic and cultural diversity*

	Interpretation of linguistic and cultural diversity			
	1. Diversity as deficit	2. Diversity as difference	3. Not diversity, domination	4. Deficit, difference and domination as discourse
View of culture:	Culture is equated with the elite canon ('high culture').	Cultures are the sets of values, beliefs and behaviours developed in different settings.	Culture is a reflection of socio-economic relations.	Culture feeds, gets reproduced and emerges in people's activity together – it exists in the processes and resources involved in situated, dialogical, sense-making.
Approach to language:	'Prescriptivism': there are norms and standards that should be followed.	'Descriptivism': non-standard forms are actually systematic and authentic.	'Determinism': language is secondary to structures of political and economic domination (and/or it's a distraction from the real issues).	'Constructionism': interpersonal, institutional and collective discourse and interaction are crucial to the processes through which social realities and social identities get reproduced, resisted or created anew.
Descriptive focus:	High culture and standard language. The Other's language and culture are unworthy of study.	The language and culture of the Other, which are shown to have autonomy and an integrity of their own.	The linguistic and cultural relationship between self and Other, between 'us' and 'them', in a larger system of domination.	The interaction between global, national and local discourses.
View of research:	Research is neutral, objective and informative. It gets us close to the truth.	Research is neutral and objective, but it can also be used on behalf of the people that it studies, to advocate their causes.	Research is either part of the apparatus of hegemonic domination, a form of scientific imperialism, or it can help us see through the mystifications of the dominant ideology	Research can either be restrictive and controlling with its claims to 'truth', or it can be empowering, giving a voice to types of knowledge that have been silenced or subjugated hitherto.

Philosophical perspective:	The dominant group is superior, and the linguistic and cultural problems of the Other are their own fault.	Relativism. Cultures and languages are well adapted to the particular settings where they developed, so it makes no sense to say one is 'better' than the other.	Power, ideology and capitalist oppression. There is resistance through critical analysis and the mobilisation of oppressed groups.	Power, difference and improvisation in the face of unpredictable contingency. The Other may resist, or see things differently.
Assumptions about the world:	There are universals and grand narratives: e.g. development, modernisation, market competitiveness.	There may be grand narratives, but it's the little ones, the subplots, that we want to celebrate.	There are universals and grand narratives: imperialism, exploitation and dependency.	There aren't any universals or grand narratives, and the world is much more chaotic than we have assumed in the past.
Intervention strategy:	Assimilation: the Other should learn to become more like us.	Pluralism: the different languages and cultures in a society should be recognised, respected and cultivated.	Class war/anti-racism/anti-imperialism: structures of domination need to be critiqued and resisted.	Anti-essentialism: ideas about people having fixed identities, and about groups, cultures and languages being static and homogeneous, are oppressive.
Typical politics:	Conservatism.	Liberal pluralism.	Marxism.	Post-modernism.

Second, the points of connection between (a) late modern social conditions, (b) post-structuralist theory generally in the social sciences and humanities, and (c) recent work in sociolinguistics are themselves worth stressing. Looking back over this section and the one before it, a number of themes and issues recur in the different arenas I have pointed to: the declining influence of regulating, homogenising nation-states and the cultural hybridisation associated with globalisation find an echo in the emphasis on plurality, contingency and ambivalence (rather than regularity and system) in Bauman's postmodern sociology, and this in turn can be mapped into the shift from system to situated practice in sociolinguistics. Similarly, new rhetorics of choice in education and meta-cultural experience in global cities find parallels in the shift of interest from socialisation to 'self-assembly' in sociology, and the emphasis on reflexive language and artful performance in sociolinguistics. Other parallels could be drawn (and disputed),[16] but for present purposes, two points stand out:

- to the extent that sociolinguistics has withstood institutional pressures towards (sub-)disciplinary autonomy and instead adjusted its conceptual vocabulary and empirical interests in line with a much more widespread sense of cultural shift, it should be able to participate in broader debates about the contemporary world;
- to the extent that post-structuralist perspectives in social science attach special importance to discourse, emerging from the work of social theorists with a particular sensitivity to discourse and situated practice (e.g. Foucault 1962; Berger and Luckman 1966:172–3; Giddens 1976; Bourdieu 1977; Bakhtin 1981; Hall 1996; Table 1.2 column 4), sociolinguists may be able to use their specialist expertise to make a distinctive contribution (Fairclough 1992b:1; Coupland 1998; Kulick and Schieffelin 2004:365).

Third, there are two major topics in this book which would make little sense in a sociolinguistics governed by the belief that language and identity are determined first and foremost by our early experience at home and in local neighbourhoods. In Part II, I focus on adolescents playing around with a foreign language that they have been taught at school (German). This is probably a very common phenomenon, but it is an almost entirely new theme for sociolinguistic research, and its neglect is no doubt related to the fact that in the 'linguistics of community', this kind of language use seems simply too trivial to bother with. Then in Part III, I analyse social class as an interactional process, and again this is out-of-step with sociolinguistic orthodoxy, which instead tends to treat social class among young people as an objective matter determined by parental occupation and income, and takes it for granted that children from non-posh homes will be vulnerable to feelings of linguistic inferiority ('linguistic insecurity'). Neither of these issues merits much attention if our actions, attitudes and language are principally regarded as a reflection of the big communities we're born into, but if we shift from this essentialism to a frame in which here-and-now social action is seen as playing at least some part in the formation of potentially consequential solidarities and divisions, they both deserve a closer look.

Those then are the real world processes and the conceptual frameworks that I am using the term 'late modernity' to refer to, together with a foretaste of how they assert themselves empirically in my data (e.g. changes in the demographic and educational landscape), a list of ideological claims to interrogate or argue with (the decline of traditional authority; the ascendance of consumer identities; the demise of class), and an outline of the way they connect to perspectives and issues in sociolinguistics that have either gained momentum relatively recently or remain largely unexplored (ideologies of language, artful performance and the linguistics of practice; instructed foreign language and social class in interaction).

It is now worth focusing more fully on the other terms in the book's title, language and interaction. Precisely what approach to language and interaction do I adopt? How does it relate to the processes and assumptions I have associated with late modernity?

1.3   Language and interaction

The analyses in this book draw on interactional sociolinguistics (IS), a perspective on language and communication pioneered by John Gumperz in particular (e.g. 1982a, 1999). IS generally focuses on face-to-face interactions in which there are significant differences in participants' cultural resources and/or institutional power, and it has a relatively broad methodological base, with deep roots in dialectology, linguistic pragmatics, conversation analysis, ethnography, and Goffmanian interaction analysis (Gumperz 1982a: Chapter 2). IS generally seeks as rich a dataset on interaction as it can get, and data-collection involves the audio- and/or video-recording of good samples of situated interaction from particular events, people and groups, supplemented by as much participant observation and retrospective commentary from local participants as possible. The purpose is to produce detailed and fairly comprehensive analyses of key episodes, drawing on a range of frameworks to describe both small- and large-scale phenomena and processes (e.g. pronunciation, grammar, genres, interaction structures, institutions, social networks), and this is given coherence by the theoretical view of communication as an 'on-line', moment-to-moment process in which speakers (a) try to construct their utterances broadly in line with their recipients' understanding/experience of the social world, their communicative history together, and their sense of the interactional possibilities on hand; (b) provide and draw on a very large number of different kinds of verbal and non-verbal sign to steer listeners in the interpretation of their words and utterances ('contextualisation cues'); at the same time as (c) continuously monitoring listeners' semiotic displays to see whether they are all more or less in tune. As a whole, Gumperz's framework is driven by a commitment to doing analysis that is capable of addressing "the facts of [contemporary] urban life ... yield[ing] new insights into the workings of social process" (1982a:4, 7), and there are in fact a number of ways that it connects with the perspectives on language outlined in the previous section.

Interactional sociolinguistics regards interaction as a key site for the construction and reproduction of social identities and relationships, impacting on people's minds, lives and material conditions, and IS micro-discourse analysis is always mindful of the positions that the participants occupy in larger/longer/slower social processes, seeking to reveal how these more established identities can be reproduced, contested and maybe changed by human agents interacting. More specifically, IS invites us to see communication as an intricate process of imposition, collusion and struggle in which people invoke, avoid or reconfigure the cultural and symbolic capital attendant on identities with different degrees of purchase and accessibility in particular situations. The last section described growing interest in the part that human agency plays in what had been previously treated as the predetermined facts of social and linguistic structure. We saw how structuralist ideas about socialisation, rule-following, speech community and 'language-as-system' were being revised as researchers paid more attention to interaction – to reflexive improvisation and situated interpretation – and how social reality is now quite widely regarded as more than only the product of forces that actors can neither control nor comprehend, being seen instead as something that is extensively reproduced *and at least partially* created anew in the socially and historically specific activities of everyday life (Berger and Luckman 1966; Giddens 1976, 1984). There is a good case for saying that in the synthesis of different perspectives on communication that Gumperz has produced, interactional sociolinguistics constitutes an exceptionally sharp and flexible window on the more micro-dynamic aspects of social reality production.[17]

Interactional sociolinguistics, then, seems well-tuned to the main lines of contemporary social thought. But how do I use it to engage with the focal topics in this book? It is now worth turning to a more focused sketch of the book's central themes. In doing so, I shall provide a preliminary view of 'performance', 'stylisation', 'ritual' and 'genre', four of the most central integrative sociolinguistic concepts in my study, and also point to the places where the account moves *outside* the normal terms of IS analysis.

1.4 Empirical foci and analytic concepts

For a sharper characterisation of my interactional sociolinguistic perspective on the empirical processes reported in this book, it is useful to start with an observation by two ethnomethodological micro-ethnographers:

[i]n the routine performance of their everyday life, people seldom answer directly questions about the wide-scale constraints on their lives. Rather, they point at those aspects of their environment that at a particular moment are most salient to what they must be doing. (Varenne and McDermott 1998:20)

When people speak, they inevitably convey much more than their words and sentences articulate 'literally', and a great deal gets expressed much more indirectly, with different aspects of the communicative stream drawing on a wide range of unstated assumptions that often vary in apparentness to their interlocutors – assumptions about activities, manners, relationships, people, places, the past, the future, etc. (cf. the reference to 'contextualisation cues' in the previous section). These unstated assumptions are developed through social experience, and to the extent that they provide a baseline for the explicit part of an utterance to make sense – and to the extent that they are unquestioned by the recipients – they can be analysed as tiny pieces of taken-for-granted social structure. But without breaking through into explicit semantic propositions, people also routinely engage in more active intimations of perspective, displaying a particular orientation to the situation and the social world though innuendo, irony, prosodic emphasis and so forth, and this can be hard for analysts – as well as for unfamiliar participants – to pick up on. Varenne and McDermott elaborate:

[i]t is not easy to capture people in the real time of their practice. When we perform practical research tasks ... apparently paradoxical things happen as we notice how actors are both continually sensitive to [convention], and also slightly 'off' the most conventional version of what they could have been expected to do ... [W]hat subjects construct in the real time of their activity can never be said to be what it would be easiest to say it is. What subjects construct may never be any particular thing that any audience may label it to be. We, as analysts, must always take the position that it is something more, something other.   (1998:177)

Varenne and McDermott develop this into a political point. People have the capacity to act unconventionally, and so researchers should expect to have to struggle to make sense of what their subjects are doing. In contrast, if the process of analysis is rapid, tidy and definitive, then it inevitably favours the conventional aspects of human conduct, ignoring the distinctiveness and the creative agency in what's been said or done. And since agency and the capacity to break with dominant discourses and conventional structures are central to cultural politics, quick-and-neat analysis can be seen as a form of intellectual imperialism, promoting whatever 'parsing' framework the analyst prefers above the participants' own alertness to the matrix of constraints and possibilities problematically on-hand in any activity being investigated.[18]

In much of the book, my entry into practices that are "slightly 'off' the most conventional version of what [participants] could have been expected to do" lies in moments in the flow of spontaneous interaction when young people break into artful *performance*. These are fleeting moments when "the act of speaking is put on display, objectified, lifted out to a degree from its contextual surroundings, and opened up to scrutiny by an audience" (Bauman and Sherzer 1989:xix; chapter 1.2 above), and in **Part III** ('The stylisation of social class'), I emphasise a particular kind of performance – *stylisation*, in which the speakers produce "an artistic image of another's language" (Bakhtin 1981:362). More specifically, I focus on youngsters switching into exaggerated posh and Cockney accents. These accent shifts represent moments of critical reflection on aspects of educational domination and constraint that become interactionally salient on a particular occasion – for example, a teacher's patronising remark, or the demands of a writing chore – and they classify some feature of the interaction on hand as the instance of a more general social type. These typifications ultimately draw on a set of binary high–low, mind–body, reason–emotion oppositions that have a very substantial historical pedigree in class-stratified societies, and so here we can see a long and well-established tradition being repeatedly reanimated in contingencies of the situated moment (chapter 9).

There are, though, limits to how far an interactional perspective can carry the analysis of social class. There is a huge body of work on the pervasiveness of class and its impact on individuals, and there is a risk of trivialising the topic if class is *only* analysed as a strategic interactional identity projection, or as an ideological resource that actors can draw on to comment on particular types of social relationship that they notice from time to time in the situations around them. To avoid this reductionism, my account of posh and Cockney takes two steps outside the idiom of interaction analysis.

First, I turn to the tradition of quantitative research on speech variation associated with William Labov (1972a), and this shows that in their routine unself-conscious talk, my informants' language becomes more standard/posh in relatively formal settings and more vernacular/Cockney in informal ones. Patterns of speech stratification that can be found in the distribution of language forms across class-groups-in-society-as-a-whole get echoed in the unself-conscious behaviour of individuals as they move between situations that are more and less associated with the accumulation of mainsteam prestige, and as Bourdieu emphasised, this suggests that social class has penetrated deep into the ordinary speech of individuals (Bourdieu 1977, 1991:Part I; Woolard 1985; Eckert 2000:13). This invites a more elaborate interpretation of posh and Cockney stylisa- tion: in acts of stylisation, youngsters are bringing to consciousness – excavating – a classed sensibility that permeates their routine own activity (Chapter 7). Second, I observe the ethnographic injunction to follow wherever the data leads,[19] and when the radio-microphone recordings reveal adolescents using posh and Cockney to embellish performances of the grotesque and to portray images of unsettling, disorderly sexuality, it looks as though analytic idioms emphasising the strategic control of interacting agents aren't quite adequate, and that the class meanings of language also mingle with fantasy, anxiety and desire in the kinds of territory addressed in depth psychologies. Language is still focal and so, emphatically, this remains a piece of linguistic research, but at this point, the vocabularies of mainstream contemporary sociolinguistic analysis seem insufficient, and cultural theory provides a crucial analytic resource (Stallybrass and White 1996; Ortner 1991; Skeggs 1997). Indeed overall, starting with IS as an open, non-doctrinaire tradition that is particularly well-tuned to interaction as a point of juncture for micro/macro and structure/ agency dynamics, my analysis of posh, Cockney and social class is eventually offered as a synthesis of sociolinguistics and cultural studies, with Vološinov, Bakhtin and Raymond Williams providing some overarching theoretical coherence.

Part II of the book – 'Performances of *Deutsch*' – deals with another largely unanticipated phenomenon that emerged during fieldwork – adolescents in multi-ethnic groups improvising German in their Maths, English and Humanities lessons.[20] If ESL and minority languages are taken as the central ethno-linguistic issues in socio-educational linguistics, this sounds inconsequential and indeed peer-group *Deutsch* did turn out to be only a passing fad. Even so, IS analysis shows that *Deutsch* connected with some real and enduring tensions when it was used, and for adolescents (if not for modernist sociolinguistics), its identity as an instructed foreign language with curriculum recognition made it amenable to all sorts of entertaining appropriation among peers. As in the analysis of posh and Cockney, 'performance' features prominently as an inte- grative concept in my account of these improvisations in *Deutsch*, although the social resonances of *Deutsch* seemed very narrow in comparison. The pleasures of sound play sometimes seemed more important than the evocation of different kinds of stance or social type, and to the extent that 'stylisation' involves an 'artistic image of another's language', it is much less apposite for the analysis of *Deutsch* than it was for Cockney and posh.

Still, *Deutsch* didn't come from nowhere, and the analysis of its origins also leads beyond a strictly interactionist framework. The main source of these improvisations was the German language class, and this involved a lot of high-intensity oral work in which the teacher pushed the class through choral call-and-response sequences, emphasising the vigorous repetition of German language structures rather than the exercise of critical intelligence. At this point, *ritual* presents itself as a concept that is not only well-matched to many of the properties of these language lessons, but that also suggests a particular kind of link to the way my informants improvised *Deutsch* elsewhere. On the whole, my informants really disliked their German classes – learning German in the foreign language class meant suppressing a lot of the talk, the classroom sociability, and the experience of control and agency they were accustomed to in other lessons. Following on from this, I argue (a) that in their ritual intensity, the German lessons provided a disagreeable experience that affected the language's socio-emotional meaning, investing it with the complicated emotional associations that Sapir attributes to condensation symbolism (1949:565), so that (b) when students reused *Deutsch* in corridors and in the Maths, English and Humanities lessons, this was a 'return of the repressed', a "release of emotional tension in conscious and unconscious form" (Sapir 1949:565) that both acknowledged and profaned German's ritual force in the foreign language class.

My analysis of *Deutsch*/German invokes a tension between traditional pedagogy (instantiated in the German lessons) and the kind of classroom relations preferred by my informants, and this is a major theme in **Part I**. As noted in Chapter 1.1, recent years have seen major government efforts to retraditionalise the curriculum, with a great deal of emphasis being given to whole-class instruction fronted by the teacher. But contrary to the ideological endorsement it receives in policy and public debate, students in the inner-city school I studied seemed to experience whole-class teacher-talk as a jostling but expressively depleted style of communication, which marginalised their own judgement but threatened to drag them into the spotlight with curriculum scripted performances that in the end, didn't actually count for very much. Some students showed interest in lesson topics but generally sought to embellish the proceedings, tirelessly milking classroom talk for all its aesthetic potential (recoding it in sound play, snatches of song, non-standard accents etc.), while others generally declined to take any part, devoting their attention to more interesting business of their own. Stuck between a set of exuberantly *over*-involved students on the one hand and obdurate refusers on the other, teachers tended to favour the former, and in this way a rather different kind of classroom settlement seemed to have evolved, in which teachers tolerated the excesses of some students for the reassurance and support that could be detected in their hyper-enthusiasm.

Up to this point, the discussion in Part I takes its cue from discourses about education, but in Chapter 3, I look at the proceedings in Class 9 A with popular media culture as the central focus. A number of social theorists argue that contemporary media culture has undermined traditional authority relations quite extensively, but there has been little systematic analysis of the processes by which these large-scale cultural formations come to impact on everyday practice, and this serves as a prompt for interactional and ethnographic investigation of how students' affiliation to media culture and teachers' commitment to curriculum instruction were actually negotiated. This reveals that although popular culture's entry into classroom affairs might look chaotic and/or subversive when set against the purist models advocated in educational discourse, if the interactional habits and arrangements in this class are considered in their own terms, then pupils and teachers seemed to have come to some accommodation between their potentially conflicting affiliations. This accommodation was not especially harmonious, but it still seemed livable and it got repeated on a daily basis.

In this part of the book, *genre* features a central integrative concept. Following Bakhtin (1986), Hanks (1987), and Bauman (2001), I take a genre to be a set of conventionalised expectations that members of a social group use to shape and construe the communicative activity that they are engaged in, and these expectations include a sense of the likely tasks on hand, the roles and relationships typically involved, the ways the activity can be organised, and the kinds of resources suited to carrying it out. But generic expectations and actual activity seldom form a perfect match, and the relationship between them is an important focus in political struggle, with some parties trying to hold them together and others seeking to prise them apart. Traditional whole-class teacher-talk is a matter of intense concern to education policy-makers because like all genres, it is an encapsulated vision of the social world tuned to practical action in recurrent situations, projecting particular kinds of conduct and relationship, promising the participants particular types of personhood. But a different set of interactional arrangements seemed to have stabilised in the local practices at Central High, and when these are compared with classroom ethnographies in the 1970s and 80s, in at least one respect it looks as though they form part of a wider historical shift in socio-communicative relations. In Class 9 A, active commitment to school knowledge often combined with a lack of regard for procedural decorum managed by the teacher. There is little evidence of this in the descriptions from the 1970s and 80s, and this shift can be aligned with the increasing 'conversationalisation of public discourse' that Fairclough speaks of (1995), and with the growing separation of formality and seriousness in public culture generally.

That is probably sufficient as an introduction to the central topics and concepts in this book. To conclude this chapter, it is worth briefly describing the fieldwork and data collection on which it is based.

1.5 Fieldwork and data collection

This book focuses on data drawn from a 1997–99 project funded by the UK Economic and Social Research Council.[21] In the end, the constraints and contingencies of working academic life prevented analysis of the entire corpus assembled in this project, and instead, I have focused on two subsets of the data. In Chapter 3.2, I report on the findings of a survey of 82½ hours of spontaneous activity recorded in two schools in 1997–98. Funded by the US Spencer Foundation, these data were scrutinised by Caroline Dover during 2001–02, and Dover, Roxy Harris and I carried out the analysis (Rampton, Harris and Dover 2002). But in the rest of the book, I concentrate on a smaller data subset from only one of the schools,

Central High. I carried out the fieldwork that produced this dataset, and in doing so, I made approximately 40 visits and sat in on about 50 lessons. Though there were 28 months between my first and last contact with the school, this fieldwork was most intense in the months February to June 1997, and data-collection included: gathering various pieces of student work and curriculum material; keeping a field diary (c. 80 pages); audio-recording lessons with an omni-directional microphone in my equipment bag; and conducting interviews and replaying audio-recordings of particular interactions to elicit retrospective commentary from the participants on what had been happening, said and done (11 sessions with 10 informants in 3 groups of 2–4, with 2 to 5 sessions per group). But as I have already intimated, my central data-collection technique involved a radio-microphone that 2 boys and 2 girls wore for 3 to 4 consecutive hours for about 3 days each (11 days in all).[22] This produced about 37 hours of audio-data, spread over 5 weeks, and it merits more detailed discussion.

The radio-microphone produced most of the data fragments that are transcribed and analysed in detail in the book, but in addition to the intensive work required in interactional sociolinguistic micro-analysis (see Chapter 10.2.3), work on these recordings entailed a great deal of *extensive* listening. This extensive listening can itself be regarded as a process of 'mediated', repeated and repeatable, ethno-graphic observation, and it is a fertile activity for the emergence of the 'contrastive insights' that Hymes identifies as the starting point for ethnography (1996:6). 'Contrastive insights' involve the appre-hension of a disparity between the claims that prevailing discourses make about social life, and what you can see, hear and experience in social life as it actually seems to happen, and simply because it is not done as often as it might be in social and educational research, 'trawling' with radio-microphones can be an abundant source of such insights. In academic research and professional debate in edu-cation, for example, the participants in a lesson are often simply described as 'pupils' and 'teachers'. If the recording equipment is placed in a position that provides a view of the class as a whole, it is usually the teacher's talk that comes out most clearly, and what the teacher says and does is regarded as the main influence on what happens in a lesson. But if a radio-mic is pinned on pupils at the start of the day and they are followed through the morning, it is self-evident that in the first instance, adolescents relate to each other as individuals with different personalities, tastes, interests and so forth, and that makes it hard to ignore the difficult processes by which a collection of disparate individuals get turned into a class of pupils – processes that are often a central worry for teachers, but that get ideologically erased in research transcripts that reduce all the human individuality to the label 'Teacher', 'Pupil 1', 'Pupil 2', 'Pupils' etc. (see Pratt 1987:51–52). This vivid decentring also has obvious consequences for the interpretation of specific actions. With the analysis of a lesson focused primarily on the teacher, unsolicited talk among the students tends to be regarded as a distracting interruption, but when you listen to radio-mic recordings, it is apparent that youngsters are often committed to talking about themes and issues that either began at the start of the day or have carried over from the day before, and it is much less clear who's distracting who. Equally, who is being rude to whom when a teacher tells a pupil to stop talking in the lesson? Pupils frequently carry on nevertheless, and you can hear on the radio-mic that it is often basic considerations of interpersonal politeness that compel kids to provide a decent completion to whatever they've been saying to their neighbour.

The gap between official representations of classroom talk and the discursive practices I heard in my radio-mic recordings of Class 9 A was obviously one of the 'contrastive insights' that motivated the analysis in this book. Another lay in the disparity between students' voluntary use of German at Central High, and the widely reported difficulties that the subject seemed to be facing everywhere else. The third centred on the split between youngsters doing class accents again and again in my data, and the wider retreat from class analysis in social theory and education policy. Hymes goes on to say that after the contrastive insight, ethnography involves 'a [systematic] seeking of specific information', and in the study of German and exaggerated posh and Cockney, part of this occurred during fieldwork: I asked interview questions about practices that I had noticed, replayed relevant extracts from the radio-mic recordings for the participants to comment on, and formulated speculative claims in my fieldnotes and on the data protocols. But the most extensive and systematic search for specific information came afterwards, and for the analysis of German, of posh and Cockney and of popular music, topic-focused datasets were assembled that included instances of their use – all the instances for German and singing, and a lot for posh/Cockney – which were then supplemented with all the potentially relevant participant commentary, fieldnotes and documentary data that had emerged in lessons, interviews or elsewhere around the fieldsite.[23]

Last, says Hymes, after the contrastive insights and the search for specific information, comes 'a general interpretation'. The previous section presented a summary of my 'general interpretations', and Chapter 10 contains a set of reflections on the analytic and interpretive procedures that produced them. I also address more specific methodological issues at different points in the ensuing chapters, and so at this juncture, it is probably worth just restating that this book has been written with a conviction

  a) that classrooms, language and discourse are all significant sites, indicators and stakes in social contestation, reproduction and change, and
  b) that the ethnographic and interactional sociolinguistics pioneered by Gumperz and Hymes provides a set of frameworks and procedures that can make a useful contribution to our understanding of these processes, feeding off and into discussion beyond the confines of both language research and the academy more generally.

These views are hardly very controversial, but the studies they inspire are necessarily different at different times and places, and this introduction has given a preliminary sketch of how they work in the accounts that follow.

Notes

1. This section draws very heavily on the work of Roxy Harris and of Constant Leung, some of which we have co-published as Harris, Leung and Rampton (2001); Rampton, Harris and Leung (2002).
2. In 1970, there were just under 150 LEAs in England.
3. Many were relatively well-established in the industrial work force, sympathetic to the labour movement (Goulbourne 1998:84; Ramdin 1987:362), and could draw on discourses of equality and rights that had been successful in relatively recent struggles for colonial independence.
4. Asylum applications in UK from 1985–88 averaged about 4,000 a year, whereas in 1998 there were 46,000 applications (Watson and McGregor 1999). In 1998, the British Home Office estimated that it had a backlog of 93,000 asylum seeker cases (Fiddick 1999:10).

5. They also tend to be politically voiceless: "there is a strong incentive for those who are here illegally to keep as low a profile as possible, and avoid unnecessary contact with Government agencies" (Grabiner 2000:17).

6. In the late 1990s in the North East of England, 2.6% of pupils in maintained primary schools were described as belonging to ethnic minorities, and in the South West, the figure was 2.7%. In contrast, the figures for Inner London were 56.5%, Outer London 31.2%, and West Midlands 15.9% (DfEE 1999). The linguistic consequences for schools are shown in a recent survey of the languages of London's schoolchildren (Baker and Eversley 2000:5), which states that in Greater London the range of home languages spans more than 350 language names, with English dominant amongst 67.86% of the 850,000 schoolchildren surveyed.

7. See, for example, Qureshi and Moores 1999 on Glasgow and Sansone 1995 on Amsterdam, and on processes within the UK, closely connected to Hall's 1988 'new ethnicities' framework, see also Mercer 1994, Gilroy 1987, 1993. For work focusing on the linguistic dimensions of these processes, see e.g. Hewitt 1986 on London; my own work in the South Midlands of England (Rampton 1995a/2004, 1995b); Heller 1999 on Toronto; and Auer and Dirim 2003 on Hamburg.

8. By the year 2000, 82% of the money spent on schools was controlled by head-teachers and school governors, compared with around 5% in 1990 (Audit Commission 2000).

9. More specifically: the decline of area-based manufacturing industries like mining, steel and shipbuilding; the growth of the service sector; and with women and black people almost 50% of all manual labour, a major shift in the demographic composition of the work force (Abercrombie and Warde et al. 2000:167; Gilroy 1987:19; Reay 1998; chapter 6 below).

10. See e.g. Barber 1997: "Whilst general societal factors (such as the status given to school learning or the prevalence of television viewing amongst adolescents) may be responsible for some of the poor British perform-ance, most are agreed that the educational system bears the main responsibility" (1997:10).

11. Cf. Estelle Morris, *Times Education Supplement* 6 October 2000.

12. Periodising the 'pre-modern', the 'modern' and the 'late modern' is notoriously difficult, and within sociolinguistics figures like Sapir, Hymes, Gumperz and LePage had been showing sociolinguistics how to reposition itself at the modernity/late modernity interface long before 'post-modern' became a common term in academic dis-course. Nevertheless, it takes time for the insights of ground-breaking researchers to work through into everyday academic practice, and a line can perhaps be drawn somewhere in the (mid-)1980s, even if this only turns out to be a matter for convenience (cf. Kroskrity 2004:500).

13. Certainly, sociolinguistics long fought against the idea that language and society were homogeneous, but on encountering diversity and variation, its strongest instinct was to root out what it imagined to be the orderliness and uniformity beneath the surface, an orderliness laid down during early socialisation. This instinct can be seen, for example, in the variationist's quest for the vernacular; it has led code-switching researchers to look for *conventional* syntactic and pragmatic patterns in the mixed speech of relatively well-established ingroups; and when sociolinguists have looked at intercultural contact, there has been a strong tendency to emphasise the integrity of tradition *inside* particular social groupings, the concern being that 'sociolinguistic interference' is likely to occur in cross-cultural encounters where people with very different backgrounds interact.

14. In the debates about race and ethnicity in British education, they are fairly easily recognised as assimilation, multiculturalism and antiracism (Brandt 1986), and in discussions about the global spread of English, they are broadly in line with the views expressed in Quirk (1990), Kachru (1982) and Phillipson (1992) respectively.

15. There are two other assumptions quite often made about late/post-modernity which I ought to put at some distance from my own appropriation of the notion. First, and most cursorily, it is sometimes suggested that research in a late modern, post-structuralist frame erases issues of power, domination and inequality – that this doesn't accord with my perspective should be clear from main text in this chapter. Second, in terms of method, it is sometimes proposed that any even half-favourable mention of late or post-modernity means the abandonment of all commitment to scientific method, and I have tried to contradict this view by citing some of the ways in which the relatively 'grand theory' claims summarised by Bauman translate into different sociolinguistic research programmes. All of these sociolinguistic research programmes are committed to empirical analysis that is logical, careful, sceptical and systematic, and although they would no doubt admit that these investigative values cannot reveal a final truth, they would insist that they are important for the discovery, analysis and reporting of phenomena beyond our ordinary imagining. At the same time, they would accept the limitations of the methods they employ, and recognise the historical specificity of the research traditions and the wider ambience that they are working in. In fact, the perspective I adopt might most aptly be described as 'neo-modernist', following Comaroff and Comaroff's formulation of a

neo-modernist method [that] ... takes seriously the message of critical postmodernism yet does not lose the possibility of social science; ... [that] takes to heart the lessons of cultural Marxism, seeking a conception of power, yet does not reduce meaning to either utility or domination ... [that] builds on the techniques of cultural history, pursuing the dialectic of fragment and totality ... [and that] proceeds, as it must, by grappling with the contradictions of its own legacy, seeking to transcend them – if only provisionally and for the moment. (1992:45)

16. Late modernity has been described as a era of networks and flows rather than 'centres', and in line with this, sociolinguistics has moved beyond its traditional focus on language use within very carefully specified cultural niches to analysis of the way linguistic texts and meanings get shaped, disembedded and then recontextualised as they travel across a range of different sites (e.g. Silverstein and Urban 1996). Indeed at the end of his essay on "A sociological theory of postmodernity", on which Table 1.1 is based (1992:204), Z. Bauman gives credit to the inspiration/stimulation provided by a number of figures, and several of these are now a staple reference in contemporary sociolinguistics (Beverly Anderson, Bakhtin, Bourdieu, Giddens and Goffman).

17. These social constructionist ideas are not new in themselves to sociolinguistics (see e.g. Sapir [1931]1949:104; Bauman and Sherzer 1974:8, 1989:xvii–xix, Halliday 1978:169–170), but Gumperz has probably done more than anyone to address them with "a general theory of verbal communication which integrates what we know about grammar, culture and interactive conventions into a single overall framework of concepts and analytic procedures" (1982:7).

18. In this regard, analysts need to be particularly careful with modernist linguistics, since as many scholars have noted, it has often been prone to neglect creative improvisation (see Chapter 1.3 above and Chapter 10.2.2 below; also e.g. Vološinov 1973:45–63; Garfinkel 1967:70; Williams 1977:21–44).

19. See Chapter 10.2.2 for fuller methodological discussion of ethnography.

20. Admittedly, the analysis of both *Deutsch* and stylised posh and Cockney is foreshadowed in theoretical speculation about practices with a family resemblance to 'language crossing' in my 1995a book (page 289).

21. The project was entitled 'Multilingualism and Heteroglossia In and Out of School' (Rampton 2000) and it focused on two schools, described in more detail in Part I. The fieldwork was conducted by myself and Alissa Shethar, and Annie Gillet and I worked on the initial analysis in 1998–99. The total dataset comprised:

   a. c. 180 hours of radio-microphone recordings of social activity centred around 9 boys and 11 girls aged 13–14, backed up by c. 60 hours classroom recordings with an omni-directional mic (c. 180 hours, of which 120 hours were extensively annotated [see main text])

   b. retrospective commentary from participants on extracts from the recordings (25 hours, all given broad transcription)

   c. interviews discussing school, local life and language use with approximately 30 youngsters (19 hours, transcribed as above)

   d. field diaries covering 75 visits, and field jottings made during the recording of lessons

22. The use of radio-microphones inevitably raises ethical issues. One of the principal virtues of radio-mics is that both the individuals wearing them and their (easily audible) friends often forget that they are being recorded, and this raises the risk of breaching privacy. To off-set this, all of the class and their teachers were informed of the recording, and as the fieldworker, I was generally visible in the vicinity. The microphone transmitters also had an off/on button controlled by the informants, and in addition, I agreed to erase the recording if a participant asked me to.

23. Rather than assembling a fourth data subset for the analysis of class-room talk in Chapter 2, I drew on the corpora that had already been assembled on German, posh/Cockney and popular culture.

PART II

Urban classroom discourse

Talk in class at Central High

After the 1960s and 70s, when child-centred theories of learning
were ascendant in British education,

there was an overt and persistent attempt to impose or re-impose the teacher's
voice as the centre of a transmission model of knowledge transfer: '... by
1979 many [members of the Conservative Party] had gained the impression
that schools were chaotic and teachers were lax, or – worse still – militant
egalitarians who used the classroom for subversive political activities. The
right wing feared that schooling had ceased to be a means for promoting order
and obedience, and had taken on the role of encouraging the young to be
critical of authority and disrespectful ... [In general the Tories expressed] a
wish to return to traditional curricula and teaching methods' (Lawton
1994:47, 147). In the mid-1990s there was also fierce debate ... on the
desirability of whole-class teaching. This tide of sentiment was joined by the
Labour Party before the 1997 election: 'The Labour Party intends to launch a
back-to-basics drive in the classroom if it wins the next election. More
emphasis on basic skills, classroom discipline and whole-class teaching will
become part of a drastic overhaul of teacher training' (*Times Educational
Supplement* 31.5.96).[1] (Harris 2002)

A great deal of more recent political and public discourse, then, is
very much in favour of whole-class teacher-talk. And yet, continues
Harris,

class teachers have long known that in the new communicative order it is
extremely difficult to hold pupil attention with their voice as central,
unchallenged, authoritative source, and they have settled for a low conflict
resolution in which competition from pupil voices is accepted or only
weakly challenged.[2]

So just how easy is it to impose whole-class teaching in contemporary urban classrooms? What actually happens when teachers
adopt this pedagogic style? And what is going on if and when they

give up the idea that they will be listened to as a "central, unchallenged, authoritative source"?

This chapter is intended as an empirical, case study contribution to our understanding of these issues, and from the two schools where we carried out our fieldwork in 1997–98, it focuses on the one where whole-class teacher-talk seemed particularly problematic, Central High.

At Westpark, a more prosperous school in the suburbs,[3] teachers could generally talk to the class for substantial periods of time, relatively free from interruption or distraction by the students, and they had few difficulties maintaining the conventional 'IRE' pattern of classroom discourse – a pattern in which the teacher initiates e.g. a question or instruction (I), the pupil(s) responds (R), and the teacher then evaluates the response and/or provides feedback (E or F). Unauthorised talk between students was largely hidden from the teacher, and in some regular classes where students were working through textbooks, there were protracted periods of total silence. The five students we focused on at Westpark were by no means always equally interested in the content of their lessons, but for the most part, they were relatively subdued in their displays of involvement in other matters and though it might not be full-throated, they generally maintained a public show of willingness to participate in class.

In contrast, at inner-city Central High it was usually quite difficult for the teacher to use his or her voice to develop a topic free from interruption or distraction. Students could often be seen and heard talking to each other about other matters while the teacher was trying to address them, and there were a lot of comments called out across the class unbidden by the teacher. One of the Central High informants that we focused on was a top student, but by no means all of his contributions to classroom discussion adhered to the conventional IRE structure. At the same time, two of our focal students routinely declined to answer questions from the teacher, and they spent substantial periods of class-time talking to each other about issues unrelated to the lesson. Exactly what was going on at Central High? What kind of an environment was this? Why weren't the teachers and students more effective in producing the kind of discourse that politicians call for?

Section 2.1 of this chapter provides a general overview of Central High, combining some quantitative information with fieldwork impressions. I then shift to a more detailed account of classroom discourse in

Class 9A,[4] and Chapter 2.2 compares interaction in Class 9A with the canonical IRE structure of pedagogic discourse, pointing to a decentring of pedagogic authority. Chapter 2.3 describes a penchant for embellishing the main instructional line among of a number of over-exuberant boys, and Chapter 2.4 focuses on the refusal of a number of fairly disenchanted girls. In Chapter 2.5, I suggest that these three elements – pluralised authority, hyper-involvement and resistance – were mutually reinforcing, and that they had their primary roots in the local exigencies of trying to teach and learn in a difficult environment (rather than in gender *per se*). At the same time, at least for teachers, life was easier when they weren't trying to hold a whole-class discussion – when the students were writing or engaged in role-play – and this leads to a review of exactly what it could have been about traditional teacher-led discourse that the students found so unappealing (Chapter 2.6). After that, I ask whether or not whole-class discourse dynamics like those at Central High could be a relatively new historical phenomenon, and consider some of the wider processes undermining whole-class teacher-talk as a discursive genre (Chapter 2.7).

This chapter also provides important contextualisation for the ones that follow.

2.1 Central High and Class '9A': an overview

In England in 1999, on average, £5,460 was spent on each pupil attending a fee-paying private school, while £2,732 per head was spent in schools funded by the state (Davies 2000:116). Substantial differences also existed in their end-of-compulsory-schooling exam performance. In the same year – the year when my informants sat their end-of-school exams – over 65% of private school pupils in the inner London borough where this study took place gained 5 or more GCSE grades at A*–C, while in state and voluntary aided schools, the figure was less than 40%. This fits, of course, with a wider pattern, where "pupils from more economically advantaged backgrounds achieve the highest averages [in GCSE examinations at 16]" (Gillborn and Gipps 1996:1). Social class, say Gillborn and Gipps, "is strongly associated with achievement regardless of gender and ethnic background: *whatever the pupils' gender or ethnic origin,* those from the higher social class backgrounds do better on average" (1996:17 [original emphases]). This inequality shows up on other indicators as well: in the private school sector in this borough, 5% of the year group were registered as having special educational needs, while in state-funded schools, the figure was about 20%.

'Central High', the school my informants attended, was a state secondary school for 11 to 16 year olds, with a sixth form for 16–18 years olds as well. But on both of the 1999 indicators of disadvantage mentioned above, it appeared to be in a position that was worse than the borough average: less than a quarter achieved 5 or more GCSE grades A*–C, and almost a third were registered as having special educational needs. Approximately half the students at Central High received free school meals, and the school's pupil population was also relatively unsettled in its geographical mobility – in the estimate of a senior teacher responsible for ESL, about 30% of the students moved away from the school (and sometimes back) before they completed their compulsory education. This was not an affluent 'middle-class' school in a settled suburban community, and the demographic profile of '9A', the class of thirty 13 and 14 year olds that I followed in 1997–98, was broadly consistent with this.

Out of 24 class members for whom the data was accessed, 11 received free school meals, and 7 were entered on school records as having both parents unemployed. Among those with working parents, 4 pupils had parents in jobs that could be classified as technical and professional (e.g. accountant, nurse), 3 had parents who were self-employed, and 9 had parents in semi- or unskilled work (e.g. driver, dinner supervisor, porter, shop assistant). 3 of the pupils in the class had arrived at the school as non-English speaking refugees from abroad, at least 2 others had received/were still receiving special learning support for literacy, 2 were regularly absent, and there was 1 who hardly ever attended. The composition of the class also changed over time: of the 28 pupils registered in the tutor group at the start of the 1996–97 school year, only 20 remained in 1999. In their last year (1999), only 3 of the class achieved 5 or more grades A*–C at GCSE.

Those, then, are some quantitative/demographic indicators. What about the atmosphere? At this point, it is worth reporting some impressionistic observations from fieldwork.

In the school as a whole, I was told, there was a relatively low turnover of teachers, and staff were said (and appeared to me) to be generally committed to comprehensive education (the idea that children of all backgrounds and abilities should go to the same school). In fact, there was also a good deal of mixed-ability teaching, and between the ages of 11 and 14, the students in each tutor group were taught together for all of their lessons except foreign languages (after that, the situation became more complicated as students split up to follow different exam courses). The impression I gained from the subset of staff that I encountered was that this was a thinking, left-of-centre, independent-minded group of teachers, intellectually committed to trying to get to grips with the complex urban environment where they worked, with a significant number actively interested in research (doing MAs and in some cases PhDs).

They also seemed to me to like, and to be generally fairly committed to, their pupils. Of course, as in any staffroom, you could quite often hear some grumbling about individual students, but on several occasions I was told that these were "nice kids", making it "a nice school to work in". At the same time, there was a clear interest in hearing youngsters' 'voices' and in talking to them honestly and openly about social life, whether this was to do with interpersonal or subgroup conflict at school, or with identity and status in society at large. As their tutor Mr Alcott said to the class in a tutor group session where they were discussing an incident the previous day:

```
there are some people in the country who think education
should be about telling kids things - 'we shouldn't talk
about racism and that stuff, it's not important' - but I
happen to think that ideas of racism are very very - I'm
not saying racism is a good thing - you know but talking
about racism is essential to your education. There are
some people whose lives are crippled by racism, suffering
from it, and some people (who maybe are racist), and that
will stop 'em learning.  (42/188: simplified transcript)
```

It was no doubt partly because of this that my interviews with young people at Central High felt different from the three other schools (including Westpark) where I have talked to adolescents about language, ethnicity, school and local social life. I seldom got the sense that pupils were excited by the novel opportunity to air issues that they often felt inhibited in talking about elsewhere. Equally, some of the lessons (especially Humanities) sometimes seemed to be as good a place to hear adolescents expressing their perspective as interviews can be.

Both the school and the class that I followed were multi-lingual and multi-ethnic – an informal estimate put the number of home languages in the school at 70+, while among the pupils in 9A, at least 12 different languages were reported (none of them with more than 4 speakers in the group). The school took this diversity very seriously. For example: pupils were entered for, and did well in, GCSE exams in minority languages (e.g. Hindi, Bengali, Arabic, Turkish); the Humanities curriculum materials addressed race relations and colonial history; there were special 'Respect' days and there was an extra-curricular 'Black History Group'; the library was well-stocked with books in languages other than English and with ethnic minority newspapers; staff were specially appointed to liaise with the larger ethnic minority communities; in communication with parents, regular use was made of translation services; and there was a large team of English Language Support teachers, very well integrated into the mainstream classroom teaching.

Overall, then, the school was very responsive to its urban population, and rather than assuming that pupils' development would be driven by their respect for the teachers' status and authoritative knowledge, a lot of emphasis was put on the importance of students taking responsibility for their own learning, as could be seen in the following notice displayed in the Maths classroom:

> Working together isn't CHEATING.
> Using a calculator isn't CHEATING.
> Finding out the answer from the back of the book and trying to work out how they got it isn't CHEATING.
> CHEATING is pretending to understand when you don't.
> That's when you're cheating yourself.

Not that this necessarily made life much easier. After I had been to an assembly for all the pupils in Year 9, I mentioned to the Head of Year who had conducted it that I'd been very impressed by genuine dialogue that seemed to take place – in my opinion, assemblies were generally among the hardest (and ghastliest) of school events. "Oh you are nice," she said, "only the trouble with interaction is that the kids talk back." Similarly, at the end of morning school, I came alongside the Deputy Head on patrol in the school entrance area and asked him how's life. "Thinking about early retirement, but that's another 15 years. Maybe I'll just chuck it in and go and work in a grammar school – Oops! I didn't say that!"

Beyond the ups and downs of everyday life at school, there was also quite a general sense that the staff were working against the tide of national policy in education.

The school's general ethos had taken shape during the 1970s and 80s, in a period when local education authorities controlled funding, when individual schools and teachers had considerable curriculum autonomy, and when both ethno-linguistic diversity and pupil-centred pedagogies were looked on favourably in dominant and official discourses. During this period, as a resident member of staff explained to a peripatetic supply teacher, Central High had been "a star in the borough, peaking in the 1980s. You got a lot of middle-class kids. But not now". Nowadays, the conversation continued, the upper echelons of the local education authority tended to be "technocrats" and they were less impressed with the school. The background to observations of this kind lay in the radical changes brought in by the 1988 Education Reform Act. During the early to mid-1990s, the legally binding National Curriculum had been introduced, and this shifted most of the control over curriculum content from schools and individual teachers to central government. Centralisation of the curriculum was accompanied by the growing advocacy for teacher- rather than student-centred pedagogy; increasing emphasis was given to standard English; and there was less and less space for attempts to cultivate linguistic diversity. Simultaneously, a system of national tests for 7, 11 and 14 year olds was introduced, and the results that each school gained in these tests were published in league tables. Among other things, this was designed as 'consumer information' to help parents to exercise their new freedom to choose which state school their children went to, and since funding now followed pupils, there could also be serious financial consequences. At the same time, these league tables gave no recognition to differences in the kinds of pupil that attended different schools, and this often put institutions like Central High at a competitive disadvantage. (See Chapter 1.1 for more detail.)

Those, then, are some demographic, descriptive and historical indicators, some fairly standardised, others more impressionistic. It is worth now turning to a closer view of the classrooms themselves.

2.2   Classroom authority and the IRE

Edwards and Westgate (1994) provide the following summary of "the deep grooves" along which whole class talk tends to run:

> communication is centred on the teacher. It is he or she who talks and decides who else is to talk, asks the questions, evaluates the answers, and clearly manages the sequence as a whole ... (A)ppropriate participation requires of pupils that they listen or appear to listen, often and at length. They have to know how to bid properly for the right to speak themselves, often in competitive circumstances where a balance has to be found between striving so zealously to attract attention that the teacher is irritated, and volunteering to answer so modestly that their bid is ignored ... In orderly classrooms, the teacher takes turns at will, allocates turns to others, determines the topics, interrupts and re-allocates turns judged to be irrelevant to those topics, and provides a running commentary on what is being said and meant which is the main source of cohesion within and between the various sequences of the lesson (Edwards and Westgate 1994:40,46; see also Mehan 1979, 1985; Cazden 1985)

Edwards and Westgate are careful to add a number of qualifications to this portrait, and in Chapter 2.7 I will consider studies where rather different patterns emerge. Even so, this was how whole-class talk generally operated at Westpark, and it is an account that chimes with a lot of contemporary education policy ideals (Lawton 1994; Davies 2000).

In contrast, these discursive structures looked rather 'frayed' at Central High, and authority in both instructional and regulative/disciplinary talk seemed to have been somewhat pluralised, with pupils – and one group of boys in particular – contributing loud interactional moves[5] that, in Edward and Westgate's account, seem to be the exclusive preserve of the teacher. This decentring was evidenced in a range of different kinds of talk.

There were occasions, for example, when teachers were contradicted, criticised, and had their comments on student conduct publicly contested (these moves are marked in bold):

Extract 2.1

Tutor period at the start of the day. Mr Alcott is talking to the class about the exams coming up. (The radio-mic is being worn by Joanne. n47:279; BL73:117)

```
MR A     HANG ON
         there are
         no: (.)
```

```
              language (.)
              SA/Ts
HANIF         there are
SEVERAL       ((chorally:)) there are
ANON          (          )
ANNA          (      it)
MR A          thank you
              (.)
              there are no: (.)
              language
              S:AT:s
              okay ((Mr A goes on to distinguish language SATs and
              language assessments))
```

Extract 2.2

Maths (a few weeks after Extract 2.3). Mr Davies is talking to the whole
class (n43:173, BL89: 25)

```
MR DAVIES     what should we use to draw
              a
              margin
NINNETTE      /ruler
ANON S        rule/r
MR D          Hanif
HANIF         ruler
              (.)
MR D          a ruler
              what else should we use
              /to draw a margin
GIRL          Sir you never use the ruler
NINNETTE      pencil
MR D          a pe:ncil
```

Extract 2.3

English. Mr Newton is giving the class guidelines on their oral assessment
tasks, and he appears to single out John. (Radio-microphone: Hanif.
n14:290ff; '15':1362)

```
MR N          the way you get a high score (.)
              is by actually encouraging others to speak
              and valuing their opinions (1.0)
              NOT (1.)
GIRL          ((with exaggerated delivery:))
              being ru: (de       )
```

```
GUY     ((funny voice:   ))
        saying (they're         )
MR N    running them down at all
BOY     yeh
MR N    so-
JOHN    hey what did I do
        why are you pointing at me
MR N    listen
        ((sound of other pupils' voices is increasing))
HANIF   /what?
MR N    shshsh
```

Extract 2.4

Tutor period with Mr Alcott. The class are in discussion about homophobia,
following an argument between Simon (wearing the radio-microphone) and
Hanif (n26:515)

```
MR A    I personally think
        and it is my- just my opinion
        (.)
        it's like accusing somebody of having blue eyes
        or brown eyes
        what's WRONG with being gay
        personally I would say
        'Excuse me Hanif
        (.)
        and others
        I would say
HANIF   ((very loud:)) WHY JUST ME:
MR A    because you were the one who
HANIF   ((fast, and even louder:))
        THAT IS WHY I DON'T WANT TO HAVE CONVERSATION
        WHEN- WHEN YOU'RE around (.)
        ((slower:)) that is why:
MR A    well
        all right then
HANIF   cos you're ALWAYS
MR A    /ALL RIGHT
        (  check  )
HANIF   ((very loud:)) (         )
MR A    okay
        (.)
        all right
```

Students could complain if the teacher appeared to ignore them:

Extract 2.5

English lesson. Mr Newton has asked why Romeo and Juliet died. (Radio-mic being worn by Hanif. n14:290ff; '15':953)

```
HANIF   love took ⌈over them
ANON               ⌊alright why did they (die)
MR N    love took over ⌈them
JOHN                    ⌊incorrec⌈t    (        )
HANIF                             ⌊yesh:
MR N    so the (point about ⌈                 )
ANON                        ⌊ah shut up
HANIF   ⌈YEH
JOHN    ⌊learn to express yourself
HANIF   ((sounding quite cheery:))
        SIR YOU⌈DON'T APPRECIATE MY ER what-d'you-macall-it
               │                                my comments
?MR N          ⌊((makes 5 taps, after which the class
        gradually quietens))
MR N    ((very quietly:)) Joanne
```

The imputation in these challenges was that the teacher was incorrect or unaware of the real situation (Extract 2.1), was inconsistent (Extract 2.2) and/or unfair (Extracts 2.3, 2.4, 2.5), but their tone varied and they could be good-humoured or angry (Extract 2.4), maybe either intended to subvert (Extract 2.2) or simply to correct (Extract 2.1?). In response, the teachers might take up the challenge (Extract 2.1), ignore it (Extracts 2.2, 2.3, 2.5) or accept it (Extract 2.4). But it's clear that even in what I've loosely designated 'challenges', students didn't necessarily lack interest in the subject matter that the teacher was focusing on (see Extracts 2.1, 2.4).

In fact, there were plenty of other occasions where these students displayed engagement with the discussion topic on hand, while at the same time breaching the canonical 'teacher-initiation → pupil response → teacher evaluation' structure so often described in the classroom interaction literature.

For instance, they sometimes jumped in to complete a sentence being uttered by the teacher:[6]

Extract 2.6

An English lesson. Mr Newton is about to tell the class about league tables comparing the performance of different schools (Radio-microphone: Simon. Blex 33; n19/210)

```
MR N     if you look at the big newspapers today (1.0)
         You'll find that they've all got these/erm
JOHN     car crashes
MR N     charts: (1.5)
         /they're called the league tables
ANON M   of schools
MR N     about all the primary schools
JOHN     /of schools
         good and bad yeh
```

Or encouraged the teacher to carry on when he seemed to be flagging:

Extract 2.7

Tutor period in the morning. There has been an incident in the school and Mr Alcott is talking about racism to the class, who are listening quite quietly. (Radio-microphone: Joanne. n42:209)

```
MR A     so we've got to make sure
         that these ideas
         which I think we all-
         you know
         we- we've
         discussed and analysed
         (.)
         um
         are connected
         in some ways
         with how we behave
         (1.5)
         I seem-
         I seem to be doing lots of talking
         ((quietly:)) I'm sorry
BOY     ⌈no you're not
ANON    ⌊((light laugh))
SIMON    no go on
ANON M   carry on
ANON     ((light laugh))
SIMON    it's very interesting
BOY      ((in a funny voice:)) go on/ (          )
SIMON    ((light laugh))
MR A     okay
         but you're the ones who are experiencing:
         (.)
         this erm:
         (1.0)
         this situation
```

Even though the tone/key varied a good deal, the boys were also
often active providing the teacher with 'back-channel cues', either
showing they were tuned to what the teacher was saying, or asking
for clarification:

Extract 2.8
Humanities. The class have to do a time line. (Radio-microphone: Hanif.
n2:592; BL2:1135)

MR A	if you really are stuck what to do
	you should be doing
	time
	line
HANIF	yeah
BOY	(all) right?
MR A	and
	if you've got the p-
	(2.0)
	and
	t- to help you
	cos we don't have a lot of time
	((sing-song intonation:)) for the time line
HANIF AND OTHERS	*((mocking:))* **oer:::::**
BOY	**oh very funny Sir**
MR A	sh
BOY	**cracking a joke there**
	((laughter, including Hanif))

Extract 2.9
An English lesson. (Radio-microphone: Hanif. n14:430)

MR N	(can you) look this way a minute (1.5)
	/er this is
BOY	*((whistles opening bars of 'Good bad and ugly'))*
	((carries on/a little))
MR N	*((softly:))* excuse me (.)
	this is like a test because (.)
JOHN	*((sounding ironic:))* **wow**
MR N	because I want you as well-
	you're gonna
	act it out
	next lesson in front of the rest/of the class
?	*((exaggerated inbreath: mock gasp))*
MR N	so- (.)
	/you've got this lesson to practise it

They also joined in actively evaluating the responses given by other students:

Extract 2.10
A Humanities lesson. The students have been role-playing lawyers trying to explain how a slave-ship lost all its cargo (Radio-microphone: Hanif. N/14:210; BL20:14).

```
ARUN       the slaves were mad
           and decided (          ) to leap over board
MR POYSER  /ah
           blaming the slaves
           that's (          )
HANIF      aha
           I like that one
```

Extract 2.11
In the discussion of why Romeo and Juliet died, Hanif takes a locally heterodox line and believes that their love was over-indulgent. Mr Newton has solicited Arun's view (n14 '15':909).

```
ARUN    (it be'd like they're sort of like) love survive in
        this sort of environment
MR N    their love couldn't sur ⌈vive in that sort of
                                 ⌊            environment=
HANIF                            ⌊WHAT A LOA:D OF RU:BBISH
MR N    =that's a nice phrase ((: referring to Arun's
        formulation))
```

Lastly, they quite often aligned themselves with the teacher and with scheduled curriculum activity by either telling other pupils to shut up or to do as they'd been asked:

Extract 2.12
Mr Newton is giving Hanif, Masud and their group final instructions about role-playing the coroner's inquest into the deaths of Romeo and Juliet (Radio-microphone: Hanif. n14:290; '15':1899).

```
MR N    one of you being Balthazar (.)
        /one of you being Benvolio (.)
MASUD   ((laughing: )) (          )
MR N    one /of you being the coroner
```

```
HANIF   what page is it-
        writing assignment
JOHN    I'll be the coroner
BOY     /no
HANIF   but we need paper (.)
        paper
BOY     ((to someone else outside the group:))
        (no you don't)
        pissmouth (.)
        (         )
HANIF   ALRIGHT
        SHUT UP THE LOT OF YOU (1.0)
        shut up
        (.)
MR N    one rule
        no shouting
```

Extract 2.13

English lesson (Radio-microphone: Hanif. n14:379; '15':1330)

```
MR N    is (.) (say back) in 1590 (.)
ANON F  ooh ooh ((giggles)) ((a mock gasp on the context
        tape))
MR N    just suppose (1.5)
        they/had such a thing as a coroner's inquest
BOY     (can't) you two shut up
?       (ooo)
MR N    we gonna do it in gro/ups (.)
```

What these extracts show is that the authority inscribed in the traditional IRE structure of classroom talk wasn't obeyed without question. Pupils – mostly Hanif, John and Guy – often challenged out loud what teachers told them (Extracts 2.1 to 2.4), and criticised them for the way that they distributed their attention (Extract 2.5). Neither did they observe the traditional relationship between speaking role and institutional position, and this is summarised in Table 2.1.

Of course, it would be a serious mistake to exaggerate this and to claim that traditional IRE relations had collapsed, that teachers and students had an equal role determining the course of each lesson. It was the teachers who knew most about curriculum requirements, who had planned particular lessons, who gave out marks, and who could quickly call on institutional punishments, and students never spoke to the whole class for a protracted period on their own

Table 2.1: *Teachers, Hanif and company, and the IRE*

Type of act	The canonical incumbents	Non-canonical incumbents and acts at Central High (with extracts)
	(cf. e.g. Mehan 1985; Edwards and Westgate 1994:chapter 2; Cazden 1985)	
Initiative	Teacher	a) Students: Boys provide the teacher with (unsolicited) 'utterance completers' (e.g. Extract 2.6) b) Students: Boys tell other students to keep quiet and do what they're told (e.g. Extracts 2.12, 2.13)
Response	Student	✓
Feedback/ Evaluation	Teacher	c) Students: Boys evaluate the answers given by other students (e.g. Extracts 2.10, 2.11, 2.21) d) Students: Boys provide unsolicited feedback on what the teacher is telling them (e.g. Extracts 2.8, 2.9, 2.16)

initiative, unlicensed by the teacher. Conversely, if we *are* foregrounding the ways in which these youngsters departed from the conventional structures of classroom talk, it would be wrong to say that these were the actions of youngsters who were disruptive and alienated (see also Chapter 2.6 below). On the contrary, some of their non-canonical activity helped to carry the lesson forward, and indeed in the extracts here, there is only one case where it results in a (mild) reprimand from the teacher involved (Extract 2.12).

Even so, in thematising students' non-compliance with traditional institutional discourse structures, so far the description of talk in class has been largely framed in negative terms of what it's not. Indeed, if the account was left like this, one might infer from this mixture of interest with IRE non-observance that these youngsters really were just a little 'communicatively incompetent', and that the patterns seen here really did derive from their deficient 'listening skills' (as Mr Poyser often told them). To correct this, to thicken the account, and to capture more of the tone or spirit of such episodes, it is worth moving to a characterisation of the non-standard 'aesthetic' commitments that were also often in play among the students, although to appreciate this, we should begin with a few more observations on the normative features of whole-class teaching.

2.3   A contrapuntal aesthetic

In whole-class teaching, teachers are supposed to work with their students to try to build a cumulative public record of authoritative knowledge (Heap 1985). Teachers formulate questions to draw students into the subject matter, and once a student has responded, they use third-turn evaluations as 'turn-stiles', either editing the student's answer down/out, or certifying it as a valid contribution to the shared lesson corpus that they are aiming for. This evaluation is not just for the immediate respondent's benefit but for the edification of all the others in class, and all of the students are expected to keep up with whatever it is that this process as a whole has identified as worthwhile curriculum knowledge.

Whether the subject is Romeo and Juliet, solar systems, or eighteenth century slavery, these interactional procedures are intended to induct students into realms of thought, imagery and experience that extend a long way beyond the here-and-now. Commitment to these curricular realms means that when they are talking to the whole class, teachers struggle with the same 'precarious ideal' that Goffman identifies in lecturing:

> games, joint tasks, theater performances, or conversations, succeed or fail as interactions in the degree to which participants get caught up and carried away into the special realm of being that can be generated by these engagements. So, too, lectures. However, unlike games and staged plays, lectures must not be frankly presented as if engrossment were the controlling intent. Indeed, lectures draw on a precarious ideal: certainly the listeners are to be carried away so that time slips by, but because of the speaker's subject matter, not his antics; the subject matter is meant to have its own enduring claims upon the listeners apart from the felicities or infelicities of the presentation. A lecture, then, purports to take the audience right past the auditorium, the occasion, and the speaker, into the subject matter upon which the lecture comments. (1981:166)

Like lecturers, school-teachers engage in all sorts of 'antics' to try to get/keep their audience engrossed, but in the end, such performance features should serve only as adornments supporting curriculum content, rather than the main business itself. In addition, the 'antics' of school-teachers are constrained (at least)

   i)   by the need to tune their talk to the kinds of understanding they attribute to their students (as evidenced for example in the latters' answers to questions);

   ii) by the textbook representations available in class and by the need for formulations which students will be subsequently capable of rendering in their own writing.

Getting all these elements to work in synchrony is often hard, but as pressures and constraints, they generally mean that whole-class subject pedagogy attaches a lot of weight to conceptual/thematic relevance and to lexico-grammatical propositions,[7] to the extent that researchers have sometimes conceived of learning as a primarily cognitive process (Delamont 1983:119; Edwards and Mercer 1987).

So although a host of other stylistic, interpersonal and institutional dynamics are obviously always also in play when they teach the whole class, teachers normally attach special importance to the articulation of conceptually relevant, lexico-grammatical propositions. This didn't appear sufficient, however, for some of the boys in the Class 9A, and instead of simply taking classroom talk for what it contributed to the cumulative construction of intersubjective mental models of the curriculum topic, allowing it to transport them "past the [classroom], the occasion, and the speaker into the subject matter upon which the [lesson] comments", they appeared to attend very closely to the talk's formal, interactional and stylistic properties, emphasising these as additional or alternative foci for the class.

So, for example, they often treated the utterance they'd just heard as an opportunity for formal linguistic recoding, producing sequences characterised by 'parallelism' (repetition with contrast), picking up pieces of relatively ordinary classroom talk and reworking them into forms that were conspicuously different from the original and often incongruous in the immediate context. These repetitions added little to the development of the propositional argument, and instead, they drew out the poetic rather than the referential potential of the words that they responded to (Jakobson 1960). More specifically, ordinary utterances in instructional and regulative exchanges were transcoded into song (see Chapter 3),

into German (Chapter 4), into non-standard accents, into a different
tempo, prosodic contour, word-stress, etc. For example:

Extract 2.14

In an English lesson. Mr Newton, the English teacher, is calling the class to
order.

```
 8   MR N    erm DONT WASTE- time
 9            everybody
10            js look this way
11            (1.5)
12            ₁thank ╲ you (.)
13            er  we've        ⎡finished- ((5.0 till turn 15))
14   HANIF   ((quite loud: ))  ⎣╲ danke
             ((trans: thank you))
15   ANON              is that gum or (        ) (.)
16   HANIF   gu/m
17   MR N    can I please have-
18   ANON    (       )
19   ANON    (   /   )
20   MR N    can I please have some complete attention
             everybody
21            cos I want to talk for about 5 or 10 minutes
```

Extract 2.15

Same lesson. Role-playing the coroner's inquest into the deaths of Romeo
and Juliet. (Radio-microphone: Hanif. n14:355)

```
ANON M       ╲Tibault ╲Tibault
             he says Tibault
                [tɪbəɫ]
JOHN/ANON   OI ˈTAI╲BOLT
                [taɪbəʊɫt]
JOHN        What did you say?
```

Extract 2.16

The English lesson. (Radio-microphone: Hanif. n14:290ff; '15':782)

```
MR NEWTON   can I please have some complete attention
            everybody cos I want to talk for about 5 or 10
            minutes
            then you're gonna have plenty of time to talk ( )
            yourselves
            in fact that's what I want you to do
HANIF       ((loudly:)) ˈEH?
```

```
MR N        but
JOHN?       ((low pitched, more open, and in the manner of
            wehay – yeah!:))
            \eh!
MR N        what I want- we finished- (1.0)
```

They also often appreciatively recycled anomalous utterances –
musical blurts, bits of German, incongruous back-channelling,
obtuse comments – iconically revivifying a comic or dramatic
moment, savouring some aspect of the very recent here-and-now,
attending *precisely* to the "felicities or infelicities of the presentation" that ought, according to Goffman, remain secondary in an
academic setting. These 'echoings' (which also normally involved
some contrast with the repetition) were often performed with a
half-laugh, co-constructing the salience, memorability, amusement
value of the original (cf. Tannen 1989:64 on 'savouring').

Extract 2.17[8]

The English lesson. (Radio-microphone: Hanif – '15' n14)

```
MR N        as I've said before
            I get a bit fed up with saying (.)
            shshsh
JOHN?       LOU/DER
MR N        you're doing your SATs now
HANIF       |VIEL |LAUTER \SPRECHEN
            |VIEL |LAUTER \SPRECHEN
MR N?       /((emphatic:)) sshh
JOHN        ((smile-voice:)) |lauter \spricken (.)
            whatever that is
```

Extract 2.18

The English lesson – see Extract 2.14. (Radio-microphone: Hanif –
'15':910 n14)

```
ARUN        (  it be'd like they're sort of like) love survive in
            this sort of environment
MR N        their love couldn't sur⌈vive in that sort of
            ⌊                            environment
HANIF                               |WHAT A \LOA:D OF \RU:BBISH
MR N        that's a nice phrase
            ((higher:)) that's a nice phrase you try it
JOHN        |LOAD \o:f \cr:: ((laughing))
```

Extract 2.19

Humanities. Mr A is telling the class about the appropriate language for a court-room (Radio-microphone: Hanif. BL19:92; n14:142)

```
MR A     you can chat in the playground
         using whatever language
         but in a (        ) court
         (.)
         you know
         you're not going to say
         (.)
         `hi there \judgey
HANIF    ((coughs)) \judgey!
         (       ) words
GIRL     (        )
MR A     even if you know the judge
         (even if he's your best fri/end)
HANIF    (("all right mate" greeting quite quietly in broad
         Cockney:))
         a'wi' mate
MASUD    ((quietly:)) all right
MR A     okay
```

In parallel and echoic utterances like these, the students were closely tracking the main discourse on the classroom floor. At the same time, both types of repetition impacted on the lesson's momentum. The boys lingered on utterances beyond the point of comprehension where words yielded their contribution to the development of a propositional argument, and in this way, they appeared to insist that it wasn't simply the rational and disciplinary requirements of the curriculum that propelled the unfolding of activity.

Such utterances also displayed an interest in artful 'performance' as an option within the the official lesson. According to Richard Bauman,

[p]erformance in its artful sense may be seen as a specially marked way of speaking, one that sets up or represents a special interpretive frame within which the act of speaking is to be understood. In this sense of performance, the act of speaking is put on display, objectified, lifted out to a degree from its contextual surroundings, and opened up to scrutiny by an audience. Performance thus calls forth special attention to and heightened awareness of the act of speaking and gives licence to the audience to regard it and the performer with special intensity. Performance makes one

communicatively accountable; it assigns to an audience the responsibility of evaluating the relative skill and effectiveness of the performer's accomplishment. (R. Bauman 1987:8)

In repetitions-with-contrast, students pushed themselves momentarily into the spotlight, bidding for acclaim for their quick wits, resourcefulness or droll humour, while in 'echoings' they acted as the responsive audience that performance plays to.[9]

Overall, these boys engaged in a set of practices which we can characterise as a kind of contrapuntal aesthetic, pulling against the lesson's prioritisation of semantic propositions, working tangentially to its normative drive for intellectual relevance to the curriculum topic (for comparable characterisations of classroom activity, see e.g. Grahame and Jardine 1990:298; Gutierrez et al. 1995; chapter 2.7 below). Rather than tuning out from the main proceedings in class, these boys appeared to intensify their enjoyment by embellishing them, seizing on a wide range of different aspects of the talk they were listening to.

In the previous section, these boys finished sentences for their teachers and peers, reprimanded others for being disruptive, and provided evaluative feedback of a kind that is traditionally the preserve of the teacher. If we search for a more general characterisation that combines this section with the last, inattentiveness and a lack of adequate 'listening skills' are clearly insufficient as descriptions of the classroom behaviour of these boys, and instead, it looks as though they were often actually *hyper-involved*, positively *exuberant* in their lesson participation. Indeed, the performance of Hanif and his circle often provided a sharp contrast to others in the class. "I'm sorry," said Mr Alcott pointing to Hanif's table in one lesson, "look, these people are bursting with enthusiasm – I'd like that to happen on this table too," and then, right at the end of the same class: "by the way (.) I- I've noticed that these four girls haven't answered one single question all morning (.) I noticed that, you're very difficult to ignore in the centre." It seems quite likely that when it combined with the decentring of discursive authority described in Chapter 2.2, these boys' hyper-involvement was a significant factor in the exclusion of most of the girls from whole-class discussion.

2.4   The exclusion of girls

Alison Lee gives the following account of a series of geography lessons for 15 and 16 year olds that she observed in a working-class inner-city secondary school in Australia:

Boys appear in this account as relatively free inhabitants of the space of the geography classroom, producing themselves as particular kinds of masculine subjects within the social/academic language of the site. Through various tactics, boys controlled the physical and spoken discursive space and, in doing so, constructed solidary relations with each other and with the teacher, Alex D, which functioned to 'other' the girls in the class in a number of ways. Together, these process produced a tangibly masculinist cultural dynamic in the classroom.

   It will probably surprise no one that the most lasting impression that I have of this classroom is of boys' voices. This impression accords with much of the earlier research into interactional dynamics in coeducational classrooms (Kelly 1987; Stanworth 1981, 1984; Wolpe 1988). The sense was of male voices physically swamping girls. The boys were generally a very sociable group, chatted (outside the procedures of the formal lesson) constantly across quite large spaces, to each other and to Alex D, with whom they had an easy and informal relationship. Their voices were often loud ... Many of the formal lessons consisted of whole-class discussions, which were dominated by boys. Boys most typically addressed Alex D directly, but occasionally they also addressed each other when an issue became contested. They rarely spoke to girls in these discussions, and when they did, it was to challenge the status of girls' knowledge and of their claims to know.   (1996:72–73)

Lee focuses in particular on a boy called Robert:

Robert's work in class was often to be primary producer of social cohesiveness and solidarity across the boys' subgroups and with Alex D. It was his sociability and interactive skill with boys which, as much as any other single feature of the class, effected a social exclusion of the girls ... This happened through particular kinds of interactive strategies ... Robert produced a ready mixture of formal and informal language accompanied by expansive arm and body movements. He interacted directly with Alex D, finishing his sentences, coughing loudly, and commenting in ways calculated to amuse and entertain the other boys. In doing so, he also managed to perform the part of the involved and productive student, and all of his production remained within the bounds of politeness and friendliness.

   In the meantime, the girls ... were seen but rarely heard.   (1996:74)

Much of Lee's description resonates with my account in the two previous sections, and there are parallels between Lee's Robert

and Hanif in my own research. The English and Humanities teachers
at Central High were worried that the girls in 9A generally kept
quiet in their lessons, and whenever there was a class discussion,
the two girls that I recorded with radio-microphone spent most
of their time talking quietly to each other about other issues.
It was clear that they didn't like speaking in front of the rest of
the class:

Extract 2.20
In the corridors. (Radio-microphone: Ninnette. nr34:187)

```
NINNETTE   no we ain't got a test in Humanities today
           we got it tomorrow
           but we gotta read
           (1)
           today
           (2)
           we gotta report back
           to the stupid
           idiotic
           class
           (.)
GIRL       (and people) are say(in')
           ((half-laughing: )) are you thick
           or something
NINNETTE   (yes)
           I know I know
```

Ninnette's reluctance to speak in front of the class was partly due to
the way boys like Hanif and his friends responded:

```
if I say something, the boys they'll take they'll start
saying 'oh what're you saying that for' and start on you
((Interviewer: yeh)) and laugh at you if you answer this
question and it's wrong and like the girls ain't got
much confidence I don't think, but they need to boost
it up.   (Interview with Alissa Shethar (SI: 571))
```

In an early morning recording before school, Joanne told Ninnette
she wasn't going to go into one area of the playground because
Hanif, Masud and "their shitty little crew" were
"gonna start on me again" (n47:28), and in class, there was
ample evidence in the radio-microphone recordings of boys putting
pressure on the girls whenever they were called to speak. In

Extract 2.21 below, for example, Mr Newton calls for girls to participate and nominates Ninnette. John flags up the girls' potential embarrassment (line 5), and then he and others 'embellish' Mr Newton's
questions with disparaging comments on Ninnette's knowledge (line
12), facetious remarks about dating (lines 19, 21–23), and competition
for her speaking turn (lines 18, 20, 31):

Extract 2.21

English lesson on Romeo and Juliet with Mr Newton (Hanif wearing the
radio-mic. Gex4:116; n14::350).

```
 1   ?MR N      shsh sh shsh
 2    MR N      ((light voice: )) first of all
 3               can I have a couple of girls hands up
 4               (1.5)
 5    JOHN       the girls are (.) embarrassed
 6    MR N      ⎡erm (.) let's try
 7    ANON F    ⎣(             )
 8    MR N       (we) 've had the feud already
 9               Ninnette, you (    ) about these characters
10               Ninnette (.)
11    ANON       feudal system
12    GUY        /Ninnette don't know
13    MR N       Ninnette (.)
14               why do you think
15               apart from the feud
16               that Romeo and Julie might have died
17               can you blame it on any particular people
18    GUY        I CAN
19    JOHN      ⎡yeh Joanne
20    GUY       ⎣Sir I can / (              )
21        JOHN      ((continuing in a quieter side-
                    conversation: ))
                    for going out with Simon
22        ANON      (did she?)
23        MASUD     /Joanne went out with Simon ((half-
                        laughs))
24    MR N      (         ) Ninnette have a go (.)
25               shshshsh
26        JOHN          she did
27        ANON        /((quiet laughs))
28    MR N       IF YOU HAD TO PUT IT ON ONE PERSON Ninnette
29               who would you say was most to blame (.)
30    NINNETTE?  (         ) erm (         )
31    ANON M     Tibault Tibault
```

Here the boys produced a mixture of deviation and conformity to
the line of questioning being posed by Mr Newton, some seeking to
interpose their own answers while others introduced extrinsic issues.
Elsewhere they could be seen taking the teacher's side in disciplinary
issues:

Extract 2.22

The English lesson. Mr Newton is in the stages of telling the class about the
role-play (Radio-microphone – Hanif. n14:290ff; '15':803)

```
MR N    what I want- we finished- (1.0) ⌈we finished erm-
ANON                                    ⌊((in a deep slow
                                          funny voice:))
                                        (          )

MR N    ⌈watching the play
LARA    ⌊((laughing quite loudly about some side business))
MR N    and we've done some exercises
        ⌈to show you understand what happens in it
JOHN    ⌊((to Lara:)) shut up
MR N    ((quite quietly)): Lara
LARA    ((more high-pitched laughing))
ANON M  ⌈(          )
JOHN    ⌊send her out
```

And on other occasions, they urged the teacher to interrogate the
girls more closely.

   In general, these boys' hyper-alertness to their teacher's agenda,
their incessant embellishment of whatever line the teacher was trying to develop, must have made a lot of the girls feel that these boys
and the teacher were working in concert, with the adult using his
power to put them in the spotlight so the boys could prance around
them. Certainly, rather than targeting Hanif and his crew, it was
towards the teachers and their capacity to single them out by name
that Ninnette and Joanne directed a lot of their discontent at being
drawn into the main class business and/or interrupted in their independent conversations:

```
NINNETTE  some of the teachers in the class disturb you
          ((laughter)) ... they start trouble
```
                                              (Interview SI:489)

Extract 2.23

Humanities class. Mr Alcott is asking the class to name the four factors
leading to the abolition of slavery. Ninnette, who is sitting next to Joanne

(wearing the radio-microphone) has evidently been making a (relatively rare) bid for his attention (n42:348).

```
 1   NINNETTE   /becau:se
 2   MR A       Joanne's table
 3              ((to the rest of the class:)) SHSH
 4   NINNETTE   becau:se
 5   MR A       can you give me another factor
 6   NINNETTE   because the slaves rebelled
 7   MR A       excellent
 8   JOANNE     ((in a whisper:))
                Joanne's table!
 9   MR A       so action by the /slaves
10   JOANNE     ((whispering:)) fucking bastard
11              ((light laugh))
```

Extract 2.24

Maths lesson. Joanne (wearing the radio-microphone) has just had a short run-in with Mr Davies, and complained to Ninnette that 'he's a bloody trouble-maker'. Now Joanne and Ninnette are in the middle of talking about the 'Karate Kid' which was shown on TV recently (48:315):

```
 1   JOANNE     ⌈and his son's really important or something
 2   MR DAVIES  ⌊RIGHT
 3              TOO MUCH NOISE FOLKS
 4              (.)
 5              JOANNE
 6              you know what you're supposed to be getting
                on with
 7   JOANNE     ((approximating Mr D's intonation:))
 8              okay::
 9              (5.0)
10              ((quietly:)) won't leave me alone!
```

Joanne appears to accept the reproach in Extract 2.24 (lines 5–8) but it is followed in line 10 by some critical muttering to her friend (cf. Goffman on 'afterburn' 1971:152–153). Elsewhere, she was more up-front in her rejection of reproaches:

Extract 2.25

Early on in the Maths lesson. Mr Davies is going round looking at their work, and now he's talking to Joanne (wearing the radio-microphone), who's sitting next to Ninnette. (48:285, 48:315)

```
 1   MR D      you haven't finished this:
 2             you're tellin' me
 3             or askin' me
 4             to sign it off
 5             and you still haven't finished
 6   JOANNE    yeh: well-
 7             I'll finish it
 8             but
 9             (.)
10             /js sign it
11   MR D      I've got-
12             I've told you what to do
13             haven't I
14   JOANNE    ((impatiently:)) ye:s:
15             ((quieter:)) okay::
16   MR D      (        ) create problems
17   JOANNE    ((loud and emphatic:))
18             I'm not creatin'
19             the problems!
20             (2)
21             ((suppressed laughter))
22             ((quietly to Ninnette:)) don't create pro-
23             am I the one that's-
24             no::
25             ((laughs quietly))
26             he's a bloody trouble-maker
27   NINNETTE  ((laughs))
```

Mr Alcott described Joanne as quite alienated, and she certainly didn't argue when on separate occasions in the radio-microphone recordings, Ninnette said Central High was "a shitty school", and that "it's shitty, the playground". In fact Ninnette made it clear in interview that neither she nor her parents were particularly enthusiastic about the education she was receiving:

```
NINNETTE   they didn't like the education in the school
           it's really awful
           but they finally got used to it
           (interview S1:516)
```

But there were others in the class who displayed much more vehement disenchantment. After a period of refusing to apologise to Mr Alcott for a serious misdemeanour, Lara was suspended from the school for a period, allowed back only with letters of apology,

and most of her teachers found her very difficult to handle. Early on
in fieldwork I witnessed the following episode in an English lesson:

Extract 2.26

There was much more noise throughout this reading session
than there had been in the previous class, and among other
things, in the far back corner of the class, there was a tall
boy called Luke who was enjoying himself ostentatiously
telling people to 'Please keep quiet'. On the other side
of the class at the front, there was a tall good-looking,
mixed race girl [Lara] who at one point, after some loud and
strong words about I don't know what, stood up and stormed
out of the class, slamming the door behind her. 'A moody
girl', one boy commented to me loudly from across an aisle
a few rows up, but Mr Newton, who was away from his desk
talking to someone in the middle of the class, made no
acknowledgement that anything had happened at all
(didn't turn or register her departure).[10]

Overall, the challenges to the authority of the teacher that
I have described in this Section seemed to carry rather different
implications from the ones described among the boys. The disagreements articulated by Hanif and his friends were set within a
more general pattern of close attention to, and sometimes vocal
support for, what the teacher was trying to do. So their challenges
seemed to be framed within a wider agreement on the importance
of the matters on hand. In contrast, the active dissent of Joanne,
Ninnette and Lara was off-set by very few signs to reassure the
teachers of their broader interest and commitment to the proceedings. Their challenges seemed more profound, questioning the
relevance and legitimacy of the classroom enterprise as a whole.
In fact, there was a conspicuous split in the class, between a subgroup of male students who showed an energetic, albeit often
rather anarchic, enthusiasm on the one hand, and on the other, a
number of girls who seemed rather obdurately – and indeed sometimes quite explosively – disaffected.

At this point, however, it's worth standing back a little, (i) to
avoid the risk of a simplistic and exaggerated depiction of over-keen
boys and alienated girls; (ii) to suggest some links between the
different elements described in this chapter; and (iii) to try to clarify
the part that gender played in all this.

2.5   Power relations and the classroom settlement

The broad contrast between boys talking and girls keeping silent was very striking in whole-class talk at Central High, but the situation was more complex than the account so far suggests, since:

a)   there were a number of boys (like Gopal and Khalid) who kept fairly quiet in class discussion;

b)   there were a lot of quiet girls who were far less disaffected than Ninnette and Joanne.[11]

Gender (and sexuality) certainly mattered a lot in these classrooms, and it is very possible that gendered-orientations to speaking in public may have made it easier for boys to talk than girls. But empirically, the male–female split wasn't absolute, and as a matter of theoretical principle, it is important to consider how this relationship between gender and discourse might be shaped by the kinds of activity that these youngsters were engaged in (Goodwin and Goodwin 1987:241), as well as by the wider conditions affecting their lives.

To understand the social and interactional matrix that gave shape to the discourse patterns we have seen, it is necessary (1) to formulate a more encompassing view of how power figured in these interactions; and (2) to consider the ways in the participants' different strategic reactions to unequal power relations might stabilise in something of a self-reproducing system.

To begin, all of the conduct described so far can be analysed as opposition, in different forms, to the educational power-relations that are expressed so obviously and so insistently in the traditional IRE structure of classroom discourse. When students answer a teacher's question – or indeed work on an exercise, or write an essay – their performance is liable to get ranked by teachers on an ordinal scale of better and worse, and this judgement is tied into a very complex educational apparatus, involving a huge array of categories and explanations, rewards, punishments, remediations and so forth. Varenne and McDermott describe what can happen when they discuss a child hesitating to read aloud the letter 'I':

And then, the child's delay is *noticed*. It is noticed by another human being, but not just any human being in a neutral setting. It is noticed by *a teacher* (not a janitor), *in a school* (and not at home), *during classtime* (and not on the playground). Suddenly, the difference between performance and the teacher's expectation has been made into a difference that can make a difference in the biography of the child. The delay has become a 'failure' in need of explanation, evaluation and remediation. The child's act (in this case, the nonact) has been recognised and identified as a particular kind of act that must lead to further actions by possibly a host of other people. In certain schools but not in others, the act-made-into-an-instance-of-school-failure can itself be used as a token justifying an even more consequential identification. The particular act is taken as exemplary of the kind of acts performed by this kind of person; it is now the child, rather than the act, that is identified as a success or failure. The act may be used as a token justifying the school as a whole; there are successful and failing schools. This can be extended to characterise a group with whom the person is identified.   (1998:5 [original emphases])

Returning to whole class talk and the traditional pattern of (i) teacher Initiates (I) => (ii) pupil Responds (R) => (iii) teacher Evaluates (E), the teacher's first turn orients the students to the area they are expected to address in their reply; in the second turn, the particular student takes a shot within the zone that the teacher has identified; and in the third, the teacher indicates how well or badly the student has done. The sequence as a whole demands students' attention and regulates their participation, and the third turn constitutes one of the most micro forms of the classification process described by Varenne and McDermott. Borrowing Foucault's formulation, the IRE can be identified as one among a number of 'techniques of disciplinary power' that "structure the possible field of action of others" (1982:221) and try to "reach . . . into the very grain of individuals, [to] . . . insert . . . [themselves] into their actions and attitudes, their discourses, learning processes and everyday lives" (Foucault 1980:39; 1977:170–194).

   But as we have seen, this technique did not work very well in Class 9A, and to characterise the opposition to it, we should follow Foucault a little further. Surveying "a series of oppositions which have developed over the last few years: opposition to the power of men over women, of parents over children, of psychiatry over the mentally ill" etc. (1982:211), Foucault warns against identifying these struggles with particular political causes and interest groups too quickly. At least in the first instance, this resistance is associated with a concern for self-determination and an objection to the insidious disciplinary techniques that try to stop people from being individuals in the way that they want, and that seek to turn them into the types of person desired within the regimes of expert knowledge. These struggles, Foucault suggests, are 'immediate' struggles for two reasons. In such struggles people criticise instances of power which are the closest to them, those which exercise their action on individuals. They do not look for the 'chief enemy', but for the immediate enemy. Nor do they expect to find a solution to their problem at a future date (that is, liberation, revolutions, end of class struggle) ... [T]hey are anarchistic struggles.   (1982:211–212)

Linking this with Foucault's emphasis on disciplinary techniques, the 'immediate enemy' in the data in this chapter seems to be a set of conventionally structured actions – the IRE – which, if implemented in the traditional way, would give the teacher a good deal of control over students' conduct. At the same time, if a sense of self-determination is the first stake in struggles over power, there is a case for saying that Joanne, Ninnette, and Hanif and company were actually rather *similar* in rejecting docile submission to the teacher's will, but that they differed sharply in their strategies of opposition. Joanne and Ninnette did their best to keep away from IRE-structured discourse, retreating into private conversation, and when they were forced into it, they often made it clear that they experienced this as coercion. In contrast, Hanif and his friends appeared to have 'invaded' the IRE, often inserting themselves into the discursive spaces traditionally reserved for the teacher, and as they were relatively emancipated within it, they moved it along with the kind of noisy consent described in earlier sections.

   In fact, as already noted, the teachers generally seemed relatively willing to relinquish some of control inscribed in the IRE, winning the consent of Hanif and company through co-optation, and this points towards a degree of stabilisation in the relations of talk in Class 9A. My analysis so far has drawn attention to three features of the whole-class discourse – decentred authority, over-exuberance, and refusal. If the focus is widened and these IRE dynamics are set in a broader context, a plausible case can be made that these three characteristics were mutually reinforcing, and the emergence of an at least partial settlement among these potential antagonisms can be modelled as follows:

   1)   For a large number of reasons (including the school's commitment to teaching students of this age in mixed-ability groups), it wasn't easy for all the people in these classrooms to work together to meet the institutional requirements expected of them. The apparent enthusiasm of some of the interested students threatened to spin out of control; there were others

who were quite seriously disaffected; there was a substantial turnover of pupils (with new ones arriving at different times); quite a few had only a very limited command of English; and all this was set against a background of the material disadvantage which so often intensifies conflict over educational power-relations (Davies 2000:3–22).

2) The English, Humanities and Tutor Group classrooms weren't rigidly governed by the traditional IRE structure of classroom talk. I have already presented a number of practical reasons why this was difficult to implement in its pure form, although there were also philosophical justifications for the pluralisation of authority that emerged instead. Oral discussion and the voicing of student views obviously held an important place in the teachers' professional beliefs, and in fact up to a point, it was also expected in parts of the National Curriculum. There is a long tradition of educational thought which sees the IRE pattern of classroom talk as a negative constraint on authentic communication and learning (e.g. Barnes, Britten and Rosen 1969), and indeed freed from the constraints of a rigid IRE, there were occasions when (some of) the students produced some really scintillating intellectual debate in class.

3) At the same time, as others have often noticed (e.g. Gilbert 1988; Czerniewska 1992:Chapter 7), giving students more space to express themselves often means that they say things that don't fit the official agenda, and among other things at Central High (as elsewhere), this involved over-exuberant kids making noisy, provocative and disparaging comments to/ about other students, some of whom didn't want to participate at all in class discussion.

4) Often, rather than putting a stop to this over-exuberance, the teacher seemed much more preoccupied by the conduct of those who were conspicuously disengaged. Faced with the latter's persistent refusal/rejection, it is easy to imagine how teachers could become increasingly – even existentially – dependent on (over-)enthusiastic talk for reassurance, particularly if this talk seemed closely linked to the lesson's intended trajectory. Indeed, in situations where interested students felt that the teacher was getting distracted, they could lend a hand (in whatever way) to get the lesson back on track,

intensifying the processes in (3), exacerbating the alienation of the classroom's 'others'.

5) In sum, we can see the teacher and the keen students developing a strategic alliance that managed to hold the lessons more or less on course. Within the alliance, teachers were inclined to be tolerant of the excesses of apparently keen students, and this is likely to have intensified the exclusion of the disengaged, but as long as the alliance held up, at least some sense of progress and value could be derived from the lessons.

Turning back to the issues that opened this section, it is clear that gender was factored into this system in a number of significant ways. Maybe influenced by culturally gendered dispositions, the main talkers were boys, while the girls were much more reluctant to participate. A fair amount of the boys' attentiveness to the girls seemed to be animated by sexual interest, and their disparaging comments often contained sexist and sexual content (Chapter 9.5). Widespread knowledge of research findings about *girls* talking less in class than boys probably sharpened the teachers' concern about female students keeping quiet, and whatever their motivation, they sometimes directed a lot of effort towards girls in particular (who are quite likely to have experienced all this as concerted male harassment). Even so, if the five points above are correct, it would be a mistake to see the interactional settlement having its primary origins either in sexism or in gendered dispositions *per se*. In identifying self-determination as the first stake in struggles over disciplinary power, Foucault leaves open the question of what student conduct might mean in terms of the wider politics of gender, race and class, and in this model, the main source of polarisation is located in the pressures, opportunities and constraints of the institutional activity in which they were all engaged. There certainly were a range of occasions when gender featured as a category that participants themselves used to try to make sense of what was going on and as such, it undoubtedly did feed into the way that teachers and pupils conducted themselves. But even so,

i) as an interpretive map for trying to understand what was happening, gender had only a rough fit with the territory it sought to describe, leaving, for example, quiet boys and keen girls out of the picture.

ii) With the origins of this classroom dynamic located in pressured situations more than in types of person, it is possible to conceive of *other* social category memberships becoming salient in these processes of micro-institutional polarisation. In fact, loosely comparable accounts where *ethnicity* gets foregrounded can be found in e.g. Foley 1990: chapter 4 and in McDermott and Gospodinoff 1981.

Having said that, it is important to stress that this analysis is focused on a specific interactional genre, whole-class instruction fronted by the teacher, not the entirety of these students' educational experience. A brief discussion of their participation in other genres is now necessary, and this will help to further clarify the difficulties involved in classroom interaction fronted by the teacher.

2.6   Canonical teacher-talk: a meagre genre

Schooling involves a great deal of written text. Lee states that in the classes she observed, "while boys talked, girls wrote" (1996:80), and it was obvious from the radio-microphone recordings that both Ninnette and Joanne were a lot more attentive to curriculum business when they had a written tasks to do. But they were not alone in this. The complex impact of written text was obvious early on in fieldwork:

Extract 2.27
An English class (fieldnotes 12)

After a very noisy period of silent reading, Mr Newton tried to call the class to attention and move into the main business of the day, which was a reading of (an abridged version of) the early scenes from Romeo and Juliet. He didn't really manage to get the attention of the class as a whole (and he certainly didn't hold it for any period), but the play texts were distributed and as they arrived on people's desks, for a brief period there was a semblance of common focus. This recurred later on whenever the play was being read aloud by the pupils allocated to different parts. They generally read their parts very badly – faltering, misreading, late on cue and inexpressive – but for the

```
first half at least, I was surprised that reading aloud
the Shakespeare held them all more or less on task. They
weren't reverential: Mr N reminded them to be polite even
if someone made a mistake, and when a foreign-accented girl
at the front was late on cue as Lady Capulet, there was a
small chorus (3 or 4 boys) of very accented 'Zainab'
('Zainab' was her name I imagine). As soon as the reading
aloud stopped, the class became like a market place, with
many persons and diverse foci of interest. Mr N only moved
towards getting all the different people in the class to
synchronise when he got his 'eyes down everyone' heard
above the tumult, and everyone returned to the script.
```

In one of the German lessons, the teacher declared to the class as a whole:

```
okay, how come every time we do oral work, you get out of
hand. The only time this class can actually (1.5) be man-
ageable is when we do writing
```

And pedagogy in the Maths lessons relied almost totally on individualised worksheets. Reading-and-writing certainly didn't turn everyone into model pupils, but it certainly did seem to change the atmosphere in class.

Beyond reading-and-writing, a lot of lesson time was spent with pupils working in small groups, and in 4 of the 15 Humanities and English lessons recorded at Central High, the preparation and performance of student role-plays was a focal curriculum activity (there were none in the 7 English and Humanities lessons recorded at Westpark). Here and in the weekly drama classes, there was normally some point at which students were required to perform in front of the whole class, and when this happened, the rest of the students were generally far quieter and much more attentive than they were when the teacher was trying to talk to them. Indeed, there was one remarkable instance in a rather disorderly drama class where the students were clamouring to stage a Ricki Lake talk show, the teacher gave way and handed over to Simon, who then took the helm as 'host' and proceeded to manage really sustained, disciplined discussion on the pros and cons of different ways of caring for unwanted babies.

Pupils, then, were much more compliant with curriculum demands when it came to writing, and during role-plays they were generally fairly attentive and sometimes quite inspired. In contrast, they were either over-exuberant or obdurately disengaged when it came to whole-class discussion. The comparison of students' conduct in either or both of these other activities points to three properties intrinsic to teacher-talk in its canonical form that are likely to have made it particularly problematic at Central High: inconsequential assessment; restrictive forms of audienceship; and for some, forced platform performance. I can elaborate each in turn:

- *Inconsequential assessment*: *Written* work was normally quite carefully assessed by the teachers, and their evaluation was entered next to the student's name in a mark book. Students were concerned about their grades, they generally behaved well in tests, and weaker ones often tried to copy the answers off friends who were known to do better. Compared with this, it's clear that even though laughter from the rest of the class or a critical comment from the teacher could make the moment of evaluation very vivid in a whole-class discussion, the evaluative acts in a fast-flowing IRE sequence were relatively fleeting and trivial, contributing much less to the documentary records on each student than the written texts that they produced. Writing fed into records and reports on each individual much more directly than an oral contribution to class discussion, and the concern of students for their documentary profile is one obvious factor encouraging more orthodox conduct during writing.
- *Restrictive forms of audienceship*: When they are listening to an ordinary whole-class discussion, students may well have personal views on the quality of what has just been said, and they may think it's dull or ridiculous. But, in the standard version, if they express their distaste, they are likely to be censured and told to be supportive, and overall, they are expected to subordinate their own assessment to the evaluative criteria and curriculum knowledge possessed by the teacher. In addition, for the audience of peers, active listening in the approved style involves a continuous process of semiotic reduction. Student spectators can often see whoever's talking in all their idiosyncrasies (Goffman 1967:123; Foley 1990:126), but from the midst of this semiotic plenitude, they are supposed to abstract and remember the concepts and propositions that the teacher deems relevant to the development of the curriculum topic (see Chapter 2.3). But as we have already seen, things didn't generally work like this at Central High. None of my

informants deferred without question to the teacher's judgement – Hanif and his crew argued with the teachers and offered
their own evaluations, while Ninnette and Joanne kept busy
with private interests of their own. Nor did they restrict their
focus to the intellectual concepts and arguments that their teachers were trying to communicate: one group volunteered all
sorts of aesthetic embellishments to the main flow of instructional discourse, while the others entertained themselves chatting, singing, and eating sweets. In contrast, in *role play*, there
wasn't a particular concept or 'teaching point' that they were
supposed to abstract and retain from the flow of speech. They
could attend to many different aspects of the performance, and
there was more leeway to respond as you wanted to the proceedings. Rather than being disruptive, laughter, gasps and
comments could enhance the general activity, and if you were
asked for your views at the end, the aesthetic framing of the
activity gave more scope for a take-it-or-leave-it response.

• *Forced platform performance*: Whole-class talk involves what
  Goffman calls a 'platform format':

> The presenters will either be on a raised platform or encircled by
> watchers. The size of the audience is not closely geared to what is
> presented ... [T]he format itself very much answers to the require-
> ment of involving a potentially large number of individuals in a single
> focus of visual and cognitive attention. (1983:7)

Moving beyond the socio-spatial arrangements, it also entails
'performance' in Bauman's sense – "the act of speaking is ...
opened up to scrutiny by an audience ... license[d] ... to regard ...
the performer with special intensity... evaluating the relative
skill and effectiveness of the performer's accomplishment"
(1987:8; Philips 1972:376,381; Arthur 2001:66ff.) – and
although Hanif and his friends relished this,[12] Joanne and
Ninnette generally loathed it. For them, there were advantages
in both writing and role-play. Occasionally, if you did a particularly good piece of written work, you might be asked to
asked to read it aloud, but overall with written work, individuals weren't called to become the "single focus of visual and
cognitive attention" for the whole class, and it was more the
written product that was carefully scrutinised than the practice

entailed in its production. There was a chance that persons sitting close-by might comment on what you'd written, make disparaging remarks to you or your friends (but not the whole class) about your handwriting, etc., but for the most part in writing, neighbours-as-audience tended to be friendly. Turning to role-play, it was obvious that neither Ninnette nor Joanne relished the prospect of actually having to take the stage in sessions devoted to role-play, but while role-plays were in progress, the boundary between performance and audience was fairly clear, and students had a better sense of how long they could relax in an audience identity. Compared with this, whole-class interaction involved cycles of spotlighting, performance and evaluation that were both rapid and insistent, not just cramping you within evaluative criteria you didn't control but also nagging you to participate.

This comparison of whole-class discussion with writing and role-play helps to eliminate a range of factors that one might otherwise consider in the attempt to explain the kinds of conduct described in this chapter. The pupils' behaviour in writing allows us to discount the idea that students like Joanne and Ninnette were completely alienated, involved in a wholesale rejection of the grading and assessment integral to schooling, and it also shows that under different conditions, they were perfectly capable of participating in activities that entailed an element of semiotic narrowing, following the logo-centric rationality of the curriculum, focusing their minds on curriculum ideas and turning these into writing. Equally, we can discount any suggestion that there was an endemic inability to participate in orderly platform events by referring to the evidence of role-play. Instead, the comparison suggests it was the particular blend of elements brought together in the canonical form of whole-class, teacher-led discussion that students found distasteful and that they subverted in their different ways. Indeed, the evidence of how pupils actually did and didn't participate in different activities in class invites a characterisation of whole-class teacher-talk that is strikingly at odds with the standard view, at least as this is represented in the quotation from Edwards and Westgate 1994 at the start of Chapter 2.2. Using the data in this chapter to produce a definition that seeks to reflect the experience and perspective of

Class 9A students, whole-class teacher-led instruction in its traditional form emerges as *a jostling but expressively depleted style of
communication which marginalises students' judgement but threatens to drag them onto the platform with curriculum-scripted performances that in the end don't actually count for very much.*

All of this can be productively placed in a broader context by focusing on the notion of genre. From one angle, genres can be seen as
relatively stable, conventional structures of expectation, mediating
between what happens in interaction and the understanding that members of a social group or network have of the socio-communicative
situation in which they're participating – their sense of the likely tasks on
hand, of the relationships involved, of the ways the activity should be
organised and carried out (cf. Bakhtin 1986; Bauman 2001:79–81; also
Levinson 1979 on 'activity types'). But what actually happens does not
necessarily match the participants' generic expectations, and indeed,
participants themselves do not necessarily have the same generic expectations. According to Hanks, genres "consist of orienting frameworks,
interpretive procedures, and sets of expectation that are ... part of ...
the ways actors relate to and use language", but although they involve a
set of focal or prototypical elements, these elements never become fixed
in a unitary structure:

neither the genre nor the individual work can be viewed as a finished
product unto itself, but remain partial and transitional. The actuality
of discourse changes with its reception, and social evaluation is always
subject to revision. Because they are at least partly created in their enactment, then, genres are schematic and incomplete resources on which
speakers necessarily improvise in practice. (Hanks 1987:681; see also
Bauman 2001:79–81; Foley 1997:Chapter 18)

Hanks identifies a tension between idealised expectations on the
one hand and talk and activity as it actually transpires on the
other, and this corresponds closely to my discussion of the gap
between teacher-led, whole-class discourse in its form as a canonical
genre, and the ways in which Ninnette, Joanne, Hanif and their
teachers actually conducted themselves, introducing successive
adjustments that led to the rather different interactional settlement
described in this chapter.

In a context such as this, one might ask whether the traditional
image of whole-class teacher-talk still has any relevance at all as a

reference point, but Bauman provides the answer when he points to the 'ideology and politics of genre':

[w]ithin any speech community or historical period, genres will vary with regard to the relative tightness or looseness of generic regimentation, but certain genres may become the object of special ideological focus. Prescriptive insistence on strict generic regimentation works conservatively in the service of established authority and order, while the impulse toward the widening of [the gap between the inherited generic ideal and the actuality of behaviour] is more conductive to the exercise of creativity, resistance to hegemonic order, and openness to change.   (Bauman 2001:81)

This applies very closely to teacher-led, whole-class discussion. Whereas the account of Class 9A suggests a number of ways in which this genre has been reconfigured in "the exercise of creativity, resistance to hegemonic order, and openness to change", the quotation from Harris at the beginning of chapter 2 draws attention to the conservative, "prescriptive insistence on strict regimentation" that circulates in a great deal of the public debate about contemporary classrooms. Youngsters like Hanif, Joanne and Ninnette may in practice have negotiated a new settlement with their teachers, but in wider debates about education, the IRE is still an important political emblem.

As Bauman and many others also note, these tensions are shaped in the fluctuating currents of history, with genres both influencing and being affected by wider social conflict and change. In fact, in the penultimate section of this chapter, it is worth trying to situate whole-class teaching at Central High in a larger time-frame. According to Furlong 1985, moral panics about urban classrooms have a very long historical pedigree, and so the question arises: Is there actually anything new or different about the particular pedagogic settlement witnessed at Central High? Are the dynamics of whole-class pedagogy in Class 9A responding to some kind of "new communicative order", or is it just business-as-usual in working-class education in Britain?

2.7   Historical change in the genre?

In the 1970s and 80s, the British sociology of education produced a flurry of classroom ethnographies (e.g. Hammersley 1974, 1976; Furlong 1976, 1985; Pollard 1979, 1985; Turner 1983, Measor and Woods 1984; Hammersley and Woods 1984; Beynon 1985;

Woods 1990). How far do their portraits of classroom life resemble the descriptions in this chapter? Has the discursive organisation of classroom discourse in urban secondary schools stayed much the same over the last thirty years, or were there new ingredients in Class 9A which might be linked to more general cultural change?

There are a range of major methodological differences which inhibit the comparison of my data with these classroom ethnographies from the 1970s and 80s, and these include their relatively limited use of audio-taping, together with the absence of radio-microphones from their fieldwork repertoire.[13] Even so, a lot of their findings resemble the kinds of pattern identified at Central High. Among other things, these studies showed:

- how classes were often split between those who wanted to work and those who didn't;
- how both the most deviant and the most conformist students varied in the extent to which they conformed or deviated, with lots of people in the middle;
- how quite a lot of pupil acts looked both ways, satisfying the demands of both school and peer group – either doing the work without any show of enthusiasm, or putting on shows of enthusiasm that peers understood to be digressive, ironic and/or subversive;
- how work and non-work activity were often closely intertwined;
- how a certain amount of acceptable deviance was taken as routine – "laughter, talking in class, running in school, jostling in line, fidgeting, staring out of windows, not listening to teacher, failure to hand in work, failure to 'try your best' etc." (Pollard 1979:83);
- how teachers drew the line differently, with different classes at different moments (deliberately ignoring a lot of the goings-on);

Nevertheless, at least on the evidence available, it looks as though there might actually have been two quite substantial shifts:

1) in British classroom ethnographies of the 1970s and 80s, there was generally a basic contrast between, on the one hand, lessons as a place/period for work, and on the other, the high priority that young people attached to enjoyment.

In working-class areas anyway, pupil peer groups were seen as normatively oriented to pleasure and amusement, to the extent that keen students felt pressure to conceal their commitment to schoolwork (e.g. Beynon 1985; Turner 1983). In contrast, at Central High in the late 1990s, instead of being defensive about an interest in the lesson, pupils were often quite aggressive trying to keep the lesson on track, making space for curriculum work by challenging the unofficial activity of other pupils (see Extracts 2.12 and 2.13). Of course the motives for this might be mixed (e.g. when telling particular girls to shut up – Extract 2.22),[14] but at other times – for example when the speaker was only addressing friends close at hand – it is hard to see their purpose as anything other than serious (e.g. Extract 2.12).

In addition,

2) ethnographies from the 1970s and 80s painted a picture in which academic work went hand-in-hand with orderly talk along the lines directed by the teacher. When pupils prioritised their own concerns and ways of talking, moving outside the terms of reference/engagement offered by the teacher, this was generally construed as 'deviance' (albeit often in mild forms that teachers were prepared to accept). At Central High, on the other hand, discursive moves traditionally reserved for teachers were appropriated again and again by a group of boys whose oral participation teachers actually rather appreciated. Indeed, there were also some quite confrontational challenges to the teacher which were framed within what looked like – and what the teacher evidently saw as – quite intense commitment to the officially ratified whole-class issue or activity on-hand.[15]

In sum, in the 1970s and 80s, British classroom ethnographies assumed/reported a set of normative oppositions and links which can be loosely described as:

$$\text{lessons} + \text{work } versus \text{ peer group} + \text{fun}$$

and

orderly talk ⇔ deference to teachers ⇔ respect for knowledge and learning

At Central High in the late 1990s, these patterns appeared to be less stable. Talk among *peers* could be aggressively *school*-oriented, while at the same time, there was often a noticeable *lack* of deference in the way that pupils spoke to the teacher about session topics. Valued classroom knowledge – or in Heap's formulation, the public record of authoritative knowledge – was no longer inextricably tied to a procedural decorum managed by the teacher.

There is actually an early glimpse of the destabilisation of these normative patterns in the accounts of black girls at school provided by Furlong 1976, Fuller 1984 and Mac An Ghaill 1988. The equation of fun with peer interaction, for example, is disrupted when Furlong describes how Carol sometimes worked alone, afterwards saying in interview:

Valerie ... and them lot sometimes start to muck about, you know, and I says to them all, 'Why can't you lot behave?' – you know start to tell them off. (1976:164)

And in all three studies, the girls are described as being pro-education but anti-school, keen to learn but opposed to many of the ways that they were treated and expected to behave. At the same time, from Mac An Ghaill's account of a sixth-form college in 1983–85, it doesn't look as though there was any room for non-deferential intellectual commitment in class. Teachers are reported as being critical of girls like these "for not communicating with them in the manner that high-achieving students normally did" (1988:27), and according to one of the girls in Mac An Ghaill's study,

A teacher actually admitted to me, some of my friends were really good but they just did not like their attitude to them, so they put them down [in a lower set]. They didn't even try to understand. (1988:16)

At least in this institution, a commitment to learning was not deemed acceptable if separated from conventional displays of deference.

Elsewhere in the research I have read from the 1970s and 80s, Delamont expresses considerable interest in pupils challenging the teacher's epistemic authority (1983:130–135), but in 1983 anyway, produces only one instance of such a 'crisis', involving the daughter of two research scientists questioning her private school biology teacher on a point of experimental method. Hammersley and Turner suggest that "with recent changes in attitudes to children and in the social organisation of the family, there may be a mismatch between the way pupils are treated in school and outside: outside, certainly among some strata, they are increasingly treated as 'semi-adults'" (1984:169). And Woods (1990:159, 168) also wonders whether "mass communications, changing patterns of child-rearing, career opportunities and so forth" might alter prevailing notions of work at school. But they present no evidence to support such speculation, accepting instead that "the school's authority relies to a considerable extent on [pupils] being 'children'" (Hammersley and Turner, 1984:189), and that "schools are enormously conservative institutions" (Woods 1990:159). So overall, even in those part of the research from the 1970s and 80s where one might most expect to find it, it is difficult to find anything similar to the combination of rather non-canonical classroom talk with intellectual engagement identified at Central High.

So there were certain aspects of whole-class talk at Central High that might be read as evidence of historical shift in the classroom interaction order. Of course, the example of Westpark shows that any such shift is far from universal across schools in London (let alone England), but in different parts of the world over the last ten years or so, there have been a number of other studies showing broadly comparable patterns.

For example, focusing on science lessons in an elementary school in a shanty town in Mexico City, Candela (1999) describes students reversing the traditional interactive roles in IRE, contradicting the teacher, forcing him/her to justify his/her position, nominating speakers, asking evaluative questions, evaluating each others' turns. But this isn't, she argues carefully, a resistance to learning: this redefinition of classroom interactional relations "is [often] constructed around a real interest in knowledge, a collective commitment to try to understand" (1999:158). In a ninth-grade classroom in Los Angeles, Gutierrez, Rymes and Larson (1995) draw attention to what they call "the third space", moments when the division between student and teacher discourse is eroded, and the dialogue enters a new key, with students "not [just] tossing out yet another [random association], but … ask[ing …] question[s] of personal and social import". Focusing on 9–10 years olds in the US Mid-West, Kamberellis describes similarly "hybrid discourse practices", which "help children forge productive linkages between the disparate worlds of school and everday life" and "disrupt traditional power relations and passive forms of student participation"

(2001:120–121; 2000; Kamberellis and de la Luna 1996). And lastly, I have already pointed to the interactional parallels between Central High and the geography classrooms that Lee describes in Perth, Australia, where "the official language of the geography curriculum appeared to pass relatively readily into the social or everyday language of the boys" (1996:77), and where boys "regularly took up positions of authority as information providers, with each other and with the teacher" (page 78).

So overall, (a) the combination of intellectual involvement with a lack of interactional deference that we sometimes saw at Central High has been hard to find in the British classroom ethnographies of the 1970s and 80s, while (b) more or less similar patterns have been described among 10–11 year olds in Mexico City, 14–15 year-olds in LA, 9–10 year olds in the US mid-west and 15–16 year-olds in Perth, Australia. What could this signify?

Given the methodological difficulties involved in the comparison of our data with research from the 1970s and 80s, it is conceivable that these differences and similarities might ultimately have more to do with a global shift in the perspectives and sensitivities of academics than with any historical changes in classroom interactional practices themselves. The last thirty years have seen a shift in the academy from structuralism to post-structuralism and this has generated a new concern for the carnivalesque, the agency of subordinates, and the co-construction of social systems. So taking a sceptical perspective, these patterns could be construed as a simple case of researchers finding what they're interested in.

But to take that line, it would be necessary to discount the influence of a more general tendency that Fairclough calls the "conversationalisation of public discourse", both in Britain and elsewhere (1992a:204; 1995:137–138). Citing Giddens 1991, Fairclough associates this with the emergence of a 'post-traditional' society in which

traditions have to be justified against alternative possibilities rather than being taken for granted; ... relationships in public based automatically upon authority are in decline[; and ... r]elationships and identities therefore increasingly need to be negotiated through dialogue, [in] an openness which entails greater possibilities than the fixed relationships and identities of traditional society, but also greater risks. (1995:137)

And in post-traditional society, conversational discourse gets

> projected from its primary domain, in the personal interactions of the
> private sphere, into the public sphere. Conversation is colonising the
> media (Kress 1986; Fowler 1988), various types of professional/public dis-
> course, education and so forth.   (Fairclough 1992:204)[16]

Public culture, in other words, has experienced a growing separation
of formality and seriousness, and if the unruly curriculum activity in
Class 9A is located within this context, the likelihood that this is a
real rather than merely imagined change in the order of classroom
discourse increases.

Secondly, to hold to a no-change, business-as-usual view of classroom discourse, we would have to assume that over the last twenty
years, teachers have remained both obstinately insensitive to the
commitment to learning of students like the ones reported by
Furlong, Fuller and Mac An Ghaill, and deaf to their criticisms of
schooling in its traditional form. Mac An Ghaill (1988) makes it
clear that the pro-education, anti-school stance of the black girls he
researched in 1983–85 was informed by their political criticism of
prejudiced teachers, racist structures, and a monocultural, imperi-
alist curriculum, but the inflexibility of their schools and colleges
meant that they had to suppress these views in class, adopting an
instrumental attitude that "caused great confusion among their
teachers" (1988:31). At Central High, there was also long history
of black students coming to the school, but there is plenty of evidence that the school was actually very sensitive to criticisms of this
kind. During the 1970s and 80s, it had been in the forefront of
national efforts to develop a politically aware, culturally open curriculum, and in spite of the National Curriculum, there were still a
great many signs of this during my fieldwork (see Chapter 2.1)
above). Staff at Central High had, it seemed, not simply listened to
the complaints of students like Mac An Ghaill's 'Black Sisters' – they
had also reorganised their teaching so that these students' critical
analysis could be both developed and rewarded within the curriculum itself. In sum, it looks as though the combination of commitment with a lack of traditional orderliness in Class 9A formed a
small but significant part of the legacy of post-colonial history in one
specific locale – more specifically, the legacy of a history of negotiation between teachers, minority parents and their children in which

challenges to authority could be accepted as a legitimate part of the life and growth of Central High.

Of course not all schools have shared this experience. But the conversationalisation of public discourse is a very widespread phenomenon, and there has obviously also been global circulation of the ideas informing curriculum developments at Central High ('progressive' educational philosophies and the black and minority rights movement). So when we encounter broadly comparable alterations to the traditional IRE in classrooms in Australia, Mexico and the US, it is easy to imagine that broadly comparable currents and processes might have contributed to the local dynamics in each of these settings as well.

2.8   Summary

In this chapter, I have concentrated on a traditional educational genre – teacher-led, whole-class discussion – and described in some detail the ways in which it was challenged and revised at Central High. Whole-class teacher-talk has become something of an ideological cause in public discourse, where there is a tendency to represent urban classrooms as little more than the chaotic product of incompetent teaching, supported by a bankrupt child-centred educational 'progressivism'. This leaves the teachers and students who work in these schools with little room for anything but feelings of failure and shame, and so one of my aims in this chapter is to try to undermine the hegemony of official discourse with an empirical description of how teachers and pupils actually adapt to the complex array of pressures and constraints that they face in inner-city schools like Central High.

I certainly don't want to suggest that Class 9A was an ideal learning environment; I am not trying to building a moral justification for everything that went on in class; and recommendations for practical action lie well beyond my expertise and present purposes. At the same time, without a realistic account of the ways in which teachers and pupil actually manage to get by in their everyday lives, pedagogic interventions are bound to flounder, and even within the much narrower confines of debate, a lot of ready explanations for the behaviour in this class look questionable when we look at the proceedings more closely. Defective listening skills, gender and sexism; student alienation, and an incapacity to handle semiotically depleted (a.k.a. 'context-reduced') communication, might all be invoked to account for what went on, but when we try to look at how things hold together in such environments, we can see that these are either wrong or only very partial explanations. On an admittedly more moral level, it is also essential to recognise the difficulties that students and teachers work under, the adaptive utility of the strategies they develop, and their hard-won achievements (among which, incidently, one might want to include the development of a probing, non-deferential intelligence). So, in the first instance, my empirical analysis is intended as an attempt to help reset some of the basic terms of engagement with urban classroom issues.

Beyond that, I have also compared the data from Central High with the description of British classrooms in ethnographies in the 1970s and 80s, and from this I suggested that the rather unruly commitment to learning evidenced among some of the students at Central High might represent a new historical development, finding parallels in recent work in other countries. To support this contention, I pointed to a particular history of curriculum change at Central High, and suggested that widespread conversationalisation of public discourse, and the circulation of political and educational philosophies across global 'ideoscapes' (Appadurai 1990), could assist the development of comparable patterns in other parts of the world.

Of course, any impact that discourses in global circulation have on local interactional practice is going to be mediated by a very wide range of different factors, and indeed the same can be said of more 'mid-level', institutional processes like curriculum change. This means my references to conversationalisation and curriculum history can only be taken as circumstantial evidence. They are potshots at 'contextualisation' that increase the plausibility of the case for real historical changes being involved the discrepancy between my own data and data from the 1970s and 80s, but they do not actually tell us much about how such processes work their way into the details of interaction in particular settings. Maybe this is all one can hope for in historical analysis, but in the next chapter I will dwell in more detail on the problems and issues involved in trying to understand how quite general processes impact on everyday life.

Notes

1. As Harris also notes, "[A]fter 1997 ... these ideas were consolidated in extreme form in the National Literacy Strategy (NLS 1997)" 2002.

The National Literacy Strategy legislated for primary schools and focused on the basics of print literacy and standard English grammar, not only dictating what to teach, but also how: in its concern to "train teachers in using the most effective ways of teaching literacy" (Secretary of State David Blunkett DfEE 1998: Foreword; Barber 1997:13), the NLS prescribed a minute-by-minute programme for 'the Literacy Hour' in which whole-class teaching, with pupils' eyes and ears tuned to the teacher, form the main part (two thirds) (Harris, Leung and Rampton 2001). See chapter 1.1 above for an account of the wider context.

2. Indeed as long ago as the early 1970s, Bernstein also proposed that the practical difficulties involved in managing classrooms in the traditional way were an important factor in the development of 'progressive' pedagogies. Teachers had moved to more egalitarian social relations, to increased rights for the taught, to space for diversity, and to interpersonal rather than traditional institutional ('positional') modes of regulation, "*for purposes of [the] social control ... of deviancy*", at least in part (Bernstein 1971b:58 [my emphasis], 61, 65, 67; 1996).

3. Quantitative data comparing students' active engagement with popular media culture at Westpark and Central High can be found in chapter 3.

4. Two methodological notes are in order. First, the extracts that I cite were not drawn from a systematic sample of the structure of classroom interaction. Instead they are a relatively random selection from episodes that had already been transcribed for the analysis of 'posh', Cockney, *Deutsch*, and singing. Even so, the fact that it was very easy to find these examples – readily accessed in transcripts intended for other purposes – is some indication of the recurrence of the kinds of talk I draw attention to, and they are also broadly consistent with most of the rest of my experience of sitting in lessons at Central High, as well as with the quantitative data in Chapter 3.2. Second, my analysis of these extracts falls short of the intensive micro-analysis that forms the basis of my interpretations of German, posh and Cockney in Parts II and III of the book – instead, I only dwell on them long enough to exemplify my sense of the general tendencies (cf. Chapter 10.2.3).

5. Unless otherwise indicated in the 'stage directions', all of the utterances in the extracts in this section that are marked in bold (as well as others) were audible by the teacher (and often picked up by an omni-directional hand-held microphone that I used to augment the radio-microphone recordings).

6. Teachers quite often provide carefully uncompleted sentences in their talk to students, leaving a final part open for students to fill in with 'key' words (see e.g. Hammersley 1974; Chick and Hornberger 2001:35; Arthur 2001:67). But the teacher in the episodes here hardly seems to be engaged in that kind of fishing-for-pupil-knowledge (or oral 'cloze' talk). They're not pausing for terms that they expect the students to know, or hoping that they'll produce a word or phrase that's crucial to the building up of a shared understanding of curriculum content.

7. Of course, teachers often make metalinguistic comments and attend to the poetic functions of language (Jakobson 1960), but when, for example, they commend a pupil's utterance for its formal felicity, its thematic relevance to the topic on hand is also likely to be a major consideration.

8. Here and in the rest of the extracts in this section, underlining points to the elements being transcoded while bold indicates the new form.

9. There is also of course an element of enforced 'performance' whenever an individual pupil has to respond to a teacher's questions (see also e.g. Philips 1972:376,381), and we will return to this in the next section.

10. Lara wasn't the only girl who was capable of this kind of overt resistance.

11. Zainab, for example, said in interview: ``well I don't speak a lot in the classroom because I have to concentrate on my work''. It also seems highly unlikely that boys' derogatory remarks were a major factor in the intense disaffection of someone like Lara. Lara tended to treat Hanif and his friends as either comically or contemptibly immature, and when she was interested, she was actually very well able to argue against them in public discussion (see http://www.cambridge.org/0521812631).

12. Performance in the 'Response' slot of the canonical IRE differs from the 'performance' involved in Hanif et al.'s incessant contrapuntalism (a) in the element of obedience involved in the IRE, and (b) in the teacher's domination of the "special interpretive frame within which the act of speaking [was] to be understood" (Bauman 1987).

13. The studies I have mentioned generally relied heavily on fieldnote observations, and without radio-microphones, they were unable to gain the kind of intimate insight into classroom life we achieved at Central High (cf. Edwards and Westgate 1994:44). Beyond that, there was very little systematic discourse analysis in these studies as discourse analysis itself was only in a very rudimentary stage of development in the 1970s. Instead, they relied very heavily on what pupils said in interview, taking folk categories at face value and using them for the description and analysis of classroom practices, effectively ignoring problematic and varied 'map' and 'territory' relationships. Lastly, relying on observational fieldnotes in an interactional arena where conduct itself is often highly ambiguous, it was harder for resulting accounts to escape the researcher's presuppositions than it is in studies which present transcripts of interaction for the reader's independent inspection (cf. Chapter 10.2.2 below).

14. Of course, in line with the contrapuntal aesthetic described in Chapter 2.3, a lot of the students' talk was polyvalent, only *partly* committed to the terms of engagement being offered by the teacher. But this doesn't mean that at such times the youngsters were really *only* messing about. Research in the 1970s and 80s might have been inclined to classify ambivalent acts as essentially 'deviant', privileging only those dimensions that oriented to peer group entertainment, discounting the fact that in certain respects, those acts *did* engage with curriculum

meanings. But that was their particular analytic bias, not an encompassing description of activity in its fullness.

15. For example:

Extract 2.28

Drama class. In a role-play discussion of abandoned babies, Hanif has been playing the role of 'Professor Simpson', and in the course of this, he has used the words "bitches" and "they know bloody well". Ms Briggs has frozen the action and is now pulling him up on this. (Radio-microphone: Ninnette. N29 – rl 1316)

```
 1   MS BRIGGS      now I don't think that a professor of philosophy
 2                  you did really well in the beginning and then for
                                                             some reason
 3                  you decided to swear
 4   ANON           (      swear   )
 5   MS B           which actually wasn't/appropriate
 6   ANON M         ((high falsetto:)) woo-ow!
 7   ANON M         you wouldn't do that (.)
 8   ANON M         /whe::re? (('jokingly'))
 9   ANON M         you:: wouldn't do that
10   ANON M         /((laughing:)) where
11   ANON M         ((laughing:)) you (weren't) thinking it
12                  ((others also laughing))
13   MS B           (    )
14   JOHN           ei bitches/is a swearword
15   ANON           yes
16   ANON MS        ((talking at same time, volume increasing)) (2.0)
17   ANON M         it's in the way you use it
18   HANIF?         (       )
19   ANON           shshshsh
20                  ((noise dies down a bit))
21   ANON M         it's in the way you use it
22   HANIF          I mean (.) I mean erm
23   MS B           let me just explain (1.0)
24   ?              shsh ((Anon Ms talking))
25   MS B           it was probably not-
26   ANON M         ((laughs))
27   MS B           I'd like you all to be listening to this
28                  (2.0) ((noise dies down))
29   MS B           it was probably not/appropriate for that
                                              character to choose
30                  that kind of language
31   ANON M         (     )
32   HANIF          but that's how I felt though
33   ANON M         ((laughs))
34   HANIF          I felt that those women (.)/who-
35   ANON M         (     )
36   HANIF          and I still do that that-that-that
37                  /(.) that wrap up their children in a=
38   ANON F         (       )
39   HANIF          =rag cloth and put them in a (.)
40                  a-a-a-a a cardboard box (.)
41   ANON M?        I agree
42   HANIF          m-mind my French right
43                  they're bitches
```

```
44              that's how I feel
45   MS B       as a philosopher
46   HANIF      as a philosopher and-and as a- and (        )
47   MS B       okay (2.0) so
48   ANON       (                    )
49   MS B       I'm saying that for your assessment
50              (you'd need to think) about your language
51              (      ) appropriate (.) to character yeah (.)
52   ANON M     ((funny voice in the background: )) mind your
                language
53   MS B       okay
```

16. If we assumed that this conversationalisation process simply entailed the trivialisation of public discourse, then there would be no reason to link it to the specific changes in classroom interaction that I have suggested. Researchers in the 1970s and 80s equated high levels of informality in class with low levels of educational commitment – in Bernstein's formulation, "the weakening of [the traditional] frame occurs usually with less 'able' children whom we have given up educating" (1971b:58) – and if Fairclough were only talking about 'dumbing down' and a deterioration in public standards, there would be little relevance to the combination of informality and intellectual engagement that we found at Central High. But he's not. The conversationalisation of public discourse also embraces the dialogical, non-deferential articulation of very weighty matters (and as Harris notes, this can be seen any time on the floor of the British House of Commons).

3

Popular culture in the classroom

In the last chapter, I concentrated on an educational genre, whole-class discussion fronted by the teacher, and I outlined a number of modifications to its canonical form evidenced in Class 9A. Teacher-fronted discussion was now open to quite a wide variety of different expressive practices, and in this chapter, I focus on some of the practices associated with popular media culture. The centre of attention shifts, in other words, from a genre associated with learning and work to practices associated with consumption and leisure, and the guiding question is: How far, and in what ways, was classroom activity influenced by popular media culture in general, and by popular music in particular?

I won't be able to engage directly with the question of historical change in this chapter, since I haven't accessed any loosely comparable datasets or reports on popular cultural practices in class from the 1960s–80s (compare Chapter 2.7). But instead of trying to achieve time depth empirically, I shall try to work quite systematically through some of the very different kinds of process that are necessarily involved when, for example, it is claimed that changes in popular media culture are altering the way kids listen to their teachers. A shift in the production values governing television (Eco 1992) or the availability of a new communications technology, may be widely noticed, but if we are to understand how this impacts on the small details of everyday life, we need to see how the new cultural style, form or object gets received in particular social networks and institutions, and how it is apprehended, appropriated and/or refashioned in particular relationships, locations, activities, against a background of fairly specific opportunities and obstacles (cf. Silverstone and Hirsch 1992). In fact, these are important questions whether or not one believes that there have been major social changes – it is impossible to understand either change *or* stability without some kind of map of the relationship between phenomena and processes that differ in time-scale and socio-spatial scope, and so in thickening the description of discourse in Class 9A, I shall also try to locate their media cultural practices within this kind of differentiating, macro-'meso'-and-micro framework.

The chapter begins by pointing to claims about the impact of media culture on schools and classrooms (Chapter 3.1). It then outlines a project in which Roxy Harris, Caroline Dover and I set out to examine the ways in which young people's participation in 'techno-popular' culture[1] influenced their conduct at school. The project combined quantitative, ethnographic and interaction analysis, and Chapter 3.2 describes the findings of our survey of Central High and Westpark. Overall, youngsters oriented to popular media culture quite a lot more often at Central High than at Westpark, and music and song proved to be popular cultural forms that youngsters at Central High engaged with most often. In the sections that then follow – Chapter 3.3 to 3.6 – I explore the positioning of popular song within everyday activity: how it enters the class, the kinds of sociability it offers, the ways it gets woven into different kinds of friendship, and its place in the kinds of classroom dynamic I described in the previous chapter. Then in Chapter 3.7, I argue that instead of seeing the proceedings at Central High as a chaotic corruption of the canonical patterns of teacher-talk, there is a strong case for seeing teacher-fronted interaction in Class 9A as a mixed genre with a distinctive momentum of its own, emerging at the point of encounter between curriculum priorities and popular culture (as well, no doubt, as a range of other influences). After that, in Chapter 3.8, I review the different levels covered in the analysis, and conclude that, as Bakhtin and a wide range of others suggest, it is essential to focus on genre in any effort to understand the interaction between macro and micro processes.

This chapter, then, has two principal objectives: first, to enrich the account of everyday life in Class 9A by describing popular culture's intimate role in classroom activity, and second, to explore the relationship between large- and small-scale social processes.

3.1   Classrooms and popular media culture

The development of fast, digital, multi-media communications in the globalised, 'networked' society is quite often said to be weakening "the symbolic power of traditional senders external to the system" (Castells 1996:374–375), and school-teachers are frequently identified among the 'senders' that are now vulnerable (Tiffin and Rajasingham 1995:73; Richards 1998). It is often proposed that contemporary mass media are changing social relationships in society at large, encouraging more egalitarian, informal and familiar forms of communication (O'Sullivan 1998:199; Eco 1992), and it is also suggested, for example, that moves from mass communication, where the few speak to the many, to a new set of more mobile, decentred, interactive communicative media, are likely to have a significant impact on discourse relations in schools (Holmes and Russell 1999). In a summary of some of the debate, Sefton-Green notes, for example, that "young people who regularly 'surf the Net' at their own pace may well find the regimented structure of a teacher-led curriculum tedious" (1998b:12).

In the last chapter, we saw that quite a few members of Class 9A indeed did seem to find "the regimented structure of the [traditional] teacher-led curriculum tedious", at least in its traditional form. In fact, when this class was compared with research from the 1970s and 80s, I identified certain aspects of the talk in Class 9A that were hard to find in the accounts of classroom interaction twenty to thirty years ago, and I suggested that the emergence of these features might be linked to socio-cultural changes such as the conversationalisation of public discourse in society at large, and, more locally, the revision of curricula in the light of post-colonial critique. Sefton-Green broadens "the directions" from which "traditional notions of authority and transmission are being undermined", and he goes on to add an important cautionary note:

Of course, we have to question the idea that it is the digital technologies, the Net or the computer game, [or any other factor] which is/are solely responsible for undermining these power relations. If attitudes to learning are changing, we have to consider an extremely broad range of influences from the intellectual challenges of progressive education to the market's subversion of paternalism. Yet again we need much more evidence about these changes, rather than allowing theoretical speculation about such changes to stand for the facts. The co-existence of digital technologies and post-modern theory is more than a coincidence obviously, but the matrix of influences that create social change are complex and highly variable between different local situations.   (1998:12)

It was against this background of debate that Roxy Harris, Caroline Dover and I set out to look more closely at the influence of techno-popular culture at school, aiming to provide some of the evidence on "different local situations" that Sefton-Green says is so sorely needed. Our project involved reanalysing the dataset collected in 1997–98, and we were guided by two questions:

- Who engaged with what aspects of techno-popular culture, how, when, where at school, and against what background of obstacles and opportunities?
- How was the relationship between students' affiliation to media culture and teachers' commitment to curriculum instruction actually negotiated in classroom interaction?

Our methods of analysis involved:

- an ethnographically oriented survey of media-related activity at Central High and Westpark, focusing on 9 students[2] in over 80 hours of radio-microphone recordings, covering interaction in 70 lessons and in lunch- and breaktimes.
- Intensive case studies of the media engagement of individuals over several continuous periods of 2–4 hours, also drawing on fieldnotes and interview data wherever we could.[3]
- Transcription and micro-analysis of particular episodes, focusing on the ways in which media-oriented discourse fitted in with the social relations and curriculum activity in class.

This meant that in one way or another, our discussions ranged across processes that differed very substantially in their scope and duration. We considered:

i) historical and communicative processes in society at large. Here we drew on the literatures in education, sociology, media and cultural studies,[4] and some of this has obviously provided the introductory framing for this section;

ii) the conditions and ethos in particular schools and classrooms;

iii) the cultural resources and dispositions that students brought
with them (their wealth, linguistic abilities, educational expectations, and positioning within (sub-)cultures of consumption);
iv) the positioning of individuals at school and within the peer
group.

For (ii), (iii) and (iv) we drew on our own ethnography, some of which
has already been presented in Chapter 2.[5] Lastly we focused on:

v) the discourse within specific communicative events, and the
kinds of interactional use to which different media lent themselves (drawing on the synthesis of interaction analysis and the
ethnography of communication that informs interactional
sociolinguistics).

The intensity and depth with which we engaged with these areas for
analysis varied very considerably. But we could map them into the
four dimensions of social reality identified in the realist social theory
of Layder (1993) and Carter and Sealey (2000),[6] and if popular
culture does impact on classroom conduct, then in one way or
another, we would expect to see processes associated with this
impact operating in all five analytic areas.

At the same time, we were not aware of any empirical studies of
techno-popular culture among young people which did actually
address each of these areas and their inter-connections, and the
absence of interactional micro-analysis was particularly striking.
In a programmatic statement on *Media and Everyday Life in
Modern Society*, Moores concludes that

[media studies] must ... account for the complex ways in which communication and information technologies are 'knotted into' everyday encounters between co-present participants. Those relationships which people
form in places like households, neighbourhoods, work and leisure contexts
are frequently negotiated around electronic media – in the course of using
television, radio, telephones or computers. (2000:145)

He goes on to suggest that:

[b]eyond the front door, in the neighbourhood setting, there are also occasions when media technologies [and their symbolic contents] can serve as
props for the performance of identity – or else for struggles over the meaning
of local community ... Reception analysts in media and cultural studies
have [now begun, for example,] to document the circulation of TV

narratives in public workplaces and leisure interactions too. (2000:146, 147; see also Bausinger 1984; Spitulnik 1997, 2001)

According to Hesmondhalgh (2002:118–119), there is a pressing need for similar kinds of analysis within popular music studies, the field of enquiry closest to the data I analyse later on in the chapter. There is a commitment to asking the big questions:

> if we lose sight of the historical circumstances in which we experience music, and in which we live our everyday life, then there is a risk of evading questions concerning history, power and meaning. (Hesmondhalgh 2002:128)

But exactly how the movements of history connect to the details of ordinary life remains largely uncharted.

In what follows, I shall outline some of our findings, paying particular attention to the links *between* the different levels of analysis outlined in (i) to (v) above. But I will start with our survey.

3.2   Popular culture in class: a survey

Most of this book focuses on Central High, but this was not the only site for fieldwork in 1997–98, and in our 2001–02 study of media and popular culture at school, we also looked at Westpark.

As I hinted in Chapter 2.1, Westpark was rather different from Central High. It was located in a suburb rather than in the centre of London and it served a much more stable student population, most of whom had family roots in the Indian subcontinent. Students at Westpark tended to be better off than those at Central High (about a quarter received free school meals, compared with more than half at Central High); only half as many were registered as having special educational needs (15%); and in 1999, when informants took their 16 + GCSE exams at the end of compulsory schooling, more than 60% of Westpark students got 5 or more GCSE A*–C results, compared with less than 20% at Central High. In all, the inclusion of Westpark gave us some purchase on the relationship between popular culture in class and different levels of material and educational advantage.

For our survey of media practices, Caroline Dover, the project officer, listened to 82½ hours of spontaneous interaction recorded on radio-microphone at both schools, and she identified episodes where there was an orientation to media and popular culture in the talk of either students or teachers.[7] More specifically, she noted every occasion in the 82½ hours when the 9 youngsters wearing radio-mics (4 at Central High, 5 at Westpark), their friends and their teachers either referred to, alluded to, used or performed music, television, film, computers, electronic games, telecommunications (phones, mobiles, pagers), newspapers and magazines. In all, she identified about 275 episodes.

First, we compared the overall findings with a very large self-report survey of young people's media and popular culture, conducted in the UK over the same period by Livingstone and Bovill (1999). From this, it emerged that there was nothing particularly idiosyncratic about the youngsters in our sample: music and television featured much more often than other media;[8] boys oriented to computers and electronic games more than girls;[9] and mobiles had not yet had much impact.[10]

Next, we looked at the 'when' and 'where' of these media involvements, and we found that pupils oriented to media and popular culture at some point in most of the lessons that we recorded (51 out of 70). At the same time, at both schools students tended to treat the official curriculum and popular media culture as normatively separate realms. Teachers did occasionally make film, television, print-media or computers an important focus for discussion in class, and they also made a few incidental references.[11] But inside class, out of 166 episodes when students oriented to media culture in interaction with their peers, youngsters tried to use it in a serious contribution to curriculum work on only 3 occasions, and outside class, there were only 8 out of 84 episodes when students linked media culture to curriculum work.[12]

So far, then, the survey suggested that:

• these youngsters' spontaneous media talk at school conformed to more general patterns of media consumption among youngsters in Britain at the time,
• popular media culture (PMC) was indeed a fairly routine element in their lived experience of lessons and school,

while at the same time

• PMC did not appear to have been assimilated to the curriculum as an integral part of students' learning – at least not with anything like the frequency that kids themselves oriented to PMC.

In sum, the findings so far suggested that there could indeed be some substance to the original contention that we had set out to examine: popular media culture and classroom relations at school might be at odds.

Moving to a closer look at each school, it then emerged that there were substantial differences between them. During lessons, pupils at Central High oriented to popular media culture more often than pupils at Westpark: media-oriented activity featured in about 90% of the lessons we surveyed at Central High (28/31), while at Westpark, it featured in about 60% (23/39). In pupil–pupil talk during lessons (rather than in pupil–teacher interaction), episodes featuring popular media culture occurred at an average rate of 3.8 per hour at Central High, whereas between peers during lessons at Westpark, the rate worked out at 1.7 episodes per hour.[13] There were also noticeable differences in the ways in which youngsters displayed these popular cultural involvements. Dover's survey distinguished between (a) 'performative' invocations of popular media culture – mimicry, tapping, humming and singing – and (b) explicit references to it as a topic. Performative invocations were much more frequent at Central High than at Westpark – 2.8 per hour (74 episodes) compared with 0.5 per hour (18)[14] – and a great deal of these turned out to involve music. Indeed, there was far more unofficial music-making in class at Central High than Westpark. Central High students engaged in informal music-making episodes in about two thirds of the lessons we recorded (20/31), at an average of 2.5 episodes per hour (67 episodes in all). In contrast, there were only 13 episodes of singing, humming or tapping at Westpark, occurring in around a quarter of the lessons (10/39), averaging 0.3 per hour (13 instances).[15]

The comparison between Central High and Westpark invites us to situate the relationship between popular culture and schooling in a larger socio-economic landscape. Judged by objective indicators, the students at Central High experienced greater material disadvantage than those at Westpark, and twice as many were classified as having special educational needs. Conditions of this kind are quite often associated with noisier, less monologic classrooms (e.g. Davies

2000; Kapferer 1981; Collins 1987:311), and indeed as I mentioned at the start of Chapter 2, it was generally harder for the teacher to control the talk in lessons at Central High. Beyond that, unruly classrooms allow more space for spontaneous popular cultural performance, and so these associations can be sketched as:

greater socio-economic disadvantage ⇨ noisier classrooms ⇔ more popular culture in class

On its own, this pattern is hardly very surprising, but it actually covers a number of different 'levels', ranging from general processes (such as socio-economic stratification) to more local and specific ones (like pupils interacting in a lesson). The processes and activity at different levels are organised in ways that are often fairly distinctive, only partially shaped by processes at the other levels (Goffman 1983; Layder 1993), and as the rest of this Chapter will show, this makes the connection between wealth, classrooms and popular culture a lot less predictable than the 'arrows' above ('⇨' and '⇔') might suggest.

To take forward this examination of the links between processes that differ in time-scale and socio-spatial scope, I shall focus on the popular cultural practice that appeared to be most common in our survey – humming and singing – and I shall start right at the 'bottom', working 'upwards' step by step. How did pop songs get into school? What did they contribute to everyday life there? How far and in what ways did they present a challenge to the main business of school? And how should a song's 'career' at school influence the characterisation of contemporary urban classrooms?

3.3   Songs stuck in the head

According to Simon Frith, scholarly analyses of music often emphasise

structural qualities, rather than … the qualities of a work in time, the qualities of immediacy, emotion, sweat – suspect terms in both the library and the classroom [so that in the end] how people (or, rather, critics and scholars) talked about music became detached from how people (musicians and listeners) felt about it. There was always an excess in musical experience, something unreasonable, something that *got away*.   (1996a:116; see also e.g. Sontag 1967)[16]

I do not know whether or not Frith is being fair to music scholarship, but there was plenty of evidence from the lapel radio-microphone that certain tunes had a compulsive appeal to particular individuals, and that in Frith's words, these youngsters "absorb[ed] songs into [their] lives and rhythm into [their] bodies" (page 121). Joanne, for example, spent one morning humming and singing "It's gotta be you" by 3 T, while Hanif spent a lot of time with a tune from a Skips crisp advertisement:

Extract 3.1: Joanne's morning with 3T

One morning during the first lesson of the day, while Mr Alcott is talking to the class as a whole, Ninnette asks the girls on her table (Joanne, Anna & Rita): "Who likes 3T?", an African American boy band. Joanne says she does – 'kind of' – and Rita says she particularly likes their song 'It's gotta be you'. Ninnette agrees, and Joanne then breaks into quite a loud rendition of the first two lines ("It's gotta be you/no one else can do the things you do"), singing this over the top of some further chat between her friends. After momentarily interrupting the topic to make a derogatory remark about the teacher's appearance, they briefly discuss whether anyone has got the song, and then they move on to other issues. A few minutes later, just after she's been commenting on the general election result with Ninnette, Joanne does a rather staccato performance of the second line, much to the amusement of Ninnette, and then when the chat closes, Joanne hums a few notes to herself before lapsing into silence. Half a minute or so later, during another spell not talking, she hums another phrase from the song very softly to herself, a couple of seconds later transposing this to (what sounds like) the imitation of an electric guitar, again very softly. The words and musical phrases from "It's gotta be you" now stay with her for the rest of the morning, reproduced in a variety of different interactional formats: referred to ("can I borrow that tape" [see Extract 3.7]), sung in partnership with Ninnette or another girl (with varying degrees of loudness), announced to a friend ("I was just singing"), hummed or sung to herself when she is temporarily a side-participant in a conversation or the conversation lapses, while she is walking down the corridor between lessons, waiting to go into the classroom, listening to the teacher talking, fetching her book, working on a Maths exercise, and so on. It isn't the only tune in her repertoire that morning, and she also sings or hums the refrain from Queen's 'Bohemian Rhapsody'

(made popular again by the film 'Wayne's World'), lines
from 'You're gorgeous' by Babybird, and the Whitney
Houston signature tune from the film 'The Bodyguard'.
But at lunchtime, shortly before I collect back the radio-
mic, 'It's gotta be you' is still circulating. Joanne and
another girl briefly organise a short chorus together –
Girl: "one (.)" Girl and Joanne together: "two (.) three
(.) 'Gotta be you [etc.]'" – and then Joanne reverts to
singing it to herself. As she herself says a few days
later, the song has got "stuck in my head". (Summary from
notes on radio-microphone recordings)

Extract 3.2: Two fragments from Hanif's morning

DURING MATHS: Hanif likes Maths and he's one of best in class
at it – indeed, at the end of the lesson, he asks if he can
come back after school to carry on. Today most of the lesson
has been taken up with a mental arithmetic test, and he's
been quiet throughout. But when the test is over and
they've all reported on how much homework they've done, he
starts working alone on a worksheet and begins humming off-
and-on till the end of the lesson (31 times in all). At its
fullest, he hums two lines of six notes each (we haven't
been able to identify the tune) but it is often only the
last three notes. This is interspersed with brief flurries
of talk – for example, there is one 3½ minute period where he
asks the teacher if he can ask him a question, lapses into
silence, hums 4 lines, lapses into silence, hums 2 more
lines, keeps silent for 16 seconds, half-hums, falls
silent, gives some help to Anna nearby, falls silent, hums
another four lines and then declares that his pen's run
out. Most of the humming is within his normal pitch range,
but as the lesson ends and there is the noise and animation
of clearing away, he switches to falsetto for the last
seven renderings before he leaves the room. Once he's
left, he half vocalises these lines three times (not in
falsetto), and then whistles them once on the way out to
break.

AT THE END OF HUMANITIES: The instructional part of the history
lesson has finished, and the class is packing up. After a
brief flurry of talk about the homework expected for the
next lesson and some kind of non-word closure of the topic,
Hanif lapses in silence for about 2 seconds, and then
starts singing a few bars quite loudly: "just driftin'
away/just driftin' away/ ah hah hah" (a jingle advertising
Skips crisps). This is overlapped by some procedural

directives from the teacher, and Hanif stops for a few
moments, and then resumes very quietly, transposing it
into falsetto, and with the words only half-articulated.
Continuing to sing softly like this, he fiddles with
the radio-microphone transmitter, turning it on and off,
and then suddenly breaks off with "aah!", commenting that
the transmitter in his pocket is uncomfortable. A friend
addresses him with a few words about the arrangements
for a game of soccer later on at lunchtime, he exchanges
a couple of words with his neighbour, and after another
three seconds of silence, he quietly resumes the Skips
tune. (Summary from notes on radio-microphone recordings)

With a video-recording, a lot more might be said about how
Joanne and Hanif's humming and singing synchronised with their
physical activity and surroundings. Even so, it was obvious that
when they hummed and sang to themselves from time to time, the
varying combinations of words, stances, voice and melody that this
involved (Frith 1996b:159–160) provided quite an insistent but
pleasurable soundtrack overlaying visual and physical experience.
At the same time, this data qualifies the survey finding that education and popular media culture were broadly counterposed. Schoolwork and popular song could be complementary when soft solo
humming and singing served as an accompaniment to writing or
reading.

   Of course in addition to its interior resonance, music is also
obviously shared, "provid[ing] us with an intensely subjective
sense of being sociable" (Frith 1996b:273):

At the same time [as absorbing it] ... music is obviously collective. We hear
things as music because their sounds obey a more or less familiar cultural logic,
and for most music listeners (who are not themselves music makers) this logic is
out of control ... The experience of pop music is an experience of identity:
in responding to a song, we are drawn, haphazardly, into emotional alliances
with the performers and with the performers' other fans.   (Frith 1996a:121)

One very good way of analysing this 'experience of identity' is
to explore the imagined realms, styles and (sub-)cultures associated with particular songs (Frith 1996b:273ff.), but we can also
gain some purchase on the kind of sociability that music affords
by temporarily holding to the interactional level that Moores
referred to (Chapter 3.1), comparing song's interactional potential
with some of the properties of talk.

3.4   The interactional potential of humming and singing

Humming and singing in school provide opportunities for a particular kind of sociability, and a rudimentary comparison of singing with conversation can help to make this clear.

Canonically in conversation, a turn-at-talk is addressed to identifiable recipients; it claims some relevance to him/her/them; it makes reference to the world around; it is internally organised with local situational exigencies in mind; and very often it expects – and sets up the lines for – a reply from the interlocutor(s) (see e.g. Goffman 1981:Chapter 1; Schegloff 1988; Heritage 1997:162–163). So for example, when Ninnette asked ``Who likes 3T'', the girls around the table understood she was speaking to them, rather than talking to herself; they took it as a sensible question, addressed to an issue they were likely to have an opinion about; they could identify who and what she was referring to when she said "who", "likes" and "3T"; they recognised that they were being addressed as a group (rather than singled out as a particular individual, as in 'do you like …'); and they knew that the thing to do next would be to provide some kind of answer (``me – kind of'' from Joanne, and ``I like their song 'It's gotta be you' '' from Anna).

In contrast, the words of a song are normally pre-formulated, created by the original lyricist in a setting that is far removed from the particular situations where the song is being revoiced, and so, usually, the sentence structure is not organised in a way that requires a reply. When Joanne sang ``It's gotta be you / no one else can do the things that you do'', nobody said "thanks" or "look I'm really busy right now", and in a similar vein, when Hanif sang ``they're melting away/just melting away'', no one asked "where?" or "how can we stop it?" And of course when they *hummed* these tunes, there weren't any words for their friends to reply to. Instead, informal solo music-making in company was normally passed off as 'exuded' rather than intended expression, 'given off' rather than given (Goffman 1959:14). Indeed, on the occasions when Hanif wanted his friends to respond to his singing in kind, he had to say so in so many words: ``come on you f***** – he does it – he does it – he does it – then me'' (Gex4:1473ff.).

Solo humming and singing, then, don't demand a reply in the way that a turn in conversation does. But that does not mean that they cannot be noticed by those nearby, and instead, in company, solo humming and singing contribute to the 'hummer's' interactional 'demeanour', their self-projection as someone who is or isn't reliable as an interactant, who is or isn't poised for communication, who is or isn't likely to endanger others, etc. (Goffman 1967:77). When either Joanne or Hanif hummed or sang on their own, it certainly did not signify that they were obsessively abstracted/ 'away', incapable of responding to happenings-on-hand and the approaches made by others. But opting for music rather than silence had implications. On the whole, when they are not talking, people lapse into silence:

> Silence ... is very often the deference we will owe in a social situation to any and all others present. In holding our tongue, we give evidence that such thought as we are giving to our own concerns is not presumed by us to be of any moment to the others present, and that the feelings these concerns invoke in ourselves are owed no sympathy. (Goffman 1981:120)

When Joanne and Hanif hummed within easy earshot of their peers, they appeared quite happy for their interior feelings for a tune to be noticed rather than hidden, relatively confident that their expressions of personal taste at least wouldn't meet with antipathy.[17] I will look at how Joanne and Hanif negotiated the peer group status of their tastes in the next section, but on the topic of interactional affordance, it is worth noting that even though solo humming and singing did not require a reply, they often allowed or invited an *evaluation/appreciation*. On one occasion, for example, after a loud snatch of "they're walking away/just melting away" from Hanif, Satesh responded with "oh yeh, Skips, I like that", and later, after a particularly passionate rendition, Hanif turned to Satesh with his friends around and asked: "are you [the] only one that likes that song?"

And sometimes, of course, rather than either treating a bit of song as private expression that they were simply overhearing, or limiting themselves to a laugh, groan or comment on it, one or more of the people around actually joined in, singing alongside or taking up the tune at the point where their friend left off. For example:

Extract 3.3

Humanities lesson, while Mr Alcott is conducting a discussion with the whole class. Joanne (wearing the radio-microphone) is sharing a table with Ninnette, Anna and another girls (N43:wm177).

```
 1  JOANNE    ((responding to a question from ?Anna:))
 2            no
 3            it takes me longer when I try and do (that)
 4            (2)
 5            ((quietly, whispering the last syllable:)) it
              takes me longer
 6            (3) ((during which boys are laughing at
              something said in whole class discussion with
              Mr Alcott))
 7  GIRL      ((singing:)) "gotta be you"
 8            (.)
 9  JOANNE    ((continuing the song:)) "no one else can
              (do-  )
10            all  [(the-
11  NINNETTE  all) [the things you do"
12  JOANNE    can I borrow that tape and disco
```

Extract 3.4

The start of a Maths lesson at little later. Joanne and Ninnette appear to have just taken their seats next to each other. (N43:wm325)

```
 1  GIRL AT SOME  [((hums several notes from 'It's gotta
 2  DISTANCE:     [  be you' quite loudly))
 3  JOANNE        [(just one) (( : referring to the
                  exchange of sweets?))
 4                ((echoes four notes from 'It's gotta be
                  you' very softly))
 5  NINNETTE      ((sings:)) "no one else in this world/
                            but you"
 6  JOANNE        ((referring to Mr Davis, as she later
                  clarifies to Ninnette:))
                  why does he keep staring over at us
```

Overall, when a person says something in conversation, there is an expectation that the addressee will respond, more or less along the lines laid down for them in the utterance they have just heard (cf. e.g. Schegloff 1988:111ff. on 'adjacency'). In contrast, when someone reciprocates in song, it seems more voluntary than required, a coming alongside in active appreciation of a mutually available tune, rather than an alignment controlled by guidelines that the speaker has designed very specifically there-and-then for the respondent. A conversation involves a mandatory exchange structure, with participants taking it in turns to speak, each one proposing in some detail the terms of engagement for the turn coming up. But if singing gets reciprocated, it 'catches on' and 'spreads' in non-obligatory displays of atunement, with participants sometimes singing along together at the same time.

Frith summarises something of these dynamics when he says that "songs ... have a looseness of reference that makes them immediately accessible" (1996a:121), and argues that

[m]usical response is, by its nature, a process of musical identification ... The crucial issue ... is not meaning and its interpretation – musical appreciation as a kind of decoding – but experience and collusion: the 'aesthetic' describes a kind of self-consciousness, a coming together of the sensual, the emotional, and the social *as* performance. In short, music doesn't represent values but lives them.   (1996b:272)

Table 3.1 summarises my rudimentary observations on the interactional affordances of singing.

Returning to the broader question of the relationship between schooling and popular song, it is clear that even at relatively micro-level, song offers something different from mainline curriculum activity. With all its textbooks, its writing, and its overarching commitment to getting students to understand particular subjects, schooling attaches a lot of weight to verbal rationality, articulated in lexico-grammatical propositions (see Chapter 2.3). Music obviously doesn't,[18] and it looks as though this contrast could be very relevant to the debates about schooling being undermined by media culture. In fact, though, I have only attended to *potentials* in this section. If we want to know whether and how popular culture could actually conflict with schooling, the focus will need to be widened further. So in the next section, I shall try to describe the way popular music meshed with Joanne and Hanif's positioning at school and among peers.

Table 3.1: *Comparison of some of the typical interactional properties of talk vs singing/humming*[19]

Talk	Solo humming and singing
Intended communication.	'Exuded' communication.
Involves a grammar and semantics, flexibly formulated *in media res* to refer to some feature of the situation on hand.	Grammar or semantics often not involved. If there is a grammar and semantics, these are generally fixed, having been formulated in real situations unknown to the current performer.
The production of a turn canonically expects a response from co-present individual(s), and often positions them as addressees. ('Self-talk' and 'response cries' figure among the exceptions to this [see e.g. Goffman 1981; Rampton 1995a: 183–185])	The production of a tune generally neither demands a response from co-present individual(s), nor positions them as addressees. It can be noticed but legitimately ignored. (There are some similarities to 'self-talk', though humming, whistling and singing are often more acceptable [Goffman 1981:82])
Working to the issues and guidelines laid down in the prior utterance, responses articulate the recipient's own perspective on the matters on hand.	If there is a response, either this takes the form of an evaluation/appreciation, or it involves joining in, submitting oneself to the other person's musical choice.
Participants normally take it in turns to speak.	Participants often sing together simultaneously.
During conversationally disengaged co-presence, silence keeps the participants' concerns private.	During conversationally disengaged co-presence, humming/singing actively displays your musical taste.

3.5 Humming and singing with friends in class: Joanne vs Hanif[20]

Joanne and Hanif both hummed and sang quite a lot during the 20-plus hours we recorded them – this averaged out at about 4¼ times per hour for Joanne, and about 3½ times for Hanif. But there seemed to be sharp differences in how music fitted into their daily lives at school.

Although *Joanne* had been very keen to wear the radio-microphone and seemed to enjoy doing so for most of the time, there were a couple of occasions when Joanne stopped humming and remembered the radio-microphone, saying things like "Oh no, I forgot about this!". And more generally over the two days when I recorded her, she projected an image to her friends of being absent-minded

and slightly out of control.[21] But music wasn't cast as the cause of
this distraction, and song didn't operate as a realm that separated her
from her friends. Instead, it seemed to serve as an enrichment of their
activity together. There were at least six occasions when she embellished a conversational remark with a brief solo:

Extract 3.5
A maths lesson. Ninnette and Joanne (wearing the radio-microphone) are
talking about people wearing electronic ear-pieces in the film 'The
Bodyguard'. (N43:440)

```
JOANNE    Kevin Costner
          /or whatever his name is had it
NINNETTE  he's beautifu::l
JOANNE    he's gorgeous
NINNETTE  aaah
JOANNE    ((sings softly from "You're Gorgeous" by the
          British pop singer Babybird:))
          "because you are gorgeous
          I'll do anything for/you"
NINNETTE  I loved ''The Bodyguard''
```

Extract 3.6
Ninnette and Joanne are indoors during break-time. They have been trying
without success to get someone who is up the stairs to join them:

```
NINNETTE  ((quite quietly to Joanne:)) come on
          (.)
JOANNE    she won't come down
          (1.5)
NINNETTE  ((emphatically:)) come on::
JOANNE    ((breaks into the old Gary Glitter hit:))
          "come on co:me on
          come on co:me on"
```

On the morning described in Extract 3.1, the two songs that she sung
most often to herself – 'It's gotta be you', followed in poor second by
'The Bodyguard' theme tune – had been initially invoked, and
broadly ratified as good songs, in conversations that included
Ninnette, the main overhearer of her hummings. It has already
been shown that the girls quite often joined in each other's singing
(Extracts 3.3 and 3.4), and in fact after asking Ninnette if she could
borrow the 3T song, Joanne responded to Ninnette's enthusiasm for
the 'The Bodyguard' by volunteering to bring in the video for her the

next day. Joanne's hummings, in other words, were embedded in her friendships, particularly with Ninnette, and in class, they formed part of ongoing exchanges that also included posters and, most noticeably, sweets, another source of pleasure that helped them through the lessons.

In terms of its wider institutional status, Joanne's involvement with song seemed to get constructed as illicit, opposed to the main business of the classroom. Early on in the circulation of 'It's gotta be you', Joanne momentarily broke off the discussion to observe that "Sir looks like a poof"; she curtailed Ninnette's appreciation of her staccato performance in Extract 3.1 with "Sir's watching us"; and early on in the Maths lesson, she interrupted her friend's rendering with "why does he ((Mr Davis)) keep staring over at us" (Extract 3.3 line 8). Joanne and Ninnette generally paid very little attention when the teacher was talking to the class as a whole (see Chapter 2.4) and in fact the teachers certainly did monitor their activity, as can be seen in Extract 3.7:

Extract 3.7
Humanities class. Mr Alcott is talking to the class about the results of a vote they've had on reasons for the abolition of slavery. Joanne (wearing the radio-microphone) and Ninnette have been participating only spasmodically, and after a short duet on the song "It's gotta be you", Joanne stops singing. (n43:80)

```
 1   JOANNE     can I borrow that tape and disco
 2              (2.0)
 3              and I'll bring it back
 4              I swear
 5              I'll bring it back tomorrow (.)
 6              ah: (.)
 7              you won't be able to give it to me today
 8              will you
 9   NINNETTE   I'll give it to you- (1.5)
10   JOANNE     tomorrow,
11              and I'll give it to you on Monday
12              (2.0)
13   MR A       ((who has been talking continuously))
14              and JOANNE
15              I would like your ATTENTION
16   JOANNE     ((as if impatient with Mr A's nagging:))
                all right:::!
```

```
17              (2.0)
18  GIRL
    NEARBY:     ((quietly:))
19              she (was) workin
20  JOANNE      ((also quietly:)) I'm only tryin to catch up
21              on the work I haven't done
22  GIRL
    NEARBY:     yeh
23              innit
```

Whereas Joanne spent most of her lessons sitting next to Ninnette, there was a lot of variation in the people that *Hanif* sat next to, and only a couple of these were close friends who he socialised with outside school. There were a couple of occasions when he was critical of other boys' for their taste or knowledge of tunes on television – "only you would think Star Trek's fun" – and when he hummed and sang by himself, he certainly didn't always assume that his neighbours shared his taste. Earlier on the morning reported in Extract 3.2, he had started singing some falsetto phrases from the Bee Gees 'Staying Alive':

Extract 3.8

End of a German lesson, just after the teacher has told them to pack up. Hanif (wearing the radio-microphone) has been sitting next to Gopal (n11:620)

```
1   HANIF   ((hums several bars of 'Staying Alive', slowly in
            falsetto for about 8 seconds, quite softly))
2           (.)
3           do you like the Bees Gees
4           the- the song?
5           (1)
6           ((sings another 8 notes, louder for the benefit
            of the person he's addressing))
7           I like that song
8           (.)
9           (it's quite good innit)
10          (6)
11          ((sings the chorus, varying the volume, going on
            for more than 20 seconds))
12  BOY     ( ) Bee Gees
13  HANIF   they did a remix
14          they did a remix of the Bee Gees
```

Joanne started singing *after* she and her friends had established a
verbal agreement on a tune, but here Hanif sang first and asked
questions later. At least from what is audible on the tape, it was he
who first introduced 'Staying alive', and he only asked his neighbour
whether he liked it after he had already displayed his own involvement with it. These comparatively assertive displays of his individual taste were common, and they often initiated rather than
responded to talk:

Extract 3.9

During group work in a Humanities lesson. (n2:510)

```
1  HANIF    ((hums several notes from the theme tune of
            Zeffirelli's film 'Romeo and Juliet'))
2  ?MASUD   you love that song
3           don't you
4  HANIF    I love (that song)
5           I dunno why
6           it's really nice /song (.)
7           really nice tune
8  ANON     ((overlapping, whistles a few bars))
9  HANIF    ((continues with the next few bars, also
            whistling))
```

More than that, there were two occasions when he stopped singing
to himself, turned to his friends and started trying to organise them
to sing along with him in harmony. This forcefulness was particularly clear in the way that he developed the Skips jingle in
Extract 3.2. It started off as a mainly private involvement, as
the extract shows, but over a 15 minute period stretching from
the end of the Humanities class into the start of an English lesson, it
underwent changes that moved it from being a tune that he had
on his mind and sometimes hummed softly, often only in fragments,
to being one among several musical motifs combined in a spurt of
loud, harmonic, multi-part singing, with Hanif now the leader of a
'barber shop' group. In the process, the tune also shifted from being
merely 'exuded' expression to become a topic of discussion, and, with
the words altered to fit circumstances on hand, a song of derogation
focused on one of the girls in class ("she scares them away" etc.).

Indeed, Hanif's expressive urges did not simply confine themselves to the performance arena provided by his friends. Throughout

the morning described in Extract 3.2, Hanif seemed to get a lot of pleasure in falsetto singing (maybe inspired by the Bee Gees, who it started with in the first lesson), and this was also a part of his contribution to the group singing sketched in the previous paragraph. But on three occasions that day, he also projected falsetto onto the main floor of classroom discourse. At one point, for example, he produced it at the juncture when Mr Newton was trying to get everyone's attention at the start of the English lesson:

Extract 3.10

At the start of an English lesson. Mr Newton is calling the class to order. (Radio-microphone: Hanif. '15':614)[22]

```
 1   MR N    just start by ( keep quiet looking) this way (3.0)
 2            quickly ⌈please settle down
 3   HANIF           ⌊((high pitched and very brief:)) (?did
             he?
 4           (1.0) yip?)
 5   MR N    shoosh shoosh shoosh shoosh (1.5)
 6           ⌈e::rm
 7   ANON    ⌊( rubber?) (.)
 8   ANON    what?
 9   ANON F  ((quite a high pitched laugh, descending?: ))
             heh heh heh (heh)
10   ANON    ( )
11   ANON    Good (1.0)
12   HANIF   /((brief but high pitched and loud three note
             singing [glissando down a major third]))
             [u u: u::]
13   MR N    now (.)
14           erm don't waste- time
15           everybody
16           js look this way (1.5)
17           thank you (.)
```

Stepping back, it is clear that both Hanif and Joanne got tunes 'stuck in their heads', but these were woven into their routine activity in very different ways on the days I recorded them. When Joanne hummed songs, she already knew that her closest friends liked them too, and these companions often joined in of their own accord, but for Hanif, there was often no background consensus when he asserted the songs he liked, and instead he worked quite hard to promote them. At the same time, Joanne's musical tastes were more particular to her friendship, and once she and Ninnette had agreed on what they liked, they talked of lending and borrowing tapes, videos, and posters from home. There was no evidence of any comparable support for Hanif's musical interests. The repertoire he performed while being radio-microphone recorded wasn't noticeably smaller than Joanne's,[23] but there seemed to be nothing special or exclusive about the circulation or origins of the songs that he made most of. 'Skips' was merely a TV jingle, and when a boy nearby couldn't identify it, Hanif laughed at him with the suggestion that he'd ``just never seen television before''. And three days before, he had spent much of his time humming the theme tune from a film they'd all been shown in their English class (Zeffirelli's 'Romeo and Juliet').

There was also a striking difference in the way that their music-making got positioned within official classroom business. Joanne and Ninnette generally kept their singing fairly quiet, whereas the singing of Hanif and his friends was often very noisy. But as we have seen, for Joanne, musical involvements were a cause for censure from the teacher, both potentially and actually, whereas Hanif et al. almost always got away with it. There was no concealing artfulness, for example, when he burst back into Bee Gees on hearing his friend Masud coincidentally use the phrase 'stayed alive' in discussion with Mr Newton:

Extract 3.11

Later in the same English lesson as Extract 3.10. Mr Newton has asked the whole class to think of reasons for Romeo and Juliet's deaths, and he's now talking to Masud and John, who are sitting next to Hanif (wearing the radio-microphone). ('15':1136; Gex4/N14:358)

```
1   MASUD       cos if they stayed alive and the/whole thing ( )
2   MR NEWTON   the only way to be together/was in death
3   HANIF       ((very high pitched and loud rendition of Bee
                Gees 'Staying Alive', continuing until the
                middle of line 7)):
                ``her
                herher
                herher
                staying alive
                staying alive
                hr-'' ((stopping abruptly))
```

```
4   MASUD    yeh
5   MR N     ((fast: )) (yes I agree)
6            ((to the whole class, optimistic tone: ))
             ALL RIGHT (2.5)
7            listening skills everybody
```

Yet Mr Newton's regulative efforts in line 7 are directed to the whole class, not just Hanif.

The debate I started out with – are traditional forms of authority being undercut by contemporary media culture? – look very relevant here, but there is a serious anomaly. Of the two students considered, one (Joanne) kept her musical interests confined within a fairly close friendship circle, while the other (Hanif) worked hard to recruit other youngsters to the tunes he liked, and hurled loud snatches of song onto the main floor of classroom discourse. Yet it was Joanne, not Hanif, that the teachers picked on. If popular culture and the traditional pupil–teacher relations are supposed to be opposed to each other, how could this be?

The teachers' different treatment of Hanif and Joanne can be partly explained by referring to their broader educational profiles. Hanif was one of the top students in the class, happy to talk in front of the rest of the class and, without being submissive, very attentive to the teachers. In contrast, Joanne was receiving extra literacy support, made no effort to disguise her dislike of speaking in front of the rest of the class, and spent most lessons sitting next to Ninnette, chatting quietly and sharing sweets. Hanif generally seemed to help the lesson forward, while Joanne appeared to question its whole purpose and value.

So the difference in the school profile of these two kids may have had something to do with the way teachers responded to their music-making. But there is still an explanatory gap in the account: How was it possible that Hanif had such high status if he engaged in musical acts that, from the outside anyway, look so transgressive? At this point, we need shift the focus once again, to look at how both singing *and* educational profiles like these fitted into the organisation of local institutional discourse.

3.6   Talk in class at Central High

Up to a point, Hanif's singing may have escaped censure because he produced some of his loudest contributions either during or close to

interludes *between* periods of officially focused classwork – entering
the class early on, reseating for group work, packing up at the end of
a lesson. During these noisier phases of movement and spatial
reorganisation, teachers allowed low-levels of informal chat and it
was no doubt easier for them to either miss or ignore these performances. But this could not explain Mr Newton's lenient reception of
his falsetto in Extract 3.11, and indeed even in periods before and
after focused classwork, a certain level of decorum was still
expected, as Mr Poyser explained in 3.12:

Extract 3.12
The end of a Humanities lesson, in which Mr Poyser has complimented
them on their performance of a series of role-plays – "Right very good, very
impressive . . . I'm afraid we have to end there". ('15':267; Gex4):

```
 1  MR P       that was quite a good session
 2             but again you were very noisy (at the end of it)
 3             (5.5)
 4             I would like (a few of you) to train yourself
               (2.0)
 5             into behaving yourself
 6             at the end of lessons (.)
 7             because if you do this at upper school
 8             you're going to dri::ve people round the bend
 9             basically (.)
10             which is a pity
11             because you're ( ) a group
12             in a/way
13  HANIF      ((very loud high pitched note))
14             aa aa
15  HANIF      ((c. 14 secs of repressed giggles before next
    AND        turn))
    OTHERS
16  MR P       what's going on now
17  HANIF      ((quietly:)) nothing Sir
```

For a more general explanation of the processes that rendered
Hanif's singing officially ignorable/inaudible, but turned Joanne's
into a potential or actual offence, it is worth briefly recapping
several of the main points made in Chapter 2.5 about the classroom
'settlement' in 9A:

1) This was a very mixed class: some of the kids were very keen
   and obviously very clever, others had only recently arrived in

the country, while there were one or two who seemed very seriously disaffected.

2) For one reason or another, the traditional IRE structure of classroom talk – teacher Initiates, pupil Responds, teacher provides Evaluation – didn't work very well at Central High (see Table 2.1). Much of this was simply due, no doubt, to the intractability of the students, though there is a long tradition of educational thought that sees the IRE pattern as a constraint on authentic communication, and freed up from the IRE, there certainly were some really scintillating intellectual debates in these classrooms.

3) But if students are given more space to express themselves, they often say things that either don't fit the official agenda, or fit it only tangentially. In Class 9A, there was a group of boys who attended very closely indeed to whole-class discussion, but rather than sticking strictly to thematic relevance and lexico-grammatical propositions, they milked the main line of talk for all its aesthetic potential, recoding the official discourse into melody, German, non-standard accents etc, etc. On top of that, these hyper-attentive kids also made noisy, disparaging comments about others in the class, some of whom didn't want to participate at all.

4) Rather than putting a stop to this over-exuberance, the teachers seemed much more preoccupied by the conduct of the youngsters who were conspicuously disengaged. Indeed, faced with their persistent refusal, it is easy to imagine the teachers becoming dependent on the hyper-involved ones for reassurance. More than that, in situations where interested students felt that the teacher was getting distracted, it is not hard to understand these keen kids lending a hand (in whatever way) to get the lesson back on track, exacerbating the alienation of the classroom's 'others'.

5) In sum, the teacher and the enthusiastic students appeared to form a strategic alliance that managed to keep the lessons on course. Within this, teachers were inclined to be tolerant of the excesses of the apparently keen, and this is likely to have intensified the exclusion of the disengaged, but as long as the alliance held up, at least some sense of progress and value could be derived.

If Hanif is now slotted in as one of the over-exuberant pupils and Joanne as one of the disaffected, we can see how it could be that the teachers ignored Hanif's noisy singing but censured Joanne's much quieter musical involvements. Looking back at Extract 3.11, it is clear that Hanif's burst of Bee Gees was sparked by Masud's serious reply to Mr Newton, and to that extent, it was closely tuned to what was supposed to be happening in the lesson. Under the circumstances I have described, we can imagine teachers coming to terms with such outbreaks, grateful for at least some complementarity to what they were trying to achieve.

The micro-political 'settlement' within Class 9A, then, helps to explain the contrast in the official acceptability of Joanne and Hanif's singing. But there is more to be said about the different kinds of value and experience offered in curriculum instruction and popular song, and about their relationship within whole-class discussion.

3.7   Teacher-talk and student song

In the previous chapter, students' (mainly non-musical) behaviour during whole-class discussion was compared with their conduct during writing and role-play. They were generally much more attentive in the latter than the former, and pulling all the evidence together, I suggested that either actually (for Joanne and Ninnette) or potentially (for Hanif and co, if they hadn't partly reconfigured it), whole-class teacher-talk involved

[i] a jostling but expressively depleted style of communication which [ii] marginalised students' own judgement but [iii] threatened to drag them onto the platform with curriculum-scripted performances that [iv] ultimately didn't actually count for very much.   (Chapter 2.6)

Popular song typically contrasts with this:

a) It is semiotically rich (mixing particular voices, words, and rhetoric with tunes and rhythm in a huge array of combinations), and it allows the listener a lot of interpretive freedom (contrast [i] above).

b) The listener's judgement is vital, and in a very heterogeneous field of singers, bands and musical styles, the process of preferring some more than others can play an important part of social self-definition, selections often being sanctioned informally in friendship groups. Popular music is a field where a great deal of the authority and decisive assessment lies with youth and a set of generally rather non-school adults (contrast [ii]).

c) Whereas at school, you are a pupil/apprentice and your capacity to rearticulate curriculum styles and issues is put at a premium (and graded), most people are simply consumers of popular music, their taste counts much more than their ability, and relatively muted appreciation is often more than adequate as a mode of participation (contrast [iii]).

d) Popular songs often have a great deal of personal significance for listeners, drawing them into 'emotional alliances with the performers and the performers' other fans" (Frith 1996a:121) (contrast [iv]).

Song, in other words, possessed in abundance the very properties that, from their more general conduct, youngsters seemed to find quite widely lacking in the standard forms of teacher-led discussion. It was not, of course, the only popular cultural form that youngsters oriented to during whole-class teacher-talk, and even though our four informants hummed and sang at an average rate of about 2 to 3 times an hour, there were only 67 episodes in the c. 1600 minutes of lessons that we listened to altogether. So it would be an exaggeration to say that music was an obsession with these youngsters, and that Class 9A was a battle ground for a clash between whole-class instruction and popular music. Even so, music was the popular cultural form they invoked most often, and it was one important crystallisation of a set of social and expressive values (in (a) to (d) above) that could no doubt also be found, to different degrees and in different combinations, in other kinds of peer and popular culture activity (going shopping, watching television, chatting with friends etc.). Overall, there are grounds for seeing humming and singing as emblematic of a wider orientation among these youngsters, and this can be used as the base for a more general interpretive gloss on student conduct in Class 9A. Running with its metonymic connection with popular cultural values more generally, music can be used to propose a more encompassing characterisation of the different kinds of adaptation, involvement and identity that students

and teachers sought from whole-class discussion *in the particular
non-standard form that the participants actually gave to it.*

Hanif and his friends participated very fully in teacher-led discussion, they were uninhibited about offering their own assessments, they attended closely to what was being said, and they
frequently embellished the instructional discourse, changing words
and phrases into other languages, accents and forms of pronunciation etc., appreciatively recycling anomalous moments in what
I described as a 'contrapuntal aesthetic' (Chapter 2.3). Even though
they used language much more than music in the pursuit of this
contrapuntal aesthetic, I would like to suggest that their experience
of participating in whole-class discussion bore some similarity to the
sense of dynamic collectivity that Frith attributes to musicians playing together:

What I want to suggest . . . is not that social groups agree on values which are
then expressed in their cultural activities . . . but that they only get to know
themselves *as groups* (as a particular organisation of individual and social
interests, of sameness and difference) *through* cultural activity, through
aesthetic judgement . . . [musicians experience] a simultaneous projecting
and dissolving of the self in *performance* . . . in the moment of enactment of
musical fellowship.   (Frith 1996a:111. Original emphases)

Joanne and Ninnette no doubt also experienced "this coming
together of the sensual, the emotional and the social as performance" when they sang together. But they hated speaking in front of
the class, they usually switched off from teacher-led discourse, dis-
dainful, among other things, of the displays put on by Hanif and co.
Instead, they spent their time privately chatting, eating sweets and
sometimes singing either together and with other girls close by.
So overall, "the simultaneous projecting and dissolving of the self
in performance" seems less representative of their participation in
teacher-fronted discussion that it was with the boys. Rather than
standing as an emblem of efforts to transform the lesson experience
by intensifying it (in the manner of the boys), a different aspect of
musical experience can be used to stand for these two girls' attempt
to transcend their institutional surroundings:

what makes music special . . . is that musical identity is both fantastic –
idealising not just oneself but also the social world one inhabits – and
real . . . enacted in activity . . . We all hear music we like as something that

defies the mundane, takes us 'out of ourselves', puts us somewhere else. 'Our music' is, from this perspective, special not just with reference to other music, but, more important, to the rest of life. It is this sense of specialness (the way in which music seems to make possible a new kind of self-recognition, to free us from everyday routines, from the social expectations with which we are encumbered) that is the key to our musical value judgements. 'Transcendence' is as much part of the popular as of the serious music aesthetic, but in pop transcendence articulates not music's independence of social forces but a kind of alternative experience of them.   (Frith 1996b:275)[24]

At this point, my account has obviously shifted from empirical description to more general and much more loosely framed cultural interpretation,[25] but there are both analytic and ideological justifications for this move.

First, the use of musical experience as a interpretive figure helps to bring out the 'interdiscursivity' of whole class interaction in Class 9A. In Norman Fairclough's formulation, interdiscursivity occurs when a "discourse type is constituted through a combination of elements of orders of discourse" (1992b:118). Translating this into present context, teacher-fronted discussion is the 'discourse-type', the 'orders of discourse' are education and popular media culture, and their 'elements' comprise, among many other processes and phenomena, the IRE, curriculum topics, disciplinary concerns on the one hand, and humming, singing, styles of sociability on the other. The musical frame, in other words, pushes us to see these proceedings as a complex, hybrid genre, a way of interacting that emerged at the point where teaching priorities ran together with resources, interests – even sensibilities – that had their roots in popular music and popular culture more generally.

Of course, to refer to the goings-on in Class 9A as a genre, however complex and hybrid, implies quite a high level of stable organisation, or in Bauman's terms, "a set of conventional guidelines for dealing with recurrent communicative exigencies" (2001:80; see also Günthner and Knoblauch 1995:6; Blommaert 2004). But the case for this has already been stated. The students certainly did differ very sharply in their commitment to the teacher's oral instructional discourse, and keen and disaffected students habitually adopted very different strategies to make the talk tolerable. In relatively hushed voices, the girls chatted to each other about music, sweets, and a host of other matters, while the boys engaged in

rampant aesthetic embellishments of the main discursive line. But
these differences were openly displayed – Hanif and company had a
good idea of Joanne and Ninnette's preferred styles of participation
in the lesson, and no-one could miss the boys'. In consequence, the
behaviour of the one group was partially shaped by the conduct of
the other. The teachers were also caught up in this, using school rules
and sanctions to keep the proceedings on track for part of the time,
but also accepting some children's over-exuberance for the support
it gave them in the face of refusal from others. Overall, centrifugal
tendencies were generally held in check, prevented from spinning off
into activities of a completely different kind, and the strategies used
by different participants meshed together to produce the patterns my
account has made familiar.

Analytically, then, foregrounding popular music as an experiential dimension underscores the interdiscursivity of whole-class discourse as a genre. Of course, it also brings out some of its
substantial, sustaining features. One interpretive option is to look
at the proceedings in Class 9A through the lens of teacher-talk in its
canonical form, and when this is used – as in Chapter 2 – the
proceedings seem, at first sight anyway, to be characterised by
breakdown, with humming and singing featuring as mere fragments
in the ensuing chaos. In contrast, if teacher-fronted discourse is seen
as an *interdiscursive* genre with popular cultural practice as one of
its constitutive ingredients, the educational 'deficit' perspective loses
its supremacy, relativised by a fuller view of aesthetic pleasures that
also help to keep the participants going.

At the same time, recognition of interdiscursivity holds this shift
of emphasis in check, preventing one simplistic account taking over
from another.

As already discussed at some length in Chapter 2, there is "an
ideology and politics of genre" (Bauman 2001; Chapter 2.6). Genres
are encapsulated visions of the social world tuned to practical action
in recurrent situations, projecting particular kinds of conduct and
relationship, and promising the participants with particular types of
personhood. As such, they play a central role in socialisation (e.g.
Heath 1983; Kress 1994[1982]), and become a matter of intense
concern to education policy-makers. At the same time, there is actually no "timeless closure" or "unlimited replication" intrinsic to any
genre (Hanks 1987), and so a great deal of ideological work is often

needed if the preferred genres are to remain steadily in place. In recent years, the IRE model of teacher-led classroom discourse has been ideologically dominant, with the result that a 'chaos' interpretation is overwhelmingly privileged when it comes to urban classrooms like Class 9A. Reacting against this hegemony, it might be tempting to claim polemically that if popular culture were used as the principal interpretive frame, all the pedagogic strain would evaporate and the real satisfactions and orderliness of the proceedings would flood into view. But when the interdiscursivity of whole-class teacher-talk is reckoned with, it is clear that popular culture is no more adequate as a total representation of the proceedings than the canonical IRE model. Both were present as sets of "schematic and incomplete resources on which speakers necessarily improvise in practice" (Hanks 1987:681, cited in Chapter 2.6), but neither reigned supreme. Joanne and Ninnette's enjoyment of music may have been rooted in their desire to transcend their circumstances, but their talk and singing were still modulated by the teacher's gaze. Similarly, whenever teachers reprimanded individuals for not attending, or made a show of waiting for silence before they started to talk themselves, they appealed to the IRE as a normative ideal, but in the event, they generally made do with much less than total compliance to their calls for attentive silence. Both traditional 'transmission' pedagogy and popular music were available and active as cultural resources in this classroom, but they were hybridised and intermingled with each other and with a lot other influences. The practices, styles of participation and the mix of curriculum and popular culture in this class certainly were not euphonious, but they seemed to be adapted in interdependent ways to the difficulties that institutional demands posed for them all, and these patterns of interaction could be witnessed again and again in Class 9A's collective activity, with the predictability and regularity that we associate with genres.[26]

It is worth now stepping back for a methodological review of the chapter as a whole.

3.8 Summary: levels and genres in the analysis of cultural process

Contemporary media and social theorists make a range of potentially very consequential claims about the way our daily lives are being changed by techno-popular culture in late modernity

(Chapter 3.1). But it is essential to reckon with the ways in which very large-scale processes and phenomena could filter down into the way people interact together in particular activities in particular settings, and there are a lot of empirical contingencies on the path between global cultural trends and the details of everyday life.

My investigation started off with an interest in cultural debates about the tension between techno-popular and traditional authority relationships at school. I reported a survey of media-practices in two schools, where it was found that

- yes, popular media culture was a routine, regular element in young people's lived experience of lessons, while at the same time,
- popular media culture had *not* been assimilated as a standard part of curriculum activity itself with anything like the same regularity.

Our survey also found that

- greater socio-economic disadvantage coincided with noisier classrooms, which coincided with a greater incidence of popular cultural practices in class.

Picking up on the frequency with which kids hummed and sang at Central High, I then shifted to a more differentiating, micro- and meso-analysis of popular song in class, a genre with very deep roots outside school. Here it emerged that:

- music has an insistent interior resonance, songs stick in people's heads, and in the recordings of Joanne and Hanif, solo humming and singing served as a pleasurable overlay across a range of work and recreational activities.
- compared with conversation, song allows a particular kind of sociability, and
- when it is used in reciprocal communication (rather than in quiet solo humming), it is generally going to be marginal to the logo-centric rationality of the curriculum.

Analysis like this of the properties and usability of a text, a genre, or an object, is going to be important in any analysis of popular culture, and a broadly comparable account would be needed in an analysis of some other aspect of popular culture – film, clothes, sweets, etc.

However, it is impossible to extrapolate straight from this kind of text-, object- or genre-analysis to the ways that the items will actually get used in particular environments (Hymes 1980:95;1996:10; Fischer 1985). Yes, it did turn out that peer interaction, not curriculum tasks, provided the main arena for joint singing, but individuals drew music into very different kinds of practice, shaping/ shaped in different kinds of friendship. Stating the contrast starkly, Joanne's singing helped in the consolidation of intimacy, while for Hanif, song assisted a quest for social influence.

Similarly, it would be a mistake to run too far with the broad lack of congruence between popular song as a mixture of orality and music, and traditional curriculum discourse, heavily committed to literacy and reason. It is essential to look empirically at the speech economy in particular classrooms, and in the ones I looked at in the inner city, discursive power was far less clearly concentrated in the teacher than it had been in the suburbs. I have not taken a very close empirical look at exactly what the broader social and institutional pressures, warrants and possibilities were that underpinned the mesh of decentred authority, hyper-involvement and resistance found at Central High, but there was something of an interactional system here, and among the wider influences that this responded to, one might identify migration and material poverty among students, educational philosophies that valued mixed-ability classes and the pupil's voice among the teachers, and a local post-colonial history of curriculum negotiation that involved them both (see Chapter 2). But whatever the broader factors involved in its emergence and/or stabilisation, this classroom 'settlement' provided a certain amount of scope for musical exuberance in the polyphonic soundtrack that accompanied curriculum activity at Central High, although *again*, the acceptability of any given performer's contribution depended on the nature of their educational profile and their classroom demeanour more generally.

Up to this point in the resumé, then, the analysis has covered a wide range of micro to macro processes.[27] But it would be very hard to take any one of these and to read off its more general implications for the relationship between schooling and popular culture, or to say which counted most. Thus far at least, this 'multi-level' analysis simply seems to corroborate recurrent calls for empirical caution in the theorisation of media influence (see e.g. Bausinger 1984;

Fischer 1984; Sefton-Green 1998b). But a concern for empirical complications need not amount to a rejection of theory *tout court*, and if we take the notion of genre, focusing more intensively on the relationship between popular music and teacher-fronted whole-class discussion in particular, the different dimensions of the analysis so far can be pulled together and reshaped in a more coherent formulation with certain claims to generality.

Drawing on Hanks (1987), Bauman (2001) and Bakhtin (1986) here and in Chapter 2, I said that a genre is a set of conventionalised expectations that members of a social group or network use to shape and construe the communicative activity that they are engaged in. These expectations include a sense of the likely tasks on hand, the roles and relationships typically involved, the ways the activity can be organised, and the kinds of resources suited to carrying it out. A genre, in other words, involves practical perceptions of how the social environment should come together with the details of meaningful activity in different types of situation, and as such, it integrates phenomena and processes that, from an analytic point of view, are often seen as operating at different levels. For most of the analysis in this chapter, I moved up one level at a time: music's interior resonance, the interactional affordances of humming and singing in company, the impact of an individual's school profile and peer-relations on a song's informal reproduction, the receptiveness of different educational environments to spontaneous music-making, and the effect of educational philosophies, demographics and wealth. And in terms of my guiding interest in the relationship between schooling and popular culture, the cumulative effect of this step-by-step progression was to pile on the caveats and provisos, emphasising the unpredictability of the 'cross-level effects'. But then, when the analysis started to consider teacher-fronted interaction as an interdiscursive genre, the different levels and elements in my account coalesced, and it was possible to see how rather regular patterns of collective activity could emerge from the insistent tunes in the heads of different kids, from their different responses to the tedium of teacher-talk, from their contrasting orientations to school and peer group, and so forth.

So, in defining genre as the integrated, multi-level analyses that participants themselves implicitly formulate for their own practical activity, it has been possible to move from an enumeration of the processes relevant to the impact of music on schooling, to a view of how these processes combine for specific situations. But in fact, of course, genres are much more than assembly instructions on how the different bits of social process fit together, helpfully provided by the participants for the benefit of analysts. As integrated-configurations-of-'readings'-of-the-social-world, as units of socio-communicative sensibility oriented to particular situations, genres get continuously exposed to the experience of interaction itself. Where there is a significant degree of correspondence between these socio-communicative expectations and what actually transpires, the genre is likely to be relatively stable. Where there is a significant mismatch, people may adjust their generic expectations, limp on, or aggressively reaffirm them. But there is always some gap – "the fit between a particular text and the generic model ... is never perfect" (Bauman 2001:80) – and the crucial question is whether the gap is sufficiently large to change the participants' generic expectations now and in the future, or whether the difference between expectation and experience is relatively minor, easily assimilated within generic form as it is currently conceived.

This is where to look if one is interested in the impact of popular media culture (or any other macro process) on everyday practice. "[S]peech genres ... are the drive belts from the history of society to the history of language," said Bakhtin (1986:65), and many others have agreed (e.g. Hanks 1987; 1996; Fairclough 1992b; Guenthner and Knoblauch (1995); Bauman (2001), Blommaert 2004). Since a genre represents a temporary stabilisation between the different components in a given group's multi-dimensional representation of the social world, drawn up for interaction in specific types of situation, one can ask: How far do the details of concrete experience continue to ratify these generic representations, suggesting that they're still intersubjectively valid? And how far does a change on one dimension of these integrated representations destabilise the whole, reverberating across subsequent implementations-and-interpretations of practical action?

Unfortunately, my data and analysis do not cover the longitudinal formation of the main instructional genres at Central High, and I cannot actually tell whether or not the development of particular popular cultural forms or practices has led to the significant changes that can be called generic. I have identified quite a range of wider factors that could be relevant to the patterns of teacher-fronted interaction found in Class 9A (including student backgrounds, and teacher philosophies); any or all of these might have been more important in the stabilisation of this interdiscursive genre; and logically anyway, popular media culture may simply have flowed into the spaces created by other influences, more a camp-follower or carpet-bagger than vanguard. But set within the pressures identified, it is easy to see how as a genre, teacher-fronted interaction could now absorb quite a lot of developments in media culture without much change. We can imagine, for example, a scenario in which popular music producers release a new song, it sticks in Ninnette's head and she starts humming it while Mr Alcott's talking to them all. Joanne notices Ninnette humming as usual, but she hasn't heard the song before, asks about it, joins in a little bit. But nothing much has changed. Alternatively, working in the other direction: Mr Newton wheels in a TV, and instead of telling the class about Romeo and Juliet himself, he plays the Zeffirelli film. This certainly does change the communicative dynamic and everyone attends. But it only lasts a couple of lessons, and on the Thursday session, it's back to Mr Newton's voice (though there's still space for Hanif to hum the theme tune). Of course there are other innovations that might be of more consequence. What happens, for example, if and when pupils bring in Nintendo Game-Boys, Sony Walkmans or start text-messaging? Are they banned, concealed, or accommodated, in what phases of the lesson, and what is their impact on the communicative economy within different activities in class? Unfortunately, these are questions I cannot answer. Even so, in centring all these questions on the notion of 'genre', the journey through this chapter has arrived at a much sharper view of the 'units' to focus on in the effort to understand how and how far changes in popular media culture impact on everyday life.

Notes

1. Participation in 'techno-popular' culture covers both uses and references to electronic technologies on hand (TVs, videos, audio-tapes, CDs, computers, mobile phones, pagers, etc.) and to the contents, genres and practices which these technologies promote or facilitate.
2. 2 White Anglo descent (1 male, 1 female), 5 South Asian (3M, 2F), 1 African Caribbean (F), 1 African (M).

3. The interviews were not designed with media culture specifically in mind.
4. e.g. Castells 1996:374–375; O'Sullivan 1998; Eco 1992; Hartley 1997; Sefton-Green 1998:12; Holmes and Russell 1999. Personal experience was also an important resource here.
5. For other ethnographies of school, media and/or adolescent identity e.g. Willis 1977; Hammersley and Woods 1984; Woods 1990; Foley 1990; Silverstone and Hirsch 1992; Gillespie 1995; Sefton-Green 1998a.
6. The four overlapping dimensions/domains described by Layder (1993) and Carter and Sealey (2000) are:

- the self (the subjective dispositions, the psycho-biography and life career of the individual)
- situated activity (face-to-face activity, intentional communication, emergent meanings and definitions of the situation)
- settings: the physical and social contexts of social activities and specific social practices, such as workplaces, schools or places of worship, and their routinised ways of doing things
- macro-social organisation and contextual resources: values, traditions, forms of social and economic organisation and power relations; the anterior distributions of material and cultural capital which social actors inherit as a consequence of being born into a particular place at a particular time

As social processes, each of these involves different time-scales and 'units' of change (Layder 1993:Chapter 5).
7. An episode was defined as a sequence of talk introducing and often sustaining a media-cultural theme, bounded by periods of talk and activity devoted to other matters.
8. The figures were: music – 130+ episodes; television – 68; film – 43; PCs – 11; electronic games – 3; telecommunications – 5; newspapers – 4; magazines – 6. Compare Livingstone and Bovill 1999:29.
9. There were 14 spontaneous references to PCs and computer games. 13 of these were produced by boys, almost all of them at Westpark, and one was produced by a girl at Central High. When adolescents' engagement with PCs, games and communication technologies [pagers, mobiles, email] was compared across the two schools, the difference was very sharp: at Westpark there 17 episodes involving these media, whereas there were only 2 at Central High.
10. Livingstone and Bovill 1999:29; compare Annual Childwise Monitor (*Childwise Insights: Boys Kick the Reading Habit*. http://www.childwise.co.uk/reading.htm. Consulted by Roxy Harris, 9/5/02): "In October 1999, one in three young people aged 13–16 had their own mobile, up six fold on the previous year."
11. Teachers introduced media culture as an issue in 13 (out of 70) lessons. In 3 of these, they made it central, in 4, they made it significant, while in 6, it figured in only incidental references.

12. And 7 of these consisted of Hanif humming the theme tune from Zeffirelli's 'Romeo and Juliet' – see Chapter 3.3.

13. Central High: 100 episodes of media-oriented peer-talk in 26½ hrs of lesson time recordings. Westpark: 66 episodes in 38¾ hours of recorded lesson-time. The quantitative data also suggested that Westpark students made a clearer distinction between lessons and recess (break-time and lunch) as occasions for media-oriented talk: in contrast to the 1.7 episodes per hour during lessons, Westpark students oriented to popular-media culture *outside* class at a rate of about 4 episodes an hour. The figures for Central High were 3.8 episodes per hour in class, and 5.2 outside.

14. The average rate of explicit references was broadly comparable – 1.2 per hour at Central High (33 episodes), and 1.4 at Westpark (53 episodes).

15. Informal music-making was not restricted to lessons with any particular teacher – at Central High, 7 teachers were involved in the 20 lessons where there was unofficial music-making, while there were 6 taking the 10 lessons at Westpark.

16. This view can be matched in the discussions of *language* offered, for example, by Becker, who suggests that "Grammar rules and dictionaries are our ... substitutes for lingual memories, but they are poor ones. They lack the richness of prior texts, the particularity and special memorability that come only with languaging in context" (1995:12). Indeed, it also connects with a Bakhtinian view of language (see Chapter 9.6 below).

17. Of course, this isn't always the case, and there was one quite protracted period in a Science lesson when in a spirit of jocularity, Simon persisted in a solo performance of the theme tune of 'Star Trek', much to his peers' clearly stated distaste.

18. Frith cites Lenin and Freud on this: "It is noteworthy that the two great European rationalists of the early twentieth century, Freud and Lenin, were both disturbed by their response to music. Lenin was reluctant to listen to Beethoven because the music made him want to pat people on the head; Freud remarked that his pleasure in art lay in comprehension: 'Whenever I cannot do this, as for instance with music, I am almost incapable of obtaining any pleasure. Some rationalistic, or perhaps analytic, turn of mind in me rebels against being moved by a thing without knowing why I am thus affected, and what it is that affects me'" (1996b:260). As Frith also notes, "one cannot summarise or paraphrase a musical message, or translate it into a different language" (1996b:146).

19. The table says nothing of different types or parts of conversation, different institutional settings, ironic co-performance, etc.

20. The analysis in this section also owes a great deal to the work of Caroline Dover.

21. "I was in a dream just then" (n42:408); "I don't really know what I'm talking about – I'm in a funny mood again" (n43:15); Ninnette: "you still

mad?" – Joanne: "eh?" – Ninnette: "are you still in the weird mood?"–
Joanne: "eh?" – Ninnette: ((*laughs*)) – Joanne: "yes" (n51:330).

22. It's difficult talking of falsetto's interior resonance for Hanif, but there
were at least two ways in which it was well-suited to the very public
display in this episode. When combined with a certain loudness, duration and interactional timing, Hanif's pitch selection contributed to a
performance that created the risk of teacher censure but was able to
escape it. The high frequency made it very easy to hear (van Leeuwen
1999:108), but the deviation from his normal pitch range served as a
useful disguise, making it harder to identify exactly who the source of
this intrusive sound might be.

23. *Tunes in Hanif's repertoire*: 'I shot the sheriff', the 'Romeo and Juliet'
theme tune, 'Sitting by the dock of the bay' (Otis Redding, Pearl Jam), a
Hindi song he couldn't name, 'Staying Alive' (Bee Gees), a jingle for
Skips crisps, one or two others which we couldn't identify, and some
local improvisations. *Tunes in Joanne's repertoire*: 'I Believe I Can Fly'
(R. Kelly), 'It's Gotta Be You' (3T), 'You're Gorgeous' (Babybird), the
theme tunes from the film 'The Bodyguard' (Whitney Houston) and the
TV soap 'East Enders', 'Bohemian Rhapsody' (Queen), 'My Gang'
(Gary Glitter), plus one or two others we were unable to identify.

24. The *teachers* never actually invoked popular music themselves, so there
is less warrant for using different aspects of musical experience in any
more general typification of their participation in whole-class discourse. Nevertheless, just for the sake of completeness, it is worth
including them in this exploration of musical experience as a frame
for interpreting the different styles of participation in Class 9A (accepting that in doing so, the characterisation is much more metaphorical
than metonymic). To elaborate this, it is useful first to invoke Frith's
comments on the distinction between noise and music being a matter of
interpretation (as well as concentration and experience – 1996b:100),
and then to draw on Silverstein's careful clarification of Bakhtin's
distinction between heteroglossia and polyphony (Silverstein
1999:103–104). Heteroglossia refers to the range of voices and languages in a social group or arena, and these often move centrifugally, in
a lot of different directions. Polyphony, in contrast, involves a variety of
isolable voices coming together more or less harmoniously in the production of a unified text (see also van Leeuwen 1999:80). Situated
within the provisional classroom settlement outlined in Section 3.6,
the response of teachers to the heteroglossic soundscape in Class 9A
went two ways: some of the material they treated as distracting, caco-
phonous noise (Ninnette and Joanne), while at the same time, there
were other sounds and voices (from Hanif and company) that they
accepted, *faute de mieux*, as contributions to a curriculum discourse
that they learned (or strained) to hear as polyphonic.

25. In fact, this could be taken much further. It would be interesting, for
example, to construe Class 9A proceedings through the lens (?) offered

by the aesthetics of 'rap', where, for example, a premium is placed on
"'linguistic slippage', a [type] of discourse in which form and association are more important than a coherent denotative meaning", and
where "the fundamental practice of hip hop is one of the citation, of
the relentless sampling of sonic and verbal archives" (Potter 1995, cited
in Androutsopoulos and Scholz 2003:501, 496). How far could this be
linked, for example, to the contrapuntal aesthetic practised by Hanif
and his friends? Indeed, could we go further and suggest that the
experience of participation in urban classrooms like these plays a significant part in the development of a rap/hip hop sensibility?

26. Complex genres encompass a range of smaller generic types, and so this
    claim is compatible with the fact that classroom activity involved a wide
    range of discourse forms – story, jokes, instructions, etc. – that were
    well-formed in themselves.

27. Of course there are also dimensions that I have left completely
    untouched: for example, the characteristics of particular songs, their
    emotional tone and (sub-)cultural associations, and the links between
    social background and musical taste.

PART III

Performances of Deutsch

4

Deutsch in improvised performance

Every weekday, either by choice or compulsion, vast numbers of children and adults all round the world participate in foreign language learning classes, focusing on languages other than English. This process is often the focus of intense local and national dispute, and although very substantial sums of money are devoted to it, in Britain and other English-dominant countries, massive educational underachievement is one of its most striking outcomes (Boaks 1998; Branaman and Rhodes 1998; Schulz 1998). And yet looking back either over the last twenty-five years of the leading sociolinguistics journal (*Language in Society*), or through introductory textbooks on sociolinguistics, there are no detailed analyses of instructed foreign language practices, and it is hard to find even a cursory reference.[1] So the question of why sociolinguistics has shown such little interest in instructed foreign languages is one issue to address in this chapter, and for me, it sprung into salience when I heard the young people in my radio-microphone recordings using *Deutsch* among themselves, playing vigorously with its sound properties and re-styling it in their maths and English lessons.

Admittedly, peer group *Deutsch* turned out to be a passing fad. Eighteen months or so after I last recorded it, its principal exponents said in interview that they no longer used the language among themselves, and they were very negative about the German classes that they continued to attend. So there are no grounds for supposing that their japes with *Deutsch* spurred them on to become enthusiastic modern linguists. Still, it provoked my curiosity, and from what people have reported of their own experience when I have presented this material to academic audiences, the playful but ephemeral re-use of curriculum languages is quite a common practice, even though it is seldom documented (though see Preston 1982; 1989:206). And, most crucial to this Part of the book, ethnographic and interactional sociolinguistic analysis disclosed more going on than one might initially suspect.

In the first part of this chapter (4.1), I consider the reasons for this neglect of instructed foreign languages, arguing that it reflects the historical influence of some deeply rooted assumptions in sociolinguistics that are now changing. After that, I report the frequency and distribution of improvised *Deutsch* in my data, also giving some initial consideration to where its origins might lie (Chapter 4.2). In the section after that, I present a range of instances, dwelling on a number in some detail (Chapter 4.3), and I then pull these together, invoking Richard Bauman's notion of performance, suggesting parallels with music, and identifying some aspects of ritual *á la* Goffman (4.4). In the penultimate Section (Chapter 4.5), I look at how the status and ethnic neutrality of school German could facilitate improvised *Deutsch*, as well as having particular appeal to children who wanted both to do well and to enjoy themselves with their friends. In Chapters 4.4 and 4.5, I point out ways in which the *Deutsch* data contradict the assumptions that have led sociolinguistics to neglect instructed foreign languages in the past, and in the last section – Chapter 4.6 – I discuss the relationship between 'performance' and 'ritual', paving the way for Chapter 5, which analyses the German lessons and their links to *Deutsch* much more intensively. Throughout the book, I use the term '*Deutsch*' to refer to the spontaneous improvisations, and 'German' to refer to the language taught in the foreign language (FL) class.

I would like to begin with a sketch of three disciplinary assumptions which might explain why instructed FLs have seemed uninteresting to sociolinguistics in the past, at the same time pointing to a number of critiques and revisions that provide a clear path for their revaluation.

4.1 Reasons for the sociolinguistic neglect of instructed foreign languages

a) The first reason for the historic neglect of instructed foreign languages in sociolinguistics probably lies in the traditional idea that language *reflects* society, and that the social symbolic meaning of a language is principally derived from the positions in social structure occupied by its speakers (cf. Cameron 1990). With an instructed foreign language, the 'authentic' speakers live apart from the students learning it, often hundreds of miles away, and in the reflectionist logic, this makes the language's social significance and connotations seem remote and indeterminate (or else tediously tied to the national stereotypes that everyone is all too familiar with).

Trudgill and Giles (1983) illustrate this view when they argue that our feelings about any given variety are based on its association with particular social groups and that sociolinguistic analysis can by-pass aesthetic judgements of linguistic value:

> evaluations of language varieties, unlike those of, say, music ... are the *direct* result of cultural pressures ... [A]lthough there is some broad degree of agreement as to what is good and bad in music, there is nothing at all like the striking total uniformity of response in relative evaluations that we find in evaluations of language ... [A]esthetic judgements of linguistic varieties are the result of a complex of *social connotations* that these varieties have. (1983:214–215, 217; original emphases)

Similarly, in research on code-switching, the domains in which particular languages are used has often been regarded as the principal determinant of their symbolic meaning. In Auer's description of what he sees as a reductionist account,

> [e]ach language in the repertoire is said to have a unique context of usage (domain), defined primarily by the roles of the participants, but possibly also by its local and institutional setting. Thus, one language may be appropriate for interaction with members of the 'local team', whereas another language may be appropriate for interaction with outsiders etc. (1990:76).

Auer himself questions whether meaning can be solely derived from the allocation of languages to domains, and rather than seeing the meaning of code-switching being 'imported from outside', he instead argues that the attitudes and values associated with each language are generated by the way that code-switching is actually used in conversation itself.

b) The second long-standing assumption that makes instructed foreign languages seem uninteresting is closely related to the first, and it holds that the central empirical problem space for sociolinguistics lies at the interface between home language and the language of the nation-state. The resurgence of sociolinguistics in the 1960s owed much to widespread concern about the educational underachievement of working-class minority groups, and the central question was whether the roots of this lay in the school's failure to understand the different linguistic and cultural patterns which children brought from home (cf. e.g. Cazden, John and Hymes 1972):

> When a child from one developmental matrix enters a situation in which the communicative expectations are defined in terms of another, misperception and misanalysis may occur at every level. As is well known, words may be misunderstood because of differences in phonological systems; sentences may be misunderstood because of differences in grammatical systems; intents, too, and innate abilities may be misevaluated because of differences of systems for the use of language.   (Hymes 1972b:287–278)

This can be seen as one manifestation of what has been a formative problematic across the social sciences, the encounter between 'tradition' and 'modernity' (Giddens 1990:15–16), and in line with this, the vast bulk of research on code-switching, on cross-cultural communication, on non-standard dialects and on language maintenance attended to the same disjunction between modern institutional expectations and local community inheritance. Again, there is no real place for instructed foreign languages within this binary perspective, since they are neither a community inheritance brought to school from home, nor anything like the most salient feature of the dominant language regimes in education.

c) Thirdly, much of sociolinguistics in the 1960s and 70s was preoccupied with 'competence'. This entailed a set of social assumptions which Bernstein characterises as follows:

1. an announcement of a universal democracy of acquisition. All are inherently competent. There is no deficit;
2. the individual as *active* and *creative* in the construction of a *valid* world of meaning and practice . . .;
3. a celebration of everyday, oral language use and a suspicion of specialised languages;

4. official socialisers are suspect, for acquisition is a tacit, invisible act, not subject to public regulation or, perhaps, not primarily acquired through such regulation;

5. a critique of hierarchical relations, where domination is replaced by facilitation and imposition by accommodation. (1996:150)

In what he sees as "an extraordinary convergence across the social sciences in this period", Bernstein associates this view of competence with anthropology (Lévi-Strauss), with the ethnography of communication (Dell Hymes), with the study of child development (Piaget), with linguistics (Chomsky), and with conversation analysis (Garfinkel et al.) (1996:149). It was also central to child-centred education (Bernstein 1996:Chapter 3).

With this set of intellectual and political commitments, it is easy to understand the sociolinguist's historic lack of interest in instructed foreign languages. These are 'specialised languages', taught in accordance with a publicly regulated syllabus rather than developed in 'everyday, oral language use'; if the 'official socialiser' is removed, there is almost no contact at all with the language; and very low levels of proficiency – indeed, spectacular deficits – make it very hard to believe in a 'universal democracy of competence'.

So clearly, there was no space for instructed foreign languages in a sociolinguistic research agenda shaped by this combination of social scientific assumptions about competence, reflectionist ideas about the origins of social meaning, and an overarching preoccupation with the home–school interface. In sharp contrast to Panjabi in London, or African-American Vernacular English in New York, with instructed foreign languages the speakers who were considered to be symbolically significant lived miles away in other countries, and prospects for the sociolinguistic discovery and emancipation of rich but repressed community knowledges looked distinctly limited. Together, these beliefs suggested that if you were interested in the politics of languages and inequality, you really only needed to concern yourself with ESL, non-standard dialects and minority languages, and that for language learners, issues of power and domination could only arise in the encounter with 'native speakers'.

The neglect of foreign language education in sociolinguistics stemmed, then, from quite deeply rooted ideas.[2] In more recent years, however, there have been a number of intellectual developments which help to make instructed foreign languages a potentially more interesting topic for sociolinguists:

i) The macro-structural determinism of 'reflectionist' sociolinguistics was criticised by Auer for overlooking the extent to which the meaning of a language could be generated locally in interaction. This chimes with 'social constructionism', the emerging consensus among social theorists that although pre-existing social structures are undoubtedly influential, social reality (and hence the social meaning of linguistic varieties) is also at least partially created anew in the historically situated discourse of everyday life (see Chapters 1.2 and 1.3 above). This has important implications for instructed foreign languages. If the social meaning and importance of a language is at least partly created in the ways in which it is actually used in interaction here-and-now, then its lack of a birth-link to speakers who occupy clearly marked positions in large-ish social structures close at hand no longer matters so much, and instructed foreign languages are at least partly liberated from the hazy no-man's land to which they were banished by reflectionism.

ii) The binary division between home and school (and their associated values) also starts to look a lot less secure when cultural theories about globalisation and late modernity begin to interrogate notions of 'high' and 'low', 'elite' and 'folk'. Appadurai and Breckenridge, for example, propose an alternative notion of 'public culture', which challenges notions of culture predicated on such hierarchies and polarities as high and low, elite and popular. These terms, they argue, clearly need rethinking in situations where "popular culture is often the product of urban, commercial and state interests, where folk culture is often a response to the competitive cultural policies of today's nation-states, and where traditional culture is often the result of conscious deliberation or elaboration" (Appadurai and Breckenridge 1988; also Chapters 1.1 and 1.2 above).

    Sociolinguists traditionally conceived ethno-linguistic identity as being rooted at home and in the family, but in recent years, there has been a good deal of interest in the often ephemeral ways in which young people sometimes use language associated with ethnic groups that they themselves weren't born into, being influenced instead by friendship and/or the circulation of ethnic forms as commodities, life-style options and art-objects (e.g. Hewitt 1986; Hannerz 1992a,b; Hill 1993, 1995; Rampton 1995a; Hoechsman 1997; Bucholtz 1999; Cutler 1999; Lo 1999). There is now a large body of research that construes 'community' either as an interactional production or as ideological construct, rather than as a matter of where you were born and brought up (Chapter 1.2; Pratt 1987; Rampton 1998b), and overall, with the decline of the old certainties, the sites of identity investment and the resources for identity construction look much more mobile than before. In this less predictable, more volatile terrain, instructed foreign languages also start to lose the irrelevance they were guaranteed in the earlier dispensation.

iii) Finally, the 'competence' perspective loses it dominance when its claims are themselves identified as an ideology that masks rather than relinquishes power and social control (Bernstein 1971b, 1996). During the 1960s and 70s, sociolinguists took it as their professional mission to recover, celebrate and advocate the official recognition of capacities and resources that had been hitherto denigrated or neglected (e.g. Trudgill 1975; Labov 1982), but more recently, researchers have started looking at how academic ideas about language and ability themselves shape and are shaped within wider processes of political domination, defining the identity, value and distribution of different kinds of language, and through that, influencing the distribution of symbolic and material resources more generally (Hymes 1980; Pratt 1987; Gal 1989; Cameron et al. 1992; Pennycook 1994; Woolard and Schieffelin 1994). In this context, the 'naturalness' of mother tongues and the 'competence' of native speakers falls open question (Bourne 1988; Rampton 1990, 1995a:336–344), and by the same token, instructed foreign languages are no longer automatically disqualified for their 'artificiality'. 'Mother tongues' and 'foreign languages' may be different, but are these differences 'intrinsic', or are they produced within social and ideological processes that embrace them both?

Together, these developments promise to rehabilitate instructed foreign languages as a sociolinguistic research topic. They allow us to imagine

- how the value and social meaning of a school foreign language might be reshaped within the micropolitics of classroom interaction,
- how an FL might serve as a significant resource in the maintenance and accumulation of vernacular prestige,
- how minority bilinguals might draw on it in their self-constitution beyond essentialist conceptions of ethnicity,
- and how we could have been blinded to all this by the orthodoxies of modernist sociolinguistics.

At this point, it is worth turning to the data.

4.2   Discovering *Deutsch* in Inner London: frequency and sources

Adolescents at Central High used quite a lot of *Deutsch outside* their German classes, in breaktime, in corridors, in English, Maths or Humanities lessons. Approximate figures on this are presented in Table 4.1, and it can be seen from this that there was a notional frequency of about one *Deutsch* sequence every two hours.

Table 4.1 also shows that boys used *Deutsch* a lot more in my recordings than the girls. There is some social psychological evidence that German is quite often felt to be rather a 'masculine' language (Ludwig 1983), but this is not conclusive (cf. Esarte-Sarries and Byram 1989:157), and instead, the difference is better explained in terms of the interactional dispositions that these children displayed in class. Put very simply, Hanif and his friends liked to show off, Joanne and Ninnette didn't, and *Deutsch* was something to show off with. I discussed the relationship between gender and classroom participation in detail in Chapters 2 and 3, and I shall elaborate on 'showing off' with *Deutsch* in the course of the chapter. But this means that in what follows, I shall focus mainly on the boys, and indeed, as I was not able to record either of the girls in German lessons, this gets no better in Chapter 5.

What about the origins of *Deutsch*? First, did the *Deutsch* that these youngsters were using have neighbourhood or home community roots? Were there influential students in the class who had lived in

Table 4.1: *Summative data on* Deutsch *in one tutor group in an Inner London comprehensive school*

The 37 hours of radio-microphone recordings from four 14 year olds (2 male, 2 female) covered a period of 2 months (5 weeks without the holiday break), and spread over this period, outside German lessons, there were about 20 episodes involving a spontaneous use of German. These 20 or so episodes can be broken down into the following figures:

Total turns-at-talk in German:	c. 70
Number of turns by pupils:	c. 63
Number of turns by teachers:	3
Number of turns by boys:	c. 63 (of varying lengths; out of 20.5 hrs of boys wearing radio-microphones)
Number of turns by girls:	4 (all of one word; out of 16.5 hrs of girls wearing radio-microphones)
Maximum number of German turns in a sequence:	c. 14
Minimum number of German turns in a sequence:	1
Maximum length of turn:	c. 28 syllables
Minimum length of turn:	1 word
Maximum number of turns per user:	c. 20 (Hanif)
Minimum number of turns per user:	4 (Ninnette) 1 (Mr Newton)
Total number of identified speakers:	8
Number of boys:	5
Number of girls:	1
Number of teachers:	2

In contrast, there seemed to be only 3 episodes involving French.

Germany or had relatives there that they regularly visited? There did not seem to be, and none of my informants had any family ties to Germany. In addition, if they had accessed the language through school-independent, vernacular channels, one might have expected to find a larger vocabulary in peer group *Deutsch*, and at least some vulgarity and rude words. But there was nothing to compare with the lexical focus on parts of the body, bodily shape, bodily functions, ingestion, violence, animals and ethnic groups that had turned up in my earlier research on white and black adolescents using Panjabi (Rampton 1995a:167), and there didn't even appear to be a second person singular pronoun, an indispensible asset in any foreign language abuse exchange.[3]

Instead, there seemed to be two potential sources, and one lay in popular culture. Germany has had quite an historic role in the lore

and language of British schoolchildren, and in 1959, the Opies
found children still singing about 'Kaiser Bill' from the First World
War (Opie and Opie 1959: Ch. 7). Germany's involvement in the
Second World War is often a source of humour in the popular press
and the broadcast media,[4] and as recently as 2002, the German
ambassador to the UK complained publicly about the continuing
circulation of war-based stereotypes and clichés about Germans
being aggressive, intolerant and stupid, blaming among other things
the emphasis in British history teaching on the Nazi period
(*Guardian* 9/12/02). These connections were certainly available to
my informants:

GERMAN TEACHER	they put the 'auf' to the end of the sentence
ANON1 *((a little later))*	why?
ANON2	they wanted to start a war
OTHERS	*((laughter))*

Indeed, traditional associations between Germany and racism could
also be up-dated:

HANIF	do you like Germans?
GOPAL?	(yeah)
HANIF	well they bloody well don't like you cos you're (a) Paki (2.0)

Even so, in the contexts where adolescents spontaneously switched into
peer group *Deutsch*, Germany, Germans, Nazism and racism hardly
ever figured as issues either mentioned or implied by the participants.
British popular representations of Germans as authoritarian, aggressive
and so forth certainly cannot be ruled out as one part of the connotational resonance, but when these youngsters used the language, they
certainly weren't just indulging in anti-German stereotypes.

The most obvious source of *Deutsch* was the German language
lessons that the students attended three times a week, and some
of the students were actually quite emphatic that this was its origin:

Extract 4.1 (PB7. 16/3/97)
Interview with Guy, Satesh and Simon.

1	BEN	German gets used a bit
2	SATESH	mmm

```
 3  SIMON    mm hmm
 4  BEN      um why?/why do you think?
 5  GUY      cos (.) it sounds funny
 6  BEN      it sounds funny yeah I mean why German rather
             than Spanish
 7  SATESH   cos we're not doing Spanish
 8  GUY      mm
 9  SIMON    yeh
10  BEN      so if you're doing Spanish
11  SATESH   yeah we'd probably speak Spanish
12  BEN      right right (.)
13           is German- it's not to do with kind of German-
14           Germany being on the news more or
15  GUY      no
16  SATESH   no
17  BEN      no no no yeah
18           but why- why German rather than for example
             Arabic
19  SATESH   cos none of us /are learning Arabic
20  GUY      we don't know ( )
21  BEN      uh
22  GUY      cos none of us know Arabic
23  SIMON    we wouldn't know what it meant
24  SATESH   yeah
25  GUY      (it's true)
26           even with German we make (it) up anyway
27           but we only make up cos what the teacher looks
                                                      like
28           when she does her faces (.)
29           and (so) / when the teachers do it
30  SATESH   Entschuldigung
             ((trans: pardon))
31  GUY      they- they do like ((gesture))
32  BEN      what she puts-
33  GUY      she (goes)/like that
34  BEN      oh there's a gesture which goes with that
35           is there
36  GUY      yeh
37  SATESH   m/m
38  SIMON    yeh
39  BEN      which is- which is:
40  GUY      Ent/schuldigung
41  SATESH   that
42           Entschuldigung (.)
43  BEN      which is exactly what Miss::/( ) does
44  GUY      Wilson does
```

```
45  BEN      Miss Miss Wilson does
46           yeh yeh
47  GUY      yes Miss Wilson
```

Likewise, as Hanif explained:

```
HANIF   the way the teacher says it,
        she basically makes us laugh
        and so we just take the mick,
        and we say enshudigen
               [ənʃuːdɪgən]
BEN     why does she make you laugh
HANIF   the ways she says it
        it really cracks us up
```
                                                                    (29:180)

Indeed, it also looked as though the German lessons had provided at least those parts of peer group *Deutsch* that were sufficiently standard to be intelligible – simple formulae (*danke*, *Entschuldigung* – 'thanks', 'sorry'), negative and affirmative particles (*nein*, *ja* – 'no', 'yes'), a few evaluative and directive words or phrases used by the teacher in classroom management (*gut*, *Moment*, *schnell*, *komm nach Vorne* – 'good', 'wait a moment,' 'quickly', 'come to the front'), and the constructions, words and phrases presented in elementary language textbooks (addressing topics like 'myself' – *Schwester*, *Bruder*, *mein Lieblingsfach* – 'sister', 'brother, 'my favourite subject').

In the next chapter, I will explore the relationship between instructed German and improvised *Deutsch* in much more detail. But before doing that, we need a clearer view of these improvisations themselves, and for that I should now turn to the interactional recordings.

4.3   *Deutsch* in interaction

The first example comes from Ninnette, who was recorded on radio-microphone for more than 15 hours and who used 'danke' with her peers on four occasions. This is one of them:

Extract 4.2
Ninnette (wearing the radio-microphone) and Joanne are settling themselves at the start of the Maths lesson. The speech turns set in from the left

hand margin are voices on the main floor of classroom talk. 'Skittles' are sweets. (Gex13; 48:200)

```
1   NINNETTE ((quietly:))         we still got Skittles left (.)
2   JOANNE ((whispering:))        yeh I know (1.5)
3                                 ((noise of velcro clasp being
                                  opened))
4        MR DAVIES
         ((addressing
         the whole
         class))
5                                             right
6                                             when it's quiet
7                                             can I/call the register
8   NINNETTE ((to Joanne))        ˎdanke
9        ANON                     (                              )
10       ANON                     (                              )
11  JOANNE ((to Ninnette))        it's easier with that thing
12                                on now
13                                ((4.5 till Joanne's next
                                  utterance))
```

As earlier chapters showed, neither of these girls were particularly keen participants in lessons, they spent a lot of their time talking quietly together in class, and though they were officially forbidden, sharing and eating sweets was one way of making lessons more enjoyable. In this particular extract, Ninnette's remark about still having Skittles (line 1) is taken as an indirect request by Joanne, who then opens her bag to get them out (line 3). Ninnette uses German *danke* to express appreciation of Joanne's effort (line 8), to which Joanne responds with a minimisation in English (lines 11–12). The switch to German is unspectacular. Phonetically, Ninnette's pronunciation of *danke* is fairly 'nativised' and the first vowel sounds very much like her *a* in *thank*. The utterance is semantically meaningful (a translation of *thanks*), it is pragmatically appropriate, and Joanne takes it without comment. There is nothing here to suggest that Ninnette's switch into German signals irony or insincerity, and when they are finally fished out from the bag, she seems to enjoy the skittles as much as Joanne. In the 15 or so hours of radio-microphone recordings involving Ninnette, there were about 12 thanking sequences, and her 4 *danke*s

occurred (variably) only with peers, never with the teachers or
shopkeepers that she thanked. Overall, it is difficult to read a
great deal of symbolic or micro-political freighting into the way
that Ninnette used German: both here and elsewhere in the recordings of her, *danke* seemed like a device available for the unostenta-
tious, lightly playful rekeying of interpersonal rituals in friendly
interaction.

Ninnette's *danke* examplified one of the ways in which these
adolescents used German, and there are both similarities and differences to this in the next episode, which involved Simon:

Extract 4.3

A Humanities lesson in the library is coming to the end. Mr Poyser has just
completed a slow (c. 40 second) count to three, at which point pupils are
supposed to have finished their work, returned their library books, and got
out their homework diaries. After spending some time at a table on the other
side of the room sitting chatting to Ameena, Simon (wearing the radio-
microphone) has just rejoined the table with Marilyn, Joanne and
Michelle where he was placed when the lesson began. The speakers whose
names are indented (Mr P, Guy, the Librarian) can be heard on the radio-
microphone recording, but are not members of Simon's immediate conversational circle. (G Ex 7)

1	MR P *((some distance from Simon))*	hurry up
2		John come on
3		and Guy
4		get a move on now (.)
5		Mansur get a move on
6		Ninnette get a move on
7	GUY *((some way off: chant- like))*	(( )*ES* is YOUR pen) (2.0)
8	LIBR	Ninnette put them here would you please
9		This is ( ) (.)
10	SIMON	₁**es** ₁**is** ˈ**nicht** ₁**goot** [es ɪs niːxt guːtʰ] *((Translation: it is not good))*

11		₁**es** ₁**is** ₁**goot** ˆ**i: n** ₁**nik**
		[es ɪs guːd ĩᵊn nɪk]
		((*it is good ????*))
12		((*a gulp-like sound:*)) **ehn** (2.5)
		[ʔẽĩʔ]
13	MR P ((*in the*	quick quick quick
	background))	
14	SIMON	you love my language innit
15		₁**es** ₁**is** ¹**nicht** ₁**goot**
		[eɪs ɪs nĩŋkᵗ gʊtʰ]
		((*it is not good*))
16		₁**es i** ˆ**mioo** ₁**kineginin** ₁**chim** ＼**ineya**
		[eɪs i mĩʊ̃ kə̃nə̃gɪnɪŋ ʃʊməneɪe]
		((*Translation: ???*))
		(1.5)
17		I didn't do any work yesterday
18	MARILYN	(dinya) (.)
19	SIMON	I did a bit of work (.)
20		lan:guages (.)
21		I had to go sit with miss (.)
22		and she helped me do my work
23		and I went
24		((*in a 'thick' voice:*))
		"what's this what's this"
25		she went (.)
26		((*more ordinary voice:*))
		"you're not in the mood"
27		I goes
28		((*nasalised:*)) 'no'
29		she goes
30		((*ordinary voice:*))
		"alright then just sit there"
31		and I went
32		((*more normal but constricted:*))
		"ye::h" (1.0)
33	GIRL	((*half-laugh*))
34	JOANNE?	(did G＿follow her)
35	GIRL	(oh yeah? or ?I have)
36	JOANNE?	(did G＿follow her)
37	SIMON	find it really hard though
38		not to- (.)
39		you know (.)
40		not to do wo:rk (.)
41		I'm- I'm (.)
42		really (.)
43		always on the ball an- (1.5)

44   ((*said with energy and a bit of a*
                            growl:)) ALWAYS READY (.)
45   to face another bit of work (.)
46   tackle another bit of maths
47   ((*quiet laughs for 4.0*))
48   LIBR   (people) make sure you've
                            got your
49   diaries and a pen out
50   so that you can copy your
                            homework
51   from the board
52   /and all books in to me
53   if you haven't already
54   ((*Simon moves across the room to*
                            Ameena's desk))
55 SIMON ((*to a girl*))   ˈent ˈschu ˈli ˌgung (.)
                            [enʃʊlɪgʊn]
                            ((*excuse me*))
56   ˈen ⌈ ˋschu ˈli ˌgung=
                                 ⌊ [enʃʊlɪgʊn]
57 GIRL   ⌊((*subvocalising a word*
                                 she's writing down?:))
                            (could)
58 SIMON   =can you read (from   )
59 AMEENA?   yeh /sometimes I get a word from it
60 GIRL   got it
61   MR P   right will you now-
62   /I need your cooperation
                            //please
63 SIMON   ( ) can I see (.)
64   ((*very softly:*)) cnIsee
65   MR P   will you now sit down /
66   TANNOY   ((*pips signalling the end*
                            of the lesson))
67   MR P   and take your diaries out
68   Simon (2.5)
69   diaries out please (3.0)
70   can you just copy this from
                                                  the board
71   I'll explain it in a moment
                            (.)
72   copy this/ from the board
                                        very quickly
73   (.)
74 SIMON   ((*quietly, high pitched:*))
                            someone-

Although I observed and noted Simon's movements around the room during this lesson, it is not clear what Simon is evaluating in line 10, and nor can I say whether the gulp-like ``ehn'' in line 12 is an extension of the repetition with elaboration/corruption in line 11, or whether instead it comes as the response to e.g. a friendly punch from Marilyn. In the absence of any verbal ratification, however, Simon proclaims the approval of his audience and repeats the first half of the German of a moment ago (line 15), which he then corrupts more dramatically than before by sliding into a stretch of sound that it is hard to identify with any language. He then gets Marilyn's attention (lines 17, 18, 19) for a story about being picked out by the German teacher for not doing enough work (lines 19–32), and follows this with an ironic portrait of himself as a hard worker (lines 37–46). Apart from Marilyn's response to his story preface in line 18 and the delayed and constrained appreciation token in line 33, there is little (audible) indication that the girls are particularly interested in what Simon is saying, and in line 54 he goes back to Ameena's table, apologising for the intrusion and prefacing an interrogative in English with a couple of German *Entschuldigung*s. His approach is accepted, but he doesn't seem to get very far in the pursuit of his question/request before he is sent back to his table by Mr Poyser.

There are three points worth making about the German in lines 10 to 16. First, sound play features prominently, and it seems to be organised into two couplets (10 + 11 and 15 + 16): each line begins with [e]; the grammar and prosody of the first line of the first couplet (10) is repeated in the first line of the second (15); and the second half of each couplet elaborates/corrupts the first, the deviation increasing from the first couplet to the second (11, 16). Second, German is made salient as an object of self-conscious metapragmatic comment (line 14), and becomes the first of three guises that Simon runs through in efforts to constitute himself as an entertaining figure to the girls. Third, he immediately links it to German lessons at school (lines 17–32), contextualising it as the output of an unenthusiastic FL learner through an account which focuses its comic exaggeration on his own lack of involvement (lines 24, 28 and 32) rather than on the teacher (lines 26, 30).

All three points distinguish the German in the first part of this extract from Ninnette's *danke* in Extract 4.1, but in the second part, Simon's *Entschuldigung*s are much closer. Both are relatively unspectacular and pragmatically appropriate, they both occur in small group talk that is not officially approved, and they are selected as alternatives to English at interactional junctures where low-key displays of respect are customary.

Extract 4.3 shows *Deutsch* being used in cross-sex interaction, and in fact Simon was generally more confident with girls than a lot of other boys in the class (see Chapter 9.5). Generally speaking though, more important arenas for nourishing, performing and ratifying peer group *Deutsch* lay elsewhere, both in interactions between male friends, and on the central floor of official classroom business.

After the lesson in the library, Simon joined Hanif, Guy and others in the line waiting outside the Maths classroom:

Extract 4.4
Waiting outside the Maths classroom:

```
18   HANIF    ˈaufmachen
                ((trans: open))
19   GUY      JOHN (.)
                talk (some German to )
20   HANIF    she's going (.)
21   ANON     die ˈtoor
                ((trans: the door))
22   BOYS     ((chorally:)) ˈzoo::ˈma:ˌche:n
                                  ((close))
23   SIMON    ((laughing:)) THIS IS ˈAUFˈMACHEN
                                      ((open))
24   MASUD?   ˈauf (ˈmachen    )
25   SIMON    ((laughing:)) (oh ˈshudigung)
26   HANIF    Entˈshuˈdigung (.)
27   JOHN     Entshudigung
28   MASUD    eh
29            Moˈment (.)
                ((trans: a moment – wait a moment))
30            Hanif Moˈment
31   HANIF    Moˈme:nt
32            Moˈme:n⌈t
33   GUY           ⌊Moˈme:nt
34            Moˈme:nt
```

((the choral interplay continues until the Maths teacher comes out of the classroom))

In this (and other) episodes, Hanif plays a leading role, taking the first part in the choral call-and-responses that led up to this sequence, and figuring as the person that Masud appeals to when there is no immediate response to his first introduction of *moment* (lines 29 and 30). In fact, Hanif produced more turns in German than anyone else (c. 20, in comparison with c. 14 from Guy, the second most frequent user), and in interviews he was cited by others as one of its principal exponents. Some more of his German can be seen in the next two extracts, the second illustrating one of its most public uses on the main floor of classroom interaction.

Both extracts come from the first ten minutes at the start of an English lesson, and during this period, Hanif's German is interwoven with humming, singing and music (in 4 sequences in all – see also Extract 4.8). This begins before the lesson starts:

Extract 4.5
Hanif (wearing the radio-microphone) is moving along the corridor from the Humanities lesson to the start of English, then waiting outside the classroom (probably), and then finally moving into the English classroom. 'Skips' are a brand of kind of potato crisps advertised on TV. (The indented speakers (Guy and Boy) are not talking to Hanif.)

```
             ((in the corridor))
 1   HANIF   ((half-humming Skips tune to himself in
             falsetto for 8.0))
 2           (.)
 3           ALRIGHT then ( )
 4           ((Liverpool accent:)) aright
 5           (1.5)
 6   BOY     ((from some way off)): A RIGHT ( ) (2.0)
 7   HANIF   ((carries on humming to himself as before
             for about 7.0))
 8                    BOY:  ((away from Hanif)) (        )
 9                    BOY:       (                 )
10                    BOY:       (                 )
11   HANIF   ((half-humming and half-singing in falsetto
             for another 10 seconds))
12           ((Hanif making no sound for about 7 seconds
             until line 15))
13                    GUY:      ((not directed to Hanif))
14                         ( ah Masud )
15   HANIF   ₁Ich ˈschreize ˈmusst (le   ) ˈsteinen (.)
             [ɪch ʃʁaɪze muʃtʌ lɛ  ʃtaɪnəːn ]
             ((I ? must (teach) stones))
```

```
16            'jagen `meine (.)
              [ jɑːɡən maɪnə]
              ((hunt my))
17            ˌhaben
              ((have))
18   BEN      ((from a little way off:))
              can I just have a look/ at your=
19   HANIF    ((very quietly:)) sorry
20                     BOY:        (        )
21   BEN      =your battery (.)
22            to see that your b/attery's okay
23            ((a single noise from furniture being moved))
24   BEN      yeh it's okay
25            /I've given you one (            )
26   HANIF    yeh?
27            /Okay
28                     BOY:        (mind the door)
29            (5.0)
```

In the soft singing to himself at the start of this Extract, Hanif is involved in two simultaneous frames: one is the institutional world of changing classrooms, crowded corridors and milling bodies, and the other is the musical realm of rhythm and melody – here a moderate swing – that he is involved in by himself. He is by no means totally lost in his tune, he breaks off to greet passers-by (lines 3 and 4), and in all, the music seems to operate as a mildly pleasurable soundtrack overlaying visual and proxemic experience. There is in fact nothing exceptional about this musical involvement: high levels of engrossment in the business of getting from A to B are not routine in places like corridors, and as a form of civil inattention, there is a certain situational propriety in singing to oneself. This changes, of course, once one moves inside classrooms, where although there is obviously a lot of variation in normative expectations, pupils are generally expected to show higher levels of involvement in activities authorised by the teacher, and verbal representation usually takes priority over music. It is impossible to say whether these considerations occur to Hanif, but around the time that they move into the classroom, he code-switches into German (lines 15–17).

In fact, it is very hard to identify any external cues motivating this switch,[5] and instead, there are several ways in which Hanif's German looks rather like his humming. As before, Hanif continues as a 'single' (Goffman 1981:79), outside any conversational engagement, and

when I approach him without any mitigating display (line 18), pre-
sumably assuming his accessibility for talk, he apologises very softly
(line 19), thereby constituting the speech he has been using as an
illegitimate alternative engagement, providing no grounds for rejecting my interruption. In this respect, the German looks like self-talk
(Goffman 1981), *except* that here it is *very* hard to comprehend.[6]
Admittedly, it is difficult to know what is and isn't a well-formed
proposition in very rudimentary FL learner idiolects, but above and
beyond questions of conceptual coherence, Hanif's German is striking
for the tension in its manner of articulation, for the assonance of [ai],
and for the energy he puts into sounds and sound combinations outside the normal English repertoire (most notably, word-initial palato-
alveolar voiceless fricatives first with uvular R (*schreize*) and then with
[t] (*steinen*)). As before, Hanif seems to be maintaining a double frame –
on the one hand, he's co-present and accountable to a social situation
and a gathering (that is now turning itself into an English lesson), while
on the other, he is tuned to a partly autonomous world of sound. But
whereas before he was attending to pitch register, melody and synco-
pated rhythm, now it is segmental and phonotactic production.

Admittedly, the German is also different from the music in being
much louder, and this gives it a rather more public, declamatory
character. To the extent that pupils know that they should enter
lessons in a quiet, orderly fashion, this also edges Hanif's German
towards the transgressive, and this becomes plainer in subsequent
sequences, of which this is one:

Extract 4.6

Mr Newton has started on the introduction to the content of the day's lesson
(though it is hard going), and this involves getting the students to think about
why Romeo and Juliet died, in preparation for role-playing a coroner's
inquest on the subject. Hanif and his friends have been quite active in these
preliminary discussions, and they have had some disagreements about the
causes. In fact, Hanif's last utterance was ''Sir you don't appreciate
my er what do you macall it my comments,'' and there have now been
at least 30 turns since he last spoke. In contrast, his friends John and Masud
are carrying on in the discussion with Mr Newton (see also Extract 3.11):

```
1    MR N         ((claps once)) (.)
2                 alright
3                 (2.0) ((conversations continue in the
                 background))
```

4	JOHN	Sir
5		(.)
6		(because)first they were in love
7		and they wanted to be:
8		(.)
9	MASUD	togevver
10	JOHN	to:ge:ther:
11	MASUD	cos if they stayed alive
12		and they/( )
13	MR N	the only way to be together/was in death
14	HANIF	((begins a very loud, fast, falsetto rendition of the Bee Gees 'Staying Alive', carrying on until mid-way through line 24))
15	JOHN OR MASUD	yeh
16	HANIF	((singing:)) "huh
17		huh /huh"
18	MR N	yes I agree
19	HANIF	"huh huh
20		hu/h"
21	MR N	((optimistic intonation addressed to class:)) ALL RIGHT
22	HANIF	"staying alive
23		staying alive"
24	MR N	listening s/kills everybody
25	HANIF	/((uvular trill:)) [RRR:]
26	KUT?	((a long low drone:)) (mau:::)
27	HANIF	one more
28	KUT	/(mau::)
29	MR N	as I've said before
30		I get a bit fed up with saying (.)
31		shshsh
32	JOHN	ˈLOU⌈ˌDER
33	MR N	⌊you're doing your SATs now
34	HANIF	**ˈVIEL ˈLAUTER ˋSPRECHEN**
		[**viː** lʊtɛː ʃpʁɛxən]
		((speak much louder))
35		**ˈVIEL ˈLAUTER ˋSPRECHEN**
		[**viː** laʊtɛː ʃpʁɛxən]
36	JOHN	((smile voice)): ˌlauter ˋspricken (.)
		[laʊtɛː ʃpʁɪkən]
37		whatever that is
38	ANON	the guy said (.) spastic (.)
39	MR N	as we listen supposedly
40		(not as we speak) (2.5)
41	SATESH	why ev they got a/(nineteen on there)
42	MR N	Michelle

```
43  BOY        (            )
44  SATESH     (alright)
45  MR N       ssh
46             (.)
47             shsh shsh shsh
48  BOY        you're holdin' ('im) up
49             ((lots of people laugh out loud))
```

Extract 4.6 starts with Hanif's good friends John and Masud involved together in analytical discussion with Mr Newton (lines 4–13). Hanif seems to be attending to this and responds to Masud's turn in line 11. But in contrast to Masud's earlier collaborative turn completion (line 9), this does not contribute to the propositional development of their analysis. Instead, cued by the phrase *stayed alive*, Hanif floods into their discussion with a musical 'translation' into disco rock – *Staying Alive* by the Bee Gees, from the film *Saturday Night Fever* (lines 14, 16,17, 19, 20, 22, 23). There is a certain creative interanimation of semiotic modalities in this mode-switch, with Hanif showing how alive he is to any chance to bring different realms of expression/experience into conjunction, but it is only tangentially linked to the interaction between Masud, John and Mr Newton. Mr Newton quickly closes his conversation with Masud and John (line 18), and goes back yet again to class management (line 21). While he is trying to restore order, Masud evidently turns his mind away from curricular to masculine peer group matters, and overlaps Hanif's final uvular trill in line 25 with a long low droning taunt directed at one of the girls in the class (line 26). This is then picked up by Hanif, who confirms that he is now fully reincorporated into the team by shifting from performer to conductor and telling Masud to repeat his taunt (line 27). Masud complies (line 28), while Mr Newton continues his efforts to restore order, admitting now to exasperation (line 29). John's *LOUDER* in the next turn (line 32) is open to more than one interpretation, but it makes most sense to me as a directive to Mr Newton, construing the teacher's *ssshhh* in line 31 as inadequate to the task of getting the class to keep quiet. Mr Newton doesn't raise his voice any further, but perseveres by invoking their national oracy tests (line 33), and it is after this that Hanif comes in with a couple of loud *viel lauter sprechen* (lines 34 and 35). As before, there are some clear similarities between the code-switch into *Deutsch* and the mode-switch into song a few instants earlier. Both take their cue from a friend's words and then provide expansions (two words in English in line 11 => several bars of song; one word in English in line 32 => three words in German), and both entail a greater expenditure of vocal energy than usual, taking Hanif beyond his habitual speech range, most obviously in rhythm, melody and pitch with the song, and segmental pronunciation with the German. The German is grammatically, semantically and pragmatically quite well formed as an imperative, and indeed as such, it is a better display of Hanif's resourceful alertness to what has just gone on than he could expect to achieve with a string of German-sounding nonsense. But it is not clear how far the linguistic properties of his turn count for his audience. John reiterates part of Hanif's utterance (line 36), preserving some but not all of its non-English phonology, and then disclaims any knowledge of its meaning (line 37). Mr Newton meanwhile makes no verbal show of paying specific attention to either of them, and continues his disciplinary endeavours.

Deutsch was actually quite often used at moments when problems of classroom management were being foregrounded, and indeed in terms of the occasions that seemed to prompt the use of it, *Deutsch* appeared to be rather narrowly oriented to issues of classroom conduct and control, emerging at points when the heterogeneous activity of adolescents ran up against the institutional priorities of teachers. In this regard, it was more specialised than the stylised varieties I analysed in earlier research on adolescent crossing into Creole and Panjabi (Rampton 1995a), where in addition to bodies and sex, there was a lot of jocular abuse between friends. And it was also much more limited in scope when it is compared with the ways in which these youngsters put on exaggerated posh and Cockney accents. Stylisations of posh and Cockney certainly did sometimes engage with issues of classroom order, but they also thematised sexuality, bodily demeanour, peer rapport and a range of other issues. In contrast, about half of the *Deutsch* sequences occurred during moments when classroom order was being established (reasserted) and youngsters were being called (back) into their official institutional role as pupils. For example:

Extract 4.7
Mr Alcott is taking the register at the start of the school day. (24/4/97).

```
1  MR A   erm::
2         A_____
3  A      yes sir
```

```
4   MR A   (.) is ˇJane-
5           (1.0)
6   JOHN   \nicht hier
           ((trans: not here))
7   MR A   \Marilyn (1.0)
8           ₁Jane nicht hier ⌐eh (.)
```

Extract 4.8

Mr Newton, the English teacher, is calling the class to order.

```
 1   MR N    shoosh shoosh shoosh shoosh (1.5)
             /e::rm
 2   BOY     ( rubber?) (.)
 3   BOY     what?
 4   BOY     (           )
 5   BOY     Good (1.0)
 6   MR N    /now (.)
 7   HANIF   ((brief, loud and falsetto glissando:))
             [u u: u::]
 8   MR N    erm DONT WASTE- time
 9           everybody
10           js look this way
11           (1.5)
12           ₁thank₁you (.)
13           er we've          ⌐finished- ((5.0 till turn 15))
14   HANIF   ((quite loud:))   ⌐\danke
                               ((trans: thank you))
15   ANON    is that gum or (    ) (.)
16   HANIF   gu/m
17   MR N    can I please have-
18   ANON    (              )
19   ANON    (        /        )
20   MR N    can I please have some complete attention
                                         everybody
21           cos I want to talk for about 5 or 10 minutes
```

About three quarters of the episodes registered the significance of teachers: teachers were either addressed in *Deutsch* (Extracts 4.7, 4.10 [lines 6–8]), or they responded to *Deutsch* (Extracts 4.7, 4.9, 4.12), or they provided English words or expressions translated into *Deutsch* (Extract 4.8).

Extract 4.9

Tutor period. The class is arranged in a circle for a discussion, and the idea is that only the person holding a 'ceremonial' pen designated as such by

Mr Alcott should be entitled to speak. Attempting to hand speaking rights over to Lara, Rafiq has thrown the pen across the room and hit her in the face. Mr A has told Rafiq to leave the room, and is now addressing Lara. (13/3/97)

```
 1   MR A   I'm really sorry Lara
 2   JOHN   Lara (.)
 3          Lara (.)
 4        ┌ ent`schuligen
          │ [enʃu:lɪgən]
          │ ((trans: sorry))
 5   MR A └ okay
 6   GUY    ent`schludigung
            [enʃˡu:dɪgʊŋ]
 7   ANON   ent`schludigung
            [enʃˡudɪgʊn]
 8   GUY    ent`schlu┌digung ((laughs))
 9   MR A            │ ent`schuligung ent┌ `schuligung
                     └ [enʃu:lɪgʊŋ]      │ [enʃu:lɪgʊŋ]
10   GUY                                 └ Lara
                                           ent`schludigung
                                           [enʃˡu:dɪgʊŋ]
```

Extract 4.10

In preparation for groupwork activity in the same English lesson as Extract 4.8, Mr Newton has asked pupils to change their seating arrangements. (7/3/97)

```
 1   JOHN   Hanif
 2          get up
 3          ( )
 4   HANIF  ˌdas ist ˈnein ˌgut
            ((trans: that is no good))
 5          (6.0)
 6          SAA:-
 7          Sir (.)
 8          ˈist ˈmagd `keine ˌneine
            ((?trans: is ?like? no no))
```

And in the ten or so exchanges when it articulated apologies (Extract 4.9), disapproval (Extract 4.10), and commands seeking to enhance the flow of classroom affairs (Extracts 4.6, 4.12), it encoded speech acts that were directed to repairing, noting or preventing breaches to social propriety, at least on the surface.

   Those, then, are some examples of peer group *Deutsch* at Central High, and at this point, it is worth turning to a more general characterisation of the data we have seen, pointing as well to some of the methodological implications for sociolinguistics.

4.4   *Deutsch*: performance, music and ritual

In Chapter 2.3, I showed how students' participation in Class 9A was often framed as performance in Richard Bauman's sense, "involving the assumption of responsibility to an audience for a display of communicative skill, highlighting the way in which communication is carried out, above and beyond its referential content", "offered for the enhancement of experience", and "call[ing] forth . . . heightened awareness of both the act of expression and the performer" (1986:3). I also distinguished between on the one hand, the voluntary 'performance' of exuberant students intent on embellishing the curriculum discourse in whatever ways they could, and on the other, the compulsory performance enforced on students when the teacher nominated them to respond to a question in front of the rest of the class (Chapter 2.6). *Deutsch*, it seems, was a resource for the former.

The example of Ninnette in Extract 4.2, however, points to the importance of another of Bauman's observations. Performance "isn't all or nothing – [it] may be dominant in the hierarchy of multiple functions, as in . . . full performance, or it may be subordinate to other functions – referential, rhetorical, or any other" (Bauman 1983:3; also Hymes 1975). As we have already seen, Ninnette detested full-blown performance in front of the rest of the class (Chapter 2.4), but she was happy to perform within the semi-private enclosure of conversation with Joanne and one or two others, and the *Deutsch* in Extract 4.2 represents one of the quieter forms this took, her unspectacular *danke* being a light rekeying for the 'enhancement of experience', supplementing the ordinary functioning of speech with a hint of playfulness.

In Simon's *Deutsch* in Extract 4.3, the performance was more amplified, and 'heightened awareness of both the act of expression and the performer' are shown in quite extended self-reference and self-dramatisation (lines 14–46). With Hanif, John and Guy in Extracts 4.6 to 4.10, *Deutsch* was projected outside specific conversational enclosures onto the main classroom floor, and it probably reached its fullest form in Extracts 4.6 and 4.8. By superimposing the language from one set of lessons onto the speech in another, Hanif produced an effect that seemed to be broadly burlesque, a kind of comic intensification and *over*-involvement in current events, and when he timed *danke* and *viel lauter sprechen* to coincide with periods of heightened surveillance – lines 8–14 in Extract 4.8 and lines 24–40 in Extract 4.6 – he stepped out into the cross-current between two kinds of evaluative attention. On the one hand, there was the risk (albeit not huge) of Mr Newton disapproving and sending him out of the class, and on the other, there was the possibility of applause from his male friends (i) for his brinksmanship, (ii) for the range of his resources, and (iii) for his varied contribution to livening the classroom up for them, running different semiotic lines in precarious counterpoint to the lesson's main development.

As such, *Deutsch* formed a part of the more general 'contrapuntal aesthetic' that I described in Chapter 2.3, picking up elements from ordinary classroom talk and reworking them into forms that flouted the normative requirements of thematic relevance. These embellishments of lesson-talk often involved a shift of emphasis from the referential to the poetic functions of speech, directing attention to the formal rather than the propositional dimensions of language, and in Chapter 3.5, we saw that these youngsters also occasionally shifted from talk to singing. *Deutsch* participated in these processes, and in fact in Hanif's performances in Extracts 4.5, 4.6 and 4.8, the connections between *Deutsch* and music were rather striking. There, there was close sequential proximity between the two modes: *Deutsch* was used to repeat interactional moves and displays that had been very recently initiated through singing (self-talk in Extract 4.5 [lines 1, 7, 11 => 15–17], amplifying the utterances of friends in Extract 4.6 [lines 11, 12, 14 => 32, 34, 35], waylaying the introduction of an instructional sequence in Extract 4.8 [lines 6, 7 => 13, 14]); and contiguous stretches were also broadly similar in length – sustained in Extract 4.5, and then more extensive than the phrases that cued them in Extract 4.6, and then very brief in Extract 4.8. The similarities in length were no doubt partially due to the different kinds of interactional space available in the periods when *Deutsch* and music were performed together, but it is likely that Hanif could only manage the longer linguistic stretches of *Deutsch* because he wasn't too worried if like music, the *Deutsch* was semantically meaningless. Instead, rather than being regulated by questions of conceptual relevance, Hanif's productions were often marked by extra vocal exertion, and if it is uncontroversial as a reason for singing, then it is reasonable to suggest that Hanif's *Deutsch* was at least partially driven by the intrinsic pleasures of vocalisation and sound:

Extract 4.11

Interview with Hanif, Masud and John

```
BEN      so erm you enjoy German lessons?
HANIF    nweer
MASUD    no it's the teacher
HANIF    yeh
MASUD    the teacher gets (on your nerves)
HANIF    no I kinda like the language, I kinda like the
                                         language,
         because I dunno, the accent, the accent you can use
```

And Hanif obviously wasn't alone in this, as we saw from Simon's sound play in Extract 4.3 (lines 10 and 11, 15 and 16), and from the variations in the pronunciation of *entschuldigung* in Extract 4.9.

The last general point to make is that there was a distinctly ritual dimension to these youngsters' use of *Deutsch*. Goffman argues that talk and interaction are permeated by a sense of the respect due to the individual, and in encounters, participants continuously work to maintain 'face', the claims to positive social value implied in their speech and actions together. "One's face", says Goffman, "is a sacred thing, and the expressive order required to sustain it is therefore a ritual one" (1967:19). This line of thought has been hugely influential in research on politeness in sociolinguistics and pragmatics (Brown and Levinson 1987), and when *Deutsch* was used in thanks and apologies (Extracts 4.1, 4.2, 4.3, 4.4, 4.8, 4.9), in expressions of disapproval (Extracts 4.3, 4.10), in commands (Extracts 4.4, 4.6, 4.12), and in transitions into different social spaces (Extracts 4.3, 4.4, 4.12), it is readily associated with Goffman's 'interpersonal verbal rituals':

face-to-face interaction ... is the location of a special class of quite conventionalised utterances, lexicalisations whose controlling purpose is to give praise, blame, thanks, support, affection or show gratitude, disapproval,

dislike, sympathy, or greet, say farewell and so forth. Part of the force
of these speech acts comes from the feelings they directly index; little
of the force derives from the semantic content of the words. We can
refer here to interpersonal verbal rituals. These rituals often serve a brack-
eting function ... marking a perceived change in the physical and social
accessibility of two individuals to each other ... as well as beginnings and
endings – of a day's activity, a social occasion, a speech, an encounter, an
interchange. (Goffman 1981:21)

Ritual concerns, though, are not confined to verbal formulae, and in
Goffman's analysis, they are motivated more generally by the principle that "each individual ought to handle himself with respect to
each of the others, so that he [does] not discredit his own tacit claim
to good character or the tacit claim of the others that they are
persons of social worth whose various forms of territoriality are to
be respected" (1981:16). As we saw, *Deutsch* often emerged at points
when the priorities of students and teachers came into conflict –
at moments, in other words, when the independence, 'territoriality'
and 'good character' of the participants were at issue – and so in this
wider sense, there is also a case for saying that there was a significant
ritual dimension to *Deutsch*.[7]

Of course overall, the sincerity of these other-language acts was
very far from self-evident, and in the next chapter, I will go into
greater detail into the relationship between ritual, performance and
subversion. Even so, the very fact that *Deutsch* often emerged in
ritually pregnant moments when classroom order was in question, con-
tradicts the traditional sociolinguistic assumption that instructed
foreign languages are remote and inconsequential when it comes
to either the contestation or reproduction of social hierarchy.
Indeed, the limitations of these traditional assumptions became
clearer if we reflect on the identity dynamics around *Deutsch*.

4.5 *Deutsch* and the dynamics of identity

Given German's position as a respectable, instructed and heritage-
neutral language at Central High, one can see its lack of appeal to a
sociolinguistics committed to 'the social logic of competence', with
its prioritisation of everyday language and egalitarian suspicion of
'official socialisers' (Chapter 4.1 above). In contrast, German's
status as an 'acquired' or 'educated taste', as standard language

taught and assessed by teachers, brought a number of practical benefits which the youngsters in Class 9A seemed quick to embrace. Firstly, as also seen in Extracts 4.7 and 4.9, teachers themselves sometimes participated in sequences initiated by pupils:

Extract 4.12

The start of an English lesson.

```
MR NEWTON   sit down, coats off
HANIF       SCHNELL SCHNELL
MR NEWTON   schnell schnell exactly – vite, vite
```

Teachers, it seemed, quite liked this reuse of a curriculum language, and the respectability of German probably made it a very shrewd alternative to singing in moments when disciplinary surveillance was intensified, as in Extracts 4.6 and 4.8.

Beyond its acceptability to teachers, the institutional provenance of German made it widely accessible to pupils. On the one hand, this was a very diverse school linguistically, with about 12 languages spoken in this tutor group alone. Out of 30 members of the class, there were never more than 4 who spoke the same minority variety, and so there was only limited value in home languages as vehicles for public communication. At the same time, German didn't belong to anyone, and so its use as an additional language was safe from the issues of racist mockery and/or expropriation that can arise with crossing into other local codes (cf. Hewitt 1986; Rampton 1995a).

Thirdly, the educational status and provenance of *Deutsch* may also have made it particularly appealing to Hanif, its most frequent user. Hanif held a leading social position in the friendship cluster where *Deutsch* was used most, but he was also a very able student, ambitious about study and one of the most highly rated by the teachers of the class. As a subject on the school curriculum, German/*Deutsch* allowed him to look two ways in a larger identity project, towards the contrasting value-orientations of both school and peer group. On the one hand, German was the only subject where pupils were separated into different ability classes, and Hanif was in the top set. On the other, one of his oldest and closest friends from primary school was now starting to bunk off. The effect of recycling German could be to keep school firmly in focus for the peer group, allowing Hanif to distinguish himself with his German-like pronunciation, while at the same time providing solidarity and latitude enough for those like Simon who were placed in the bottom set, who declared themselves lads rather than 'ear'oles' and for whom, in Satesh's words, the language was less about 'accent' and more about making ``the phlegms to come out of your mouth''.

Hanif was evidently quite successful promoting the use of *Deutsch* among his peers, and he was acknowledged by others as the main innovator. But we can only understand this catching on if we dispense with the reflectionist belief that the social meaning of a language is wholly determined by macro-social structure, and recognise instead that the symbolic associations of a language can be generated locally in interaction (as Auer suggested in Section 4.1). We might have been able to hold to traditional ideas about foreign languages being principally associated with native speakers in foreign countries if Hanif, John, Guy and Simon had been either 'nerds' or incipient/crypto-Germanists, so keen on learning German that they created opportunities to practise among themselves wherever they could outside the language class. But they obviously weren't, and instead, the emergence of *Deutsch* as an ingroup fad points, *contra* Trudgill and Giles 1983, to the power of aesthetic performance in sidelining Germany – or school – as the language's main social connotation, instating alongside or in its place either Hanif, or the group's history of collective improvisation together.

These findings would also make very little sense within traditional ideas about the overwhelming importance of the division between home and school, since *Deutsch* symbolised a collective energy that was associated with neither the warmth of the hearth, nor the weight of the state. At home, Hanif actually used a good deal of Bengali, and he also had two other Bengali speakers in his close friendship group at school. But he didn't use Bengali much more often than *Deutsch* in our recordings (c. 14 sequences, compared with 9 in German). This certainly cannot be interpreted as evidence of a shift in young people's allegiance, from home languages to the standard languages of Europe – it was obvious in interview that like others, Hanif took the language used in his family very seriously. But English and his home language were not the only languages he and his peers were exposed to. At one time, dominant ideologies might have wanted to frame their voices and identifications within the confines of an ESL

and minority language problematic, but the reality of young people's
experience and affiliations is actually much fuller and more complex
(see also Harris 1997; Harris et al. 2001:41–42).

4.6   Explaining *Deutsch*

In this chapter, then, I have considered some of the reasons why
instructed foreign languages might have been historically neglected
in sociolinguistics, and I have illustrated the part that *Deutsch* played
in spontaneous language practices in Class 9A. I have also linked its
currency to two factors. First, to the aesthetic enjoyment derived, for
example, from play with its sound properties, or associated with the
(low) drama generated by heterodox interactional timing. Second, to
German/*Deutsch*'s strategic value as a curriculum language – acceptable to teachers, accessible to everyone, and attractive to the aspirational. I have also tied it to both 'performance' and 'ritual', and in
concluding this chapter, I would like to dwell on the balance between
performance and ritual in the evidence so far.

Performance – in Bauman's sense and the sense I have used it here –
is an essential element in ritual, and so there is a close relationship
between them (see Rothenbuhler 1998; Rappoport 1999:37;
Chapter 5 below). But performance is not *necessarily* associated
with the seriousness, the high ideals and the sense of the 'sacred'
that are typical of ritual, and it emerges, for example, in the telling
of very worldly jokes and stories as well as in just showing off.
Performance involves "a specially marked way of speaking" but
this does not have to be symbolically linked to any higher powers,
and in being "offered for the enhancement of experience", it can be
designed for the audience's enjoyment quite independent of any sense
of responsibility to more noble values. Performance can just be
entertainment.

To treat *Deutsch only* as fun or entertainment wouldn't do justice to the data we have seen. *Deutsch* featured in interpersonal
rituals, which are motivated according to Goffman by a sense
that the recipients of our thanks, apologies and so forth are in
"possession of a small patrimony of sacredness" (1971:63; also
Brown and Levinson 1987:44). It also occurred at stressed classroom management moments, where "good character" and a respect
for "territoriality" were at issue (Goffman 1981:16). But the sense of

'rituality' here needs to be qualified in two ways. First, to the extent that *Deutsch* occurred in interaction ritual, the rituality was only rather mild. Participants in Goffman's facework may operate with an active sense that there is an element of sacredness in each other, in themselves and in the interaction, but this pervasive feeling is generally low-key – the "patrimony" is only "*small*". Second, *on the evidence so far*, it looks as though the rituality of *Deutsch* emerged more from the actually or potentially problematic interactional moments in which it was used, than from ritual associations of the language *per se*. Admittedly, the popular stereotype of Germans being bossy and disciplined might have made it feel quite apposite for giving orders, as in Extracts 4.4, 4.6 and 4.12, but the stereotype's relevance to apologies and thanks is less obvious, and in the *schnell schnell* in Extract 4.12, Mr Newton evidently thought French was just as good. So, so far anyway, the ritual in *Deutsch* seems to have been produced in *performance*, more 'brought about' than 'brought along', and the case for discounting any distinctly ritual connotations attached to German itself looks stronger when we remember that interpersonal verbal rituals are actually a prime site for code-switching and language crossing much more generally.[8] As with most people, the youngsters in this study often shifted into another language, variety or speech style for ritual actions of this kind, and so rather than there being any special or exclusive links between *Deutsch* and ritually pregnant moments, this language can be seen as just one among a wide range of usable resources. Of course, the very act of switching to *Deutsch* added something extra to what was happening at these moments, and the repeated use of *Deutsch* on such occasions might well begin to imbue the language with more abiding ritual associations. But for the time being anyway, performance seems to be the key element in the *Deutsch* data we have examined.

So far, though, the German lessons that these youngsters attended have been rather taken for granted, and so I should now turn properly to these. In doing so, our sense of the significance of ritual will substantially increase.

Notes

1. Admittedly, this claim rests on a distinction between *foreign* and *second* languages that is often controversial, and it is also particularly hard to

apply to English. But it certainly holds true if a *foreign* language (FL) is taken to be a language like French or Dutch in Britain, where for most people, extensive engagement with the language starts in the classroom, where instruction is organised around the anticipation of interaction 'off-shore', where the non-educational opportunities for exposure to the language seem limited, and where 'native' speakers don't constitute a salient local or national political interest group (cf. Jernudd 1993).

2. Although this is now certainly changing (see e.g. Kramsch 1993; Roberts et al. 2001), foreign language education (FLE) generally operated with a set of assumptions that did little to endear instructed foreign languages to a sociolinguistics characterised by the perspective of the 1960s–80s. There was quite a lot of uni-directional flow from sociolinguistics into FLE, but in the UK anyway, instructed foreign languages lacked interest for sociolinguistics because

  • FLE was intent on preparing students for mobility, for interaction abroad, or for the reception of foreign visitors (rather than e.g. cultural self-awareness);
  • FLE emphasised referential and interpersonal meanings rather than the social meaning and connotations of different types of language (the latter being a major concern for sociolinguists);
  • FLE concentrated on primarily monolingual people entering bi- and multilingual futures (whereas sociolinguistics prioritised bi- and multilingual people entering primarily monolingual institutions);
  • FLE was associated with policy rhetorics of international competitiveness (rather than access and equity);
  • FLE worried about foreign languages being elitist within selective educational settings, and about working-class students being xenophobic in mass education (at a time when sociolinguistics ignored elites and celebrated minority working-class competences);
  • FLE oriented more to Bernstein's 'performance' models of pedagogy, emphasising: product rather than process; carefully graded inputs from the teacher; texts and skills the learner had to acquire; and gaps and errors in their knowledge and production.

3. Knowing the word for 'you' in a foreign language means that whenever an unknown but potentially abusive word gets directed at you, you can return it to the sender by simply repeating it, prefaced by 'you' (in whichever language) (Goodwin and Goodwin 1987).

4. See e.g. 'Allo Allo' and 'Fawlty Towers'.

5. If the switch had been motivated by a noteworthy visual event missed on the audiotape, one might have expected a little bit of further talk about it, or alternatively, something more like a response cry (brief and more highly contoured than the rather steady, level tune actually used).

6. In self-talk, "we kibitz our own undertakings, rehearse or relive a run-in with someone, speak to ourselves judgmentally about our own doings . . . and verbally mark junctures in our physical doings. Speaking audibly, we

address ourselves, constituting ourselves the sole intended recipient of our own remarks. Or, speaking in our own name, we address a remark to someone who isn't present to receive it" (Goffman 1981:79).

7. Surface features of *Deutsch* such as propositional obscurity (e.g. Extract 4.6 lines 34–37, Extract 4.10 line 8) and parallelism (Extracts 4.3, 4.4 and 4.9) could also be said to contribute to its ritual properties (see Chapter 5).

8. The process can be explained as follows: 'Interpersonal verbal rituals' occur at moments of heightened interactional uncertainty – on meeting new people, at the start of an encounters, close to a breach of etiquette, etc. These difficulties temporarily jeopardise the comfortable, orderly flow of interaction, and they intensify the need to show respect for social relations and social order to compensate. To do this, people generally increase the symbolic dimensions of their conduct (Goffman 1967, 1971), shifting briefly away from the (appropriately modulated) production of propositional utterances geared to truth and falsity. Instead, they turn up the ritual aspects through a range of inherited symbolic formulae – farewell and greeting routines, apologies, thanks, expletives, expressions of dismay or surprise, even proverbs (Drew and Holt 1988, Luger 1983) – and by invoking well-established material authored by tradition, they display an orientation to wider social collectivities capable of overriding the temporary disturbance immediately on hand. Very often, these ritual actions are convergent, providing the participants with some common ground on which to (re)establish synchronised, affiliative action, affirming dominant social orders, drawing on shared cultural inheritance, and one way of doing this is to code-switch into a shared language that is either more intimate or more elevated. But these showcase moments for the symbolic display of social allegiance can also be used more divergently, and they are a prime site for all sorts of creativity. They 'hosted' a great deal of the language crossing I studied in earlier research on youngsters using each other's ethnic languages, and one often hears people putting on 'funny voices' at junctures like these.

5

Ritual in the instruction and inversion of German

In the last chapter, I looked at the ways in which (mainly male) students in Class 9A improvised *Deutsch* in corridors, Maths, English and Humanities lessons, and I identified two potential sources for this – the representation of Germans in British popular culture, and the German lessons that they were attending for 45 minutes three times a week. There is no reason why these two influences should be mutually exclusive, but the boys themselves stressed the foreign language classes as their main source, and with several *guts*, *danke*s and *Entschuldigung*s, and no *Achtung*s, *Fritz* or *Donner und Blitzen*s, the words they used seemed more rooted in elementary textbooks than, say, comics. But so far, I have said very little about these German lessons. What were they like? How did youngsters respond to them? In what ways could they actually be linked to the improvisations in *Deutsch*?

In the first part of this chapter, I provide a description of these foreign language lessons (Chapter 5.1), and I suggest a little later that the students didn't enjoy them very much, making it all quite hard work for the German teachers (Chapter 5.3). These lessons were highly ritualised (Chapter 5.2), and although as *institutional* rituals, the lessons were much more elaborate than the *interaction* rituals in which students improvised *Deutsch* outside the German class, both kinds of ritual were embedded in competition for support and influence (Chapter 5.4). In fact, the boys' use of *Deutsch* can be seen as an inversion of the authority associated with instructed German (Chapter 5.5), and to explain how this could happen, I reflect on the students' socio-emotional experience in the German class, drawing on Billig's discursive interpretation of Freudian repression (1999) to suggest that the rituals of instruction had turned German/*Deutsch* into a

'condensation symbol' (Chapter 5.6). After a resumé and some speculation on links to these youngsters' longer term underachievement in
curriculum German (Chapter 5.7), I consider the way different areas of
language research have responded to the mixture of politics, symbolism and emotion that ritual potentially involves (Chapter 5.8), and I
conclude by affirming ritual's value as a concept for the analysis of
school and social change (Chapter 5.9).

'Ritual', then, is the central concept in this chapter, and before
turning to the data, a preliminary definition may be useful, together
with some introductory comments on it.

Ritual is a very broad and encompassing concept. As well as being
a term in everyday talk, it has a long history in a number of disciplines
(cf. Grimes 1985), and it can be used to describe a huge range of
activities and processes, from the international to the interpersonal.
Within my analysis, ritual will be conceptualised broadly in the
tradition of Durkheim (1912, 1972:219–238), Douglas (1966),
Goffman (1967) and Turner (1969, 1978, 1982, 1987), and although
certain aspects of it will need to be elaborated later on, it can be
initially characterised as follows:

In its clearest and most traditional forms, ritual involves a concern with
the 'sacred', but it is often also found in more secular contexts where we
can speak of an orientation to matters of high import (cf. Rothenbuhler
1998:23–25). Ritual can sometimes take comic forms, but there are serious
concerns lying at the heart of it, with an intensified orientation to issues
of transgression and respect. Ritual can be performed in a huge variety
of ways, in a wide range of arenas, but it is fundamentally oriented to
moments and periods where, for one reason or another, there are actual
or potential changes or problems in the flow of ordinary life. Ritual is a
form of action that is typically (though not invariably) intended to help
people get past such difficulties and on with normal life, albeit often in a
new state, and to do this, it draws on traditional material that is produced
in relatively rigid patterns, and that holds special significance above and
beyond the practical requirements of the here-and-now (Goffman
1971:62–94, 1981:20–21; Rappoport 1999:46ff.). While a ritual is being
performed, there is "time-out from normal social roles, responsibilities,
rules, orders, and even modes of thoughts" (Rothenbuhler 1998:15),
and the mood is often what Turner calls 'subjunctive' rather than 'indica-
tive', characterised by an orientation to feeling, willing, desiring, fanta-
sising and playfulness rather than by an interest in applying "reason to
human action and systematis[ing] the relationship between means and
ends" (Turner 1987:123). Rituals tend to generate an increased feeling

of collectivity among (at least some of) the participants, and they also involve the participants in 'performance', "an aesthetically marked and heightened mode of communication, framed in a special way and put on display for an audience" (Bauman 1989:262, cited in Rothenbuhler 1998:8–9).

In this definition, the notion of 'ritual' can be applied to a very wide range of activities, from coronations to apologies, and this scope and elasticity can certainly make it a difficult concept to employ. Over-use of the term can rapidly lead to diminishing returns, and in starting out on any piece of discourse, it can be no replacement for the kind of apparatus provided in phonetics and phonology, functional grammar, micro-sociology and conversation analysis, the ethnography of communication and so forth (see Duranti 1997; also Chapter 10.2.3 below). But although ritual is a far looser and more general concept than a fall–rise or an adjacency pair, one can still use it to say that some strips of action are more ritualised than others, and when this is done, among other things, particular modalities in the operation of power move into focus, as a number of anthropologists have emphasised (e.g. Bloch 1975; Lukes 1975; Parkin 1984; Myers and Brenneis 1984; Gal 1989). Within a political frame, it becomes appropriate to ask questions such as: What kinds of change, tension or uncertainty are particular strips of action orienting to? How are they trying to deal with them? Who is making or calling for what kinds of investment? And what kinds of contestation are there around the identities, lines and values that particular rituals seek to enshrine? In due course, we will have cause to refer to other aspects of ritual, but to begin with, it will be these (micro-)political issues that feature most prominently in my account of the relationship between instructed German and impromptu *Deutsch*.

We should now turn to the German lessons.

5.1 The organisation of the German lessons

Gaining access to the German language classes attended by my informants proved difficult,[1] and in the event, I was only able to record two 45 minute lessons and sit in on one double-lesson. This was obviously a small sample, but I have no reason to think that these classes were unrepresentative either of the rest of the foreign language teaching the students received at Central High, or of FLT more generally in England. The teachers were competent, committed and experienced, and they were well-practised both in broadly audio-lingual methods and in methods based on structural linguistics (Rivers 1964; Stern 1983; Lightbown and Spada 1993:73, 119). They were well-tuned to the requirements of national assessment schemes (Mitchell 2000:288–289), and there was also a great deal in common with the much larger corpus of foreign language lessons analysed by Mitchell and Martin (1997). In short, there was nothing to suggest that as foreign language lessons, these classes were unusual.

In terms of organisation, the lessons had a clear structure. Each was divided up into fairly well-demarcated sections, each required a good deal of collective synchronisation from pupils, and the teacher did her best to maintain one central line of activity.

Both the recorded lessons fell into about 10 or 11 major segments. The first one, for example, consisted of

(1) doing the register of attendance;
(2) a listening comprehension, noting down the times of the day in eight short German dialogues performed by the teacher;
(3) going through the answers, with a quick hands-up survey of individual results;
(4) choral repetition and translation of seven German sentences describing the early morning routine activities hand-drawn on flashcards introduced by the teacher (`ich wache auf' ((`I wake up')), `ich dusche mich', ((`I have a shower')) etc.);
(5) aural revision, with one pupil standing at the board being asked to point at the picture described in each of the sentences spoken by the teacher;
(6) teacher questions to the class about the flashcards (`Can anyone remember what we've just seen');
(7) questions to the class about the flashcards now hand-held by different pupils (`Can anybody tell me what J___ is doing');
(8) copying the sentences from the blackboard into exercise books;

(9) writing down the homework in homework diaries;
(10) a brief preview of the next lesson to fill up the remaining lesson time;
(11) packing up.

Within most of these segments, there was a steady and relatively predictable progression though the subcomponents – all the names in the register, all eight answers in the dialogues and all seven flashcards. And within brief exchanges, pupils were sometimes led word by word through the German sentences they were learning:

Extract 5.1

Wednesday afternoon. During segment 6, Ms Wilson (not her real name) is focusing on **ich ziehe mich an** ('I get dressed'):

```
 1  MS W    ′ANYBODY? (.)
 2          ′anybody? (.)
 3          ′quickly (.)
 4          ˈich (.)
            ((trans: I))
 5  JOHN    I just (     )
 6  MS W    ˈzie: :he::
            ((trans: dress))
 7  ANON    ˈziehe ˋ(hafzeg)
 8  ANON    ich ˈhabe mein ⌈ˋhess
 9  ANON                   ⌊(     )ziehe
10  MS W    ich ˈziehe ˈmi: :ch
11  ANON    ˈmick
12  ANON    ˈmick
13  ANON    ˈmick
14  MS W    ˋa: / :n
15  ANONS   ˋan
16  HANIF   ((quite loud:)) that's the one
17  MS W    ich ˈziehe ˈmich an
```

The teacher generally pursued all these sequences to the end, seldom abandoning any half-way through, but she tried to off-set this predictability by frequently changing the channel and the configuration of participants and participant roles. In the lesson outlined above, for example, after the register, which involved pupils listening and replying individually, they were supposed to listen and write (segment 2); look, listen and repeat chorally (segment 4); observe one of their number listen to the teacher, look and point (5); listen and volunteer replies (6); either hold a flashcard or reply to teacher questions as selected (7); read and copy (8). Overall, pupils were expected to stay alert to what was happening on the main floor of the German classroom – ``everybody listen cos I'm gonna pick on you'', said the teacher.

The purity of this progression through the skills and content specified in the curriculum was preserved by a pedagogy which kept the students' own agendas and experience at arm's length. The teacher told pupils several times not to worry if they didn't provide an accurate or truthful answer to her questions about their morning routine:

``you can give me any time, I don't really mind too much ... we're just practising this construction''
``pretend you do for a minute ... just give me a time''

The emphasis was on pupils' memory of recent lesson content rather than on their analytic intelligence, which might lead the lesson off in unpredictable directions. Pupils were often asked to try to remember:

``very quickly let's just see how much we can remember''
``let's see what you can remember''
``half EIGHT remember''

and the sentence patterns were presented as matters of convention to be memorised rather than as the instantiation of more general grammatical principles that one might work from:

``the **auf** goes to the end of the sentence, you put the time (.) in the middle (.) Germans do that''
``I wake (1.0) AT seven o'clock up ... that's just how Germans do it''.

The articulation of students' own concerns and perspectives wasn't prohibited, but it was generally allocated to controlled spaces specified by the teacher. There were phrasal slots for this in the teaching of German sentence patterns,

Ms W ((*speaking while writing on the board*)):
   ich (1.0) **putze** (1.0) **mir** (1.0) **die** (1.0) **Zähne** (1.0)
   um (1.0)

```
    ((translation: I brush my teeth at))   (GL2:387)
    and then whatever time you do that
```

and when students raised complications, the teacher postponed
a response either till the end of the sequence she was engaged
in, or to a time when it wouldn't interfere with the lesson's
development:

```
((Moira has replied to the question ''wann isst du
Fruhstuck'' (''when do you eat breakfast'') with
''I don't'':)):
MS W  du isst nicht ((trans: you don't eat))
      I'm gonna put that sentence up on the board in a
      minute
      pretend you do for a minute
      just give me a time

((Lara is complaining that Ms W doesn't mark their books:))
MS W  Lara can you just leave it now
      we're gonna go on to something else
      you can talk to me at the end if you want (.)
```

Indeed, whenever Ms Wilson judged that a pupil was misbehaving in
a way that deserved punishment, she often just wrote their name on
the blackboard without commenting on it. One of the teachers in
Mitchell and Martin's report said that "if they're naughty and cause
you to speak English, that's not right" (1997:18), and in the case
here, the teacher's use of the blackboard looked like a strategy for
keeping the main spoken track relatively clear of potentially distracting arguments over discipline.

Borrowing Goffman's terms, one could say (a) that the emphasis
in German lessons was on pupils operating more as 'animators' than
as 'authors', physically articulating words rather than selecting them
to compose sentences themselves, and (b) that unless they identified
closely with what they were being taught, the opportunities for them
to speak as 'principals', as people taking personal responsibility for
their speech, were limited (cf. Goffman 1974: Chapter 13). This
seemed to be a matter of pedagogic policy, and the subjugation of
centrifugal individualities was emphasised explicitly when the other

teacher I observed was reprimanding a class whose behaviour she felt was deteriorating:

```
BOY            Miss, the reason I
MS PHILLIPS    no I don't want 'I', I want you to talk as
               a class...
               ((Later:))
MS PHILLIPS    this ''I'', needing to give
               information about yourself, I don't
                                        need that
```

All in all, then, German lessons seemed to be very carefully structured events, with the teacher leading students step-by-step through the content, continuously rearranging the participation structures, doing her best to ensure that the central business of the lesson remained undisturbed by the idiosyncratic concerns of particular students.

In fact, there are a number of ways in which we can say that these lessons were very ritual events. I shall try to show this in the next section, starting with some of some of the surface features of these lessons, then moving to their position within a more encompassing definition of ritual.

5.2   Ritual in the language lessons

John Du Bois (1986) provides a useful survey of the kinds of speech used in ritual events, and these bear a striking similarity to the discourse in the German class (see also e.g. Bloch 1975). Du Bois' list is as follows, together with corresponding features from the foreign language lessons:

  a. *Obscurity in propositional meaning*: Students in the German lesson would ask ``what does that mean'' and say ``I didn't understand that''. And propositional clarity evidently wasn't the primary concern when they were expected to respond to the third-person question ``what is J___ doing according to her card'' with, for example, an answer in the first-person – **'ich wache auf'** (('I wake up')).

  b. *Parallelism, for example with couplets formed according to simple but strict syntactic rules of repetition with substitution*: This could be seen in the imitation drills, as well as in the question and answer sequences where students were expected to add their own times to the sentences that they had copied from the teacher.

c. *A mode of delivery that entails "a high degree of fluency, without hesitations, in a stylised intonation contour", accompanied by "prescribed postures, proxemics, behaviours, attitudes and trappings" (1986:317):* Again, the teacher aimed for this in the language drills:

Extract 5.2

Some choral drilling from the first German lesson (Hanif is wearing the radio-mic):

```
 1   MS W                         right
 2                                if everybody can (      ) now (.)
 3                                ICH ¦ESSE ˈFRÜH¦STÜCK
                                  ((trans: I eat breakfast))
 4   SINGLE PUPIL                 ich ¦esse ˈfrüh¦stück
 5   MS W                         ICH ¦ESSE ˈFRÜH¦STÜCK
 6                                bitte ˈalle zu˰sammen
                                  ((trans: all together please))
 7   SEVERAL VOICES, BUT NOT HANIF  ((ragged chorus:))
                                  ich esse ˈFrüh¦stück
 8   MS W                         ich ¦e::sse ˈFrüh¦stück
 9   OTHER VOICES                 ((still ragged:))
                                  ⌈ ich ¦esse ˈFrüh¦stück
10   HANIF                        ⌊ ((quite quietly))
                                    ich ¦e::sse ˈFrüh¦st/ück
11   MS W                         ich ¦esse ˈFrüh¦stück
12   SEVERAL                      ich ⌈esse ˈFrüh¦stück
13   HANIF                             ⌊esse ˈFrüh¦stück
14   BOY                          ((loud))
                                  (QUIET)
15   MS W                         BITTE
                                  ((trans: PLEASE!))
16                                ((shouting very loud:))
                                  ˈALLE ˈZU˰SAMMEN
                                  ((trans: ALL TOGETHER))
17                                ICH ¦ESSE ˈFRÜH¦STÜCK
18   OTHERS                       /ich ¦esse ˈFrüh¦stück
19   HANIF                        ((sounding less than whole-
                                  hearted:))
                                  ich esse Frühstü:
20   ANON                         (        )
21   GUY                          it's ˰breakfast ¦time
22   BOY                          what⌈˰is it
```

```
23  MS W                      ⌊ (was   das) auf English
                              ((trans: what (    ) that in
                              English))
24  GUY                       ˈbreakˌfast
25  MS W                      ˋbreakfast
26                            ˈI ˈeat ˋbreakfast
```

   d. *The use of "archaic, borrowed, tabooed or formulaic" elements that mark the ritual 'register' off from colloquial speech*: A good deal of German was learnt and used as a chunk, and its separateness from ordinary talk was emphasised when, for example, Ms Wilson criticised students for ``babbling on in English'' and reminded them **``uh entschuldigen auf Deu::tsch**: *((translation: 'oh sorry, in German'))*, otherwise it's very easy''.

   e. *Local belief in the archaism and ancestral origins of ritual speech, and a tendency for speakers to disclaim any credit or influence on what is said, paying tribute instead to a traditional source*: German wasn't construed as an archaic or ancestral language, but its origins among a distant people were stressed (``that's just how Germans do it''), and the emphasis on memory discouraged speakers from exercising much personal influence on the use of the language.

   f. *The mediation of speech through additional people, so that there is more than a simple relation of speaker and hearer*: The teacher was the main vehicle through whom German was mediated to the pupils, and on occasion, she performed multi-party German dialogues single-handed. There were also audio-taped dialogues and several permutations through which pupils mediated German to one another (``according to S____'s card, what is she doing?''; ``excellent, **ich stehe um vier fünf nach sieben auf** *((= 'I get up at five to seven'))*. Moira what time does erm Alan get up at''.)

There were, then, a large number of discursive features in the German lessons that matched Du Bois' list, and there is also significant correspondence if we return to the fuller characterisation of ritual offered in the introduction to this Chapter.

    The "heightened mode of communication" in the German lessons, as well as the teacher's efforts to get students to suspend disbelief and think and act collectively, have already been mentioned. Beyond that, Ms Wilson showed a strong sense of the difficulties which students faced in the repeated reassurance that she offered the class (``don't worry about this at all until Friday''; ``there's only number one number two number six to worry about''; ``you shouldn't have too many problems as long as you use th[e vocabulary section]''), and at the most general level, the German lessons can be seen as a protracted process of initiation into basic knowledge of the German language, an endstate specified in the National Curriculum (cf. Mertz 1996:240).

Moving one step beyond the definitions offered so far, there have also been discussions of ritual that provide a line into the kind of involvement that was expected of the students. According to Turner, structured collective activities like religious rituals, artistic performances and games generally aim for a state of 'flow'. Flow involves the:

holistic sensation [we get] when we act with total involvement … [There is] a centring of attention on a limited stimulus field. Consciousness [is] narrowed, intensified, beamed in on a limited focus of attention … [there are] coherent, non-contradictory demands for action, [with] … clear, unambiguous feedback to a person's actions … Loss of ego is another 'flow' attribute … the actor is immersed in the 'flow', [s/he] accepts the rules as binding which are also binding on the other actors … [and] no self is needed to 'bargain' about what should or should not be done.   (1982:56, 57)

If one looks back at Ms Wilson's sustained concentration on flashcards depicting early morning routine, at the insistent correction and remodelling, at the calls for ``**alle zusammen**'' and for the suppression of 'I', there are good grounds for suggesting that it was something like a state 'flow' that the teacher was trying to produce in the German language class (cf. van Lier 1996:105–106).

How far did she actually succeed?

5.3   Student responses

I certainly cannot give a comprehensive account of how students responded to this foreign language pedagogy, and what follows is very far from being a systematic study of 'teacher effectiveness'. Indeed, even within my very limited corpus, it was obvious that the class was much more responsive first thing on the Friday morning than after lunch on Wednesday, to the extent that Ms Wilson declared at the end of the Friday lesson that ``the board is clear, the board is clear''. And within each lesson, the pupils caught on the radio-microphone seemed to be more involved and attentive at some moments than at others. So, there are no claims here to a comprehensive sampling of students' behaviour in German language classes, and if anything, the portrait that follows is unduly biased towards misconduct.

For the present purposes, however, it is sufficient to say that there were quite a few students, my informants included, who weren't unequivocally reverential, rapt or enthusiastic during the class. They tended to be disparaging about German lessons in interviews,

```
BEN     ... so erm you enjoy the German lessons
HANIF   nwe:r
MASUD   no it's the teacher ((laughs))
HANIF   yeh
MASUD   the teacher gets on (gets on your nerves)
```

and on the Wednesday, after putting ``too many names on the board'', the teacher declared to the class:

```
okay, how come every time we do oral work, you get out of
hand. The only time this class can actually (1.5) be
manageable is when we do writing
```

As we have seen, the German lessons were heavily teacher-directed, but within these tight constraints, pupils used a range of 'tactics' – "manoeuvre[s] 'within the enemy's field of vision'" – to assert themselves as individuals unwilling to submit unquestioningly to the current regime, "'putting one over' on the established order on its home ground" (de Certeau 1984:37, 25).

Ms Wilson wanted lessons with a highly structured central line, composed of regular sequences and clearly punctuated segments. In the event, students used several strategies that might be loosely described as a kind of interactional syncopation. Syncopation in music involves "the deliberate upsetting of rhythm by shifting the accent to a beat that's normally unaccented" (*Hutchinson Dictionary of Classical Music* 1994:208), and in the lessons students used timing and emphasis to pull against the rhythms that Ms Wilson was trying to establish and maintain. In Extract 5.3

below, for example, in lines 14 and 15 Lara refers back to an issue from a lesson segment that had just been terminated, and in lines 8, 11 and 17, 'boy' and John dwell on remarks that Ms Wilson had only intended as background framing:

Extract 5.3
The students have just answered and self-marked eight aural comprehension questions, and Ms Wilson has surveyed the results. She now wants to introduce the flashcards. (Wednesday afternoon)

```
 1   MS W    I want you to have a look at these now
 2   KIDS    ((low level chat for 5 seconds))
 3   MS W    okay
 4           ˈbitˌte: (.)
             ((trans: please))
 5           ˈschau ˌmal
             ((trans: look at this))
 6   JOHN    are we to turn the radio on
 7   ?       (              )
 8   BOY     what's ˋschau mal
 9           ((two taps))
10   MS W    ˈlook (.)
11   BOY     oh schau mal
12   MS W    oˋkay
13           ((high pitched:)) ich ˈesse ˈFrühˌstück
                               ((trans: I eat breakfast))
14   LARA    miss what is the point of us/ doing it our books
15           if you never mark them
16   ANON    (              ) (1.0)
17   JOHN    ˈschau ˌmo(t)
18   ANON    ((laughs))
```

They also 'dragged their feet' at teacher questions:

```
MS W    according to K_____'s card, what is she doing?
        can anybody tell me (.)
        i:n German hands up
        in German hands up
        come on
        there must be somebody in the (class       )
        TAKE A GUESS
        take a guess
        Alan
```

In another tactic, students took advantage of the difficulties involved in knowing whether to attribute non-conformity to inability

or disobedience – the former being acceptable where the latter isn't –
so that when, for example, Ms Wilson discovered that Frankie
hadn't answered any of the eight questions about time (Wednesday
lesson, Segment 2), others leapt to his defence with ''he didn't
understand'', ''he don't know the times''. And they also
sometimes took the epistemic high ground, insisting on reality and
rational intelligence at moments when they were being asked to
suspend their disbelief:

*((Focusing on the flashcards showing early morning
routine:))*
LARA   Miss
        how come it's a girl over there and a boy is
                                        laying down
HANIF   *((fast:))* because he changed sex
CLASS   *((loud laughter carrying on for about 10
        seconds))*
HANIF   sorry *((followed by short half laugh to self))*

*((Ms Wilson has been telling the class about her own
morning routine, and has just gone from the flashcard
on 'showering' to 'breakfast'))*
LARA   do you have a shower
                and then you eat?
MS W   yeah
                that's what I do
LARA   AFTER you've had a shower
                you don't have no clothes on
MS W   well no ⌈I don't
SEVERAL PUPILS   ⌊((laugh⌈ter))
MS W   ⌊(I have a)
                              dressing gown or
                              something

In terms of their response to *particular* activities, students seemed
especially reluctant to participate in whole-class oral work. During
the Wednesday afternoon lesson, there were about 30 occasions
when Ms Wilson modelled a sentence out loud, wanting the class
to repeat it after her. Hanif, the boy wearing the radio-microphone,
provided a full response to only about half of these calls; for the rest,

he either only repeated a part, he distorted them, or he kept silent.[2] In contrast, he was much more assiduous about writing in these lessons, and he sometimes got things down in his exercise book when he should have been speaking-and-listening. When I sat in on German in another class, Mike appeared to be similar:

Extract 5.4

I'm sitting at the back, and on the last table alone in the same back row is quite a large boy, with heavy, sleepy looking features ... Interesting way of engaging with the lesson – showing a good deal of commitment to the lesson content, and not at all disruptive, but only very minimal participation in the activity directed by the teacher ...

- the map activity: Ms Phillips tells kids to repeat some words after her, and to point to the spot on the map. Mike doesn't do this, at least not at the start.
- Ms P asks oral questions. Rather than looking at the map and sticking his hand up to try and answer, Mike looks at the answers he's given in writing in the week when Ms P was away. He tells me he's got all the answers. At other times, rather than competing for the floor, he spends time looking things up in the glossary at the back of the booklet.
- Ms P: "put your pens down". Mike takes no notice.
- True or false listening comprehension related to the map: writes down 'R' and 'F' very lightly in the answer slots in the booklet, and then, when they go through the answers, rubs out any mistakes, puts in the correct answers and ticks.
- Asks me: are you an inspector. Me: no. Mike: just checking? Me: I'm working on a project, trying to see how things look through the eyes of um ... Mike: the pupils. Me: yes.
- We do some oral pairwork, which he quite enjoys (though he doesn't manage the transformation from 'ich' ("I") to 'er/sie' ("he/she")). His pronunciation seems to be English spelling pronunciation of the German words he reads.

> – During the reading comprehension towards the end
> of the class, Ms P says: guess what the word for
> grandmother is – don't look in the vocabulary [the
> class is supposed to infer that 'oma' means grand-
> mother]. Mick looks in the glossary, and then puts
> his hand up: 'Grossmutter' he says. Gets an okay-
> but response from Ms P.
>
> In a number of different ways, you could say that writing
> seems to speak much louder to him than the teacher. After
> the class, I see him outside the hall practising what look
> like dance steps with another boy.

In fact, as already mentioned, the general preference for writing over
whole-class oral work was something that Ms Wilson herself commented on, and to make sense of this, 'ritual' again becomes a useful
interpretive resource.

In trying to work out why students might have preferred writing
to oral work in the German class, there are four points worth
underlining: (a) they all knew that speaking-and-listening counted
for quite a lot in their exams; (b) they were perfectly capable of
responding in choral synchrony when something funny happened
in the class – there were a number of moments when they all
laughed outloud together; (c) in other lessons – Humanities and
English – someone like Hanif seemed really very happy talking in
front of the class as whole; (d) *outside* the German class, there was
plenty of evidence that these youngsters actually enjoyed speaking
Deutsch, as we saw in Chapter 4. With these four points in view,
their ragged and reluctant participation in whole class speaking-
and-listening cannot be attributed either to a feeling that it didn't
matter (a), or to some sort of endemic inability to respond collectively (b), or to a universal shyness about whole-class talk (c), or to
embarrassment about the very act of using a foreign language (d).
Instead, I would suggest

  i)   that teacher-led choral drills and oral question-and-answer
      sequences were activities where the ritual dimension of
      German pedagogy was at its most intense. These were the
      activities that required pupils to make their most unambiguous
      public professions of collective affiliation to the German teacher,
      to learning German, to doing it in the way they were told;

ii) that for students who weren't totally committed, this was just
a bit too much.

In contrast, writing did not require anything like the same public
exhibition: when it was time for students to copy sentences from the
board into their exercise books, they worked at different speeds and
were able to talk quietly one-to-one about whatever they wanted.

Summarising the account so far, there was a lot of fairly
intense collective ritual in the foreign language pedagogy these
youngsters received – much more, in fact, than in their maths,
science, English and humanities lessons, where they generally
spent much more time working individually and in groups,
where they were often encouraged to bring in their own views,
and where there was normally much more room to chat. At the
same time, though, there were quite a few students who were less
than enthusiastic in the German class, and this showed up particularly clearly in whole-class oral work, the lesson's most intensely ritual part.

Clarifying the ritual aspects of whole-class oral work in these
lessons a little further, it is worth adding two points that are consistent
with the evidence in this section and the two before:

- First, this was very much an *institutional* ritual (Bourdieu and
  Passeron 1977:108ff.; Bourdieu 1991: 117–126; Bernstein
  1971b:56–57; 1975), passed on between professionals, agreed
  in staff meetings, debated in ministries, universities and colleges of education. There might well be some dispute about the
  value of choral drills among the experts, but locally, in the
  classroom, they were expressions of authority, attempts to
  mobilise support for officially ratified goals and values, calls
  for youngsters to participate in socially approved lines of
  development.
- Second, there is room for manoeuvre in even the most rigid
  of rituals (Rappoport 1999:Chapter 2) and in plural stratified
  societies, people respond to rituals in different ways, some of
  them quite at odds with the original design (Lukes 1975).

That said, how does 'ritual' here compare with what was said about
ritual in the improvised *Deutsch* in Chapter 4?

5.4   Ritual both in the German lessons and in improvised *Deutsch*

If spontaneous adolescent *Deutsch* is compared with the ritual in the German class, there are some clear differences, particularly in terms of scale and elaborateness:

- with whole-class-speaking-and-listening, the activity had much of the character of a 'rite of institution' (Bourdieu 1991; Bernstein 1975) – ritual action that was authorised, quite carefully planned, supported by elaborate theories of pedagogic method, and designed to maintain the participants' respect for prevailing institutional relations.
- In contrast, adolescent *Deutsch* generally occurred as the spontaneous response to momentary problems perceived immediately-on-hand, and at first glance anyway, it looked more like *interactional* than institutional ritual, much more Goffman than Durkheim, Bernstein or Bourdieu.

But as I noted in the introduction to this chapter, a number of anthropologists look for power dynamics within ritual, and if this perspective on improvised *Deutsch* is adopted, it is easy to see that there was more involved than just interpersonal politeness, or a little face-work between friends. The interactional problems prompting *Deutsch* often involved *pupil–teacher power-relations*, and so it too was embedded in competition for support and influence within the school. The differences in the scale and elaborateness of German and *Deutsch* derived from the difference in their institutional backing: teachers had at least notional control over the whole lesson, whereas in English and Humanities lessons, *Deutsch* was generally confined to short bursts because kids normally had neither the space nor the authority to produce anything very protracted. And the kinds of mobilisation they aimed for were also clearly shaped by the contrasting institutional positions that the lead performers occupied. The teacher in the German class tried to create a unanimous community of initiands willing to embrace a process that would change them into GCSE speakers of German in a subjunctive mood of hope and belief. In contrast, adolescent *Deutsch* in the Maths, Humanities and English lessons tuned to a divided and sometimes conflictual grouping of teachers and pupils, and it played differently to each party: on the one hand, at least potentially, adults might be pleased or impressed at the eager re-use of a curriculum language, while on the other, adolescent *cogniscenti* could enjoy the performer's tactical dexterity and the exclusivity of being party to an emergent ingroup tradition.

So beneath their obvious differences, the notion of ritual points to a certain connection between (a) how the teacher taught German and the students responded in the language class, and (b) the way that the students used it outside and in other lessons. Indeed, beyond the involvement in relations of power displayed by each independently, ritual can also help to explain how (a) and (b) might be positively linked, as we shall see in the next section where the question becomes:

Exactly how far can one go in saying that the German lessons and impromptu *Deutsch* produced or influenced each other? In precisely what ways might one say that they were actively – even causally – connected?

5.5   *Deutsch* as an inversion of German

Instructed German can be linked to impromptu *Deutsch* in a political analysis if the latter is construed as a subversive appropriation of the former. To elaborate this interpretation, it is useful to start with Bakhtin's account of the "authoritative word":

The authoritative word demands that we acknowledge it, that we make it our own; it binds us, quite independent of any power it might have to persuade us internally; we encounter it with its authority already fused to it. The authoritative word is located in a distanced zone, organically connected with a past that is felt to be hierarchically higher. It is, so to speak, the word of the fathers. Its authority was already *acknowledged* in the past. It is a *prior* discourse. It is therefore not a question of choosing it from among other discourses that are equal. It is given (its sounds) in lofty spheres, not those of familiar contact. Its language is a special (as it were, hieratic) language. It can be profaned. It is akin to taboo, i.e. a name that must not be taken in vain ... [Authoritative discourse] demands our unconditional allegiance ... It is not a free appropriation and assimilation of the word itself that authoritative discourse seeks to elicit from us; rather it demands our unconditional allegiance ... It enters our verbal consciousness as a compact and indivisible mass; one must either totally affirm it, or totally reject it. It is indissolubly fused with its authority – with political power, an institution, a person – and it stands and falls together with that authority. (Bakhtin 1981:342–343)

As Sections 5.1 and 5.2 made clear, German lessons were, in Bakhtin's terms, much more about "reciting by heart" than "retelling in one's own words" (1981:341), and they pushed students to become mere 'animators', demanding levels of conformity and status renunciation – "unconditional allegiance" – unmatched anywhere else in the curriculum. Equally, as discussed in the comparison with Du Bois' list of the features of ritual speech, German was located in a "distanced zone", not in a sphere of "familiar contact". So on both grounds, instructed German can be classified as an "authoritative discourse". At the same time, though, there are difficulties applying the later part of Bakhtin's account. As seen in the description of student behaviour during the language lessons, German wasn't totally affirmed, but equally, improvised *Deutsch* shows that it wasn't totally rejected either – it did not belong to the "congeries of discourses that do not matter to us, that do not touch us" (Bakhtin 1981:342). German might, after all, have been simply forgotten and ignored outside the language classroom, but noting what youngsters themselves said about the influence of the lessons on improvised *Deutsch* in Chapter 4.3, it looks as though instructed German evidently made enough of an impression on these youngsters for them to bother to re-use it.

This re-cycling of German does not, then, strictly conform to Bakhtin's account of the 'authoritative word'. But this does not mean that German/*Deutsch* can be aligned with the second kind of 'alien' discourse Bakhtin describes, the 'internally persuasive':

Internally persuasive discourse – as opposed to one that is externally authoritative – is, as it is affirmed through assimilation, tightly interwoven with 'one's own word'. In the everyday rounds of our consciousness, the internally persuasive word is half-ours and half-someone-else's. Its creativity and productivity consist precisely in the fact that such a word awakens new and independent words, that it organises masses of our words from within, and does not remain in an isolated and static condition.   (1981:345)

In the way that impromptu *Deutsch* was concentrated around issues of order and propriety, it simply reproduced the broad association of language with authority and discipline that was epitomised in the German lesson choral drills, and there was no evidence of it being extended beyond this rather narrow moral/linguistic nexus to any concern with, for example, German places, products or people. As Chapter 4 showed, adolescents seemed to pay as much (or more) attention to the sound properties of *Deutsch* as to its denotational meaning, and overall, there was little to suggest that *Deutsch* was 'awakening new and independent words'. And so while German might not elicit quite the absolute acceptance or rejection that Bakhtin attributes to authoritative discourse, it certainly did not permeate outwards in the manner of the 'internally persuasive'.

Within the idiom that Bakhtin offers, the best way of characterising the relationship between instructed German and impromptu *Deutsch* would be to retain the sacral overtones in the account of the "authoritative word" ('hieratic', 'profaned' and 'taboo'), and to argue that the lessons turned German into a ritual language which was subsequently "taken in vain". This can be seen when students broke into some quite protracted German choral call-and-responses sequences in the corridors between a humanities and maths lessons:

Extract 5.5

At the end of a Humanities lesson in the library, Hanif and Guy are at the door about to be dismissed (13/3/97) (part of this sequence is also reproduced in Extract 4.4).

```
1   GUY     (mach der )
2           ((indistinct talk for 6 seconds))
3           die Tür ˈaufˌmachen
            ((trans: open the door))
4   HANIF   die Tür ˈaufˌmachen
5   GUY     John (.)
6   HANIF   die ˈTu:ˌer
            ((trans: the door))
7          ⌈ˈzu:: ˋmaˌchen
           ⎪((trans: close))
8   GUY    ⌊ˈzu:: ˋmaˌchen
            ((They leave the room ...
            A little later, as Simon (who is wearing the
            radio-microphone) arrives outside the door of
            the Maths classroom:))
18  HANIF   ˈaufmachen
            ((trans: open))
19  GUY     JOHN (.)
            talk (some German to        )
20  HANIF   she's going (.)
21  ANON    die ˈtoor
            ((trans: the door))
```

```
22   BOYS    ((chorally:)) ˈzoo::ˋmaːˌcheːn
                               ((close))
23   SIMON   ((laughing:)) THIS IS ˈAUFˋMACHEN
                               ((open))
24   MASUD?  ˈauf (ˋmachen       )
25   SIMON   ((laughing:)) (oh ˋshudigung)
26   HANIF   Entˈshuˈdigung (.)
27   JOHN    Entshudigung
28   MASUD   eh
29           Moˈment (.)
             ((trans: a moment – wait a moment))
30           Hanif Moˈment
31   HANIF   Moˈmeːnt
32           Moˈmeːn⌈t
33   GUY            ⌊Moˈmeːnt
34           Moˈmeːnt
```

*((the choral interplay continues until the Maths
teacher comes out of the classroom))*

The students are obviously not simply making up for the opportunities they wasted in the German lesson, and there are clear differences in the prevailing social relations. Here, it is the pupils
themselves who provide the models of German; it is their peers
rather than the teacher who evaluate the product; the interaction is
conducted in a spirit of levity, not seriousness; and their slow delivery and exaggerated pitch contours are a parody of Ms Wilson (see
line 20, and compare, for example, lines 4, 6, 8 and 22 in Extract 5.5
above with lines 3, 5 and 8 of Extract 5.2).

   Inside lessons, this profanation was no longer so extravagant and
instead involved strategic masking, in a politics of resistance "which
[made] use of disguise, deception, and indirection while maintaining
an outward impression, in power-laden situations, of willing, even
enthusiastic consent" (Scott 1990:17). As already noted, *Deutsch*
was double-edged: the alignment with a curriculum language that
Deutsch displayed could evade the censure of Maths and English
teachers, but the performer's relatively covert commitment and
skilled contribution to livening the lessons up could gain the support, even admiration, of peers (Chapter 4.5). In fact, this duality
itself involved partial 'secularisation' of the connotational meanings
of German. In the language lessons, German was given an other-
worldly significance, with the teacher tying it to a distant realm

where, for example, people put `'auf'` at the end of sentences. Outside, however, the resonances of *Deutsch* became much more local, with the German class itself becoming a central symbolic association. Indeed, not only did *Deutsch* localise these resonances, it also pluralised them, achieving its ambivalence through a combination of both indexicality *and* iconicity (cf. Mertz 1985; Clark 1996: Chapter 6). Indexicality involves a contextual association between the sign and its object, while in iconicity there is some kind of perceptual similarity between them. When adolescents switched into German to disguise the dissident element to whatever they were doing from their *teachers*, their performance would achieve its effect through German's general *indexical* association with the curriculum at school. The simple fact that German was learnt as a school subject would be enough to provide Maths and English teachers with grounds for looking favourably on pupils' voluntary uses of the language (Chapter 4.5). Any more specific allusion to German pedagogy would be lost on them, since it is unlikely that other teachers had any idea of Ms Wilson's teaching style, and there was no reason for *Deutsch* performers to expect them to. But for an audience of peers who had first hand experience of German instruction, improvised *Deutsch* could work *iconically* as a comic reproduction of, for example, the *Entschuldigungs* in Ms Wilson's rather imperative style of politeness (see Extracts 4.1, 4.3, 4.4, 4.9).

So there is quite a plausible case for saying, then, that language lessons turned German into a language with strong associations of ritual authority, and that this ritual dimension was both acknowledged *and* taken in vain in the subversive orientation to order and propriety displayed in impromptu *Deutsch*. But there is one problem of evidence.

In developing the argument that language lessons turned German into a ritual language, I have attached particular significance to whole-class speaking-and-listening, and so to clinch this proposal about the centrality of ritual in the connection between German and *Deutsch*, one might expect to find that knock-about *Deutsch* featured elements closely resembling the choral drills. In fact, this is the case in Extract 5.5, where the boys seemed to be parodying the highly ritualised oral/aural format that Ms Wilson put them through. But few of the other *Deutsch* improvisations were overtly modelled on the most ritual parts of the lessons. Instead, words and phrases like *danke, entschuldigung, Moment, schnell,* and *gut* are just as likely to have had their origins in the teacher's incidental classroom management talk as in central instructional sequences focusing on speaking-and-listening. Indeed, words and phrases like these are likely to occur in *any* foreign language pedagogy, not just in very formal ones, and the sceptic could easily claim that other types of language teaching – using *communicative*, non-audio-lingual, non-ritualised methods – would have been enough to enable my informants to produce their *Deutsch* improvisations. Beyond that, some of these phrases – *gut* and *schnell* for example – could be directly picked up from, and/or resonate with, the representation of Germans in popular culture and the mass media (see Chapter 4.2). If surface resemblance was the only guide, there would be grounds for saying that for much of the time, *Deutsch* might have nothing at all to do with the German language class, and we could return to the preliminary characterisation in Chapter 4.6, where *Deutsch* seemed to be more a matter of performance than ritual.

The difficulty is in fact two fold. First, in any study of inversion, distortion and oblique language use, there are often limits to how precise one can be in connecting stylised performance to the source that it is modelled on. In certain circumstances, this can be overcome. When, for example, Richard Bauman analyses 'parodic counter-statement', in which one performer comically distorts the words of another, he judiciously focuses on couplets of *immediately contiguous* straight and inversive utterances, arguing that this constitutes "a relatively circumscribed and accessible field of discursive practice in which controlled investigation of recontextualising transformations of the word may be carried out" (1996:302). Unfortunately, the German/*Deutsch* data afford few controls of this kind, and they are not exceptional in this. Second, the difficulties are compounded if one is examining processes that involve reproduction over a longer period, and this is made quite clear by researchers on second language learning: "longitudinal data [might be needed to] show evidence of sustained acquisition[, but t]he problem is that once the longitudinal evidence is in, it [can] be hard to link it incontrovertibly to the . . . work of yesteryear" (van Lier 2000:248; also McDermott 1993:270, Hutchins 1993:59–60). Even when they are not trying to be funny, people transform the linguistic material they are exposed to in strange and unpredictable ways, and this inevitably makes it hard to know exactly what the original material was that we think they might now be reproducing.

It is possible, however, to get past the impediment presented by the absence of a strong empirical resemblance between stylised *Deutsch* and speaking-and-listening in the German lessons if we dwell a little longer on the processes entailed in this rejection of the 'authoritative word', attending a little more closely to the socio-emotional, intra- as well as inter-psychological, dimensions of ritual experience.

5.6   The socio-emotional dynamics of ritual and its rejection

I have already associated the German lessons with institutional ritual, where the function is "to relate the individual through ritualistic acts to a social order, to heighten respect for that order, to revivify that order within the individual and, in particular, to deepen acceptance of the procedures ... which control ambivalence towards the social order" (Bernstein 1975:54). But beyond that, it has often been observed that ritual assemblies generate a mood of collective intensity – a 'collective effervescence' (Durkheim 1912:128, 136, 1972:229, 235) – from which participants subsequently depart feeling morally replenished, at least for a while (Durkheim 1912: 156; Handelman 1977:189). Turning to the German lessons, I have suggested that the teacher was trying to create a state of flow in the classroom, "an assembly animated by a common passion" (Durkheim 1912:128), but as the data showed, many of the students were reluctant to comply. Focusing on the boys who used impromptu *Deutsch* most extensively and going back to the account of their conduct in other lessons in Chapters 2 and 3, we can imagine just how strong this reluctance might have been.

In English and Humanities lessons, Hanif, John and friends were exuberant participants. They attended closely to the main instructional discourse, and exploited whatever opportunities they could to embellish the proceedings by transcoding official utterances into, for example, melody, non-standard accents, different intonation patterns and, of course, other languages (see Chapter 2.3). Indeed, I even suggested that in this incessant contrapuntal performance,

these boys experienced something broadly comparable to dynamic
fellowship felt by musicians playing together (Chapter 3.7). This
conduct was generally accepted by the teachers in English and
Humanities, and it was a significant component in the temporarily
stable social order that emerged in teacher-fronted interaction
(Chapter 2.5). The situation in German was radically different.
For the most part, the traditional pattern of teacher Initiates ⇨
pupil(s) Respond(s) ⇨ teacher Evaluates held up, and in stark contrast to the other lessons I observed, girls and boys contributed
roughly the same number of turns to whole-class discussion.
Certainly, the students pulled against it in a number of different
ways (Chapter 5.3), but rather than being pluralised, authority was
still centred in the teacher. It is hard to know how far Ms Wilson
retained this authority because she invoked the threat of punishment
much more often, writing the names of transgressors on the board,
and how far it was due to these students' semiotic creativity being
inhibited by their own incompetence in the language being emphasised. But whatever, the German lessons sharply contravened the
ways of being in a classroom that these boys liked, and were used to,
in other lessons.

   In the German class, then, there is on the one hand, a pedagogy
insistently oriented to the production of 'flow' and the emergence of
"an assembly animated by a common passion", and on the other, a
group of students with a strong preference for a style of classroom
participation that the pedagogy largely prohibited. At the same time,
these boys sat through this socio-emotional matrix of conflicting
interactional habits and preferences for periods of up to 45 minutes
three times a week, and it is not difficult to imagine how this could
involve an experience of prohibition and denial which then imbued
German/*Deutsch* with the kind of complex loading that Sapir
describes in 'condensation symbolism'.

   Condensation symbols, says Sapir, involve "a highly condensed
form of substitutive behaviour for direct expression, allowing for the
ready release of emotional tension in conscious or unconscious
form" (1949:565), and in this definition, Sapir is looking towards
the kinds of 'depth' process that interest psycho-analysts – fantasy,
repression, pleasure, fear and the unconscious (Cameron and Kulick
2003:105–107). These are also addressed in recent work by Michael
Billig (1999), but Billig argues that rather than being rooted in the

instinctual drives emphasised by Freud, such processes are grounded in everyday discourse (see also Vološinov [1927] 1976; Sapir 2002:210). Billig accepts that "the unconscious only exists to the extent that people repress" (p 82). But rather than seeing this as a "mysterious inner process, regulated by an internal structure such as the 'ego' ", repression "depends on the skills of language" (Billig 1999:1,36). Cameron and Kulick 2003:119 follow the view that repression is demanded by language, that "in conversing, we also create silences" (Billig 1999:261), and they propose that "in learning to speak, children also learn what must remain unspoken and unspeakable. This means two things: first, that repression is not beyond or outside language, but is, instead, the constitutive resource of language; and second, that repression is an interactional achievement" (2003:119). Billig, Cameron and Kulick are referring to a range of routine linguistic activities through which individuals push dangerous and awkward issues aside, and this can be adapted to the learning of German by Hanif and his friends: learning German meant learning to speak-and-listen as instructed by their teacher, suppressing a lot of the talk, the classroom sociability, and the experience of control and agency they were accustomed to in other lessons. Within the regimentation of feeling entailed in these lessons, German can be envisaged developing the kind of emotional associations that Sapir attributes to condensation symbolism, and following on from this, improvised *Deutsch* can be construed as a 'return of the repressed' – or in Sapir's formulation, "the ready release of emotional tension in conscious or unconscious form".

Billig, then, emphasises the role that everyday language and communication play in psychological repression, and he denies "that there is a sharp distinction between internal mental life and external social life" (1999:56; also Vološinov 1973:90–92; Sapir 2002:230; Williams 1977:40–41). Nevertheless, intra-psychological processes *within* the individual necessarily play some part in these processes, and as far as the data here are concerned, it cannot be assumed that everyone experienced exactly the same type of discomfort in the German lessons, with the same degree of intensity. It is much more likely (a) that the language class impacted more strongly on some youngsters than others, (b) that some individuals performed and enjoyed *Deutsch* mainly because their friends did, heedless of its echoes of the German lessons, with the result that

(c) *Deutsch* might have worked as a 'return of the repressed' to a greater extent for some than for others. I did not have a chance to probe this possibility systematically in fieldwork, but I can respond to this likelihood, and still sustain a plausible argument about German/*Deutsch* as a condensation symbol by taking the case of Hanif. First, Hanif was much more muted in the German lessons than he was in other classes. Second, he showed mixed feelings about instructed German: when I asked him and Masud whether they enjoyed German lessons, he first replied with a rather ambivalent 'nwe:r', only clarifying his position when Masud identifying the teacher as a problem (see p. 184 above, and Extract 4.11), and then he qualified this, saying ``I kinda like the language ... the accent you can use''. Third, turning to the radio-microphone recordings, in Extract 4.5 he switched from humming to talking *Deutsch* to himself – music obviously had interior resonance and got stuck in his head, but so too, apparently, did German (Chapters 4.3, 4.4). Fourth, Hanif was the central figure in his peer cluster, and he was *Deutsch*'s lead performer (Chapter 4.5). There is no need, in other words, to situate German/*Deutsch*'s effectivity as a condensation symbol in some metaphysical 'group mind' or 'collective psyche'. There was at least one student whose expressive impulses were largely suppressed in Ms Wilson's lessons and who had quite a complicated affective stance on instructed German. The language lingered in his mind, he promoted it among his friends, and to the extent that these friends shared his feelings about German classes, *Deutsch* could have operated as condensation symbol for them as well.

Of course, it is important not to exaggerate the psychological importance of all this. I am positing a persistent unease or discomfort in the German class, and this is a very long way from the terrain of, for example, trauma or neurosis. But when Sapir says that "specific forms of writing, conventionalised spelling, peculiar pronunciation and verbal slogans ... easily take on the character of emotionalised rituals and become highly important to both individual and society as substitutive forms of emotional expression" (1949:565), there is a good case for pointing to German/*Deutsch* as a mild, minor instance of this process.

And finally, of course, the association of German/*Deutsch* with condensation symbolism gets past the problem of evidence raised towards the end of the last section. Sapir contrasts condensation symbols with 'referential symbolism'. Whereas the latter constitutes the staple of linguistics and is subject to "formal elaboration in the conscious [as a conventional] system of reference", condensation symbolism "strikes deeper and deeper roots in the unconscious and diffuses its emotional quality to types of behaviour or situations apparently far removed from the original meaning of the symbol" (1949:566). That being the case, attempts to trace the origins of a condensation symbol cannot rely on any close empirical correspondence to data on its source, and there is no reason to expect anything more than only a weak resemblance between the choral drills led by Ms Wilson and the *schnell*s and *gut*s produced by the youngsters.

At this point, it is worth drawing together the strands of my analysis of German/*Deutsch* in this Chapter and the last.

5.7   Resumé, and some speculative projections

In Chapter 4, I looked at the spontaneous use of *Deutsch* outside the German language class, and on the evidence presented there, I suggested that this should be characterised first and foremost as a resource for performance in Richard Bauman's sense. The intensity with which students sought to "enhance experience" through the use of *Deutsch* varied, but it was, for example, the focus of sound play and sometimes featured as a 'daring' interjection in moments of heightened surveillance. At least in terms of its institutional origins as a school- rather than a home-language, German was a neutral variety in the multi-lingual peer group, and teachers seemed happy to hear students use it of their own accord. Indeed, as a language for peer activity in class, it was a good choice for students who wanted to enjoy themselves with their friends while remaining broadly focused on the curriculum. There was also a ritual dimension to improvised *Deutsch*, though judging just from the data in Chapter 4, this was secondary, emerging from the performance of *Deutsch* at interactional moments that were ritually sensitive in themselves.

The present Chapter, though, has looked more closely at the German lessons, and this has substantially increased our sense of the ritual resonance of *Deutsch*/German.

As well as being used in interaction rituals *à la* Goffman in Humanities and English, German was focal in foreign language classes and these bore many of the hallmarks of institutional ritual (in the manner of Durkheim, Bourdieu, Bernstein and Du Bois). Power and influence were at stake in both institutional and interactional ritual, but there was a sharp contrast between these informants' enjoyment of the unofficial improvisations and their relatively negative experience of the German lessons. Trying to clarify the ways in which German and *Deutsch* might be actively linked, I then suggested that instructed German had a ritual authority that impromptu *Deutsch* both acknowledged and profaned, repositioning the language so that its association with the German class and the German language teacher took precedence over its canonical connections with much remoter native-speaking Germans. I then speculated about the socio-emotional experience that the German lessons offered for the youngsters who used impromptu *Deutsch* most frequently. Comparing the conduct demanded in the foreign language class with their styles of classroom participation elsewhere, it looked as though these lessons involved students in an experience of suppression that could imbue the language with the kind of emotional resonance that Sapir associates with condensation symbolism. They obviously did not enjoy the oral activity in the German class, but it had an insistent intensity that got through to them, re-emerging subsequently as a 'return of the repressed' in spontaneous interventions subversively tuned to moments of potential conflict between pupils and teacher. To this, two points of clarification should be added, plus some speculation about the longer-term consequences.

First, even though I am suggesting that instructed German impacted on improvised *Deutsch*, there is no claim that the rituality of the lessons somehow programmed *Deutsch* to reappear in Goffmanesque interpersonal rituals, making it *uniquely* appropriate to the ritually pregnant moments described in Chapter 4. Such moments are endemic to interaction, these youngsters filled them with a far wider range of different resources, and there is no basis for suggesting that the lessons somehow impelled them to use just *Deutsch* at these junctures.

Nevertheless, they sometimes did, and at such moments – second – the discussion of condensation symbolism suggests more of *Deutsch*'s meaning at such moments than 'indexicality' and 'iconicity' alone, at least as I have used these two notions in my own analysis (Chapter 5.5). Referring to its dual connotations in the English and Humanities classroom, I said that *Deutsch* could index curriculum German for the teachers while serving as an icon of Ms Wilson for the students. This formulation seems adequate as an account of *Deutsch*'s situated ambivalence, but standing alone, it leaves *Deutsch* looking rather too tidy, neatly mapped into two signifieds simultaneously. When *Deutsch* is construed as a condensation symbol, the focus shifts to its more disorderly emotional resonance, and it is necessary to posit a degree of semiotic indeterminacy that is probably much more faithful to these youngsters' experience of actually producing and hearing these improvisations.[3]

Third and most speculatively, an orientation to socio-emotional experience allows the formulation of a hypothesis about *Deutsch*'s longer term impact on these students' learning of curriculum German. I have suggested that oral work in the German lessons tried to produce a state of flow among students, a state of concentration and engrossment where they would all act in concert. During states of flow and intense involvement, the organisational aspects of activity operate unobtrusively in the background, in what Goffman calls the 'directional track'. According to Goffman, "in ... sports [for example], the umpire inhabits the directional channel, his job being to bring editorial control, to punctuate the proceedings, but otherwise to be, in effect, invisible" (1974:417). In contrast, too much attention to whether or not the rules are being followed inhibits the experience of flow, and in Turner's words, "there is a rhythmic, behavioural or cognitive break. Self-consciousness makes [the actor] stumble" (1982:56). If Goffman and Turner are right, it looks as though spontaneous peer group *Deutsch* might actually be antithetical to flow. Rather than rehearsing for immersion in German lesson content, the *Deutsch* improvisations tied the language to the regulative and disciplinary activities that ought to have stayed in the background if flow were to be achieved. Overall, one might say, adolescent *Deutsch* was comparable to soccer practice devoted to dealings with the referee. Where the teacher aimed for immersion and 'flow' in collective classroom speaking-and-listening, the pupils oriented to procedural management, and in Bakhtin's terms, this entailed yet further transgression of the "authoritative word", which in its ideal form, purports to "permit ... no play with the context framing it, no play with its borders" (1981:343).

Going one step further, this view of *Deutsch* being antithetical to 'flow' might speak to the larger fact of these youngsters' under-achievement over the longer term. Eighteen months after the data described in Chapters 2–5 were collected, the principal exponents of peer group *Deutsch* were re-interviewed. They had forgotten that they had ever used the language spontaneously, they continued to be unenthusiastic about foreign language lessons, and a little after that, they emerged with very poor GCSE school-leaving exam results in German. Hitherto in my interpretation of the connections between German and *Deutsch*, the lessons have been discussed as a source model for the improvisations, but it is important to recognise that the influence could also go the other way. Impromptu *Deutsch* itself promoted a particular view of German language pedagogy, high-lighting some aspects to the exclusion of others. Potentially at least, this could wash back on the expectations and the receptiveness that pupils took back inside the German classroom, encouraging them, in metaphorical terms, to observe the frame and not the picture, creating a pedagogically stressful dissonance between the teacher's emphasis and the pupils' attention that doomed Ms Wilson's endeavours.

That concludes my interpretation of the empirical data on German/*Deutsch*. In drawing on the notion of ritual, I have treated it as intimate mixture of politics, symbolism and emotion and I would now like to try to place this in a larger disciplinary context.

5.8   Ritual in research on language and society

Within pragmatics and interaction analysis, ritual has been a signifi-cant analytic concept, but its use has generally been narrower than in this chapter. Durkheim's discussion of positive and negative rites provides an explicit theoretical foundation both for Goffman's analyses of 'face-work' and for Brown and Levinson's theory of polite-ness (Durkheim 1972:233; Goffman 1967:5–45, 47; Brown and Levinson 1987:43–44), but in both, the meaning of ritual is rapidly specialised. Elsewhere in the social sciences, researchers in the Durkheimian tradition pay considerable attention to ritual's symbolic significance and its relation to the historical experience and the political preoccupations of particular social groups (e.g. Douglas 1966; Turner 1969; Bernstein 1975; Alexander 1988). But in Goffman's analysis of face, the symbolisation of collective experience and (sub-)cultural history plays very little part (see Abrahams 1984:81–82), while in politeness theory, priority is instead given to individual speaker goals and means-and-ends reasoning (Brown and Levinson 1987:64 et passim; Strecker 1988). For the data in this chapter and the last, theories of politeness and face have made an essential contribution to our identification of interactional *Deutsch* as a micro-ritual practice, but they do not in themselves speak directly to its intimate involvement in institutional conflict (compare Chapters 5.4 and 5.5 above).

In pragmatics and sociolinguistics more generally, the term 'ritual' is usually avoided. There are a range of concepts that undoubtedly have 'family ties' to it, but they tend to be rebranded to mark their identity within specific paradigms, and streamlined to make them more tractable as analytic resources. 'Face work', 'politeness' and 'phatic communion' (Laver 1975; Coupland et al. 1992) feature with regularity and abundance in the indices of pragmatics and sociolinguistics textbooks, but 'ritual' is much harder to find.[4] 'Preference organisation' is another commonly used concept with family links to 'face' and 'ritual' (Heritage 1984a:268; Brown and Levinson 1987:38), but there is no scope in conversation analysis (CA) for consideration of the processes involved in something like 'condensation symbolism', (a) because the developmental sequences that CA attends to are very short, spanning turns-at-talk rather than 'types of behaviour or situations' (Sapir 1949:566), and (b) because there is no place in its working assumptions for the idea that "'human consciousness' has a 'deep interior'" (Silverman 1998:189; Billig 1999:50).

In contrast, in linguistic anthropology and the ethnography of communication, there is a very long and rich tradition in the analysis of ritual speech and ritual events, and this is very often informed by a sense of the psychic and emotional intensity experienced by ritual participants. Even so, it is not so often that the concept of ritual itself carries a major theoretical burden. Ritual frequently features as a consensual descriptor in initial characterisation of the object of study, but the analysis then soon moves on to the composition of the code, event or practice, its position in the local communicative economy, its role in the management and/or contestation of prevailing social relations, its historical development and so forth.[5] This situation changes when attention turns to practices that look like ritual but have not yet been consensually designated as such, and in such cases, the notion of ritual itself becomes a central focus of theorisation.[6] But it is not so usual for central analytic claims in linguistic anthropology either to rely on, or to seek to develop, explicit theories of ritual as psycho-social process. In contrast, in this chapter, I have invoked authority relations and the socio-emotional aspects of ritual as explanatory mechanisms, as the theoretical warrant for the connectedness of instructed German and improvised *Deutsch*, and in part, this is a response to educational concern for pedagogy and its influence on learner development.

5.9   Ritual, education and change

'Ritual' has actually figured quite prominently in research on second and foreign language learning, but it has tended to feature as a term of deprecation, being most often equated with old-fashioned ('traditional') formal modes of instruction counterposed to the more interactive, 'communicative' pedagogies that have been extensively advocated over the last 30 years or so (see Lightbown and Spada 1993 for a representative account). Indeed this can be seen more generally in research on language in education, where, for example, Edwards and Mercer (1987) call learner activities 'ritual' when they seem to be imitative, automatic, inflexible, practical, unreflexive, and designed to please the teacher, and contrast these unfavourably with 'principled' learning described as creative, considered, flexible, theoretical, meta-cognitive and done for one's own purposes.

My data certainly seem to point to the adverse effects of highly ritualised pedagogy, but it would be a mistake to assume that this outcome testified to a universal law of cognitive development. Instead, educational ritual needs to be situated in its social and historical contexts, and there is evidence, for example, that social class affects the impact and uptake of ritualized pedagogies. Heller 1995 gives a graphic illustration of this in her account of two classes in a Francophone immersion school in Toronto. One of the classes, *Français avancé*, involved middle-class students who were university-bound, and in it, deviations from standard French were relentlessly corrected, there was an emphasis on decontextualised writing and oral forms of written language, interaction was heavily mediated by the teacher who followed a canonical IRE format, and students observed a strict habit of speaking one at a time, which was itself taken as a mark of 'respect', "intimately tied to the school's notion of what it means to be a good students" (1995:390). In the other class, *Français général*, there was more negotiation around the forms of language that were used, the curriculum oriented towards contextualised everyday discourse, the teacher tried to rearrange the seating in discussion circles, and herself often lost the floor. This class was designed to lead direct to the workplace, it consisted of working-class and black minority students, and the academic outcomes were, and were known to be, lower. So here, students who did *better* academically worked in classrooms where the element of ritualisation was *greater*. A broadly comparable correlation between ritualisation, success and wealth can perhaps be glimpsed into my own comparison of Westpark and Central High in the beginning of Chapter 2 and in Chapter 3.2, and it is explicit in, for example, Kapferer's 1981 study of ritual in a private and a state school in Australia. Not that this association between wealth and ritualised pedagogy is itself a general rule either. As Arthur notes, "[r]ecitation routines are reported to be typical of many teacher-centered classrooms throughout the world, but seem to be particularly salient in large classes in poor countries" (2001:70).

So education ritual needs to be properly contextualised, and located in a perspective that treats pedagogy as part of local, national and even global cultural politics (Pennycook 1994).[7] Indeed in Chapters 2 and 3, pedagogic style was seen as a stake in situated struggle between pupils, teachers, policy-makers and others, and I documented the lines of tension and the provisional settlement that some of the teachers negotiated with pupils in Class 9A, enabling them to keep classroom activity broadly on track. Where do the German lessons stand in this process?

Focusing on pedagogy in the Humanities and English lessons, I characterised the *canonical* form of whole class teacher-talk as "a jostling, expressively depleted style which marginalises students' own judgement but threatens to drag them onto the platform with curriculum scripted performances that actually don't count for very much" (Chapters 2.6 and 3.7). In the German lessons, a number of these qualities were intensified. Students' own perspectives were made more marginal, both by the teacher's explicit injunctions and by the use of a language that they had very little propositional control over. At the same time, the insistence on participating orally was much greater. Chanting along with the teacher was deemed essential for the development of foreign language speaking skills (forcing the students to behave even more like a ritual congregation[8]), but the individual's voice was lost in the crowd's and it contributed almost nothing to the direction of the discourse.

As I documented in some detail, in the English and Humanities classrooms a mixed pedagogic genre had emerged which was substantially different from the model of teacher-fronted discourse idealised in education policy, and in one way or another, it allowed much more space for the agency of individual students. Unfortunately, there was little room for the foreign language teachers to make any comparable adjustments. If they had had a foreign languages curriculum that paid no attention to speaking-and-listening and laid less emphasis on grammatical accuracy,[9] or if they had had plenty of money to spend on computers, or if their classes had been filled with pupils they could trust to keep on-task when they were put in pairs and small groups, no doubt the FL teachers could have avoided the kind of collective oral work that the students seemed most resistant to. But they didn't, so they couldn't. The constraints of their working environment compelled the FL teachers at Central High to push their students through a set of activities that gave their lessons the character of formal ritual, and there were thousands of other foreign language teachers in England who were in the same position.[10] Indeed, in the end, it was Government itself that gave up on trying to force youngsters this age to learn foreign languages. In 2003 the Department for Education and Skills decided that for students aged 14 and older, modern foreign languages should no longer be a compulsory element in the National Curriculum (DfES 2002, 2003). Among the reasons given, it cited "issues of pupil motivation and relative lack of success of lower income groups and boys" (DfES 2002:12; also Boaks 1998:38).[11]

So it looks as though at Central High, the foreign language classroom was drawn into a longer and wider process of contestation over the communicative order, and that these lessons involved a set of social relations that it has become increasingly hard to sustain in contemporary working-class schools. What are the implications for the relevance of 'ritual' to the study of schooling? Does this kind of institutional shift make 'ritual' a redundant concept in educational research?

In the definition of ritual that I offered at the start of this chapter, I drew attention to the enormous variety of types of social action that participants and analysts have used the term 'ritual' to refer to – forms ranging from coronations to apologies. So it is unlikely that 'ritual' will disappear from the educational process, and instead, the forms it takes are likely to shift in line with the emergence, dominance and decline of competing social groups, in line with changing perceptions of the most pressing problems and transgressions in the routine reproduction of social relations, and in line with shifts in the prestige and symbolic force of different kinds of cultural resource. As Bernstein briefly noted during the period when 'progressive' pedagogies were ascendant and the articulation of authority was passing to more interpersonal, child-centred and 'therapeutic' styles of communication (1971a, 1975, 1996:Chapter 3),[12] "[w]e might ... expect a switch from the dominance of adult-imposed and regulated rituals to dominance of rituals generated and regulated by youth" (1975:60). In the analysis of instructed German and improvised *Deutsch*, we have seen a *struggle* – not just a switch – between adult-imposed and youth-generated rituals. Methodologically, there is also a good case for seeing 'ritual' as a 'sensitising' rather than a 'definitive' concept, 'suggesting directions along which to look' rather than 'prescriptions of what to see' (cf. Blumer 1969:148). Ritual involves displays of respect, a sense of transition or transgression, and a relatively rigid invocation of collectively ratified cultural material, but these elements do not only come together in institutionalised and relatively spectacular ritual practices of the kind witnessed in the German class. They can also combine in more muted forms, where it may then be wiser to speak of degrees of 'ritualisation' (Erikson 1969) or of 'interpersonal ritual', and indeed, in the initial stages of my analysis of improvised *Deutsch*, it seemed more appropriate to talk of 'performance' than ritual (Chapter 4.6).

In sum, ritual's continuing relevance to education depends very much on both where and how you look for it. This is not the place for a proper discussion of ritual in other areas of contemporary education, but very tentatively, there are likely to be a range of sites during the early stages of institutional instruction where ritualised activity emerges. In learning to read, as in learning a foreign or second language, there is often an emotionally tensed initial engagement with the outer surface of language and text prior to comprehension of their grammatical and referential meanings (see Sperber 1975; Bakhtin 1981:289; Collins 1996:220–224; Mertz 1996:246; Rampton 1999:491–497; Cook 2000:14–15; van Lier 2000:255–256, 258), and intuitively, similar processes seem just as likely to occur in classroom encounters with maths and science. Elsewhere in the curriculum, as I noted in Chapter 1, education policy in the UK has been retreating for some time from the 'progressive' teaching methods of the post-1960s, with teacher-led, whole-class pedagogy being enforced by legislation in literacy (and maths) teaching, and it is possible that ritual analysis would be revealing here as well.

Overall, with the analytic range and flexibility of application that it affords at both macro- and micro levels, ritual provides a broadly consistent vocabulary capable of recognising both continuities and differences in the fluctuating moral emphasis given to collective or to inter-individual relations at school. There may be times and places when interpersonal ties and the agency of individuals are privileged, and here Goffman may provide the best tools for analysing certain types of face-to-face interaction between pupils and teachers. But the notion of ritual allows us to stay in touch with political and institutional analyses like Bernstein's or Bourdieu's, and it can also be used to scrutinise the ways in which in particular locales, collective and interpersonal activity can be closely related. In this chapter, I have used ritual to move back and forwards between institutional events and interpersonal actions – between German lessons and utterances in *Deutsch* – but this has involved much more than just fancy analytic footwork. The empirical distribution of German/*Deutsch* across different occasions itself affirms that, in certain situations, there can be an intimate, real-world connectedness between ritual practices that differ very substantially in their scale and elaboration.

Much has been said of late of *ideology* and language, and both in education and elsewhere, ideology has often been construed as a process that seeks to *naturalise* social relations, reproducing and legitimising stratification and inequality in everyday commonsense, recruiting people to particular understandings of the world without their really realising it (Fairclough 1989; Woolard 1992; Woolard and Schieffelin 1994). Applied to schooling, this kind of critique can show how students are persuaded that they are bright or stupid, that their futures lie in one direction rather than another, and it invites analysis of textbooks, teacher–pupil interaction, and public and semi-public debates about education and learning (see e.g. Fairclough 1992a). But it is also vital to look at potentially formative moments of uncertainty, intensification and conflict, when groups and individuals seek recognition for their interests through actions that are special or spectacular rather than routine (cf. e.g. Shils 1969). This is an angle that ritual allows us to address, and investigating German/*Deutsch*, we have seen a range of animated and conflicting mobilisations for and against, in and around, official definitions of the social and linguistic identities that students should aim at. In short, ritual remains an indispensable resource for analysis of the shifting orders of schooling.

Notes

1. The foreign language teachers in this school were far more reluctant to allow me into their lessons than any other subject teachers.
2. The radio-microphone was unlikely to have been a significant factor inhibiting Hanif here, since he had already been wearing it for 3 hours that day, 6 ¾ hours in total, and more generally, there was little sign that it encouraged him to be unusually quiet.
3. Not that 'indexicality' and 'iconicity' cannot also operate with the 'deeper' psychological resonance attributed to condensation symbols – see Crapanzo 1993; van Lier 2000:256, 258; Sapir 2002:224.
4. See for example Clark 1996; Coulmas (ed.) 1997; Downes 1984; Duranti 1997; Fasold 1990; Holmes 1992; Hudson 1996; Levinson 1983; Mey 1993; Schiffrin 1994; Wardhaugh 1998.
5. See e.g. Labov 1972b; Ferguson 1976; McDowell 1983; Kuipers 1984, 1990; Briggs 1993; Szuchewycz 1994; Silverstein and Urban 1996; Foley 1997:Chapter 18. Ritual's position within linguistic anthropology's taken-for-granted (Blumer 1969:144) can be seen in, for example, the *Journal of Linguistic Anthropology*'s 'Lexicon for the Millenium' (9:1–2 1999), where there are frequent references to ritual but no section specifically dedicated to it.
6. See e.g. Katriel 1985, 1987; Ji and Shu 1990; Rampton 1995a.
7. Pennycook, Kramsch (e.g. 1993) and others are critical of educational theories which treat language teaching as a neutral technology, obscuring the social and historical particularity of language learning and

212 Language in Late Modernity

teaching (LLT). In fact cultural and critical perspectives are now very widespread (to the point where it might even be justified to say that the technicist tradition is now no longer dominant), and parts of my own work can be situated within this reorientation in LLT research (Rampton 1991, 1997, 1995a:Chapter 11.5).

8. "[In ritual events] the defining relationship of the members of a congregation ... is *participation* ... [In theatrical events], the defining characteristic of audience in contrast to performers on the one hand and congregation on the other is that they do not participate in the performance: they *watch* and *listen*" (Rappoport 1999:39).

9. According to Mitchell, the National Curriculum for Modern Foreign Languages "limits learner production to 'two or three exchanges', 'mainly memorised language' etc., thus clearly reflect[ing] a central preoccupation with accuracy in learner production" (2003:18).

10. Mitchell summarises Dobson's overview of MFL teaching within the National Curriculum, drawing on inspection reports: "Dobson reports that in many MFL classrooms, very limited opportunities are available to learners to do the following: (a) to acquire understanding of the grammatical structures of the language; (b) to expand their vocabulary beyond the basics; (c) to marshal and re-use existing language knowledge in new and wider ranging situations; (d) to take the initiative, ask questions, offer comments and justify opinions; (e) more generally, to develop independence in tackling and completing learning tasks (paraphrased from Dobson 2002:1–2)" (Mitchell 2003:19–20). Mitchell's own research with Martin (Mitchell and Martin 1997) "showed that ... lessons ... were in general very strongly teacher-centred and teacher-led. Pair and group work were rare, as was differentiation by task. Teachers used considerable amounts of the target language, and learners were actively involved in whole-class language practice of various kinds, with a strong focus on speaking and listening" (Mitchell 2003:20).

11. Of course there were also other factors, including a serious shortage of MFL teachers.

12. "In ... schools [where] there is ... a weakening of ritual and its supporting insignia ... Social control will come to rest upon inter-personal means. It will tend to become psychologised and to work through the verbal manipulation of motives and dispositions in an inter-personal context. We shall call this form of social control, this form of transmission of the expressive order, *therapeutic*." (Bernstein 1975:62).

PART IV

The stylisation of social class

6

Language and class I: theoretical orientations

According to Abercrombie and Warde et al., historically in Britain social class has proved

an incisive analytic tool for understanding inequality, social division and political change. For much of the nineteenth and twentieth centuries, family background, main source of income, place of residence, cultural tastes and political affiliations were closely associated, and class position condensed information about these major aspects of social difference ... Class linked together and summarised empirical description of many aspects of any individual's life. (2000:145–146; see also Bradley 1996:46)

They also show that although the twentieth century saw attempts to redistribute wealth and income, inequality and social division have persisted. Wealth has remained very concentrated – the wealthiest tenth of adults owned 50% of personal wealth in 1976, and still owned 49% in 1992 (provisional figure; Abercrombie and Warde et al. 2000:121) – and since the 1980s, poverty has grown from 9% of the population in Britain in 1979, to 24% in 1995/96 (2000:124). In addition, particularly in the higher and lower social categories, social mobility is relatively limited, and since 1972, "patterns of movement between class of origin and class of destination remain the same. Social mobility is not increasing" (2000:141).

At the same time, however, a number of commentators have suggested that although major inequalities of wealth and opportunity continue, a range of relatively recent economic, social and cultural changes have made social class itself a more difficult concept to use:

What is the working class today? What gender is it? What colour is it? How in the light of its obvious segmentation, is it to be unified? Is this unification still possible or even desirable? ... Class analysis must be opened up so that it can be supplemented by additional categories which reflect different histories of subordination . . . The complex experiential chemistry of class, 'race' and gender . . . yields an important reminder of the limitations of analysis based exclusively on a narrow conception of class. (Gilroy 1987:19)

New generations of the white working classes lack access to the broader collectivist cultures that many of their parents and grandparents grew up in. Any sense of heritage is denied them in the bleak 1990s discursive landscape. It is a terrain in which to be working-class is increasingly to be 'not good enough', and there are no longer politicising scripts of class oppression to counter the prevalence of views that it is all their own fault. (Reay 1998:267)

The analytic utility and the cultural salience of social class appears to be diminishing, undermined by a wide range of factors: the social and economic changes associated with globalisation, the decline of traditional collectivist politics, the emergence of gender, race and ethnicity as political issues, and the ascendance of the individual as consumer (Abercrombie and Warde et al. 2000:148). Some linguists have also suggested that class may be losing its clarity in everyday speech (Wells 1982:118; Coggle 1993:93; Honey 1989:82, 182; Williams 1961:249), and it is sometimes proposed that the cultural resonance of class is weakest among young people:

Young people are currently at the sharp end of the changing class dynamic. The cultural changes discerned by post-modernists manifest themselves among young people rather than the older age groups. Young people are especially responsive to media and fashion changes. They have often formed distinctive subcultures which signify their distance both from wider society and their own parents . . . [undermining] traditional working-class values. The growth of youth unemployment contributed to this process of class dissolution . . . For all these reasons the decline of class awareness is likely to affect young people most fully. (Bradley 1996:77)

So how much, and what kind of class awareness was there among the informants in my research? Their school, Central High, was located in the middle of London, outside any residential enclaves of traditional working-class culture, and the students came from a lot of different parts of the city. Approximately a third of them were from refugee and asylum-seeking families, and in the tutor group of thirty that I followed, they spoke at least a dozen different languages. From the geographic siting and demographic composition, it looked as though the school was quite extensively exposed to the "cultural changes discerned by post-modernists", and on these grounds, one might expect to find a decline of class awareness among the students. And yet on average about once every 45 minutes, my informants put on exaggerated posh and Cockney voices, using accents traditionally associated with the English upper class on the one hand, and London working classes on the other. For example:

Ninnette and Joanne are in the corridor at breaktime, and they see a friend (from Extract 7.9):

JOANNE *((in a very loud, ultra-Cockney accent))*: **awigh** *((= 'all right'))*
GIRL *((responding in an ultra-posh accent))*: **hello::**
JOANNE *((still in exaggerated Cockney))*: **why you ou' 'ere** *((= 'why are you out here'))*

Hanif is role-playing the coroner at an inquest (from Extract 8.2):

HANIF *((calling out, in quite a posh voice))*: order in the court
BOY: get on with it
HANIF *((switching into exaggerated Cockney for the fourth and fifth words))*: order in the **bloody well** court
OTHERS: *((laughter))*

Simon is talking to Ameena about attitudes to belching at dinner (from Extract 9.4):

SIMON *((switching into an extra broad London accent in the fourth line))*: sometimes girls don't mind that they go
oh go on
led it ou' *((= 'let it out'))*
you're a man

Stylised posh and Cockney utterances like these constitute the central focus in this part of the book, and I examine them for what they reveal of contemporary class consciousness.

The present chapter provides the theoretical bearings for the investigation. What do I mean by class? What do I mean by stylisation? What is the potential connection, and how does all this fit into sociolinguistics?

Having pointed to contemporary uncertainties about the value of class as a political and analytic concept, the first section specifies the aspects of class that I shall be focusing on: class formation and consciousness at the level of everyday activity, reckoning with agency and subjectivity (Chapter 6.1). To clarify the relationship between class, race, ethnicity, gender, generation, etc., I draw on a broad distinction between on the one hand, practical activity and material conditions, and on the other, secondary/meta-representations of social life. It might be very hard to separate gender, ethnicity and class at the first level, but secondary discourses *about* class, gender, etc. are more easily separated, both in their form and their effects (Chapter 6.2). This then brings me in Chapter 6.3 to the stylisations of posh and Cockney, which can be seen as small pieces of secondary representation inserted into the flow of practical activity – moments of social commentary on some aspect of the activities on hand – and after that, I formulate the research questions that will guide this part of the book (Chapter 6.4). So far, the discussion has drawn on sociology and on major figures in social and cultural theory (Williams, Thompson, Foucault, Vološinov), but the chapter now turns to sociolinguistics, and I identify those parts of the sociolinguistics literature that seem to offer useful resources for my analyses of stylisation and social class (Chapter 6.5). Admittedly, there has been a good deal of dispute and difference within this literature, and at first glance, it looks as though this might undermine the appropriations I attempt in my analyses of posh and Cockney stylisation. In fact, though, these arguments lose much of their force at the interface of 'modernity' and 'late modernity', where I locate more recent studies. At the same time, it is important to note that late modernity is not a particularly hospitable site for class analysis, and that we need to take care not to let methodological developments in sociolinguistics trick us into a 'free market' account, in which social class gets reduced to a matter of choice and style (Chapter 6.7).

So this chapter outlines the theoretical terms, questions and assumptions that inform this part of the book. The chapter following that deals with several methodological and empirical preliminaries, and then in the two chapters after that, I analyse the ways that youngsters stylised posh and Cockney at moments when questions of educational positioning and status were at issue (Chapter 8), and when the focus turned more to peer relationships (Chapter 9). All in all, the analysis draws on a corpus of about 50 episodes of posh and Cockney stylisation.

6.1   Class and situated interaction

'Class' has obviously been a massive topic in the humanities and social sciences, argued and analysed from a wide range of perspectives. But in terms of the empirical traditions and methods used to investigate class, Bradley usefully distinguishes between "those who study class structure and patterns of social mobility using highly sophisticated statistical techniques, and those who focus on class formation and consciousness employing historical or ethnographic approaches" (Bradley 1996:45; see also Ortner 1991:168–169 on research in the US). The second tradition is well-exemplified in the work of the British social historian E. P. Thompson, who insists on the central role of human agency, and on the ways in which men and women come to articulate a sense of collectivity in the struggle for resources in particular historical settings:[1]

> Class is a social and cultural formation … which cannot be defined abstractly … but only in terms of relationship with other classes … [and] in the medium of *time* – that is, action and reaction, change and conflict. When we speak of *a* class we are thinking of a very loosely defined body of people who share the same categories of interests, social experiences, traditions and value-system, who have a *disposition* to *behave* as a class, to define themselves in their actions and in their consciousness in relation to other groups of people in class ways … [I]n size and strength these groups are always on the ascendant or the wane, their consciousness of class identity is incandescent or scarcely visible, their institutions are aggressive or merely kept up out of habit; while in between there are those amorphous, ever-changing social groups amongst whom the line of class is constantly drawn and re-drawn with respect to their polarisation this way or that, and which fitfully become conscious of interests and identity of their own. Politics is often about exactly this – how will class happen, where will the line be drawn? And the drawing of [this line] is … the outcome of political and cultural skills. (1978:295–296)

Thompson's emphasis on agency, historically situated activity, and the drawing of lines will provide one important point of orientation for the analysis of class in interactional practice at Central High. Admittedly, at first glance, it looks as though it might be difficult reconciling large-scale social movements of the kind that Thompson addresses with the fleeting utterances of individuals in Class 9A, but Burawoy 1990 explains that 'class' can be examined at at least three different levels. The first and broadest focuses on epochal differences in class structures, comparing, for example, feudal and capitalist class structures, and the second addresses the development of class structures within capitalist societies, taking in more detailed complexities. The third and most fine-grained level of analysis "attempts a nuanced examination of the effects of location in a class structure on individual consciousness and action, [and requires attention to] the full range of complexities that structure the class interests of individuals in time and place" (1990:348). Burawoy's 'nuanced examination' of 'individual consciousness and action' amidst the 'complexities' of 'time and place' identifies a perspective where the stylisation of posh and Cockney can speak to the 'meaning' of social class, and Raymond Williams provides a well-developed vocabulary for exploring this.

Like Thompson, Williams objects to theories that reify class as a static, a-historical category (e.g. 1977:130), and he opens a window on social class as a subjectively experienced, lived reality, through the notions of 'practical consciousness' and 'hegemony'.

Social reputations, cultural conventions, aesthetic objects, philosophical ideas, linguistic forms, etc. can all form a part of a person's historically situated awareness, but in practical consciousness, this received knowledge mingles in incomplete, confused, and often inarticulate ways with the experience of our everyday lives. "[P]ractical consciousness", says Williams, "is always more than a handling of fixed forms and units. There is frequent tension between the received interpretation and practical experience ... [This] tension is often an unease, a stress, a displacement, a latency: the moment of conscious comparison not yet come, often not even coming" (1977:130). Turning to the significance of social class within practical consciousness, Williams identifies 'hegemony' as relations of domination and subordination absorbed in practical consciousness, in effect saturating

the whole process of living – not only ... political and economic activity, nor only ... manifest social activity, but ... the whole substance of lived identities and relationships, to such a depth that the pressures and limits of what can ultimately be seen as a specific economic, political and cultural system seem to most of us the pressures and limits of simple experience and common sense.   (1977:109)

Hegemony involves more than established ideology, manipulation or 'indoctrination'. Instead,

[i]t is a whole body of practices and expectations, over the whole of living: our senses and assignments of energy, our shaping perceptions of ourselves and our world. It is a lived system of meanings and values ... It ... constitutes a sense of reality for most people in the society, a sense of absolute because experienced reality beyond which it is very difficult for most members of the society to move, in most areas of their lives. It is, that is to say, in the strongest sense a 'culture', but a culture which has also to be seen as the lived dominance and subordination of particular classes.   (1977:109–110)

Prima facie, at least, 'practical consciousness' operates at the levels of human activity addressed in interactional sociolinguistics, linguistic pragmatics and micro-sociological accounts of interaction (Chapter 1.3; also e.g. Moerman 1988; Verschueren 1999), while 'hegemony' provides a framework for examining the ways in which class penetrates into the fine details of everyday practice. Williams repeatedly returns to Marx and Engels' idea that "language is practical consciousness" (1970:51; Williams 1977:30, 35, 37, 99), and so overall, when Bradley refers to "historical or ethnographic approaches" focusing on "class formation and consciousness" (1996), it looks as though there is scope for adding the 'interactional'.

But there is a problem. There may be a place within class analysis for the study of situated discourse, opening a window on the "emotive intimacies of class, which continue to shape individuals' everyday understandings, attitudes and actions" (Reay 1998:265), but hitherto, only 'class' has been considered in the "complex experiential chemistry of class, 'race' and gender" (Gilroy 1987:19). How can 'race', ethnicity, gender or indeed other dimensions of social stratification be brought into the analysis?

6.2   Class and other categories in situated interaction

So far, Thompson and Williams have pointed towards agency, historically situated activity, practical consciousness, and hegemony as potentially significant concepts for the analysis of social class in interaction. But to expand this frame of reference to accommodate the complex intersection of class with gender, ethnicity, generation and so forth, it is useful to refer back to Foucault (discussed in Chapter 2.5).

In some respects, Foucault's concern for the subjective dimensions of power resembles Williams' attention to hegemony. When Foucault says that "in thinking of the mechanisms of power, I am thinking ... of ... the point where power reaches into the very grain of individuals, touches their bodies and inserts itself into their actions and attitudes, their discourses, learning processes and everyday lives" (1980:39), there is some similarity to Williams' account of hegemony as "a saturation of the whole process of living ..., our senses and assignments of energy, our shaping perceptions of ourselves and our worlds" (1977:109). But as I indicated earlier, Foucault cautions against identifying domination and struggles over power too rapidly with specific interest groups or established dimensions of differentiation (such as gender, class, etc.). When people contest regimes of power, it is a mistake to jump to the conclusion that the institutionalised politics of class, gender, race, etc. are directly relevant, since in the first instance, actors may be motivated by a more elementary concern for freedom from the disciplinary techniques they feel subjected to. Their struggles, Foucault suggests,

are 'immediate' struggles for two reasons. In such struggles people criticise instances of power which are the closest to them, those which exercise their action on individuals. They do not look for the 'chief enemy', but for the immediate enemy. Nor do they expect to find a solution to their problem at a future date (that is, liberation, revolutions, end of class struggle) ... [T]hey are anarchistic struggles ... [T]he main objective of these struggles is not so much to attack 'such and such' an institution of power, or group, or elite, or class, but rather a technique, a form of power. (1982:211–212; also Williams 1977:108, 128; pp. 71–72 above)

Foucault makes it clear, then, that analysts need to be very careful in their political diagnoses, recognising that interaction can host struggles that it can be hard to describe within established political vocabularies of class, race, gender, etc. In fact, together Foucault and Williams invite us to draw a broad analytic distinction between

1. material conditions, ordinary experience, and everyday discourses, activities and practices – the 'primary realities' of
   practical activity which are experienced differently by different people in different times, places and networks; and
2. secondary or 'meta-level' representations: ideologies, images,
   and discourses *about* social groups, about the relations of

power between them, and about their different experiences of material conditions and practical activity.

This kind of distinction is a very old and well-established. It chimes with the distinction Williams makes between hegemony (working at 'level 1') on the one hand, and 'ideology' on the other ($\approx$2), and it resembles, for example, the classic Marxian distinction between 'social being' and 'social consciousness'.[2] But it also provides a way of separating 'class' from 'ethnicity', 'gender', 'race' etc., and it will serve as useful underpinning for the analyses that follow, so it is worth dwelling on in a little more detail.

Practical activity and secondary, meta-representations are intricately interwoven (Thompson 1978:3, 7, 18). Secondary representations are profoundly shaped by unevenly distributed material conditions and everyday experiences ($\approx$1), while at the same time, they play a major role in apprehending, interpreting, explaining, reproducing or changing material conditions and practical activity. The capacity of secondary representations to influence material conditions and practical activity provides much of the motivation for research (as well as many other kinds of expression) (Williams 1958:323; Bourdieu 1991:236), and any comment or statement *about* social groups and categories operates at both levels, being active *both* as an inevitably selective model of particular aspects of the social world, *and* as a historically positioned intervention, subject to a host of local and larger constraints and contingencies. The distinction is also quite helpful epistemologically. On the one hand, it avoids naïve empiricism – we can never apprehend the world independently of the cultural procedures and resources available to us as specific individuals in a particular historical period, and the fullness of everyday life and experience will always escape even our best attempts to portray it. At the same time, it resists relativism. There is a world independent of our reflection and imagining; research can vary in the success of its efforts to predict action and events, and/or in the success of its attempts to produce accounts which engage or resonate with the views and experience of other people who are also knowledgeable about the world being described;[3] and systematic inequalities in the distribution of hardship, pain and pleasure do not disappear just because people stop talking about them in the ways that they used to.

Lastly, the distinction helps to clarify the level at which it is reasonable to discuss 'class' separately from race, gender, ethnicity, generation and other dimensions of social stratification. When focusing on the primary realities of practical activity – the routine interaction of embodied individuals in real world tasks – singling out class as an influence distinct from gender, race and lots of other social categories is likely to be difficult. Embodied individuals can be construed in all sorts of different ways, and whenever analysts try to produce 'context-sensitive' accounts, they have to accept that whatever category–membership they are most interested in intersects in complicated and contingent ways with a range of other identities – discourse/interactional identities (joke-teller; questioner, invitee, etc.), institutional identities (student, father), and more 'transportable' identities (white–black, male–female, young–middle-aged) (see Zimmerman 1998). But at the level of secondary representations, there are clear differences between discourses *about* class, ethnicity, gender and generation, etc. – they have different histories and direct attention to different social processes and arenas.[4] Discourses about class and gender, for example, differ substantially in the kinds of solidarity and opposition they propose, and in the ways in which the inequalities they are associated with are described, challenged and defended. Indeed, to the extent that discourses about either class, gender, or ethnicity, have been given particular institutional emphasis within a set of practices, with the participants actively orienting to them in the course of their activity, analysts can be more confident when they attend to the identity in question that they are not simply imposing their own *a priori* intellectual interests on the processes (Williams 1977:108).

In fact, the distinction between practical activity and secondary representations is directly relevant to the exaggerated performances of posh and Cockney that constitute the main empirical interest in this part of the book, and so we should now turn to this.

6.3   Stylisation: secondary representations within practical activity

The exaggerated performances of posh and Cockney that I shall be examining all fall into the general category of 'stylisation' (see also Coupland 2001a). In Mikhail Bakhtin's classic discussion, stylisation involves "an artistic image of another's language" (1981:362), evoking the character associated with particular ways of acting or types of people, and as such, it belongs to the "level of secondary representations". But this secondary representation is often very closely tuned to practical activity, and it generates an intricate dialogue across these two levels. When someone switches into a stylised voice or exaggerated accent, there is a partial and momentary disengagement from the routine flow of unexceptional business, and the recipients are invited to use their broader under-standings of society to figure out exactly what 'image of another's language' this is actually supposed to be. At the same time, the recipients are also asked to figure out exactly what dimension of the practical-activity-on-hand the voice or accent might be relevant to – so as well as "What is this voice representing?" there is the question: "How is this voice relevant to the business-on-hand?" And on top of that, they are invited to provide an evaluation – "Is this representation any good? How does the performed image compare with your own sense of the language, people and events being modelled? And how well does it fit into what we're doing right now?" Overall, the stylised utterance constitutes a small, fleeting but foregrounded analysis, suggesting that the person, event or act that occasions the switch-of-voice can be classified and under-stood as the instance of the more general social type that the differ-ent voice evokes. This small piece of analysis is offered for public consumption, and the recipients can welcome, ignore or reject it in the interactional moves that immediately follow, celebrating or forgetting it in the activity after that. (See Chapter 8.5 for an elaboration.)

In the analytic separation, in the previous Section, of practical activity and secondary representations, there is obviously a risk of reifying processes like these, and so to underline the fluidity of the movement between what might loosely called 'activity' and 'ideol-ogy', it is worth citing Vološinov, an author who is closely identified with – often thought to be – Bakhtin, and who is a central figure in Williams' discussion of language (1977:21–44).

According to Vološinov, ideologies are the sets of signs, repre-sentations and evaluations that constitute consciousness, and these are subdivided into the two broad types. Behavioural ideologies are located in the immediate social situation, comprising "that atmosphere of unsystematised and unfixed inner and outer speech which endows every instance of behaviour and action and our every 'conscious' state with meaning" (1973:91). But despite their relatively unstable and unformalised character, behavioural ideologies are dynamically intertwined with established ones: "established ideological systems of social ethics, science, art, and religion are crystallisations of behavioural ideology, and these crystallisations, in turn, exert a powerful influence back on behavioural ideology, normally setting its tone" while also "draw[ing] sustenance from it" (1973:91).[5] He goes on:

We must distinguish several different strata in behavioural ideology ... The world of an experience may be narrow and dim; its social orientation may be haphazard and ephemeral and characteristic only for some adventitious and loose coalition of a small number of persons ... Such an experience will remain an isolated fact in the psychological life of the person exposed to it ... Experiences of that kind, experiences born of a momentary and accidental state of affairs, have, of course, no chance of further social impact or efficacy. The lowest, most fluid, and quickly changing stratum of behavioural ideology consists of experiences of that kind. To this stratum, consequently, belong all those vague and undeveloped experiences, thoughts and idle, accidental words that flash across our minds ... The upper strata of behavioural ideology, the ones directly linked with ideological systems, are more vital, more serious and bear a creative character. Compared to an established ideology, they are a great deal more mobile and sensitive: they convey changes in the socio-economic basis more quickly and more vividly. Here, precisely, is where those creative energies build up through whose agency partial or radical restructuring of ideological systems comes about. Newly emerging social forces find ideological expression and take shape first in these upper strata of behavioural ideology before they can succeed in dominating the arena of some organised, official ideology. (1973:92)

Vološinov's distinction between 'behavioural' and 'established ideologies' is broadly congruent with the distinction earlier between 'practical activity' and 'secondary representations', but here he usefully points to the fluidity with which signs and experiences move between – and beyond – these levels. Indeed, at first sight, it is likely to be somewhere in the 'upper strata of behavioural ideology' – more 'mobile and sensitive' than established ideology – that the stylisation of posh and Cockney in situated interaction might best be located, although it will be necessary to wait and see, of course, whether or not we can call this 'creative'.

In fact, I have reached a stage in the discussion where I can formulate the questions to guide investigation of the relationship between stylised-posh-and-Cockney on the one hand, and social class on the other.

6.4   Guiding questions for the analysis of stylised posh, Cockney and social class

An obvious preliminary step is to locate my informants in the 'objective' socio-economic class hierarchy:

i)   What kind of agents are they? What kinds of solidarity and opposition are they disposed towards? What struggles and negotiations over position do they engage in? Who's up, who's down, and what lines are they drawing, where, and in what kinds of activity? (Thompson).

My sample is, though, obviously very small and rather than focusing on "class structure and patterns of social mobility", my principal interest is in "class formation and consciousness" (Bradley 1996), studied "in the full range of complexities that structure the class interests of individuals in time and place" (Burawoy). With this in mind, analysis needs to focus on the articulation of 'class' in '(established) ideology', in 'hegemony', and in 'practical consciousness':

ii)   What currency do established discourses about social class have among the youngsters I observed? How do class discourses relate to discourses of ethnicity, race, gender and sexuality? Is it true that these young people have no access to "politicising scripts of class oppression" (Reay 1998)?

iii)   Are there signs of class hegemony? How far could we claim that class has been naturalised within these young people's common sense, influencing their "senses and assignments of energy, [their] shaping perceptions of [them]selves and [their] world"? (Williams)

This then leads us to the stylisations themselves:

iv)   How far and in what ways does the stylisation of posh and Cockney voices play a part in the dynamic relationship between explicit ideologies and taken-for-granted practices?

Where does it feature in the movement between 'behavioural'
and 'established ideologies'? (Vološinov)

v) What images and representations are evoked with exaggerated
posh and Cockney voices? How do they relate to the activity
on hand? How are they received?

vi) Do these voices seem to be politically engaged, and if so, what
kinds of politics do they involve? What are the (micro-)political
interests and identities at issue, and where do they seem to lead?

Of course these questions involve and generate others, and throughout Chapters 7, 8 and 9, the investigation will also need to be
mindful of Foucault and Williams' (rather ethnographic) strictures
about analysis that reduces the ambivalence and indeterminacies of
lived experience to "fixed forms" (Williams 1977:128, 130). But
before that, it is worth reviewing the treatment of class in sociolinguistics, in order to identify conceptual resources that can help to
answer these questions.

6.5 Sociolinguistic resources for the analysis of class and stylisation

The literature on language and social inequality is massive, reaching
far beyond what I could hope to review here. But for what follows,
there is research on four major empirical topics that I shall have
cause to refer to.

First, there is a tradition of urban dialectology and quantitative
(or 'variationist') sociolinguistics that focuses on *the distribution of
vernacular-to-standard language forms across social groups and
speech styles*. This work documents historical, social and geographic spread and change in a wide range of different linguistic
features, combining the analysis of phonology and grammar with
relatively standardised survey methods, and in classic work like
Labov 1972a and Trudgill 1974, social class is assessed in terms of
occupational status, education level, etc., and used as one of the
main independent variables (often alongside age and gender). In the
first instance, urban dialectology provides quite detailed descriptions of posh and Cockney as sound systems, and these will be a
useful resource in the identification and description of stylisation
throughout my analysis (see questions 6.4.iv–vi above, and

Chapter 7.4). Beyond that, at a more theoretical level, variationist researchers have repeatedly found that in class-stratified societies, society-wide speech variation is 'echoed' in the style variation of individuals – the patterns of accent difference that you can see when you compare class-groups-distributed-across-society-as-a-whole are mirrored (more weakly) within the speech repertoire of individuals, their speech becoming more like the speech of high-placed social groups as situations get more formal (Labov 1972a; Bell 1984). This has been described as the "classic sociolinguistic finding" (Finnegan and Biber 2001:241ff.), and it is impressive testimony to class reproduction, large-scale stratification being inscribed even into the apparently flexible conduct of individuals. Indeed, this finding has sometimes been linked to Bourdieu's notion of 'habitus', a pre-conscious disposition to hear and speak in class- and gender-specific ways inculcated into the individual through long-term experience of the purchase that their language resources provide in different kinds of setting (Bourdieu 1977, 1991:Part 1; Woolard 1985; Eckert 2000:13). This is potentially very relevant to my own interest in 'hegemony' as "the lived dominance and subordination of particular classes" written into the "whole body of practices and expectations" experienced by the individual (see question 6.4.iii above), and I shall turn to the methods of variationist sociolinguistics in the next chapter (7.3).

Second, there has been a great deal of work on *dominant ideologies of language*, using a range of different methods. Document and text analysis have examined the representation of different language varieties and types of speaker in education, the academy, literature, mass media, popular culture, and public life in general, both historically and contemporarily (e.g. Williams 1961:237–254; Milroy and Milroy 1985; Crowley 1989; Honey 1989, 1997; Corfield 1991; Fairclough 1992a; Kroskrity, Schieffelin and Woolard 1992; Cameron 1995; Mugglestone 1995; Silverstein 1996; Lippi-Green 1997; Agha 2003; Kroskrity 2004). There is research here on the rise (and decline) of posh accents as a British status symbol which will be very useful for discussion of explicit ideologies of language at Central High, for exploration of their relationship to stylisation, and for my attempts to place all this in a historical context (questions 6.4.ii and iv above). Elsewhere, there is also a substantial tradition of work that uses socio-psychological elicitation techniques to try to get close to the way that people feel about different accents (e.g. Giles and Powesland 1975; Ryan and Giles 1982). In this tradition, informants are asked to listen and respond to carefully selected recordings of language variation, the logic being that this "reveal[s their] more private reactions to the contrasting group than direct attitude questionaires do" (Lambert 1972:337; Labov 1972a), and these techniques repeatedly point to the workings of dominant ideology, establishing in very broad terms that whereas standard varieties strike listeners as intelligent, efficient, educated and so on, non-standard speech often sounds more trustworthy and sociable. This will be another useful reference point (relevant, for example, to question 6.4.v).

Third, *the production of inequality in institutional interaction* has been extensively studied in interactional sociolinguistics, using discourse analysis supported by ethnography. With varying degrees of detail, this work attends to situated interaction between people in unequal relations of institutional power, and it looks at the processes involved in judgements and decisions that have either an immediate or a cumulative impact on the subordinates' access to symbolic, cultural and material resources. This kind of 'gate-keeping' has been studied in a wide range of different sites – schools, workplaces, social services, legal and medical settings (cf. Bernstein 1971a; McDermott and Gospodinoff 1981; Erickson and Shultz 1982; Gumperz 1982, 1986; Sarangi and Slembrouck 1996; Sarangi and Roberts 1999). More generally, this tradition provides a valuable framework for looking closely at how social class emerges in the 'drawing of lines', and is "the outcome of political and cultural skills (Thompson, 1978, and question 6.4.i above).

Fourth – and often closely related to the third topic – there has been a great deal of work on *discourse in subordinate social groups*. In one strand of this work, there is an attempt to identify patterns of talk and interaction that are distinctive to particular communities, moving from there to an analysis of whether and how these patterns act, in one way or another, as a disadvantage when community members enter mainstream institutions (Bernstein 1971; Philips 1972; Gumperz, Jupp and Roberts 1979; Wells 1981; Heath 1983). In another strand, there is detailed attention to the contextual conditions and pragmatic processes involved when people code-switch between low and high, vernacular and standard, in- and out-group speech varieties, responding or initiating a change in the interactional situation or creating special metaphorical effects (e.g. Blom and Gumperz 1972; Auer 1998; Woolard 2004). A third strand focuses on "resistance or counter-hegemonic discourses [in] the expressive genres – songs, speeches, poems, conversations – of working class and minority speakers in core and peripheral capitalism" (Gal 1989:360; see also Mitchell-Kernan 1971; Abrahams 1976; Basso 1979; Hewitt 1986; Rampton 1995a; Pujolar 2001). Bauman's notion of (artful) performance is often central here, since "performances move the use of heterogeneous stylistic resources, context-sensitive meanings, and conflicting ideologies into a reflexive arena where they can be examined critically", by performers, audiences and analysts (Bauman and Briggs 1990:60). In what follows, the research on code-switching provides essential tools for analysis of the pragmatic processes involved in stylisation (see 6.4.v above), and questions about style, critique and resistance will also feature prominently (as indeed they already have in the analysis of improvised *Deutsch* (Chapters 4 and 5).

This overview suggests, then, that there is a great deal of sociolinguistic research on domination and inequality that is potentially relevant to the questions guiding my analysis of posh and Cockney stylisation. Admittedly, there are some substantial differences within this literature. Perhaps most notably

a) a lot of this work focuses on ethnicity and race rather than class, reflecting larger differences between the US and the UK and between anthropology and sociology,[6] and

b) a number of the researchers that I have cited have been separated by heated political argument over whether school failure was best interpreted as an indication of 'deficit', 'difference' or 'domination' (see Chapter 1.2, Table 1.2).[7]

But these are not insuperable obstacles to the present enterprise.

First, in emphasising the distinction between practical activity and secondary representation in Chapter 6.3, I articulated an interest in experiences of division, domination and inequality *prior* to their identification with the politics of 'class', 'race' or 'gender', and indeed my definition of stylisation focuses on one of the ways in which participants themselves come, for example, to classify such experiences in 'class' rather than 'race' terms (and in fact, in

Chapter 8, participants can be seen giving both class and race interpretations to some of the *same* processes). So the fact that some of
the sociolinguistic research takes race or gender rather than class as
its principal focus does not make it irrelevant – what counts is the
attention to processes of differentiation that produce inequality
prior to or regardless of its labelling.

Second, the splits between 'deficit', 'difference' and 'domination'
lose a lot of their force at the interface of modernity and late
modernity. In previous Chapters – especially 1.2 and 4.1 – I have
dwelt at some length on the ways in which sociolinguistics has built
links to late modern thinking, and for the deficit, difference and
domination debates, social constructionism has been particularly
consequential. As Gumperz notes, the "view that human interaction
[is] constitutive of social reality" throws into question "[t]he
assumption that speech communities, defined as functionally integrated social systems with shared norms of evaluation, can actually
be isolated" (1982:26), and this undercuts the earlier politics
because the arguments about deficit, difference and domination
neglected the ways in which historical and institutional power relations could be neutralised or reconfigured in interaction, assuming
instead that difference, power and subordination derived from participants' membership of established socio-cultural blocs. In the
characterisation offered in Chapter 1, these three frames have now
been challenged by a 'discourse' perspective, which accepts the role
that larger social, economic and political systems play in structuring
dominant–subordinate, majority–minority relations, but argues that
their impact on everyday experience can't be easily predicted.
Instead, the emphasis is on looking closely at how people make
sense of inequality and difference in their local situations, and at
how they interpret them in the context of a range of social relationships (gender, class, region, generation, etc.). This perspective is
wary of seeing culture and language exclusively *either* as an elite
canon, *or* as a set of static class/ethnic/gender essences *or* as a simple
reflection of economic and political processes; it takes the view that
the reality of people's circumstances is actively shaped by the ways
in which they interpret and respond to them; and in line with this, it
lays a good deal of emphasis on the cultural politics of imagery and
representation. In fact, this kind of 'discourse' view is now widely
accepted in sociolinguistics,[8] and can be found in research on the

production-of-inequality-in-institutional-encounters, in research on code-switching, and in research on counter-hegemonic-discourses-among-subordinate-social-groups. Indeed, recent linguistic anthropological work on dominant-ideologies-of-language also moves beyond just the description of linguistic stereotypes and prejudice to a more subtle and encompassing account of the (meta-)pragmatic processes involved in the interpretation and reproduction of the meta-level representations of different languages and ways of speaking (see e.g. Hill 1995; Agha 2003). All this lends support to the angle on class being proposed in this chapter. There may not be a lot of other sociolinguistic work on the interactional processes associated with social class *per se*, but with this kind of broad ontological agreement, rather than just borrowing from research on language and other kinds of inequality, it should be possible to offer something back. Admittedly, the perspective here is somewhat at odds with operating assumptions in the sociolinguistic tradition that Hymes (1996:73) says is most closely associated with the study of language and class – the quantitative/variationist tradition of urban dialectology associated with Labov – but even here, practice theory is making inroads (Eckert 2000).[9]

In this section, then, I have pointed to parts of the sociolinguistics literature that are most relevant to my own analysis of stylisation and social class, in spite of apparent differences between them. But there is one more potentially difficult issue that merits further discussion in this chapter.

6.6   Class trivialised with a late modern sociolinguistics?

For the most part, I have described the philosophical and methodological shifts associated with the modernity/postmodernity interface as an enrichment, making it much easier to understand the agency involved in processes of class differentiation, the intersection of class with other kinds of stratification, and the subtleties of how class works within situated activity in particular communities of practice. Indeed on these grounds, I might actually hope to revitalise class as a topic for sociolinguistics.[10] But it is important not to be too sanguine about this, since there is one way in which the perspectives associated with late modernity might actually be rather antipathetic to any serious treatment of class.

In Williams' account of hegemony, "relations of domination and subordination ... [saturate] the whole substance of lived identities and relationships, to such a depth that the pressures and limits of what can ultimately be seen as a specific economic, political and cultural system seem to most of us the pressures and limits of simple experience and commonsense" (1977:109). And on a slightly different tack inside sociolinguistics, Hymes criticises difference-oriented research on race and class in the US for maintaining that "as far as ability was concerned, class had no cost" (1996:187–188). For both authors, class reaches deep, exacting a heavy and enduring toll on those in subordinate positions (see also Skeggs 1997:4).

This is not a view that rests particularly easy amidst the developments associated with postmodernity. In Jameson's critical account of it, the post-modern view involves an 'emptying out' of contemporary theory, and a repudiation of 'depth models' of social, cultural and psychic life. Among these 'depth models', Jameson identifies

the great modernist thematics of alienation, anomie, solitude ... and the whole metaphysics of the inside and the outside, of the wordless pain within the [individual] ... the Freudian model of latent and manifest, or of repression ... the existential model of authenticity and inauthenticity.

"What replaces these various depth models", he says, "is for the most part a conception of practices, discourses and textual play" (1984:61–62). This is the turn to 'discourse' that sociolinguists have found so exciting, promising them a position in the centre of the humanities and social sciences (Rampton 1997; Coupland, Sarangi and Candlin 2001; Duranti 2003:331–332), and the same 'emptying out' can perhaps be seen in recurrent sociolinguistic talk of 'multiple identities', which seems to portray "a shifting sense of depthless selves – a continual 'cognitive mapping' rather than a deep emotional attachment to a few fixed points" (Billig 1995:135 [on another topic]). In fact, I have pointed to comparable developments in Chapter 1.2 and Chapter 6.5 above. Now, for example, 'community' is generally seen either as a strategic discursive projection, proposing lines of affiliation and exclusion at moments of competing interest, or it is seen as the outcome of ongoing interactional negotiation. The earlier modernist view that speakers were shaped by their early socialisation is now likely to be treated with suspicion as the essentialist legacy of the 'linguistics of community' (see e.g. Rampton

2001a). At several points in this book, I have cited the work of McDermott and his collaborators with considerable approval, but he and Varenne are particularly forceful in their objection to analyses that move from cultural description to claims about 'psychological constitution', insisting indeed that

[t]he greater our concern with individuals, the greater must be our efforts to document carefully the social conditions in which they must always express themselves. We must look away from individuals to preserve them. (Varenne and McDermott 1998:145)

Sociolinguistics (and linguistic anthropology) may be defined by their expert analyses of "practices, discourses and textual play", but over-enthusiasm about these threatens to squeeze out the concerns of Williams and Hymes, and could easily end up trivialising social class, neglecting its toll on individuals, lending support, indeed, to market ideologies which treat class position as a matter of individual will, effort and enterprise.[11]

   In fact, with the particular focus of the analyses that follows – the stylisation of posh and Cockney – there is an even greater risk of late modern sociolinguistic analysis becoming a praise-poem for a "post-modern psyche ... at home playing with the free market of identities" (Billig 1995:134). As I have said, stylisation involves "the image of another's language", or what Coupland describes as "strategic inauthenticity", and as such, it looks as though it could tune rather well with the unreality of simulations and floating images that are often said to characterise postmodernity. Jameson, for example, suggests that in post-modernism, pastiche takes over from parody:

the advanced capitalist countries today are now a field of stylistic and discursive heterogeneity without a norm ... Pastiche is, like parody, the imitation of a peculiar mask ... but it is a neutral practice of such mimicry, without any of parody's ulterior motives, amputated of the satiric impulse, devoid of laughter and of any conviction that alongside the abnormal tongue you have momentarily borrowed, some healthy linguistic normality still exists. Pastiche is thus blank parody. (Jameson 1984:65)

Which will come closest to the stylisations of posh and Cockney – parody grounded in moral and political criticism of the oppressive distortions of class, or just pastiche, pleasure in the play of voices? And what will the answers say about contemporary class consciousness?

These are central issues in Chapters 8 and 9, but before focusing intensively on stylisation itself, there are a number of preliminary issues that need to be addressed. Where should the speakers I am studying be placed within more traditional, 'objective' measures of social stratification? How did they treat social class as an issue in explicit discussion, outside stylisation? How far did class impact on their non-stylised, routine speech? How indeed is stylisation to be identified, distinguished from normal variability? These are questions I shall address in the next chapter, where I shall also touch once more on the pastiche issue, pointing to episodes of Cockney stylisation where class does seem largely irrelevant.

Notes

1. Thompson is also highly critical of the way in which 'class' is often reified: "No historical category has been more misunderstood, tormented, transfixed, and de-historicised than the category of social class; a self-defining historical formation, which men and women make out of their own experience of struggle, has been reduced to a static category, or an effect of an ulterior structure, of which men are not the makers but the vectors" (1978:46).
2. See Marx and Engels 1970:47; Goffman 1974; Thompson 1978:18; Stedman-Jones 1983; Bourdieu 1991:Ch 11; Ortner 1991:170; Bradley 1996:7.
3. Overall, this position on research can be summarised as a combination of ontological realism (a belief in 'primary realities' beyond the researcher's imagining) with epistemological interpretivism (recognition that we are only working with 'secondary representations') – see Frazer and Lacey 1993: Chapter 6 and Cameron et al. 1992: Chapter 1.
4. Bradley recognises their inseparability in concrete social relationships, but suggests that they have different 'existential locations' and can be distinguished analytically as follows: "Class is a social category which refers to the lived relationships surrounding social arrangements of production, exchange, distribution and consumption ... Gender is a social category which refers to lived relationships between women and men; gender relations are those by means of which sexual divisions and definitions of masculinity and feminity are constructed, organised and maintained ... 'Race' and ethnicity are social categories used to explain a highly complex set of territorial relationships; these involve conquests of some territorial groups by others, the historical development of nation states, and associated migrations of people around the globe ... Age as a dimension of inequality relates to social categories derived from the organisation of the life course and lived relationships between people socially located as being in different age-groups" (1996:19–20).

5. Vološinov's 'behavioural ideology' resembles Williams' 'practical con-sciousness' ("the relatively mixed, confused, incomplete consciousness of actual [people] in [any] period or society" (1977:109)), and 'established ideology' covers the same ground as 'ideology' for Williams ("a relatively formal and articulated system of meanings, values and beliefs" (1977:108)). Both are concerned with the interaction between these two levels (cf. Williams 1977:130), though as Gardiner notes (1992:182–187), Vološinov's terms do not foreground the questions of power and domination in the same way as Williams' 'hegemony.'

6. As a number of commentators have noted, in the US "class ... is rarely spoken in its own right. Rather it is represented through other categories of social difference: gender, ethnicity, race, and so forth" (Ortner 1991:164; Bradley 1996:75; Urciuoli 1996; L. Milroy 1999:192ff.). In addition, in the study of education in North America, anthropology has been much more influential than it has been in the UK, where instead, sociology has played a more important role. As a result,

> [f]or the (American) anthropologist the classroom is the site of cultural differ-ences, often ethnic in origin, and the teacher an agent of cultural imposition. For the (British) sociologist the frame of reference is a class-based social structure, in which teachers and pupils alike are subject to the everyday disciplines of work.   (Delamont and Atkinson 1995:34)

US anthropology's attention to ethnicity and home culture allows a theoretical separation of students' practices-and-dispositions from the processes of stratification they encounter at school, and this creates the prospect of eradicating inequality by closing the gap between school and ethnic culture, either making schools more hospitable to cultural differ-ence, or tuning home culture more towards education. Class analyses of education are more pessimistic. Social and cultural identities are defined *within* the central processes of social stratification, not outside. Rather than being overcome by cultural bridge-building, discrimination and inequality are seen as intrinsic to schooling, and there is the stark possibility that educational failure represents the logical destiny of cul-tural and linguistic dispositions shaped in subordination (see Hymes 1996:187–188 on this difference in perspective).

7. Among the authors cited in this Section, Bernstein, for example, was widely accused of being a 'deficit' theorist, counterposed to Labov's emphasis on 'difference' (see Atkinson 1985: Chapter 6), while McDermott and Gospodinoff 1981 criticised Heath for over-emphasising home socialisation in the analysis of educational inequality ('difference'), neglecting the influence of systemic pressures in situated classroom interaction (also Varenne and McDermott 1998: Chapter 7).

8. This can be seen in the fact that one of its most coherent formulations – Bourdieu's 'practice theory' – has, as Hymes notes (1996:188), become something of a canonical reference point in sociolinguistics/linguistic anthropology (Bourdieu 1977, 1991; Woolard 1985; Gal 1989; Heller

1989; Irvine 1989; Eckert and McConnell-Ginet 1992; Urciuoli 1996; Hanks 1996; Duranti 1997; Kroskrity 2004).

9. A discussion of social class in variationist sociolinguistics can be found at http://www.cambridge.org/0521812631.

10. During the 1990s, sociolinguists who were interested in British education moved away from survey methods to ethnography, but in doing so, they drew their inspiration from the ethnography of communication in North America, with its anthropological roots and preoccupation with ethnicity, rather than from the more class-focused, sociological ethnographies produced in Britain in the 1970s and 80s (see Note 6 above; also Chapter 2.7; Rampton et al. 1997:229, 231, 2002). In consequence, social class has been somewhat neglected in this recent British work in sociolinguistics.

11. Indeed, according to Gee et al. 1996:65 et passim, the notion of 'communities of practice' has currency in 'fast capitalist' management theory.

Language and class II: empirical preliminaries

As we saw in the last Chapter, the notion of 'class' can be used to embrace a huge range of cultural and material processes, involving social differentiation in "family background, main source of income, place of residence, cultural tastes ... political affiliations etc" (Abercrombie and Warde et al. 2000:145–146; Chapter 6.1 above). My main concern is with 'class formation and consciousness', expressed in the stylised performance of posh and Cockney accents, but to get a better idea of what stylisation can and can't tell us about class consciousness, it is important to look at class through other 'windows' as well, and that is the purpose of the present chapter. More specifically, it addresses the first three questions identified in Chapter 6.4:

(i)   What kind of agents are the individuals and groups engaged in stylisation? What kinds of solidarity and opposition are they disposed towards? What struggles and negotiations over position do they engage in? Who's up, who's down, and what lines are they drawing, where, and in what kinds of activity?

(ii) What currency do established discourses about social class have among these youngsters? How do class discourses relate to discourses of ethnicity, race, gender and sexuality? Is it true that these young people have no access to "politicising scripts of class oppression"?

(iii) Are there signs of class hegemony? How far could we claim that class has been naturalised within these young people's common sense, influencing their "senses and assignments of energy, [their] shaping perceptions of [them]selves and [their] world"?

Although a fuller account of the 'drawing of lines' in particular kinds of activity will need to wait until Chapters 8 and 9, I start on the first set of questions (i) with a sketch of the backgrounds, aspirations and school trajectories of my four focal informants (Chapter 7.1), and I then move to the second set (ii) by considering these youngsters' exposure and involvement in collectivist discourses of class and social stratification (relying largely on some evidence from lessons – Chapter 7.2). To engage with the third set of questions (iii), I turn to variationist sociolinguistics to see whether class-related speech differences at a societal level are 'echoed' in the talk of my informants as they move between more and less formal situations, using this as one sign of hegemony (or 'classed habitus') (Chapter 7.3; also Chapter 6.5 above). After that, I turn to two essential methodological preliminaries. First, if my informants shift their accents between posh and Cockney in routine, relatively unself-conscious practice, how do we actually distinguish stylised performance, telling it apart from normal variability? Second, once we have established how to distinguish stylised from ordinary speech, how do we know that social class is actually relevant? After all, these youngsters lived in London, encountered lots of different kinds of Londoners every day, and so it is logically quite conceivable that specific dialect performances could be intended to conjure the image of particular people either as individuals or as inhabitants of a particular region rather than emblems of any more general class type. These last two issues are covered in Chapters 7.4 and 7.5.

7.1   Focal informants and their backgrounds, aspirations and status

What places did my informants occupy within the dominant hierarchies of value that feed into conventional assessments of 'class position'?

As the discussion of demographic, descriptive and historical indicators in Chapter 2.1 showed, their school was rather poorly placed in a highly stratified education system. The parents tended to be less well off, their children usually left the school with relatively weak employment credentials, and in situations of this kind, educational commentators have underlined the importance of social class, "whatever the pupils' gender or ethnic origin" (Gillborn and Gipps

1996:17). At the same time, though, it was also quite clear that the school was affected by processes associated with ethnicity and globalisation, and so it is highly unlikely that 'class' alone provides an analytic vocabulary adequate to this scene.

Among the four focal informants themselves, the backgrounds were varied: ethnically Caribbean and African in Ninnette's case, Bengali in Hanif's, and white Anglo in Joanne and Simon's. Three of them lived with their mothers, apart from their fathers all or most of the time (Joanne was the exception). Two of them – Hanif and Joanne – were entitled to free school meals (a low income indicator). Ninnette's mother worked in domestic service, Hanif's was a part-time dinner supervisor, and Joanne's was a housewife while her dad was a self-employed tradesman. Ninnette had siblings abroad, Joanne had an unemployed sister and a brother at school, Simon's sister was doing a craft course, and Hanif had older brothers and sisters, some of whom were starting on professional careers.

These youngsters were only thirteen or fourteen years old, and varied in how clear they were about kind of work they wanted to be doing in ten years time. Hanif wanted to go to university and become an airline pilot, but Ninnette said she didn't know, and then ran through a range of possibilities – a vet, a teacher, a business woman (though she didn't take a business studies option). Simon thought he might do a photography course or become an actor, and Joanne, who didn't want to have children till she was 30, said she wouldn't mind working in nursery, being an air-hostess (for the travel), or joining the police. But although these youngsters were not generally very clear about the jobs they hoped for, they could be quite articulate in their images of lives to either avoid or aim for. In pair-work during drama class in which they'd been asked to prepare a scene on the theme of unwanted children, Joanne set the context – "I've got a really bad home life". Ninnette responded by rattling off the parody of a social worker:

I am considerably richer than you ((both girls laugh)).
Right now, your dad beats your face up, your mum chucks
drugs in your mouth, and you are pregnant. How did you
become pregnant – on your own, eh? You had sex with a
tramp, so what are we going – so what are we going to do
about this? I think you better have an abortion ((simpli-
fied transcription. Blex 53)). (Compare Skeggs 1997:3)

Conversely, according to Hanif (in a lunchtime conversation with me):

```
I can't forget my education, that's one thing. My brother
says "yes you've got to enjoy yourself otherwise you're
gonna have a sad life, aren't you", but then he also says
"you've got study to prevent yourself from having a sad life
and a life that doesn't lead to anything," if you know what I
mean. Basically education is the key, isn't it. I want to be
something when I grow up, so I can support myself and my
family, you might be thinking "oh a bit too young to think
about that," but thinking in the future is actually a good
thing to do. ((simplified transcription))
```

In terms of their positioning in educational hierarchies of effort and achievement, these youngsters occupied different places in the tutor group, with Joanne the weakest performer and Hanif the strongest.[1] Joanne attended individual special needs lessons to help with her reading and writing, and she felt the stigma of this very vividly, looking towards Ninnette for support. In the audio-recordings on one occasion in break, for example, she asked Ninnette to come up to the learning support classroom 5 minutes before the bell because she wanted to get into the classroom before everyone else saw her, and on another, Ninnette challenged another girl on her behalf: "and what if she was in learning support ... you got a problem with that?". Joanne was reputed by staff to be relatively alienated from the school, and was prepared to be emphatic in her disagreement with teachers (see Extracts 2.23 and 2.25). Ninnette did better than Joanne, but she was not enthusiastic about school either, and was considering moving to another one. For example, in an interview with Zainab, a keen student who was talking about doing homework in the lunchbreak, Ninnette remarked: "my God, we're completely different ((laughs)), I mess about and you just do work", and as we have already heard on the radio-microphone recordings, she and Joanne spent a large amount of their time in lessons engaged in other matters. Simon was sometimes derogatorily reminded by his peers that he had received special support for literacy when he first arrived at the school, and though this was no longer necessary, he tended to do well only in art and drama. On several occasions he called himself the class clown and was happy to speak up in class, although of the four informants here, he was generally rated by teachers as making least effort. Hanif, in contrast, was identified by teachers as one of the stars of the class, as a boffin/nerd by his peers, and indeed Ninnette complained about Hanif often getting preferential treatment. But Hanif attached a lot of importance to friendship, and was aware that there was a potentially difficult relationship between friendship and success – one of his oldest friends, Mansur, was renowned for his ambition to be a judge, but he had now started to 'bunk off' quite regularly from school.

The account in this section, then, helps us to place these youngsters *individually* in schemes of value relevant to social class (income, occupation, aspiration, school success). But what about social class as a *collective* issue related to large-scale inequalities grounded in politics and history? How did these youngsters relate to class as an explicit topic, as an '-ism' loosely parallel to 'racism' and 'sexism'.

7.2   Articulated views and opinions about class

As mentioned in Chapter 2.1, the teachers I observed were committed to talking openly with their students about society as they saw it, and social class sometimes emerged as a spontaneous topic in what the teachers said. I have already quoted Mr Alcott talking to the tutor group during their tutorial period about an incident the previous day in which there had been some conflict in the school between some white girls and some girls of Bengali descent (none of them in Class 9A). There was a possibility that racism had been involved, and Mr Alcott had said that he thought that "talking about racism is essential to your education". In fact just before that, he had referred them to their Humanities lessons and located racism in a larger historical context of economic exploitation:

Extract 7.1 (42/165)
Tutorial period, the day after a potentially racist incident.

```
MR A   you know what poison racism is, and you're doing
       you're still doing work in Humanities on slavery (.)
       and you know why racism began in this country (.)
       very simple reason? (.)
BOY    money
MR A   yeh
ANON   power
```

```
MR A   yeh quite simple
       money, greed, power and all this
       because if you want
       to have people as slaves
       you've got to show (.)
       got to think (.)
       that they're different from you from you
       and one way to do this
       a very kind of clever way to do this
       is
       to be
       racist
```

But the links between race and relations of material production were not pursued, and generally speaking, the tutor group seemed quicker to engage with questions of race, ethnicity, gender and sexuality than social class. During revision of the Humanities unit on slavery, Mr Alcott asked the class to work in groups, assessing which factors they thought had contributed most to the abolition of slavery: "the white middle class, the white working class, black people's actions, or economics". After they had discussed it, each group reported back, and the conclusions of each were tabulated on the black board. The first group proposed the "white working class" – a declaration which met with silence from the rest of the class – but then the next six declared "black people's action", each announcement being greeted with cheers and applause. The result was, in Mr Alcott's phrase, a landslide, and in this context anyway, pupils' alignment with 'the working class' was relatively muted.

Issues of wealth, privilege and opportunity, unrelated to ethnicity and 'race', also arose in other settings, as in the following episode. During a tutor period on Monday at the start of the day before assembly, Mr Alcott had started out reminding the class about the stationery that they needed for the Standardised Assessment Tests (SATs) that they'd be taking over the next two weeks. Discussion turned to the exam timetable, and a question was raised about whether there was an exam on the second Wednesday. Mr Alcott responded:

Extract 7.2 (47: 270)
Tutor period at the start of the day

```
1   MR A   AS FAR AS I KNOW EVERYBODY
2          SHSH (.)
```

```
3         EVERY KID WHO COMES TO SCHOOL ON THAT DAY (        )
4         EVERY YEAR NINE KID IN BRITAIN who's not at a
                                        po-posh
5           private schoo:l who comes to school on that day
                                        does the SATs
6         (.) if you don't want to do the SATs
7         well you- you com- come you can stay at home
8         or you go to a private school
9         all right
```

He went on to tell them that it wasn't SATs but their GCSE school-leaving exams later on that they needed to worry about, and the discussion then turned to the purpose of the SATs. One of the boys mentioned "school league tables", and Mr Alcott started to elaborate:

Extract 7.3 (Blex 73)

Monday morning tutor period, at the start of the SATs fortnight (and close to the 1997 General Election [see line 46]). Joanne is wearing the radio-microphone, and the parts of the overlapping side-conversation between her and Ninnette that relate to the topic being discussed by the class as a whole are indented. (In lines 52ff., 'Comprehensives' are non-selective schools, funded by the state and compelled to follow the National Curriculum. Grammar schools receive state funding but are selective. Private schools are selective, they don't receive state funds (directly), and they don't have to follow the National Curriculum. John Major [line 94] was Prime Minister at the time, and leader of the Conservative Party)

```
30  MR A      at the end of the SATs test,
31            the government will turn round and say
32            (.) oh look this school did well and this
                                        school- (.)
33            ((addressing a girl judged to be acting
              out of line:))
34            I'm SORRY (.) MAZAR (.)
35  JOHN?     get out
36  MR A      d'you mind (.)
37            ((returning to the main topic:))
              so that the government can say (.) this
                                        school did well
38            this school didn't do well
39            and so somebody else can say (.)
40  JOHN      let's close the school down
41  SEVERAL   ((loud laughter))
42  MR A      WELL possibly
```

```
43              the thing is of cou:rse
44              and- I want to remind you of /this
45    RAFIQ     ((chantlike rise at the end:))
46              Labour's coming /to power
47    MR A      well maybe
48              (but that's        )
49              look- the thing is (.)
50              which kinds- which kinds of school
51              >I'm not saying which kind of kid<
52              but which ki:nds of school do well in this
53              from your knowledge /of
54    HANIF     COMPREHE/NSIVE
55    BOY       private
56    HANIF     Comprehensive
57    MR A      well to some extent private schools maybe=
58    HANIF     ((loudly:)) comprehensive
59    MR A      =ALTHOUGH THEY DON'T HAVE TO DO SATs
60              (      ) You know (      )
61              it's not-
62              because they don't do the national
                                   curriculum=
63    HANIF     comprehensives
64    MR A      =well I think /comprehensive schools
65    BOY       grammar
66    BOY       (                  )
67    MR A      lemme put it this way (.)
68              and I hate- I hate to say this
69              because I don't want you to think oh my god (.)
70              this means I'm a failure
71              ((turning to address a member of the
                class:)) ((name))
72              please listen
73              (       ) including ( ((?name))    )
74              will you please listen (1.0)
75              ((returning to topic:)) IN GENERAL (.) and
                                   so I don't mean YOU
76              I mean in: general: (.) I'm not talking about
                                                   you (.)
77              in general (.) schools (.) where kids (.)
                                   have got parents
78              (.) who are wealthy (.) who are educated (.)
79              who have er you know got- got- erm: good
                                   jobs etcetera
80              TEND (.) to do better in exams (which is     )
81    JOHN      (I thought it /was people        )
82    MR A      NOW- NOW- NOW- I SORT OF STRESSED 100 TIMES (.)
```

```
83              that doesn't mean (.) that I'm saying
84              oh yeh well you know your parents can't
85              you know
86              they're not- doctors and engineers
87              (>so there's nothing you do about it<)
88              I'm not saying that
89              okay (.)
90              there are lots of teachers in this school for
                                                    instance
91              (.) come from poor families did very well
92              no problem (.)
93              ok:ay
94              even John Major his d/ad used to make garden
                                                        gnomes
95   HANIF      /yeh
96   OTHERS     ((laughs))
97                  NINNETTE:  ((tuning into the discussion))
                                (      people )
98                              (    ) rich and wealthy
99   MR A       and he's the prime minister
101  MR A       I'm not saying /(how      )
102                 NINNETTE:  and (.) erm (.) a good job
103                            and everything
104  MR A       I'm not saying you should /admire John Major
105  BOYS       /((laughs))
106                 NINNETTE:  the children tend
107                            to do better in exams
108  MR A       so
109  BOY        (was he doing   /      )
110  MR A       WELL-
111  BOY        ((loud /laugh))
112  MR A       SHUSH (.) but IN GENERAL (.) IN GENERAL
113  JOHN       (lost   / et )
114  MR A       shsh (.) ON AVERAGE and we're talking /about
115  ANONS      ((noise levels rise))
116  MR A       (Zahida sh/ush)
117                 NINNETTE:  look (.) Joanne (well I
118                            can't) but I would like
119                            to know what you (got   )
120  MR A       THOSE OF YOU INCLUDING RAFIQ WHOSE jacket
                should be now off
121                 JOANNE:    I don't think-
122  MR A       THOSE OF YOU WHO ARE DOING SOCIOLOGY NEXT
                                                    YEAR=
123  HANIF      Yeh
124  MR A       =WILL HAVE A CH/ANCE TO DISCUSS THIS
```

```
125            JOANNE:      I don't see anyone rich
126                         or anything
127                         and (they'll all) do well
128  SEVERAL   / (              )
129  MR A      and I'm very (/     )
130  BOY       (       told you)
131  MR A      Rafiq take your/ (           )
132            JOANNE:      everyone's average
133  MR A      you'll have chance to discuss this and the
                                                   reasons
134            / (               )
135            NINNETTE:      I'm a bit over average
136                           ((laughs for a bit))
137  MR A      ANOTHER THING THAT YOU NEED TO /KNOW
138            ((Other kids /talking a bit))
139  MR A      SHUSH PLEASE SHUSH (.)
140            ((when the class is silent:))
141            another thing that you need /to know=
142            JOANNE:      no you're NOT (.)
143  MR A      =I'm sorry if I'm boring /you=
144            JOANNE:    you're not rich
145  MR A      =Ninnette
146  MASUD     (they        /        )
147            NINNETTE:      I'm not rich
148                           but I'm a bit
149                           /over average
150  MR A      EH! (.) Shsh
151            JOANNE:      (wanker)
152  BOYS      ((giggle))
153            NINNETTE:    (           )
154  MR A      shush (1.5) WILL YOU PLEASE LI:STE:N
155            (3.5) ((some boys quietly talk)) sh
156            another thing that you need to know is that-
157            in this country (.) and it's shameful
158            I know about it but I'm reminded /a:gain
159            JOANNE:      (   ((sings))    )
160            NINNETTE:    (           )
161  MR A      (.) on the head-
162            front page of my newspaper (.)
```

After this, Mr Alcott started to talk about a table on child poverty in Europe printed in the newspaper, pointing out that whereas in Denmark, 5% of children lived in poor households, the figure for Britain was 32%, the worst in Europe. Some of the pupils were evidently interested and engaged in this, but the discussion was interrupted by a Tannoy announcement, ending in an instruction to all Year Nines to make their way down to assembly. Joanne and Ninnette did not participate in the child poverty discussion, though they continued to talk quietly to each other. Joanne mentioned someone she knew who was ``fucking ri:ch'', with a big house which she described, and their conversation moved on to some consequential furniture changes in her own house.

This is a complex episode. It displays a number of features of the classroom talk described in Chapter 2, and in it, Mr Alcott is in a difficult position, talking about systemic social inequality from a position of dominance within one of the institutions that produces it. The structural tension between message and position, between emancipatory commitments and coercive practices, deserves much fuller exploration, but the present context, three aspects are worth noting.

First, in spite of – or maybe because of? – its potentially sensitive relevance to them, quite a number of the students are inattentive, and Mr Alcott periodically interrupts what he wants to say in order to quieten the class down (e.g. lines 112, 114) and to get particular individuals to listen or behave (lines 33, 71–74, 116, 145). He is continuously distracted from the larger political and educational topic by the local exigencies of classroom order (including the dress code – lines 120 and 131), as well as by the institutional constraints of the time (the Tannoy). The effect is to make him feel that for at least some of the class, what he no doubt intended as sympathetic social consciousness-raising has now turned into a tedious teacher's lecture – ``I'm sorry if I'm boring you'' (line 143).

Some of the students seem actively interested throughout – to the point of sometimes supporting Mr Alcott's efforts to bring others into line (lines 33–35) and collaboratively completing his utterances (lines 39–40). As in a great many other lessons, Hanif features prominently, but just here, it is worth noting the answer that he gives with some force and insistence to Mr Alcott's question ``which kinds of school do well in [SATs]'' (lines 52, 54, 56, 58). Of the three kinds of school mentioned in response, Hanif proposes the least elite and least selective – 'comprehensives' (like Central High) normally have an open intake, while entry to 'grammar' and private school generally involves selection tests and, with the latter, an ability to pay. Hanif's answer, then, seems unaware of the links between income/

social class and educational achievement, and in fact it provides
Mr Alcott with the cue for a more direct exposition of the links
between social background and exam success (lines 63ff.).

Third, it is also worth noting the responses of Joanne and
Ninnette. Joanne is wearing the radio-microphone, and for simplicity of presentation, the transcript does not include most of the *sub
rosa* conversation that goes on between the two of them in the period
leading up to line 97 of Extract 7.3. But Ninnette has obviously been
keeping one ear to the talk on the main floor of the classroom, and
picks up on what Mr Alcott has been saying about wealth and school
success, relaying it into her conversation with Joanne:

```
"(        ) people ( ) rich and wealthy and get a good
job and everything the children tend to do better in
exams"  (lines 97, 98, 102, 103, 106, 107).
```

In lines 117–119, there is a turn that is hard to connect to this theme,
and then Joanne responds. She apparently assumes that the claim
about exams seeks to generalise about the tutor group (or maybe the
school) rather than the country, and dismisses it, along with the idea
that there are major differences of wealth between them:

```
"I don't see anyone rich or anything and (they'll all) do
well. Everyone's average"  (lines 125–127, 132).
```

This then sets up some light-hearted argument about Ninnette's
economic position – "I'm a bit over-average" "no
you're not" – which continues until Mr Alcott's (second or
third) attempt to get them to keep quiet (lines 135, 136, 142,
147–149). The topic of wealth clearly interests the two girls, but
after the initial moment of engagement in lines 97–107, they collaboratively refuse the analysis that Mr Alcott is propounding, and
their subsequent discussion of richness drops education from the
frame and focuses on personally known individuals rather than on
social groups or classes.

Looking over this and other episodes,[2] it does not seem as though
these youngsters had an 'instinctive' or rapidly accessed grasp of a
specifically class politics and class analysis. Here and elsewhere,
teachers engaged in consciousness-raising about social class, motivated by a sense of class injustice, but situations like this were hardly
auspicious for the creation or mobilisation of any feeling of collective

class pride or purpose. First, there was the problem of the teachers' position within structures of social reproduction, which meant that for quite a lot of students in Extract 7.3, Mr Alcott's institutional voice came across more forcefully than his political message. Second, in the contexts in which it had arisen as an issue, class was almost inevitably formulated as 'bad news' for these children, informing them of their lack of collective cultural capital, warning them to perform well as *individuals* in the very school tasks that produce class stratification. Admittedly, at this point, the lack of a proper analysis of the Humanities curriculum is crucial absence, since it provided a space for youngsters to think about class free from a sense of personal foreboding. But outside that relatively autonomous curriculum space, closer to the competitive assessment culture of SATs and comparative league tables introduced by government in the late 1980s and 90s, extracts like this appear to ratify Reay's view of a "bleak 1990s discursive landscape ... in which to be working-class is increasingly to be 'not good enough'" (1998:267; Chapter 6 above). I certainly cannot claim that they were without any access to "broader collectivist cultures" that could be counter-hegemonic, since I have not given any systematic consideration to ideologies of gender, religion or ethnicity. Indeed, from the evidence cited, ethnicity and race seemed to cut deeper as ways of talking about social inequality and differentiation. Nor can any inferences be drawn about the decline of class awareness among young people in late modernity (Bradley 1996:77, cited in the introduction to Chapter 6 above). Not only were there only a handful of informants, but they were also only 13 and 14 years old, not necessarily an age in which you would expect to find well-formed class analyses. Nevertheless, this discussion of their overt views of class will be an important reference point when their stylisations of posh and Cockney are considered, and it will serve as a crucial element in later exploration of the relationship between 'established' and 'behavioural ideologies' (Vološinov 1973; Williams 1977:108), between explicit lexico-grammatical articulations of class sensibility and symbolic/indexical expressions in everyday practice (see question 6.4.iv in the previous chapter).

In fact, we must now turn right to the opposite end of Vološinov's spectrum of ideologies – to these informants' routine linguistic practice, far removed from any conscious, propositional and lexico-grammatical engagement with questions of social class. Both away from discussions of class, and outside their efforts to put on particular kinds of stylised voice, what kinds of accent did my informants have in their relatively 'artless', routine talk? Where did their ordinary speech locate them in the kind of socio-linguistic class hierarchy that Labovian variationists have studied? And what might this tell us about their participation in the processes of social class?

7.3   Sociolinguistic variability in everyday speech

'Routine' speech is itself, of course, a very variable phenomenon, but as has already been noted (Chapter 6.5 and http://www.cambridge.org/ 0521812631), this variability has received particularly close attention within the quantitative sociolinguistic tradition pioneered by William Labov (e.g. 1972a). Put simply – see Labov 1972a and Hudson 1996:Chapter 5 for much fuller accounts – the 'variationist' approach involves

   i)   the identification of linguistic features that can be produced in more than one way. (For example, the -ING in 'speaking' can be realised as either 'speak*ing*' or 'speak*in*', these two realisations being described as 'variants' of the -ING variable.)

   ii) quantification of the extent to which particular speakers use particular variants of a feature in particular linguistic and situational contexts. (Nouns and verb participles are, for example, two different 'linguistic contexts' for the -ING variable [which can occur in words like 'thing' and 'going' respectively], and 'chatting with friends' and 'reading aloud' are two situational contexts.)

   iii) comparison of the extent to which different variants get used across contexts, speakers and social groups, looking, for example, at how far middle-class women use either '-in' or 'ing' in reading aloud as opposed to chatting, and how far this resembles or differs from the patterns of middle-class men and working-class men and women.

The tradition pays particular attention to two kinds of linguistic variable:

   a. 'indicators', where the frequency of the use of particular variants is just a function of the speaker's social group membership, and

b. 'markers', where the frequency of the use of a variant is affected *both* by the speaker's social group membership *and* by the (formality of the) situation.

With its attention to frequency of use, this approach can document systematic differences between speakers even when they have the same basic stock of linguistic forms in their repertoire, and among other things, frequency differences have been correlated with broad gradations of socio-economic status (cf. (a) on 'indicators' above). Beyond that, as I intimated in Chapter 6.5, the analysis of socio-linguistic 'markers' has shown that in stratified class societies, across-group language variation is 'echoed' within the speech repertoire of individuals, their language becoming more standard, more like the speech of higher-placed groups, as situations become more formal. Indeed, the findings on 'markers' have been productively drawn alongside notions of (linguistic) 'habitus', suggesting that a preconscious disposition to hear and speak in class- and gender-specific ways is inculcated into the individual through long-term experience of the purchase that their language resources provide in different kinds of setting (cf. Bourdieu 1977, 1991:Part I; Woolard 1985; Eckert 2000:13).

The present study is not centrally concerned with variability in routine speech, and what follows is very far from being either an exhaustive or sophisticated quantitative study of dialectal variation in London speech.[3] But for present purposes, the Labovian tradition is immediately relevant in two ways:

1. it is a useful way of locating my informants in sociolinguistic space, situating some of their most routine speech forms in the heteroglossia of urban life, demonstrating whether or not these youngsters are in fact identifiably vernacular speakers, irrespective of any other languages in their repertoire (this is probably only necessary to the extent that there is persistent prejudice that if you have minority ethnicity, then your speech is indelibly 'foreign'/'other')
2. more importantly, an analysis of 'markers' – of stylistic and situational variability in talk – can show us whether or not speakers have been socialised into wider patterns of social stratification in speech – whether or not their tacit speech practices seem to reproduce/ratify certain aspects of class structure.

Table 7.1: *Sociolinguistic variables identified for quantitative analysis*

---

1. *Voiceless TH* (as in 'think', 'thief', 'something'). The standard is TH ([θ]), the traditional vernacular variants are [f] ('fink') and a glottal in the middle of words [ʔ] ('nu_in' for 'nothing'). As a newer multi-ethnic London variant, there is also [t] ('tief').

2. *Voiced TH in the middle of a word* (as in 'mother' and 'another'). The standard variant is [ð], and the vernacular London variants are [v] ('muvver'), with (probably) [d] as the newer multi-ethnic variant ('anudder').

3. *Word-initial voiced TH* (as in 'then' and 'the'). The vernacular variants are [d] (e.g. 'over dere') and 'zero' (e.g. "that's the one" => "'at's 'e one")

4. *Word-initial H* (as in 'home'). The H is sounded in the standard, and 'dropped' in the vernacular ('go _ome').[4]

5. *L after a vowel and before a pause or a consonant* ('old'). The L is sounded in Received Pronunciation ([ɫ]), and replaced with a vowel ('vocalised') in the vernacular ('old' => 'o_d').

6. *T between two vowels inside a word* (as in 'cottage'). The T is sounded in the standard variant, and is replaced with a glottal stop ([ʔ]- "majori'y") or a [d] ("whatever" => "whadever") in the vernacular.

7. *-ING in participial suffixes* (as in 'speaking'). 'ing' is the standard form ([ɪŋ] – 'shopping') and '-in' is the vernacular one ([ɪn] – 'shoppin').

The task is complicated by a number of factors, perhaps most prominent among them the fact that variationist studies of urban vernacular speech in the UK tend to focus only on historically white speech forms, neglecting the extent to which urban white people's speech now incorporates features that were introduced by ethnic minorities (see Hewitt 1986; Foulkes and Docherty 1999:16).[5] Nevertheless, to carry out these two kinds of variationist analysis, I first identified seven phonological features that seemed likely, on the basis of Wells 1982:Chapter 4.2 and Hudson and Holloway 1977, to be sensitive in London to social class and/or to the formality of the situation. These are outlined in Table 7.1.

A priori, I then identified a range of settings in which the participants' exposure/orientation to official values and teacher/researcher control were likely to vary in their strength, classifying these situational contexts as either formal or informal. For the four focal informants, the settings were those outlined in Table 7.2.

Then I carried out an auditory analysis of these informants' performance on the seven variables in each of these situations.

Table 7.2: *'Formal' and 'informal' elicitation contexts*

Informant	Formal situations	Informal situations
Hanif	• A classroom role play where the teacher was carrying out a national assessment of speaking and listening and where Hanif was performing the role of a coroner	• The *sub-rosa* narration of a horror story between friends
Simon	• A drama role-play in which Simon was acting as a talk-show host in front of the whole class	• An argument with peers about homophobia and being gay • A *sub-rosa* conversation with a friend about embarrassing situations
Ninnette	• Reading aloud to Joanne the menu in a café • Being interviewed with Joanne by Ben	• messing around with drinks at breaktime • recounting tales to Joanne and Linda of a flooded toilet, of trespassing, and of being banned from a shop
Joanne	• Doing a one-to-one spelling test with the learning support teacher • Being interviewed with Ninnette by Ben	• telling Ninnette about her family, and complaining to her about Mr Davies and Arun

The results are shown in Table 7.3 – what did they reveal of these youngsters' location in London sociolinguistic space?

Because I do not have adequate comparative data on London speech, I cannot use particular frequencies on specific sociolinguistic variables to locate each of these speakers at a specific point on a general scale of, for example, social status. In addition, relatively recent discussions of the development of 'Estuary English' suggest that it may be harder than it used to be to treat particular non-standard variants as being typically working class.[6] Even so – though it is not really necessary in view of the massive weight of evidence in Chapters 8 and 9 (as well as almost everything else I have said about them!) – we can use the two *white* Londoners (Joanne and Simon) as a yardstick to point

Table 7.3: *Proportions and percentages of standard variants in the four focal informants' production of seven variables in formal and informal contexts*

	Hanif		Simon		Ninnette		Joanne	
	formal	informal	formal	Informal	formal	informal	formal	informal
1. Voiceless TH (*thing*)	10/12	2/2	3/4	1/1	5/5	4/4	8/11	10/13
2. Word-medial voiced TH (*other*)	6/6	1/1	9/9	3/4	4/10	–	2/5	3/7
3. Word initial voiced TH (*the*)	32/33 97%	35/50 70%	27/28 96%	35/35 100%	40/49 82%	34/43 79%	37/37 100%	16/17 94%
4. Word-initial H (not proforms)	16/16 100%	12/14 86%	23/26 88%	13/15 87%	14/14 100%	15/19 79%	12/14 86%	4/9 44%
5. Pre-C, post-V L (*old*)	6/9 66%	9/14 64%	16/19 89%	6/12 50%	11/26 42%	5/21 23%	18/38 47%	8/12 66%
6. Word-medial intervocalic T (*butter*)	2/3 66%	3/13 20%	7/8 87%	0/4 0%	7/10 70%	0/5 0%	(2/14) 14%	(0/11) 0%
7. -ING in participial suffixes (*running*)	17/17 100%	2/6 33%	12/14 86%	4/10 40%	6/9 66%	0/6 0%	8/13 61%	2/9 22%
Overall scores on 'markers' (the shaded areas in the table)	51/53 96%	40/69 58%	35/41 85%	10/26 38%	38/59 64%	20/51 39%	22/41 53%	6/29 21%

Key:
Shading = figures which indicate style-shifting in the conventional direction (the proportion of standard features increasing with formality).
Underlining = figures which contradict the conventional pattern

a. to the unexceptional use of non-standard vernacular variants
    in the speech of the two with minority ethnic backgrounds:[7]
    - all four informants – with both white and minority back-
      grounds – engage in H-dropping (Row 4), L-vocalisation
      (Row 5), intervocalic T-glottalling (Row 6) and de-
      velarisation of -ING (Row 7)
    - like Joanne and Simon, Ninnette uses [v] for word–medial
      voiced TH (Row 2)
b. to the unexceptional patterns of English style-shifting in the
    speech of the youngsters with ethnic minority backgrounds:
    - Hanif and Ninnette's increased use in informal contexts of
      vernacular variants of both word-medial intervocalic T
      and -ING resembles Joanne and Simon's (Rows 6 and 7),
    - Ninnette's increased vernacular L vocalisation in informal
      contexts resembles Simon's (Row 5), and
    - Ninnette's increased vernacular H-dropping in informal
      contexts broadly resembles Joanne's (Row 4).[8]

There are two cases where the use of *vernacular* variants looks as
though it might be *greater* in the *formal* than in the informal context –
see Hanif's uses of Voiceless TH (Row 1) and Joanne's uses of pre-
consonantal, post-vocalic L (Row 5) (both underlined in Table 7.3).
But since one of these involves a white monolingual, this unexpected
pattern cannot be attributed to some kind of bilingual foreignness.

So much, then, for the first issue – the urban 'vernacularity' of my
informants' speech. What about the second? To what extent did
they produce more prestigious speech variants in more formal and
official situations? How far did their speech suggest that they had
been socialised into the class-related ranking of speech contexts that
variationist research has so often revealed in the past? In fact, this
has already been largely answered in (b) immediately above. There
were two linguistic variables where it is hard to speak of any style-
shifting – voiceless TH (Row 1) and word-medial voiced TH (Row 2).
But for at least one or two of the speakers, the other five variables
functioned as conventional Labovian 'markers' (becoming more
standard in the formal contexts), and intervocalic T (Row 6) and -
ING (Row 7) seemed to be markers for all of them.

The empirical connection between prestigious standard dialects
and formal (school and literacy-oriented) situations has its origins in

the fact that situations and activities that play an important part in the production and distribution of mainstream cultural and material resources tend to be associated with more powerful social groups (and vice versa). And so in their conformity to this pattern, it does look as though Ninnette, Hanif, Simon and Joanne ratify this socio-symbolic hierarchy, unself-consciously consenting to the colonisation of status-relevant situations by the speech styles that form part of the specialised inheritance of wealthier people and higher placed social groups. Returning to Bourdieu's formulation, we can say that class-stratification does seem to have inscribed itself in these children's sociolinguistic 'habitus', or alternatively, drawing on Williams, we can refer to the routinisation achieved in hegemony and its "saturation of the whole process of living ... [by] the dominance and subordination of particular classes" (1977:109).

That said though, it is important to clarify what the reproduction of class hegemony in these youngsters' routine speech might actually signify. As noted in Chapter 6, quantitative sociolinguists focus on the more automatic levels of linguistic production, to which speakers normally devote relatively little of their processing energies and attention, but in doing so, Labovians also operate with a semiotically reduced notion of language (as Coupland 1995 emphasises in his call for a new 'dialect stylistics'). The data-processing in our analysis may have followed Labovian principles, but the numbers given in Table 7.3 amount to no more than the barest summary of deracinated fragments stripped of pragmatic meaning, and as such the analysis is still a long way from any sense of class as a 'lived reality'. Accent and dialect may participate in, and display respect and regard for, the dominant social order, but individuals generally express their agency through a highly complex combination of different dimensions of speech, and the errors attendant on 'over-reading' and attaching too much weight to the social meaning of accent and dialect on their own are demonstrated in the following extract:

Extract 7.4

A drama class, where working in pairs, everyone has been told to prepare and rehearse a short role-play discussion involving one character who is going to have a baby. They will then be expected to perform in front of the rest of the group, but Ninnette and Joanne are fairly emphatic about not wanting to, and they've used their time joking around putting pillows up their jumpers. In the end, they successfully manage to avoid having to perform, but during the final moments allocated to preparation and rehearsal, just prior to their coming together to watch individual performances, Ninnette is recorded as follows (blex 52, 30–20):

```
1   NINNETTE   ((calling out to the teacher, loudly:))
2              ˇMISS
3              (.)
4              MISS
5              WE |AIN'T |EVEN |DONE ˋNU IN
                                 [nʌʔɪ~ⁿ]
6              (.)
7              ((even louder:)) MISS WE |AIN'T |DONE ˋNOTHING
                                              [nʌfɪŋ]
8              (2)
9              ((not so loud, as if Miss is in closer range:))
10             miss we |avent |done ˆanything
                             [enɪθɪŋ]
11             (2)
12             ((to Joanne, re pillow:)) go on
13             put that little thing in- up
14             (.)
15             you look lov- you look lovely with them sandals
16             ((calling to someone else:))
               don't you think she looks pretty
```

As Ninnette perseveres in the attempt to get the teacher's attention, her language becomes increasingly standard, starting with ``miss we ain't even done nu' in'' in lines 4 and 5 and ending with ``miss we 'aven't done anything'' in line 10. Although repeated attempts to initiate an interpersonal exchange quite often involve shifts like this, the consecutive adjustments in Ninnette's speech style are rather striking and the linguistic changes produced in these three turns can be charted as follows:

Linguistic shifts in Ninnette's speech in Extract 7.7:

Non-standard ⟵========================⟶ *Standard*		
Line 5	*Line 7*	*Line 10*
ain't	ain't	=> aven't
n't (= not) + nothing	n't + nothing	=> n't + anything
nasalised -ING [ɪ~ⁿ]	=> velarised -ING [ŋ]	velarised -ING
glottal TH [ʔ]	labio-dental TH[f]	=>dental TH [θ]

(=> indicates the point where the variable becomes (more) standard)

But although her movement towards standard forms seems quite appropriate, converging to the styles of speaking likely to be favoured by teachers, these shifts in linguistic structure do not signal submission to the authority of school, since the actual content of what Ninnette is saying stays the same. The forms in line 10 may make her seem more polite and 'hearable' to the teacher, mitigating her declaration of disengagement, but the declaration itself remains unaltered and she carries on immediately after in much the same spirit as before. So although the patterns of style-shifting evidenced here and in Table 7.3 show that class structure has quite extensively shaped these youngsters' speech habits and their instinctive sense of what linguistic resources are suited to which kinds of interaction, this does not mean that their participation in the procedures and activities that reproduce social stratification is necessarily docile and acquiescent. Variationist analysis gives a feel for one part of the 'elephant', but this is still a long way from the 'lived realities' of class, and more encompassing forms of study are required.

At the same time, that cautionary note should not detract from the contribution that variationist methods have already made to the analyses that follow. At the end of the previous Chapter (6.7), I wondered whether the contemporary sociolinguistic emphasis on "practices, discourses and textual play" might be inadequate for the analysis of class, falling in line with free market ideologies privileging agency, choice and the availability of 'multiple identities', rather than the enduring restrictions and costs emphasised by Williams and Hymes. Indeed, going one step further, I asked whether the study of stylisation might trap us in Jameson's nightmare world of post-modern simulations and pastiche, where people spoke in "abnormal tongues" and no-one believed in "linguistic normality". Now, though, Labovian methods have provided empirical evidence of a classed 'habitus' and of the 'hegemony' of class-determined sociolinguistic structures in routine everyday speech. More than that, they have produced a vital baseline for analysis of the artful stylisation of posh and Cockney, helping to dispel the concern that we might be stuck in a world of pastiche without any ties to "linguistic normality". Rather than looking at 'voices from nowhere', the analyses of stylisation will focus on varieties that form an intimate part of the performer's ordinary repertoire (cf. Johnstone 1999:506).

Better still, the quantification inspired by Labov stops us jumping to the conclusion that one of these varieties is likely to have 'we-coded', in-group associations while the other is treated as 'they-coded' and out-group. Even in the most standard version of Ninnette's declaration of disengagement in Extract 7.7, there is a Cockney dropped H (``'aven't''`` in line 10), and scrutiny of Table 7.3 shows that overwhelmingly, when they style-shift, these youngsters still use some standard variants in informal settings, and vernacular ones when they are being formal. In the shaded areas in Rows 3–7, there are 6 cases of "informal context = only vernacular variants" and "formal context = only standard variants", but for the remaining 20, vernacular and standard – posh and Cockney – are intermingled, the difference being only a matter of degree. So in their penetration of these youngsters' routine talk, these two varieties are *themselves* intimately linked, and it would be a misrepresentation to suggest that, for example, the vernacular variants connoted 'ingroup' while the standard ones symbolised 'outgroup' (see Irvine 2001).

We shall have to wait and see, of course, exactly how the exaggerated performance of either posh and Cockney fits into all this, but for the time being, variationist analysis helpfully suggests that there may well be rather more involved than just the pleasure of playing in a "free market of identities".

All of which presupposes that exaggerated-performances-of-posh-and-Cockney can actually be distinguished from routine speech variability, and we should now turn to this.

7.4   Identifying stylised posh and Cockney

Given that standard and vernacular forms feature in the routine talk of my informants, how did I identify stretches of speech as involving stylised exaggerations of posh and Cockney?

As indicated in the discussion in Chapter 6.3 above, I expected stylisation to be linked to some kind of change of footing, or minor shift in key in the flow of activity-on-hand. Of course, this could take many forms, and in identifying such discursive moves as stylisations of posh or Cockney in particular, the first and most obvious resource was my own intuition as a (relatively standard-accented) speaker who was brought up and lives in the London area, and who had spent quite a lot of time talking and listening to these young-sters. In listening through my recordings for the first time, it was this that I drew on when I first identified particular strips of talk as perhaps involving stylised posh and Cockney. Phonetic descriptions of Received Pronunciation and of London speech, particularly those provided by Wells 1982 Volume 2:Chapters 4.1 and 4.2, provided essential back-up and meta-language for this, not only in ratifying particular utterances as being London rather than, say, Yorkshire, but also in helping to classify them as being particularly strong/broad versions of the varieties in focus.

These segmental phonetic clues provided a first point of entry into the analysis. But they were generally only one ingredient in an ensemble of semiotic features that constituted a stylised 'perform-ance', and the co-presence of these other elements was another important indicator. Stylised performance was sometimes signalled and set off from the speech used both before and after by an increased density in the co-occurrence of marked phonetic features, sometimes accompanied by marked grammar or lexis; by the quo-tative verbs 'say' or 'go', introducing reported speech; and by abrupt shifts in some combination of loudness, pitch level, voice quality or speed of delivery. In addition, stylised utterances were also often formulaic in their lexis and pragmatic function, as well as stereo-typical in the characteristics of the social personae which they por-trayed (cf. Bauman [1975] 2001:171).

If the audience (or indeed the speaker) subsequently responded by laughing, repeating the utterance, by commenting on it, or by switching into a different kind of non-normal dialect or voice, this could be another clue. And finally, a significant number of 'candi-date' instances recorded on radio-mic were replayed to the partici-pants, which also helped to clarify whether or not an utterance involved stylisation.

There were, then, a number of elements that helped to differenti-ate exaggerated performance from routine variability, although it is important not to underestimate the interpretive leeway involved in identifying stylisation. Sometimes, a lot of identifying features co-occur, making the stylisation very apparent, but at other times, the signals can be weaker, and for their effect on local *cognoscenti*, they might depend, for example, on social images or on network-specific practices that the analyst cannot access or understand (see Gumperz

1982:30–37; Bauman 1986:3, cited in Chapter 4.4). In fact, there were a number of instances where there definitely seemed to be some phonetic exaggeration of posh or Cockney, but where I found it hard to make much sense of what was going on. There is certainly enough reliable evidence to address the guiding questions (Chapter 6.4), but my analysis cannot claim to provide an exhaustive typology of posh/ Cockney stylisation, developed from a collection of episodes that I can confidently claim to represent all of the posh and Cockney stylisation in my corpus.

The analysis of particular episodes will inevitably bring us back to these methodological issues again and again, but to show the operation of these criteria just here, it is maybe worth saying why, for example, I do not regard the striking movement from ``miss we ain't even done nu'in'' to ``miss we 'aven't done anything '' in Extract 7.7 as a case of artful stylisation:

a) there is no disruption to our expectations of how we would expect Ninnette to behave at this juncture, given her particular purposes within the activity on hand. The shifts of style are entirely congruent with her effort to gain the teacher's attention;

b) the shift elicits no metalinguistic response from the participants – no laughter or comments;

c) the grammatical and phonological variants involved in the shift all fall within Ninnette's normal speech range.

I cannot say the same of the episode in the next Section, where we will need to address the last empirical preliminary. Establishing that a strip of speech involves stylised posh or Cockney is one thing, but how do we know that it is 'social class' that is somehow symbolically relevant there-and-then to the participants, rather some other kind of meaning?

7.5   Stylisations of posh and Cockney unrelated to social class

As I stated at the start of the chapter, these youngsters lived in London, they encountered lots of different kinds of Londoner every day, and so it's quite possible that specific dialect performances could be intended to conjure the image of particular people *as* individuals

rather than emblems of any more general social type. In fact, there
will be no stage in my analysis of stylised posh and Cockney stylisation where I will be able to take social class for granted – we will need
to scrutinise all of the episodes we look at for the emergence of issues
of power, control or social differentiation, as well as for any wider
recognition of class relations (see questions 6.4.v–vi above). So it will
not actually be possible to answer the question 'how do we know that
class is involved?' just in this Section. Nevertheless, as a limiting case
and to show that this is a relevant question, warning us not to reach
too fast for class interpretations, it is worth dwelling on some data
where it might be wisest just to stick with a relatively anodyne notion
like 'sound play'.

Extract 7.5

A Maths lesson. The teacher has just finished telling the class to be quieter in
their work, and Ninnette is fixing something with sellotape. The two girls
spend a great deal of time together at school, and Joanne has been telling
Ninnette quite a bit about her house, but they live at some distance from one
another, and they don't visit each other's houses very often:

```
1                  (1)
2    JOANNE        ((quietly, but with some urgency:))
3                  Ninnette
4                  I've gotta show you my roo::m
                                            [u::]
5                  (1.5)
6    NINNETTE      your /broom
                        [ʊ]
7    JOANNE        ((louder:)) my roo:m
                              [u::]
8    NINNETTE      ((rhyming with broom:)) your tomb
                                            [ʊ]
9    JOANNE        ((as if in exasperation:))
                   >ohh<
10                 (2)
11                 ((with high rising intonation:)) o'kay
                                            [ʌkˣāī]
12   NINNETTE?     ((a non-word, with very high, very quick,
                   rise-fall:)) ˆda
13                 (.)
14   NINNETTE      ((in her ordinary voice:)) sellotape
15                 (11)
```

The episode begins with an urgent-sounding utterance from Joanne that could be taken either as an invitation (eliciting a response like "that'd be great – when shall I come?"), or as the preface to some kind of boast ("really? Tell me about it . . ."). But rather than opting for either, after a short pause, Ninnette responds with a repair-initiator, apparently having misheard 'room' as 'broom' (line 6: ``your broom?''). Joanne corrects the mishearing, but Ninnette then mishears a second time, making it clear that her failure to understand is (now) wilful/playful rather than genuine. Joanne expresses some exasperation (line 9), and then comes back with a confirmation request – ``okay'' in 11. This is in a much broader Cockney accent than she normally uses – whereas her two previous articulations of the GOAT and FACE vowels were both fairly standard, [əʊ] and [eɪ] respectively, the two vowels in 'okay' are very Cockney, as well as being heavily nasalised (see Wells 1982:308–309, 307, 318). From the audio-tape, it is hard to know for sure who produces the very brief, high-pitched non-word that immediately follows, but it makes sense to see it as Ninnette, using a rise-fall to express approval but keeping it still very much in the play frame. Whatever, Ninnette then closes the topic in line 14, concentrating on the fixing job she's engaged in.

The two girls enjoyed a lot of metalinguistic play together, and in that regard, Ninnette's deliberate mishearing is unlikely to seem either startling or threatening to Joanne. But whatever the purpose of the initial statement, Ninnette's two repair-initiators in lines 6 and 8 still leave Joanne hanging at the end of line 8, not only without the positive expression of interest from Ninnette that she's hoping for (e.g. "oh yes, I'd love to see it"), but also adrift in an unfinished clarification sequence, short even of any acknowledgement of the repair she offered in line 7. Her Cockney "okay" sounds like a response to this uncertainty. It appears to close the clarification sequence by refocusing on the original assertion (``I've got to show you my room . . . okay?''), and at the same time, the switch into a stylised voice minimises any potential loss of face. By now she must have gathered that Ninnette is not going to provide her with the uptake she might most prefer, and if she continued in earnestness, she'd be open to being seen as insensitive, over-insistent and possibly humourless as well. Instead, she joins Ninnette in the general frame of language play that the latter has introduced, and her non-serious voice gives Ninnette the chance to express interest in Joanne's proposition without any real commitment, an option that Ninnette can perhaps be heard accepting in line 12.

It is impossible to say why Joanne switches to Cockney rather than some other speech variety – elsewhere she does versions of posh, Northern English, Midlands English, foreign English, French and baby talk. Are there connotations of solidarity and vigour that are somehow relevant here (see Chapter 9)? Or does she have the image of a particular speaker in mind when she uses Cockney? – no obvious candidate emerged in the 16–17 hours in which Ninnette and Joanne were recorded. But there is nothing here to suggest that the use of Cockney makes the interaction itself saliently political in any way, either by evoking a wider realm of class inequalities and/or by providing some pointed commentary on any institutional positioning or power-relations immediately on hand. As far as we can see, this does look like an instance of Cockney stylisation that is innocent of class consciousness, and there were other episodes in my dataset where exaggerated Cockney simply looked like language play, free of any momentarily sharpened political awareness.[9]

7.6 Summary

In the discussion of empirical (and methodological) preliminaries in this chapter, I have circled around the links between stylisation and social class, first investigating class outside stylisation in my discussion of its explicit representation in talk, and later looking at stylisation where there does not seem to be much 'class' (the language play in the previous section). Perhaps unsurprisingly in view of the age of the informants, class has not appeared here as an especially vibrant topic in explicit discourse, capable of mobilising a collective political consciousness among them, although these youngsters were aware of the possibility of futures that could be good and bad – high or low – in the stratified society they lived in, and their teachers certainly alerted them to this. We ourselves were able to see the effects of class hierarchy in the informants' routine speech behaviour, but this does not mean that an active sense of hierarchy is inherent in every piece of stylised posh or Cockney that we encounter. When we witness Cockney being simply used in sound play, there is clearly still a serious need to reckon with the possibility of stylisation amounting to not much more than playful pastiche, detached from 'linguistic normality'.

We are now ready to look more closely at the rest of the episodes where there seemed to be posh and Cockney stylisation, engaging with the remaining questions from Chapter 6.4:

iv) How far and in what ways does the stylisation of posh and Cockney voices play a part in the dynamic relationship between explicit ideologies and taken-for-granted practices? Where does it feature in the movement between 'behavioural' and 'established ideologies'?

v) What images and representations are evoked with exaggerated posh and Cockney voices? How do they relate to the activity on hand? How are they received?

vi) Do these voices seem to be politically engaged, and if so, what kinds of politics do they involve? What are the (micro-)political interests and identities at issue, and where do they seem to lead?

To do so, I shall divide these episodes into two groups, involving

a) interactions where informants' identities as school pupils are at issue, where talk is addressed to school tasks and where teachers were salient, either as interlocutors or as the topics of discussion;

b) interactions between peers, where educational identities do not seem to be relevant but where something more than just the sound properties of posh or Cockney seems to be in focus.

I shall address (a) in Chapter 8, and (b) in Chapter 9.

Notes

1. For data on official school assessments, see http://www.cambridge.org/0521812631.
2. Further illustration and discussion can be found at http://www.cambridge.org/0521812631.
3. There are, for example, no measures of social network involvement; vowels are largely ignored (primarily because they are generally more complicated to analyse – see Hudson 1980; 1996); there is nothing on interactional accommodation processes (Trudgill 1986); only a relatively limited number of tokens have been analysed; there has been no

accoustic analysis; and no tests of statistical significance. Nor has there been any attempt to situate variation in connected speech processes (Kerswill 1987) (even though, according to Milroy 2000:277, mainline variationist studies now generally neglect these).

4. For simplicity, I excluded pronouns like 'he' and 'his' from my count since these words are often unstressed.

5. In addition, as far as I am aware, there are few comprehensive, very up-to-date empirical studies of variation in London speech with which I can compare the patterns in my data – Wells 1982 is one valuable study, as is Hudson and Holloway 1977, but neither is very recent. Even so, given that my own variationist aspirations here are themselves only very limited, the available resources for comparison are likely to be sufficient.

6. A number of recent, small-scale and sometimes relatively informal studies of 'Estuary English' suggest that in recent years, some of the differences between London vernacular/Cockney and Received (standard) Pronunciation have diminished, with previously working-class forms now being used and accepted across a wider social spectrum (see www.phon.ucl.ac.uk/home/estuary/home). For example, the vocalisation of pre-consonantal/final L is said to have spread across classes.

7. For a slightly fuller account of some of the variables in Hanif's speech, see Rampton 2001b.

8. These four speakers differ in the actual degree to which they use standard vs vernacular variants in particular settings, but the elicitation contexts were not rigorously controlled to allow inter-speaker comparison, and anyway, one would not expect people with different social networks to speak identically.

9. Further illustration and discussion can be found at http://www.cambridge.org/0521812631.

8

Schooling, class and stylisation

Schooling involves rewards and penalties, reputations and identities, that can be very consequential for students' future position within systems of production, distribution and consumption, and as such it has often been associated with social class (e.g. Bourdieu and Passeron 1977). Pupil–teacher interaction is often fraught with institutional power-conflicts, and it can be a major site for the formation and the display of class consciousness (Willis 1977). So how did stylisations of posh and Cockney feature in the schooling process, when talk was focused on school tasks, or when teachers were salient, either as interlocutors or as the topics of discussion? What part did stylised posh and Cockney play in scenes where there were institutional rewards and penalties at stake, and how did they fit into the negotiation of official classifications and requirements? And within this, what kinds of politics did stylisation seem to be associated with – what aspirations, solidarities or oppositions?

These are the basic descriptive and interpretive issues addressed in this chapter, drawing on a corpus of about 20–25 episodes. But I shall link the analysis to more general debates about the educational treatment of non-standard speech. Since the 1970s, sociolinguists have claimed that if schools are insensitive in their promotion of standard English, they are likely to produce (a potentially debilitating) linguistic insecurity among their working-class pupils. The chapter begins by asking whether this is still the case today, and notes the speculative basis of these claims, the reified notion of class that they operate with, and their inconsistency with findings on style-shifting (Chapter 8.1).

I then move to some analysis of an English lesson where there is a significant degree of linguistic tolerance, created within what is now

quite a long history of language ideological dispute between govern-
ments prescribing standard language, and teachers and schools
sympathetic to the arguments of – among others – sociolinguists
(Chapter 8.2). But the creation of some space for non-standard
speech at Central High did not sever the links between linguistic
difference and social stratification, and students still used prestige
forms to caricature teachers as upper-class snobs (Chapter 8.3).
Indeed there is evidence of a critical, reflexive sensitivity to class
division in the way that pupils stylised posh and Cockney in the
transition between reading/writing and peer sociability (Chapter 8.4),
although to avoid inflated over-statements about the symbolism,
these expressions of class awareness require quite careful pragmatic
description, alert to the subtlety of the social shading that they
introduce (Chapter 8.5).

The connotations of an accent exist in a dialectical relationship
with the uses made of it in interaction, and in certain
stylisations at Central High, class and ethnic affiliations were
articulated together, giving condensed symbolic expression to
a relationship that seemed quite hard to express explicitly
(Chapter 8.6). It is not possible to comment on the subsequent
development of the class awareness displayed in stylisation,
but individuals did seem to differ in the senses of social possibility implied in their exaggerations of posh and Cockney. In fact
these differences appeared to link to their different positions
within the pedagogic settlement in Class 9A, success at school
feeding bolder visions of how the relationship between education and non-standard speech could be configured differently
(Chapter 8.7).

Turning back to the sociolinguistic commonsense about accent
and schooling first formulated in the 1970s, it is clear that there have
been important changes in the climate of language attitudes.
Education still involves the drawing of lines that will be highly
consequential for their futures, and in their uses of posh and
Cockney, my informants seemed to sense the class significance of
school relationships and activities. Even so, responses to accent
status were much more active and differentiated than a blanket
term like 'linguistic insecurity' implies (Chapter 8.8).

We should begin, however, by reviewing the orthodox sociolinguistic position on accent, school and social class.

8.1 The sociolinguistics of accent and school

In 1975, Peter Trudgill warned a British educational readership that there was a great deal of essentially class-based prejudice about non-standard accents. Non-standard accents and dialects were simply different, not deficient, and if teachers criticised their pupils' pronunciation, they risked alienating them from education (1975:63–64, 46). In the US, sociolinguists have focused more on race- rather than class-prejudice (L. Milroy 1999; Chapter 6.5 above), but otherwise, Trudgill's views represented something of an orthodoxy among Anglo-American sociolinguists, and many continue to hold such views (Labov 1969; Lippi-Green 1997; Carter 1999:164). Indeed, according to Hymes

[c]lass stratification and cultural assumptions about language converge in schooling to reproduce the social order. A latent function of the educational system is to instil linguistic insecurity, to discriminate linguistically, to channel children in ways that have an integral linguistic component, while appearing open and fair to all. All have equal opportunity to acquire membership in the privileged linguistic network. If they fail, it is their fault, not that of the society or school. (Hymes 1996:84)

Historically, there is obviously an intimate relationship between schooling, standard accent and class position, to the extent that 'educated' is often used as a synonym for Received Pronunciation (RP) and middle class, and indeed, my own variationist analyses of the routine speech of Hanif, Ninnette, Simon and Joanne showed that their pronunciation also became more standard as the activities they engaged in became more broadly school-compatible (Chapter 7.3). Even so, there is a good case for asking whether these concerns about accent discrimination are really still as relevant today as they were 30 years ago.

How, for example, does Trudgill's warning square with the emergence of 'Estuary English' as a new standard (see Chapter 7 note 6)? Cameron cites Neustupný's claim that post-modern societies put value on diversity, generating a 'variation ideology' to compete with the standard (Cameron 1995:27–28), and it would be very hard to deny that there has been a substantial change in attitudes to accent since, say, the 1950s when commentators could justifiably speak of an 'accent-bar' comparable to the 'colour-bar'

(J. Milroy 1999:19, L. Milroy 1999: 186–187). Since the mid 1970s, there have also been generations of teachers who have actually had sociolinguists like Labov (1969), Trudgill (1975) and Stubbs (1986) on their reading lists at teacher training college (cf. e.g. DES 1988), and even though the reactionary 1995 English National Curriculum orders required pupils to "be taught to speak with clear diction and appropriate intonation" from the end of primary school onwards (DFE 1995a:12), they did not actually retract or recant on the 1989 injunction NOT to teach RP (compare DES 1989 para 15.15 and DFE 1995a:12). So just how relevant is the kind of anti-discrimination stance originally associated with Labov and Trudgill? Are non-standard accents still stigmatised at school, and does linguistic insecurity still play a major part in the cultural production of class identities?

Before engaging with empirical data relevant to these questions, it is important to reflect on the conceptual and methodological foundations that the orthodox anti-discrimination stance is based upon. Looking closer, the advice that sociolinguists tend to give teachers is based on a rather problematic definition of social class; it is quite hard to reconcile with core sociolinguistic findings on language variation; and there are significant empirical blindspots.

Sociolinguists interested in class usually portray the relationship between standard English and non-standard regional dialects in the UK as a triangle, with prestigious speech at the top, spoken natively by 12–15% of the population (Trudgill 1999:124). In the orthodox view, the association of standard language with this elite minority needs to be handled very sensitively with the rest of the population:

> to become a *speaker* of standard English is to become a speaker of a clearly marked, socially symbolic dialect; and a long tradition of sociolinguistic research suggests that, whatever the teacher may do in the classroom and whatever the overall implications for assessment, children will not learn a dialect associated with a group with which they do not wish to be associated. (Carter 1999:163; see also Stubbs 1986:96; Hudson 1996:211).

In other words, if you're going to succeed teaching non-elite speakers of English, first of all you have got to show your respect for the vernaculars that the children bring from home.

It is surely right that in ideal circumstances, respect and trust provide the best base for learning at school. Even so, there is a serious discrepancy between these educational injunctions and what is perhaps the most significant sociolinguistic 'law' discovered by variationist researchers. When they discuss education, sociolinguists often conceptualise social class as an inherited identity that people acquire in particular speech communities – hence the risk that non-posh pupils will experience the learning of standard English as betrayal of family and friends. But how can this be reconciled with the classic variationist finding that actually, there is style-shifting in nearly everyone's speech, and that this develops quite early in life, well before the teenage years (Romaine 1984:97–104; Andersen 1990:36–37). Most people can move up and down a continuum of speech styles, sometimes being more standard in their speech and sometimes more vernacular, and so almost everyone is likely to have some experience of feeling now and then that sociolinguistically they are better off – posher – than somebody else (or themselves at other times) (Macaulay 1997:51, 54, 112). And if children hear their mums and dads doing this, can we really assume that they feel they are being forced to "join ... another social group" when they are taught standard English (Hudson 1996:211)? In short, there are good reasons to doubt the assumption that if students do not belong to the privileged 12–15%, then they are locked into some kind of fragile but unmoving 'basilectal' otherness, partitioned in a remote outgroup identity that teachers need to address with the utmost delicacy if there is to be any chance of progress.

The problem here lies in a reification of social class. As happened more generally in arguments about deficit and difference, classes are regarded as separate socio-cultural groups very much along the lines of the 'linguistics of community' discussed in Chapters 1.2 and 6.5 above, and this means that in turning to education, sociolinguists have often overlooked the potential implications of their own finding that at all levels of society and from quite an early age, individuals command styles of speaking that are both more and less prestigious in mainstream schemes of value. Indeed, at this point, it is worth recapping on the conception of social class that will inform my own analyses in this chapter, following through its implications for our imagining of social class in schoolrooms.

In a country with a long history of class stratification like England, occupational status is at best only a short-hand for a very considerable range of cultural and material phenomena and processes, covering social differences in "family background, main source of income, place of residence, cultural tastes … political affiliations" and a great deal else (Abercrombie and Warde et al. 2000:145–146), coalescing and diverging in enormously complex and changing patterns over time. So as soon as the focus shifts from synoptic quantitative correlation to meaning and social action, as soon as an attempt is made to address the relationship between language, class formation and class consciousness (Chapter 6.1 above), no single indicator of class will be sufficient, and an analytic vocabulary will be needed that is much more differentiating than the traditional sociolinguistic focus on occupational category membership.

If the concern is with accent, class and education, it is necessary to have an account of how class identities are produced in cultural activity, and for this, it is useful to refer back to E. P. Thompson's claim that "[p]olitics is often about exactly this – how will class happen, where will the line be drawn?", and that "the drawing of [this line] is … the outcome of political and cultural skills." (1978:296; see also Chapter 6.1 above). Class in this view is a sensed social difference that people and groups produce in interaction, and there is struggle and negotiation around exactly who's up, who's down, who's in, who's out, and where the lines are drawn. These differences, of course, are not created out of nothing or invented on the spot – actors encounter historically rooted expectations, images and discourses, and to a very considerable degree, they experience inequality and the stratification of style and other material and cultural resources as given. Nevertheless, human agency plays a crucial part in class processes, and this means that when analysts see people in better and worse, higher and lower positions in systems of production, distribution and consumption, they need to look for the cultural practices of differentiation, classification and evaluation through which this is accomplished.

Once we look beyond parental background to a fuller picture of class stratification, taking into account the practices that (re)produce it, we can get a little closer to the "lived reality" of social class that Hymes says has been sorely neglected in sociolinguistics (1996:74). If, instead of depending on parental occupation for the definition, class is seen as a process in which people negotiate and struggle for position, affiliation and advantage within unevenly receptive institutional systems that have a significant impact on their destinies, then style-shifting stops being the range of variability that is representative (acceptable or authentic) for someone belonging at a particular social level, and instead it becomes an index of each individual's structured but moving alignment with 'high' and 'low', 'lower' and 'higher'. Following on from that, the conception of classrooms changes, and they are no longer imagined merely as arenas where working-class children are dominated by middle-class teachers, whose insensitive standard language prescriptions risk alienating their students, making them feel that their families and their cultures are inadequate, and that school learning isn't for the likes of them. Instead, classrooms become sites for the still structured but more open possibilities contingent on a group of people engaging with one another, trying to work out where and how the lines are drawn, and which side of them they are standing.

This is not an especially original perspective on either education or discourse: processes of 'differentiation' and 'polarisation' were a major concern in the British sociology of education in the 1970s (see Chapter 2.7 above), and it is broadly consistent with the tradition of research on the production of inequality in institutional interaction associated with John Gumperz (Chapter 6.5 above). But this perspective is very different from the theory of society that informs orthodox sociolinguistic calls for schools to show respect for non-standard dialects at school, and perhaps more pertinently here, it also opens up the possibility of a different kind of empirical analysis of the relationship between accent, schools and social class. In order to clarify these empirical possibilities, it is worth briefly reflecting on the main methodological limitations underpinning orthodox sociolinguistic advocacy of non-standard speech.

Orthodox sociolinguistic opinion about accent discrimination tends to draw on two kinds of evidence: quantitative data on the social distribution of linguistic forms and language attitudes, and documentary data on debates about language in historical, media and educational texts (see Chapter 6.5).[1] These kinds of data have a vital part to play in an understanding of the history and politics of language, but quantitative research on language attitudes and variation provides very little insight into how people actually negotiate the symbols of social class in situated interaction (see http://www.cambridge.org/0521812631), and documentary research generally makes no claims to doing so. So there is an empirical gap.

Linguistic prejudice is supposed to have a deleterious effect on the education of non-standard speakers, but *we hardly ever get to see the damage being done*, and it is hard to find any concrete descriptions of exactly how attitudes to accent impact on young people's sense of themselves and their potential, when and where (Cameron 1995:14–15; see however Clark 1998, 2003). Instead, the claims made about accent discrimination at school need to be treated as *speculative*. Yes, there is social-stratification-among-speech-varieties, there is class-related-underachievement-at-school, and there may well be linguistic-prejudice-in-society, but that does not tell us how they all fit together. Elsewhere in educationally relevant language study, the 'new literacy studies' (Street 1984; Heath 1983) have shown that literacy is *not* necessarily always all that important, in spite of the researchers' own intense interest in the subject, and its significance needs to be assessed in the careful empirical description of actual events in which script is one semiotic dimension. This should be carried over to sociolinguistic claims about accent: if all you have got are documents, correlations and structured elicitation tests, and if there is nothing in your methodological tool-kit comparable to the concept of a 'literacy event', then the empirical adequacy of what you say about accent and school is inevitably limited.

In what follows, I shall start to try repair this empirical gap, and to do so, I shall focus on what might be called 'metalinguistic (or metapragmatic) episodes', episodes which, in analogy with Heath's definition of 'literacy events', could be informally defined as occasions in which linguistic difference is salient and "integral to the nature of participants' interactions and their interpretive processes and strategies" (Heath 1982:50). Alternatively, following Coupland's proposal for a 'dialect stylistics' (1995), the data that I shall analyse could be referred to as 'dialect performances'. But more important than the name, these episodes can be linked to theories of class as an everyday social process which make it possible to claim that particular interactional sequences play a constitutive part in the negotiation of social class relations. If our conceptualisation of class is revised and combined with careful description of metalinguistic episodes in which accent is made salient through stylisation, there is an opportunity to move the discussion of language, class and schooling from the realms of speculation to empirical analysis.

We can start by returning to the questions about the general climate of school attitudes to accent. How far was non-standard speech still stigmatised at school, and how clearly associated was it with linguistic insecurity?

8.2   Official ideologies in action

In the episode below, Mr Newton can be seen saying to the class:

```
because you're all from London, you're handicapped to a
certain extent, because if [you're at Eton], your everyday
language wouldn't include too many [ain'ts and] innits,
would it?  (Extract 8.1, lines 34-42)
```

At first sight, this looks very much like the kind of crude linguistic prejudice that Trudgill and others warned against. But on closer consideration, Mr Newton himself looks rather less culpable than one might at first assume:

Extract 8.1

An English lesson with Mr Newton (c. 30 years old, male, Anglo-descent), Hanif, Rafiq (14 years, male, Moroccan descent), John (14, male, Ghanaian descent), Masud (14, male, Bangladeshi descent). Mr Newton, a popular, committed but not very commanding teacher (admired for his sharp turn-of-phrase by these informants when interviewed), is trying to get the English class started on their oral assessment activity, and in part-exhortation, part-warning, he has mentioned some recently published league tables of schools performance, telling them that in this school, pupils of fourteen have been achieving the level expected of eleven year olds (Level 4).

```
 1  MR NEWTON        ((three claps))
 2                   Ninnette:::
 3                   listen (.)
 4                   listen (2)
 5                   to get a level Five it starts:
 6                   to be a little bit more difficult
                     because
 7                   Shahid (.)
 8                   the words Standard English start to
                     crop up
 9  RAFIQ            ((in a constricted sing-song
                     voice:)) ˆoh
10                   ┌thats ˈvery ⎡ˆ(good)
11  MR N             └           ⎣  and (.)
```

```
12   SHAHID          > I don't (      ⌈  ) <
13   MR N                             ⌊ so:
14   ANONS (MALE)     ((laughter))
15   MR N            sort of people who er answer every
                                             question (.)
16                   with lots of aints and innits (.)
17   ?HANIF          ((quietly:)) yeh
18   MR N            are in fact (.)
19                   handicappin' 'emselves (.)
20                   so unfortunately
21   HANIF           > yeh I know
22                   Daily Times <
23   MR N            because you're all from (.)
24   HANIF           > Ban⌈gla'desh <
25   MR N                 ⌊because youre all
                     from ⌄ Lon⌈don
26   HANIF                      ⌊ > Bangla'desh <
27                   oh (.)
28   SEVERAL         ((laughter, noise⌈levels rise
                                       ⌊gradually))
29   RAFIQ ((IN HYPER-               ꞌsoˌnar ꞌbanˌgla
     COCKNEY))                       ((laughs))
                                     [səʊnɑ: bæ̃ŋglɑ̃::]
30   ?MASUD          ((hyper-Cockney accent:))
                     ꞌsoˌnar ꞌbanˌgla
                     [s:ə̄ūnɑ̄ bæ̃ŋg]
31   JOHN            ((hyper-Cockney accent:))
                     ꞌsoˌn/ar ꞌbanˌgla
                     [sə̄ūnə̄ bæ̃ŋglɑ̄]
32   MR N            (you know) I'm getting fed up with
                                          (  back )
33                   (1) ((quite a lot of talk going on))
34                   because you're from London
35                   you're handicapped
36                   to a certain ext⌈ent
37   SEVERAL                          ⌊((loud laughs))
38   MR N            because erm: (.)
39                   your everyday language (.)
40                   if you're at Eton (.)
41                   wouldn't include too many innits
42                   would it (1)
43                   alright
44                   ⌈listen
45   ANON (M)        ⌊((in a posh voice:)) (because
                                     they're very) posh
46   MR N            ((fast and quieter:)) yes exactly
```

When Mr Newton says in lines 5–8 that

`to get a level five it starts to be a little bit more diffi-`
`cult because ... the words standard English start to crop up,`

he is reporting what the National Curriculum (NC) says:

"Level 5: Pupils ... begin to use standard English in formal situations" (DFE 1995a:26)

Indeed, with the phrase `"the words standard English start to crop up"`, he evokes some text *elsewhere* as the source and authority on this, rather than appropriating these requirements in a pronouncement of his own (as he might have with, say, "to get a level 5, you've got to use standard English"). From there, when he begins to speak about the `"sort of people who ..."` in line 15, he starts to situate the NC stipulations in a wider social field, and this is congruent with quite a strong local pedagogic commitment to telling these youngsters about the harsh realities of life. In fact, he is now embarked on some syllogistic reasoning, which can be summarised as:

1. SATs are hard because they require standard English (lines 5–8)
2. people who use (vernacular) ain't and innits are handicapped in SATs (lines 15–16, 18–19)
3. because you're from London (and speak the London vernacular), you're handicapped (lines 23, 25, 34–35)

This is quite an elaborate rhetorical structure and it has a momentum which carries him through a number of student interjections and responses. He postpones the conclusion on two occasions (lines 23 and 25), the second time to deal with inattentiveness (lines 32–33), and for those who are listening, these delays no doubt heighten the climax. When it comes, the upshot looks rather blunt, but it is obviously hard to hold the attention of the class – see Chapter 2 – and this rather extreme formulation may be an adaptation to these situational difficulties. As Pomerantz notes, "[i]nteractants use extreme case formulations ... when they anticipate or expect their co-interactants to undermine their claims and when they are in adversarial situations" (1986:222). In fact Mr Newton softens this immediately after, with `"to a certain extent"` and he then goes on to associate these standards with 'Eton', the elite private school. In identifying these linguistic expectations with hyper-toffs in a social stratum far above the tastes and aspirations of ordinary kids, he effectively 'others' the NC requirements and this can be seen as a gesture of solidarity and another form of mitigation.

For an understanding of the articulation of official ideologies of language at Central High, perhaps the most important aspect of this episode is the students' reaction when Mr Newton's conclusion eventually does come. When the students are told that as Londoners they're handicapped, they respond with loud laughter, one of them following up with congruent remarks that Mr Newton "exactly" agrees with (lines 45–46). Of course it is very hard to know what long term effect this kind of message might have on pupils, but at this point, anyway, Mr Newton seems to have been quite successful addressing at least a subset of the students, and they sound as though they have enjoyed his message rather than felt cowed by it.

To extend this view of teachers and pupils negotiating the relationship between non-standard speech and the National Curriculum, it is worth looking at what happens later on in the same class, when the students actually start to perform the oral assessment activity. They have been working in groups preparing to role-play an inquest into the deaths of Romeo and Juliet, and it is now time for the groups to take it in turns to perform the scene they have rehearsed. Hanif has taken the part of the coroner – the central role – in his group, and his group is also going first. The rest of the class, however, is taking a little time to settle down, and in his effort to get them to attend, Mr Newton is now acting in role as a court official:

Extract 8.2

At the start of Hanif et al.'s coroner's inquest role-play. (Blex 34–35; 19c:330)

```
1   MR N      be seated
2              (.) ((talking continues in the background))
3   HANIF     ((clearing his throat loudly: )) ehem ehem
               ehem
4              (1) ((talking continues in the background
               until around line 13))
5   ?         ((raps 6 times in rapid suc/cession on a hard
               surface))
6   BOY       (get on with it)
```

7	HANIF	((calling out, in a posh voice:))
		ˈorder in the ˋcourt
		[ɔ:dəɹ ɪn ə kɔ:tʰ]
8	BOY	get on with it
9		(1.5) ((background talk continues))
10	HANIF	((with roughly the same intonational contour
		as before, slightly quieter, but with 'bloody
		well' pronounced in a London accent:))
		ˈorder in the ˈ**bloody** ˈ**well** ˋcourt
		[ɔ:də ɪn ə blʌdɪ weʊ kɔ:tʰ]
11		((laughter from a lot of students))
12	HANIF	/TODAY
13	BOY2	((to another student:)) >be quiet ( )<
		(1) ((only one or two voices continue to talk
		softly))
14	HANIF	TODAY
15		(1)
16		((more quietly, as if addressed to a particular
		individual:))
		shudup
17		((a couple of boys/ laugh))
18	MR N	MEMBERS OF THE PUBLIC GALLERY
19		(.)
20		MEMBERS OF THE PUBLIC GALLERY
21		(.)
22	BOY3?	((sitting at the side, in very broad nasal
		Cockney, fading out abruptly on the last
		syllable:))
		awigh aw/ai
		[ãwʌ̃ĩʔ ãwʌ̃ɪʔ]
23	MR N	you're here
24	LARA	((continues her own conversation quietly))
25	MR N	to listen
26		(.)
27		to this-
28		inquest into the deaths of these unfortunate
		pair

The extract begins with a number of efforts to settle the class, with Mr Newton and Hanif acting together in role. It is not clear who simulates the gavel in line 5, but Hanif first clears his throat and then calls for order, pronouncing 'court' with a standard monophthongal realisation of the FORCE vowel and a clearly enunciated (aspirated) T. But members of the class continue to talk among themselves, and so Hanif repeats this command, upgrading it with the insertion of ``bloody well''. This is transgressive in at least three ways: first, it imports a swear-word into a formal setting, whether this is taken as the classroom or the fictive inquest; second, it breaks the rules of standard syntax, using an adverb – "well" – rather than an adjective to premodify the noun 'court'; and third, it inserts Cockney L-vocalisation into an utterance that is otherwise pronounced in a rather posh accent. ``Order in the bloody well court'' in line 10 is not spoken as loudly as the initial ``Order in the court'' in line 7, perhaps in recognition of its transgressive qualities, but it has an immediate impact, drawing from the members of the class their first collectively synchronised response as an audience (the laughter in line 11). Raising his voice (but in his normal accent), Hanif then begins to introduce the main business of the court – ``TODAY'' in line 12 – and by the time he repeats it, almost all of the class has fallen silent, to the extent, indeed, that he can now pick off the stragglers (``shudup'' in line 16). But before he continues this exposition, the court orderly (Mr Newton) intercedes with some more framing activity, casting the spectating members of the class as ``members of the public gallery'' (lines 18 and 20) and reminding them of the conduct expected (lines 23 and 25–28). One of them responds to this address in role, using the exaggerated Cockney catchphrase ``alright'' in line 22.

Hanif often stylised broad Cockney (as well as posh), but here we can see that there are a number of ways in which *official* activities could build his confidence in doing so, encouraging him to import non-standard speech into areas where standard accents had hitherto been dominant. As a rhetorical strategy, the switch to Cockney in line 10 appears to be highly effective in bringing the class to order – this is an objective that he shares with the teacher, and the teacher subsequently reiterates the appeal for order on Hanif's behalf (lines 18, 20, 23, 25–28). Within the fictive frame of the inquest itself, there is nothing especially radical in these switches to broad London – on the contrary, to the extent that they help to establish social stratification within the dramatic arena of courtroom, dividing it into those who communicate in the formal language of the inquest, and those who need to be addressed much more emphatically in a vulgar vernacular, the use of Cockney reproduces dominant sociolinguistic structures. But

Hanif's position as coroner in the fictive inquest (which comes from his position as a relatively keen and successful student) provides him with the opportunity to edge the use of Cockney in more publicly transgressive directions, and with increasing confidence, Hanif recycles this call-to-order three more times over the course of the role-play. On two of these occasions, Mr Newton steps out of role to try and rein him in, but Hanif remains undaunted, the audience stays amused, and at the end of the lesson, when Mr Newton gives pupils marks for their oral performance, Hanif comes top with a Level 6 minus – ``quite high'', says Mr N.

Plainly, this is not a pedagogy which seeks to humiliate pupils for the use of non-standard speech, picking up and correcting a mistake in enunciation at the very moment it is produced (see Mugglestone 1995:190, 293 *et passim* on educating accents in the eighteenth and nineteenth centuries), and at an institutional level there is more involved here than just an isolated teacher whose personal sensitivity impels him to shield his pupils from the unvarying, absolute force of non-standard accent stigmatisation. For their oral assessment, the National Curriculum might state that secondary students should "speak with clear diction and appropriate intonation"; to gain a Level 6 in speaking and listening, it might expect that they "are usually fluent in their use of standard English in formal situations" (DFE 1995a:26); and if this situation is compared with the 1970s and 80s when educational interest in urban multilingualism was more widespread (Bernstein 1996), one would probably want to say that in 1997, 'variation ideologies' were much more 'residual' than 'dominant' in English education (see Williams 1977: 121–127; Carter 1992; Chapter 1.1). Even so, the NC expected children to "adapt their talk to the demands of different contexts with increasing confidence" (DFE 1995a); at this school there was a surviving tradition of respecting rather than condemning vernaculars; and the evidence in these and other extracts points to an ambivalence about non-standard speech that was institutionally grounded and that emerged from a complicated history of cultural change and political argument, a history in which sociolinguists have themselves been significant actors. In short, it would be wrong to assume that there is an unchanging bedrock of prejudice in the social and educational dynamics of non-standard accent, and that principles articulated in the 1960s and 70s are still relevant. Instead, it is essential to take an empirical look at metalinguistic activity in historically specific locales.

There are good reasons, then, for looking empirically at the climate of language attitudes in particular schools in particular periods, and even though central policy directives had lain increasing emphasis on standard English over the 5–10 years that preceded my fieldwork, there was still space for actual teachers and students to give some recognition to vernacular speech. Can we in fact go on to infer from this acceptance of non-standard English in certain parts of the curriculum that at this school, posh and Cockney had been largely neutralised as symbolic weapons in the conflict between teachers and pupils, and that sociolinguistically, the main lines of class division now lay between central government (and Eton) on the one hand, and on the other, an integrated school community of teachers and pupils at Central High? Unfortunately not, and in the next sections, I shall show that although the school had managed to erode a sense that dialect speech and school learning were entirely antithetical, the resonance and flexibility of posh and Cockney meant that they were worked quite extensively into the everyday micro-politics of educational division.

8.3   Mock posh retaliations to indignity

Here are Ninnette and Joanne in the playground:

Extract 8.3
Joanne, Ninnette and Linda, and perhaps a few others. They have been talking about the radio-microphone that Joanne's wearing, when Ninnette starts to talk about Mr Alcott in line 2, who they had been talking to a couple of minutes earlier (Blex 71 44/160)

```
1   JOANNE     I keep singing
2   NINNETTE   oh this is Mr Alcott
3              (.)
4              erm-
5              no-
6              look
7              this is Mr Alcott
8              ((in a posh accent:))  |oh (.) \no
                                      [əʊʔ : nɛuː ]
```

```
 9                (.)
10   JOANNE       >he goes he's<
11                (1)
12                ((high pitched posh laugh:))  ''ohehehe`haw:
                                                 [ɒ̃ʰə̃ʰə̃ʰə̃ʰɔ:ᵊ ]
13   NINNETTE     ((loud but in normal accent:))oh I can fly
14   JOANNE       ((laughs:)) he goes
15                he looks down
16                and he goes
17                ((high pitched posh laugh:))
                  >ahahahaha haw haw haw haw<
                  [ā:hāhāhāhāhɔ̃hɔ̃hɔ̃hɔ̃]
18                /I go (.)
19   NINNETTE     I (        )
20                I want to kick /his bum
21   JOANNE       >that's how I go<
22   NINNETTE     I want to kick up /the
23   JOANNE       I will
24                where is he
25   NINNETTE     ((laughs))
26   LINDA?       (          )
27   JOANNE       ((quick three-note humming))
28                I'm not going down there with them
29                gay people
30                (3)
31                just go-
32                NINNETTE
33                (.)
34                >(   I'm a go)<
35                (.)
36                ba:ng
37   LINDA        ((seeing someone:)) OH THAT'S SIMON
```

At the start of the extract, Ninnette sets up an impersonation of
Mr Alcott – 'oh this is Mr Alcott' (line 2) – and then focuses on
some visual/physical aspect of the scene (line 6: 'look'). Without a
visual record (and no playback commentary), it is impossible to say
either what physical actions or features she is performing, or
exactly what attitude the 'oh no' in line 8 is intended to express –
whether the 'oh no' signified fear, dread, boredom or distaste might
well depend on Ninnette's facial demeanour in uttering it. But it is
articulated in a posh accent – 'oh' is Received Pronunciation, and
the 'no' is 'hyper-RP'.[2] Joanne enters the spirit of this impersonation, and elaborates the scene with a couple of high-pitched, nasal,

stereotypically very posh laughs, but before she has finished her cameo and had time to reenact her own response to Mr A (line 18), Ninnette steps out of the Alcott guise to announce that she'd like to kick him (line 20), an idea which Joanne then offers to actualise (lines 23–24).

Ninnette's facial expression in uttering 'oh no' is not the only obscure element in these data, and it is hard to know exactly how 'oh I can fly' in line 13 and 'he looks down' in line 15 fit into the unfolding cameo.[3] But from the audio-record, it is possible to identify the encounter with Mr Alcott that provoked this exchange between the two girls, and it took place a couple of minutes earlier:[4]

Extract 8.4 ('free food')
In the playground at breaktime, a couple of minutes before Extract 8.3 (*posh laughs*). Mr Alcott is on duty, and Joanne, Ninnette and Linda go up to him to ask him about whether in their tutor group lesson immediately after break, they are going to continue the discussion of racism that had been initiated in the short registration period at the start of the morning (a discussion which had been occasioned by a racist incident the previous day).

```
 1  JOANNE     Sir
 2  MR A       yes
 3  JOANNE     are we talking about racism in: tutorial
 4  MR A       well I dunno
               I got- I had these other plans
 5             whi- that Miss Ford wants us to er deal with -
 7             I'm not quite sure
 8  JOANNE     oh
 9  MR A       I mean what do you think?
10             do you think it's worthwhile talking about
11  JOANNE     I don't know
12  NINNETTE   what
13  MR A       /what do you think Ninnette
14  NINNETTE   talking about what
15             what
16  MR A       well
17             John wanted to carry on
               talking about racism and stuff like that
18             (.)
19  NINNETTE   ((high pitched:))erm /what-
20  MR A       what do you think
21  JOANNE     yeh=
22  NINNETTE   yeh (.)
```

```
23                    ((not in an especially enthusiastic tone of
                      voice:))
                      `better than ˈanything
24    MR A            ((smile-voice, and with a chuckle at the
                      start of 'anything':))
                      ˌbetter than ˌanything (.)
25                    ˈwhat
26                    ˈeven better than ˇfree:
27                    (.)
28                    `food
29                    (.)
30                    Linda
31                    what do you think
32    JOANNE          NO :/:
33    LINDA           okay
34    JOANNE          I want free foo/:d
35    MR A            (  /  )
36    JOANNE          >no I'm only joking ((laughs))<
37    ?               (            )
38    MR A            I haven't decided yet
39                    I've got something half planned
40    NINNETTE        / (like) what
41    JOANNE          half-planned
42                    what's that (.)
43                    pa:rty::
44    MR A            what-
45                    we have to do a self-assessment
46                    for- year nine
((the talk continues for a short while, briefly addressing
the possibility of doing a self-assessment in the tutor
period, before other students arrive on the scene and Mr A
drifts out of earshot.))
```

Mr Alcott actually spoke with (what was to me, anyway) a noticeably regional accent, and nothing that he said in this Extract bears any immediate resemblance to the posh 'oh no' or the extravagant 'haw haw' that Joanne and Ninnette subsequently used to impersonate him, and so if there was any verisimilitude in their impersonation of him in Extract 8.3, it had more to do with physical action than with voice. Indeed, far from being haughty and dismissive, over the interaction as a whole, Mr Alcott solicited their views about what to do in the up-coming tutor-period, and adopted a generally open and consultative tone in telling them about the other possibilities he was thinking about. There was, however, one moment when he did re-key the interaction, and this occurred within the exchange directed to Ninnette in lines 20 to 29.

In line 23, it is unclear whether Ninnette's 'better than anything' actually meant 'better than any of the other possibilities on hand'. But in line 24, Mr Alcott first recycled it as an item requiring clarification – as a 'repairable' (Levinson 1983:339–342) – and then, rather than waiting or encouraging her to specify the scope of her comparison, he hyperbolically recast the meaning of her words, presenting the possibility of her preferring a tutorial discussion of racism to free food: 'what, even better than free food' (lines 25–28). Within the normative structure of conversational repair, in the event of Ninnette failing to clarify what she meant straightaway, the politest course of action open to Mr Alcott would have been to allow Ninnette herself to clarify what she meant once he had signalled his incomprehension (see Levinson 1983:339–342). In fact, though, Mr Alcott not only pre-empted any self-repair by Ninnette, but also upgraded his turn into something that bore the hallmarks of a playful tease. The chuckle in Mr Alcott's voice in line 24 signalled a humorous intention and lines 24 to 28 bear close resemblance to the teases described in Drew 1987 (see pp. 231, 235), both in offering an extreme version of what Ninnette might mean, and in being closely modelled on the verbal material offered in the Ninnette's prior turn (lines 23 and 24). In addition, teasing changes "[s]omething which is normal, unremarkable, etc., ... into something abnormal" (Drew 1987:244), and usually, the deviant attribute or identity being conjured has at least some potential 'real-world' relevance to the person being teased. The exact relevance of 'food' is not clear: on the one hand, Ninnette was quite well-built and sometimes worried about her size, while on the other, she also liked to talk about food – it is one of the most recurrent topics in the recordings of her – and as her form tutor, Mr Alcott might well know of this. But whichever way it is (and was) interpreted, there is a sense in which Mr Alcott's rather facetious exaggeration actually cuts 'close to the bone' (Drew 1987:246).

Mr A's 'what, even better than free food' might be intended as a playful tease, but it does not appear to go down very well with Ninnette. In Drew's data,

"[t]he overwhelming pattern is ... that recipients [the persons being teased] treat something about the tease, despite its humour, as requiring a serious response: even when they plainly exhibit their understanding that the teasing remark is not meant to be taken seriously ... recipients still almost always PUT THE RECORD STRAIGHT" (1987:230. Original emphasis)

But in the episode here, Ninnette remains silent. In line 29, there is a micro-pause at the end of the tease where she could have intervened, but no one relieves Mr Alcott of the speakership, and instead he 'down-keys' by returning to the more serious business of soliciting the students' views on what to do in the tutor period by redirecting the attention to Linda. If Ninnette had responded to the extreme version offered by Mr Alcott, her rejoinder would have helped to constitute the interaction as a bit of playful pupil-teacher banter, but from her silence it looks as though Mr A's remark has been experienced as a put-down. Joanne's subsequent intervention temporarily sustains a playful key, but itself evidently runs into some difficulty – `no, I'm only joking' (line 36).

Against this background of recent experience, the girls' conversation in Extract 8.3 ('posh laughs') now looks like symbolic retaliation, fictively paying Mr Alcott back for the sense of humiliation created by `"even better than free food"`. We ourselves might find it hard to detect any imperious condescension in Mr Alcott's demeanour in Extract 8.4 – he was talking to the girls in an open and consultative manner, and it seems more likely that his teasing remark was intended in a spirit of familiarity and friendliness (Drew 1987:220). But within the stylised performance she initiates in line 2 of Extract 8.3, Ninnette's switch to a high-class accent suggests that she interprets the encounter as an asymmetrical one, and the fact that Joanne then selects laughter for her own performance of ultra-poshness in line 12 shows her own sensitivity to what it was in the interaction with Mr Alcott that caused Ninnette offence – the moment of (intended) playfulness. In actual fact, Mr Alcott's only mistake may have been to assume a reciprocity with the girls that they didn't themselves share, and immediately after the tease in line 26, Ninnette may have been prevented from setting the record straight more by her own sense of the difficulties involved in answering a teacher back than by any real threat from Mr Alcott. Now, though, Mr Alcott has now been demonised as a mocking snob in the kind of 'backstage' replay that James Scott attributes to the 'hidden transcript', where "in the relative safety of their quarters, [subordinates] can speak the words of anger, revenge, self-assertion that they must normally choke back when in the presence of the masters and the mistresses" (1990:18; 37–38). Admittedly, there's nothing in Ninnette's awkward moment in Extract 8.4 to compare with the situations of dire oppression and humiliation that Scott describes, and indeed Mr Alcott's generally consultative stance in the episode points to an egalitarian spirit that was actually quite widespread among the staff. Even so, the interaction between teachers and pupils can easily give rise to feelings of humiliation, and in elaborating their fantasy of vengeance with mock posh voices, Ninnette and Joanne were reanimating a practice with a long pedigree in British popular culture (e.g. Humphries 1981:123).

Ninnette and Joanne's performance in Extract 8.3 was probably the most hostile parody in my corpus, but it was not the only one, and here – I think – is another one, this time involving Hanif in a Humanities lesson.

Working in small groups, the class have been preparing for the role play of a trial in the eighteenth century, and Messrs Poyser and Alcott, who are teaching the class together, are now addressing them collectively, running through the kind of language that lawyers use. Hanif has been a fairly interested participant, raising queries and registering informative responses with 'oh right, okay'. A little later, Mr Alcott is offering guidance on how the students might formulate the lawyers' opening words, and the following sequence occurs:

Extract 8.5
(Blex A15 13:540)

```
 1   MR A    how can y-
 2           (.)
 3           how can you introduce your speech
 4           like writing/an essay
 5           you have t-
 6   RAFIQ   I would like to bring up
 7   MR A    I would like to::
 8   HANIF   bring forward
 9   MASUD   bring forw/ard
10   ANON    (ex  )
11   MR A    or even
```

```
12          (.)
13          I ₍in`te ::nd ₍to
14   ANON   (pro/secute)
15   HANIF  ((loudly, in an RP accent, stretched, with an
            exaggerated rise-fall:))ˆo ::: h
                              [əᴵʊ]
16   ANON   (pro )
17   ANON   ( )
18   GUY    I am going to
19          (.)
20   MR A   I- I am going to
21          or/I intend to
22   MASUD  ((talking to Hanif on another topic:))hah
23          me- remember thing (.)
24          erm
25          (.)
26          >what was I going to say<
```

The sequence begins with Mr Alcott's central question – 'how can you introduce your speech'. He back-pedals a little bit in lines 4–5, providing students with additional support by asking them to think of their experience of writing essays (see French and MacLure 1983), but this proves redundant, and Rafiq interrupts by providing an answer: 'I would like to bring up' (line 6). This answer, however, is not deemed sufficient to close the matter. Mr A solicits further views, narrowing down the range of possible answers by recycling the main verb phrase in Rafiq's contribution but leaving open the non-finite verb slot, in effect inviting members of the class to provide utterance completers. Hanif and Masud oblige, amending Rafiq's relatively informal 'bring up' to 'bring forward', a more formal version appropriate to the fictional court context (lines 8 and 9). There is no explicit oral acknowledgement of these efforts, and instead, Mr A begins to introduce an additional possibility, building up to it with the word 'even', a concessive conjunct which suggests that what's coming up will be unexpected or surprising (Quirk and Greenbaum 1973:292–293). After a micro-pause, designed perhaps to increase the suspense (line 12), Mr A reveals this addition, speaking slowly and with a stretched fall on the second syllable of 'intend' (line 13). The version that he proposes shifts the focus away from the non-finite verb slot that the class had just been attending to, back to the main verb itself, effectively trumping the sequence that has developed since Rafiq's contribution in line 6. Hanif responds with both the particle 'oh', a 'change of state' token which is commonly used to indicate that the prior talk is informative (Heritage 1984b), and with an exaggerated rise-fall, which often indicates that the speaker is impressed (Cruttenden 1986:101). At the same time, he pronounces this in a much posher-than-normal accent,[5] and in doing so, he steps back from the effort to contribute to the construction of a legal speech (line 8) and instead proposes that British upper-class identity is now somehow relevant to the proceedings.

As always in stylisation, the audience is faced with the task of working out exactly what this relevance might be (Chapters 6.3 above and 8.5 below). Unfortunately, there is nothing in the data to indicate what the participants themselves might make of it, but at a distance anyway, there seem to be two possibilities. On the one hand, we might read Hanif's posh 'oh' as an elaboration of the Mr Alcott's 'I ₁in`te::nd /to', entering into the spirit of his careful formulation, using an elite accent to amplify its specialness. Alternatively – and in my view, more plausibly – we can take his response in line 16 as a piece of sarcastic back-channelling, signalling to Mr Alcott that he has considerably under-estimated the boys' linguistic knowledge. Hanif was, after all, a very articulate student, and it is rather unlikely that he would be genuinely impressed by a word as commonplace as 'intend'.[6] In this second context, the upper-class identity is relevant to Mr Alcott's demeaning attributions of lexical ignorance – Mr Alcott, says the stylisation, is being a patronising snob.

So there seems to be ambiguity in Hanif's stylisation of posh, and it certainly does not mobilise quite the same range of images as Ninnette and Joanne did in Extract 8.3, where the initial posh 'oh no' was followed by stereotypic 'haw haw' laughter, fantasies of retribution, and attributions of homosexuality. Even so, it is clear that the Section before did not tell the whole story about the stylisation of posh and Cockney at Central High. Mr Newton's partial self-dissociation from National Curriculum stipulations – and his eventually high rating of Hanif's role-play performance – might imply sociolinguistic solidarity between teachers and students, but definitely in Extract 8.3 and quite possibly in Extract 8.5, exaggerated posh is invoked to 'other' the teacher on occasions when pupils felt degraded or patronised. One might argue that in Hanif's courtroom performance in Extract 8.2, the Cockney amounted to no more than the post-modern pastiche that Jameson speaks of (Chapter 6.6), but the stylisation of posh is now embedded (in at least one of these episodes) in a very dissatisfied apprehension of being debased by a person in institutional authority. Sociologists have often said that schooling and the pupil–teacher relationships are central to the production of class stratification, but here we can see that students also engage in small acts of critical class analysis, using linguistic emblems of class hierarchy to mark out aspects of teacher conduct that they object to.

In fact, though, the parody in Extract 8.3 looks rather spectacular when compared with the way in which these youngsters flagged up their sensitivity to class in the transition between curriculum work and peer sociability, and in turning to this in the next section, I shall show that class awareness could be more pervasive and more closely bound into their routine activity than one might infer from anything so far.

8.4   Stylised posh and Cockney transitions between work and play

The episodes in this Section involve points of transition between curriculum tasks and activity oriented to friends.

In the first, Ninnette puts on an exaggerated posh accent while she is working on a task with Joanne nearby:

Extract 8.6
(Blex 63, 38:70)
Ninnette (wearing the radio-microphone) and Joanne are doing mock SATs (written) tests in an English lesson. Joanne has been whispering to Ninnette:

```
1   JOANNE      o′kay
2   NINNETTE    okay
3               (.)
4               >how do you spell whole<
5               (.)
6   JOANNE      haitch o elle˅ee
7               (1)
8   NINNETTE    no the uvver whole
9               (2)
```

```
10  JOANNE?     with a double-U
11              (2.5)
12  NINNETTE    ((louder, and fast:))
                >double-U haitch o elle ee<
13  JOANNE?     (      ay)
14  NINNETTE    ((half-laugh:))he huh huh
15  JOANNE      um
16  NINNETTE    ((reading aloud with light laugh in the
                first word:))
                it would change her whole life
17              .hhh
18              (.)
19              \comple:tely:
20              (2.5)
21              ((in hyper-posh with very exaggerated rising
                intonation:))
                /ea:n″d: ((= 'and'))
                [εə:ṇḏ̥h]
22              (5)
23              ((starts rhythmic beat:))
24              mm mm
25              heh / leh uh=
26  GIRL        (      ) we got a problem today
27  NINNETTE    =mm mm
28              aa aa
29              ee ee
30              ee ee
31              yeh we got C-
32              ((to someone nearby:)) oh (      )
33              were (      ) looking at it
34              you can't-
35              don't peel 'em off
36              please
37              >thank you<
38              (.)
39              yeh we got
40              CDT
41              inn't we
```

After a period in which the girls have been reading and writing silently, Joanne has just whispered something to Ninnette that is difficult to decipher on the audio-tape (≈ "we're not allowed to [tell each other]"), but they have evidently come to a consensus on the matter (lines 1 and 2). Ninnette then asks her about the spelling of 'whole' and when she has got this down (lines 4–12),

she reads aloud what she has just written – ``it would change
her whole life'' (line 16). After an inbreath and a micro-pause,
she vocalises an adverbial at the end of the clause, slowing down a
little as if involved in writing it (``comple:tely:'' line 19). After
that, she remains silent for a slightly longer period, and then says
``eand'', slowly, with exaggerated rising intonation, with a very
posh articulation of the TRAP vowel (Wells 1982:281), and with a
lot of emphasis on the final consonant cluster. From subsequent
evidence, it is clear that she also writes this word down,[7] and so it
looks as though Ninnette's ``and'' announces that she is about to
embark on the writing of a new clause. She returns to silence for
another 5 seconds (line 22), but after that, she moves into sound play
and then some conversation with her friends.

Earlier in Extract 8.3, Ninnette stylised posh in quite a vehement
display of rebelliousness, but it would be hard to argue that her
exaggerated posh here represents an objection to, or refusal of,
school activity. Instead, the stylisation seems to serve as a way of
lightening it up (cf. Extract 4.2). The official writing task evidently
holds Ninnette's attention both before this sequence and afterwards
(when Mr Newton told them they should move on to the next
question), and she wants to get her spellings right (lines 4–12). At
the same time, however, when she (writes-and-)reads aloud, she uses
her voice to suggest an orientation to matters that seem to be
independent of the text itself, thereby lessening the authority of its
hold on her involvement. She may be observing the 'letter' of the
task she has been set, but she is also infusing it with extraneous
'spirit'. There is nothing comic in the text-world that Ninnette is
writing about to motivate her laughter in lines 14 and 16, and there
is no sense in which a posh English accent in line 21 might be
congruent with any of the characters within it.[8] Up to a point, the
selection of a posh accent for reading aloud falls in line with a much
wider sociolinguistic convention – quantitative sociolinguistics has
often shown that speakers seek to produce speech that is more
prestigious and less vernacular than usual when articulating written
text, and indeed in her own routine non-stylised speech production,
Ninnette also became more standard when she read aloud
(Tables 7.2 and 7.3). But the conspicuous *exaggeration* involved in
``eand''/[ɛə : ɳ d̥ h] in line 21 separates Ninnette's speech from
routine reading aloud and constructs the utterance as something

more than straightforward task-focused self-talk. Instead it displays an orientation to play and sociability which she develops further in her next turns a few moments later.

There were two other occasions when these two girls marked the transition between work and sociability with a switch to speech with exaggerated posh elements. Here is Ninnette again:

Extract 8.7

Ninnette and Joanne are in a Maths lessons, and are supposed to be concentrating on workcards. They have just been engaged together in a flurry of T-glottalising sound play, and over a series of turns and a lot of laughter and amusement, this has now transmuted into (a non-T-glottallised) "ET" (ET = the alien in Steven Spielberg's science fiction film for children). At the start of the extract, Ninnette is appreciatively replaying Joanne's rendering of ET, but after what sounds like the line from a song (10), she refocuses on her workcard (line 13):

```
1    NINNETTE          beau:tiful the way you put it
2                      you go
3                      ((with pharyngeal constriction:))
                       little ee ee
                       [lɪʔʊ ʔi : ʔi ::]
4                      ((high pitched laugh:)) ahaaaha
5    JOANNE            ((very broad London:)) little E T
                                             [lĩʔʊᵗʔ ʔĩʔĩ ::]
6    NINNETTE AND      ((laugh))
     JOANNE
7                      (.)
8    NINNETTE          ((laughing:))
                       and (   I always   you) were
9                      (.)
10                     ((with slightly US accent
                       on'can't':))
                       I can't get no sleep
11                     ((both N and J laugh for about 2-3
                       seconds))
12                     (1)
13                     ((carefully enunciated:))
                       'what's the 'date ₁of to‖day ‖man
                       [wɒs  ə   deɪtʰ ɒv tʰədeɪ mæn]
```

```
14                  (1)
15   JOANNE         e:r
16                  (.)
17   NINNETTE       the fenty tweight
                    [ðə fentʰɪ tʰweɪt]
```

Writing the date in one's exercise book is a standard work procedure, but Ninnette does not abandon the ludic frame when she asks
about this in line 13, and the articulation of her question involves
several deviations from normal style. Her syntax is hyper-correct –
*'the date of today' rather than 'today's date' – and it is also
carefully enunciated: the non-content word 'of' is fully articulated, with a non-schwa vowel and no elision of the final [v], and in
contrast to the rampant T-glottallising that was central in the sound
play that's just finished, her T's are pronounced with aspiration.
This phonological style resembles 'literate speech', and it follows in
a tradition that Mugglestone dates back to Dr Johnson's dictum:
"For pronunciation the best rule is, to consider those as the most
elegant speakers who deviate least from the written words"
(Mugglestone 1995:208). At the same time, though, Ninnette ends
the utterance with ''man'', a tag that is anomalous (a) in being a
colloquial vernacular form rather at odds with the careful style in the
utterance hitherto, and (b) in lacking the rising intonation that you
would normally expect in this position. Indeed, she carries on with
the speech play when she finds the answer (line 17).

And here is Joanne later in the same lesson, emerging from a spell
of quite sustained silent maths work:

Extract 8.8
Joanne is sitting next to Ninnette in a Maths class, and she has been working
silently for a substantial period. But now she announces that she's finished in
an ultra-posh voice, reminiscent of Brian Sewell, the television art critic (see
also Gimson 1970:102 on [ɪ] being diphthongised towards [ə] among
'advanced RP speakers'), and turns to some sweets she is sharing with
Ninnette.

```
((Joanne has been working silently))

1    ˈfie:ˌnie:shed ((= 'finished'))
     [frənɪəˑɪʃːtʰ]
2    (3)
```

```
3      but haven't finished these
4      (2) ((sound of paper rustling))
5      ((with something in her mouth: ))for now
6      (.)
7      look
```

Hanif also used exaggerated accents in the transition between workcards and sociability, but in my recordings of him, he stylised Cockney rather than posh and its significance seemed rather different. Here he is in a Science lesson:

Extract 8.9

Hanif (wearing the radio-microphone), Arun and Simon are sharing the same table in science. (Blex 8)

```
 1    HANIF    ((whistles six notes))
 2             what you doing Arun
 3             (.)
 4             what you doin Arn
 5             (.)
 6             (>shup<) leave it Dimbo
 7             (2)
 8             look what you ma-
 9             look what you made me do
10             (4)
11             ((reading the title of the exercise, with an
                 exaggerated Cockney final syllable: ))
               `Stars and `Gala\xies
               [stɑːz n gæləksə̄ĩːːz]
12             (1)
13             ((quietly reciting page numbers:))
14             one three seven
15             (3)
16             ((fast and loud to the teacher:))
17             >SIR can I go check if there's any
18             Active Sciences left<
```

Hanif had been away from the table looking around for a book he needed for the writing work he had been set, but now he had arrived back, bringing a copy with him. He asked Arun what he was doing (lines 2–4), and after that, tried to ward off some kind of territorial incursion (line 6). Exactly who was trying what is not clear from the audio-recording, but Hanif followed it with a reproach (lines 8, 9).

There was no audible apology or retort, the matter dropped and Hanif then turned to his worksheet, reading the title aloud and ending it in an exaggerated Cockney diphthong.[9]

Once again, we are faced with the question of how this stylised accent might be relevant to the business-on-hand, and taking into account the specific interactional juncture at which he produced it, we can plausibly construe his stylised Cockney as a way of managing the transition between chat and study, peer group and school. Reading the whole title itself, 'Stars and Galaxies', it looks like Hanif was engaged in self-talk, dedicating himself to the solitary work ahead. But as Goffman says (1981:97–98), self-talk is often designed to be overheard, as well as being adjusted to the audience's sensibilities, and in rounding the title off with an accent that was often associated with informal sociability,[10] he seems to combine a display of 'being on-task' with signs that he is not a nerd and is still in tune. Elsewhere, Hanif showed an active sense that peer and school activity were potentially at odds,[11] and here, his playful vernacular speech sounds like a way of mitigating the affiliation to classroom business.

In fact, as the science lesson proceeds, the play between friends and work becomes more explicit. A little after Extract 8.9, Hanif's response cries suggest he is really quite interested in the subject matter – "WO:W (2) oh my gard (7) oh my god (1)" – and he continues weaving stylised accents into the task. The next time he returns to the 'Stars and Galaxies' title, turning from talk to work, he renders it in quasi-Caribbean:

Extract 8.10
Hanif and Arun have been arguing about how long it takes to reach the moon, and Arun has contested Hanif's claims by showing him that the book he's cited is more out-of-date than Hanif thought, being published in 1993 rather than 1996. Hanif's accent in lines 9, 11 and 13 is quasi-Caribbean (see Wells (1982:572 et passim) and Sebba (1993:154) on the TRAP vowel and the non-reduction of unstressed vowels in Caribbean English)

```
1  ARUN     things can change (in four
            years)
2  HANIF    1993 was (.)
3           three years ago
```

```
4              (.)
5              >get your facts right<
6              ((very fast:))
               >>oh you (           )
7    ARUN      ((turning to John who appears to have said
               something:))
               SHUT UP JOHN
8              (4)
9    HANIF     ((with a quasi-Caribbean accent:))
               ˈguˈluˈxies ˌmun
               [galaksiz mʌn]
10             (.)
11             ˈstars ˌmun
               [stɑːz mʌn]
12             (.)
13             ˈguˈluˈxies ˌmun
               [galaksiːːz mʌn]
14   ARUN      ( your sta )
15   HANIF     shudup
```

((Hanif now stays silent for 9 seconds, breaks this by briefly noticing a textbook nearby ("someone put an Active Science Book here"), and he then keeps out of conversation for nearly a minute))

And then after a period of attentive silent reading, he begins to turn the worksheet into quiz questions for Simon and Arun. At one stage of the quiz, he uses hyper-Cockney "okay" ([əũkʌ̃ɪ]) (cf. Wells 1982:303–304) to get Simon and Arun to attend to the next question:

Extract 8.11
Later on in the lesson, with the 'quiz' underway

```
1    HANIF     ((writing down an answer:))
               Mercury (.)
2              takes (.)
3              the (.)
4              shortest (3)
5              shortest time (1)
6              to traveːl (.)
7    SIMON     all right
8    HANIF     around (3)
```

```
 9          thee
10          earth
11          (.)
12          oh-
13          thee sun
14          sorry
15          (2)
16          ((very loud, nasalised and Cockney: )) o/kai
                                               [əũkʌ̃ĩ]
17          (1)
18          number f-
19          free
20          (.)
21          all right
22          let's see if you >don't learn this< one
23          (.)
24          Arun
25   ARUN   yes
26   HANIF  and no guessin'
27          right
28          (1)
29   ARUN   I DIDN'T GUESS THE FIR/ST ONE
30   HANIF  shsh
31          shsh
```

At moments like these, Cockney stylisation seems to go further than just toning down the signs of Hanif's own school commitment. Here it contributes to a more collectively oriented effort to get his peers to focus on school-related activities, and rather than apologetic self-mitigation, switches like these look more like attempts at the *vernacularisation* of school knowledge itself, bringing the science worksheet to life with non-standard accents and popular discourse formats.[12]

When Ninnette focused on written text in Extracts 8.6, her move into hyper-posh coincided with sociolinguistic convention ('reading-aloud => more-standard-pronunciation'), and it was the exaggeration of this that signalled that her pursuit of this was not straightforward. But in Extracts 8.9, 8.10 and 8.11, Hanif seems to be running against the grain of the traditional links between literacy, education and standard speech, and the difference between them deserves further comment. But before doing so, we need to be more explicit about exactly how social class might be relevant to these episodes. This was relatively simple with Extract 8.3 – Ninnette thought Mr Alcott was putting her down, and stylisation of posh portrayed him as an upper-class snob, and much the same could be said of Hanif if the second interpretation of Extract 8.5 is accepted. Similarly, in the role-play in Extract 8.2, Hanif's exaggerated Cockney could be mapped onto the fictive division between court officials and 'unwashed masses'. In all of these cases, the stylised accents looked 'characterological', linked to particular social types or kinds of person (cf. Agha 2003). But with the data in this Section, what sense would it make to say that Joanne and Ninnette portrayed writing as an activity for upper-class people in Extracts 8.6 and 8.8, that maths workcards were cast as lower-middle class in Extract 8.7, and that in Extract 8.9 to 8.11, Hanif constructs science as an interest for black and working-class Londoners? There is a danger here of importing our own interest in accent and class too quickly into the analysis (Coupland 2001c:197; Erickson 2001:175–176), and committing what Williams calls "the basic error", "the immediate and regular conversion of experience into finished products ... the reduction of the social to fixed forms" (1977:128, cited Chapter 6.2 above).

To avoid these risks, and to clarify the way in which class might actually be relevant to these episodes, it is worth referring to Ochs' discussion of 'stance' and 'indexical valence'.

8.5 Mapping class meaning in stylised communication

In Ochs' account

> *affective stance* refers to a mood, attitude, feeling and disposition, as well as degrees of emotional intensity vis-à-vis some focus of concern; *epistemic stance* refers to knowledge or belief vis-à-vis some focus of concern, including degrees of certainty of knowledge, degrees of commitment to the truth of propositions, and sources of knowledge. (1996:410)

This fits with what I have already said about Extracts 8.6 to 8.11 – in the first instance, their exaggerations of posh and Cockney encouraged the inference that Ninnette, Joanne and Hanif were not too earnest in their commitment to the written texts on hand. As a concept, though, the notion of stance tends to focus attention on the communicative impact of symbolic associations rather than on the symbolic associations themselves – it centres on the *intersection* of indexical value and interactional meaning, on how the connotations of a linguistic form modify an act or utterance, communicating a particular perspective on what is being said or done. As such, it leaves the social specificity of posh and Cockney unaccounted for – it would, after all, be possible to intimate a stance of less than total commitment to school-work with *any* exaggerated shift away from their ordinary pronunciation. To address the connotations of posh and Cockney in particular, it is worth moving to Ochs' 'indexical valence'.

'Indexical valence' refers to the complex associative networks that underpin our expectations that particular kinds of language will be used by particular types of person doing particular kinds of thing in particular types of situation (1996:417–419). As a concept, indexical valence underlines the importance of the participants' wider cultural knowledge, and points to the fact that the meaning of an utterance is influenced by our knowledge and experience of participation in larger social systems. When a bilingual switches into another language, it is much more likely that they are doing this to qualify or emphasise the point they are making (= stance) than to display their ethnolinguistic identity, but this qualification or emphasis is often at least partly achieved by the associations that the selected language has with particular kinds of relationship, identity, network or activity. This is useful for the interpretation of Extracts 8.6 to 8.11, because if we say that class was part of the indexical valence of posh and Cockney, we can introduce class into our analysis *without* having to suggest that class types or class groups were a focal preoccupation or up-front theme for these youngsters.

But that still is not enough for the analysis of these data, since as Ochs insists,

it is important to distinguish [i] the range of situational dimensions that a form ... *potentially* indexes from [ii] the range of situational dimensions that a form ... *actually* indexes in a particular instance of use ... When a form is put to use in dialog, the range of situational dimensions that a particular form indirectly helps to constitute and index is configured in a particular way. Not all situational meanings are necessarily entailed.   (1996:418)

The implications of Ochs' scheme for accent stylisation are represented in figure 8.1. When a person stylises a particular voice or

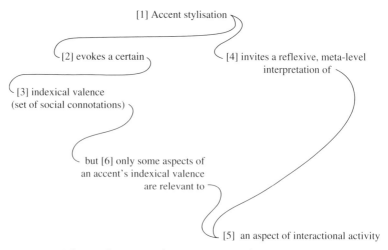

Figure 8.1: The production and interpretation of meaning in accent stylisation

accent ([1]), they evoke a particular field of connotations ([2] and [3]), and invite the recipient(s) to construe it as a meta-level representation that is somehow relevant to the interaction on hand ([4] and [5]). The recipient has to spot the shift in voice, to identify the new accent/voice that has been introduced, to link it to a particular indexical valence/connotational field, and to work out exactly *what* aspects of the indexical valence are relevant to precisely *which* elements of the interaction ([5]), moving between [3] and [5] until they have found an adequate fit [6].

Sometimes, speakers provide their recipients with a good deal of guidance, while at others, both recipients and analysts have to do a lot more of the inferential work themselves – for example in Extract 8.3 (`'oh no ... haw haw'`), Ninnette provided quite a number of cues to help Joanne make the links between poshness, Mr Alcott and snobbery, whereas in Extracts 8.6 to 8.11 (`'eand'`, `'Stars and Galaxies'` etc.), there was much less guidance on which particular dimensions within the indexical valence associated with posh and Cockney were relevant, and what aspects of the ongoing interaction they were relevant to.[13] When these elements are left unspecified by the speaker and most of the responsibility for interpretation is passed to the recipient(s), it is a mistake to assume that vagueness and indeterminacy are analytic deficiencies, to be cured perhaps with more ethnography or retrospective participant feedback. Instead, they need to be seen as properties of the communication itself (see Sperber 1975; Sperber and Wilson 1986:59–60; Blakemore 1992:Part III; Pilkington 2000 on 'weak implicatures' and 'weak communication'). Stylisation actually varies in the clarity of the imagery it evokes, for both participants and analysts. Sometimes, it can evoke a rather particular scene, social type or persona (Sebba 1993:131–135; Hudson 1996:237–240: Agha 2003), but at other times, Bakhtin's famous dictum about words *"tasting"* of the contexts in which they have lived their socially-charged lives (1981:293) points to the kind of subtle social coloration or tincture that it can bring to an activity.

This variation in the specificity of the indexical resonance of stylised utterances accounts for some of the differences in the data seen so far, and its recognition helps to avoid heavy-handed interpretation of Extracts 8.6 to 8.11 as the projection of different kinds of class persona. But if that is the case, in what way can I claim that social class has *any* relevance to these episodes, and that it is not just lying buried somewhere very deep indeed in the indexical valence of these two varieties, a historical matrix that is now more or less forgotten, recoverable only by the analyst? What is there in these interactions that would allow us to say that when kids switch to exaggerated posh and Cockney, they are responding to the processes and experiences that analysts identify with the term 'class', that they are in effect flagging up 'social class' as a framework that is relevant to the interpretation of what's happening?

My suggestion is that it is school-linked processes of differentiation and boundary marking that make 'class' a subjectively real part of the local interactional meaning of these stylisations. We know from a lot of previous work that people are particularly alert to the potential for stylised (exaggerated and non-routine) acts in moments of transition across social, spatial and interactional boundaries (see Chapter 4 note 8), and in all of these extracts, there was movement between activity oriented to school and activity oriented to friends. Recapping, there was

- a shift from work to play in Extract 8.6 (mock SATs => sound play) and Extract 8.8 (a maths worksheet => sweets), and

- a shift from play towards work in Extracts 8.7 (sound play => maths book) and 8.9 (chat => reading science).

Indeed,

- stylised speech also emerged in an effort to hold work and play in balance in Extracts 8.10 and 8.11 (getting on with the science questions while keeping Simon and Arun on task), as well as in Extract 8.2 (keeping the whole class focused while performing the coroner's inquest)

In Chapters 6.1 and 8.2, I quoted Thompson saying that "politics is often about exactly this – how will class happen, where will the line be drawn?", and I proposed that some of the patterns of social stratification associated with 'class' emerge in institutionally-embedded interactions involving the differentiation and evaluation of groups and individuals. In the extracts in the previous section, all of the boundaries being negotiated carried status implications (and in each case, lying on one side of the line there happened to be work that the students would be individually assessed on). So overall, I would say

a) that it is the correlation between stylised posh, Cockney and potentially status-freighted and socially-divisive boundaries that is significant in these data,

b) that it is the participants' sensitivity to these 'lines' that allows us to say that 'class awareness' *is* active when youngsters invoke traditional British class dialects in the situated symbolic commentary that stylisation entails, and

c) to do justice to the indeterminacy of the indexical resonance in these episodes, it would be best to say that stylisation simply introduced an orientation to 'high' and 'low' (which in an utterance like Hanif's "stars and galaxies" would translate into something like 'with you, not above').

In the transition, then, between potentially divisive interactional frames, these youngsters used traditional British class accents to crystallise an apprehension of the social differentiation of activies and people within the schooling process. To consolidate this claim, it is useful to return to Williams' view that social class entails "relations of domination and subordination ... [that saturate] the whole process of living ...: our senses and assignments of energy, our shaping perceptions of ourselves and our world" (1977:109–110; Chapter 6.2). Class certainly is associated with inequality between *groups*, but group labels and socio-economic status classifications are really only a short-hand for a far wider range of sensitivities, processes and effects. This means that although reflexive class awareness can be low key, it is no less real for that, and in fact there is a further implication. These stylisations actually did more than simply display a sensitivity to boundary demarcations – in a very small way, they also displayed critical agency, actively drawing the lines differently. The analysis of their routine, non-exaggerated style-shifting in Chapter 7.3 showed that these youngsters had a rather deeply ingrained sense of (class-shaped) sociolinguistic structure, and that in their everyday talk, they observed the conventions which link more standard speech styles to relatively formal activities, and more vernacular ones to more informal activities (Tables 7.2 and 7.3). But in the micro-processes of transition and boundary negotiation in Extracts 8.6 to 8.11, Ninnette, Joanne and Hanif responded to the conventional separation of work and sociability (and the stratification that this can feed into) by momentarily *reworking* the sociolinguistic semiotic that says

posh ⇔ formality ⇔ school-orientation
and
Cockney ⇔ informality ⇔ peer-orientation

Ninnette and Joanne kept the door open to peer sociability by exaggerating posh to the point that it lost its authority, and Hanif did the same by scrambling the convention and linking Cockney to a school orientation. This is obviously a very long way from political manifestos, mass mobilisations and industrial action, and it is not possible to extrapolate from these data to longer-term effects (see Willis 1977, and Chapter 8.7 below). But we can see (a) what Thompson means when he says that "the drawing of [the line of class] is ... the outcome of political and cultural skills" (1978:295–296), and (b) that at certain moments, people do step back from their routine practice and use the subtle flexibilities of speech to both identify *and* to refuse class reproduction in some of its everyday forms.

There is one more point to make about the episodes so far, referring once again to the model of indexical meaning outlined in this section. To a very considerable degree, the richness of a particular dialect's indexical valence – its capacity to evoke either a narrow or broad range of associations – will be determined by the extent to which the people using it have narrow or broad experience of it. As Ochs says, "[t]he indexical potential of a form derives from a history of usage and cultural expectations surrounding that form" (1996:418). As I argued in Part II, German's symbolic associations were restricted by the fact that these youngsters were most intensively exposed to it in their foreign language classes, whereas the indexical valence of posh and Cockney was far fuller, informed by my informants' very extensive day-to-day use and exposure to these speech varieties (and I shall say much more about their indexical valence in Chapter 9). Nevertheless, even though only specific dimensions of a variety's indexical potential might be made relevant in particular instances of stylisation – even though a particular utterance might only intimate this symbolic field very vaguely – indexical valence is itself profoundly sensitive to the occasions when the variety is stylised, and can itself accrete new associations through any innovative interactional uses made of it. Crucially, the fluidity of this movement between the situated use of a variety and its indexical valence/symbolic potential helps to explain how the meaning of class – how the images conjured by posh and Cockney – can change.

8.6 Stylisation in (historically) new forms of working-class identification

In sociology and cultural studies more generally, there is now a substantial body of empirical and interpretive research which describes the emergence of "new forms of working class Englishness" (Back 1996:123), "a new ensemble that both appropriates and is appropriated by British-based African Caribbean-ness, Asian-ness, Irishness and so on" (Brah 1996:209; cf. also Gilroy 1987:194–197). The pragmatic map outlined in Chapter 8.5 points to one of the ways in which this happens in the fine details of talk, and this is displayed very clearly in the Cockneyification of "sonar bangla" in the 'linguistic handicap/sonar bangla' extract (8.1).

Here again is the episode:

Extract 8.12

Background: Mr Newton, a popular, committed but not very commanding teacher (admired for his sharp turn-of-phrase by Hanif, John and Masud when interviewed), is trying to get the English class started on their oral assessment activity, and in part-exhortation, part-warning, he has mentioned some recently-published league tables of schools performance, telling them that in this school, pupils of fourteen have been achieving the level expected of eleven year olds (Level 4). He is now saying that they should be getting Level 5, and in line 8, he is referring to official curriculum specifications (e.g. DFE 1995a:26) (Blex 33):

```
 1   MR NEWTON        ((three claps))
 2                    Ninnette:::
 3                    listen (.)
 4                    listen (2)
 5                    to get a level Five it starts:
 6                    to be a little bit more difficult
                      because
 7                    Shahid (.)
 8                    the words Standard English start to
                      crop up
 9   RAFIQ            ((in a constricted sing-song voice:))
                      ^oh
10                    ₁thats ˈvery ⌈^(good)
11   MR                          ⌊and (.)
12   SHAHID           I don't (      ⌈    )
13   MR N                           ⌊so:
14   ANONS (Male)     ((laughter))
15   MR N             sort of people who er answer every
                                            question (.)
16                    with lots of aints and innits (.)
17   ?HANIF           ((quietly:))yeh
18   MR N             are in fact (.)
19                    handicappin' 'emselves (.)
20                    so unfortunately
21   HANIF            >yeh I know
22                    Daily Times<
23   MR N             because you're all from (.)
24   HANIF            >Ban⌈gla'desh<
25   MR N                ⌊because you're all
                         from ˇLon⌈don
26   HANIF                        ⌊ >Bangla'desh<
27                    oh (.)
```

```
28  SEVERAL     ((laughter, nois / e levels rise
                gradually))
29  RAFIQ       ((in hyper-Cockney))
                'so ˌnar 'ban ˌgla ((laughs))
                [səʊnɑ: bæ̃ŋglɑ:: ]
30  ?MASUD      ((hyper-Cockney accent:))
                'so ˌnar 'ban ˌgla
                [s:əʊ̃nɑ bæ̃ŋg]
31  JOHN        ((hyper-Cockney accent:))
                'so ˌn/ar 'ban ˌgla
                [səʊ̃nə̄ bæ̃ŋglɑ̄]
32  MR N        (you know) I'm getting fed up with
                                        (  back )
33              (1)  ((quite a lot of talk going on))
34              because you're from London
35              you're handicapped
36              to a certain ext⌈ent
37  SEVERAL                     ⌊((loud laughs))
38  MR N        because erm: (.)
39              your everyday language (.)
40              if you're at Eton (.)
41              wouldn't include too many innits
42              would it (1)
43              alright
44             ⌈listen
45  ANON (M)   ⌊((in a posh voice:))
                (because they're very) posh
46  MR N        ((fast and quieter:)) yes exactly
```

Mr Newton has been telling the class that under the terms laid down in the National Curriculum, candidates won't do well if they use non-standard language forms (lines 5–19), and after that, he has begun to particularise the account, shifting the focus from candidates in general to the students here in the class (lines 20 and 23). Hanif has been listening attentively, displaying familiarity with the news about school performance (lines 21–22), and in the micro-pause when Mr Newton postpones his characterisation of their (problematic) origins (line 23), Hanif proposes "Bangladesh" (24), repeating this utterance completer when Mr Newton restarts and delivers the clause as a whole (lines 25 and 26).[14] Hanif's prediction of what Mr Newton has been going to say turns out to be wrong, he registers this with a 'double-take' (line 27), and members of the class start to laugh. It looks as though the laughter in line 28 is prompted by Hanif's conspicuous error and surprise (lines 24, 26, 27), a 'fall' coming fast on the heels of rather showy claims to knowledge in lines 21 and 22, but in line 29, when Rafiq produces the first ``sonar bangla'', it is hard to know for certain whether this actually thematises Hanif's momentary stumble in the way that exclamations like 'fool!' or 'oops!' would. Nevertheless, his production of a quasi-Bengali phrase in a London accent is obviously appreciated by the two others (John and probably Masud) and they repeat the synthesis themselves, increasing the London nasalisation (cf. Wells 1982:318).

Over the week or so before this episode, 'sonar bangla' had developed into a catchphrase among Hanif, Masud, John, Rafiq and their associates. On the recordings, it had already been used more than 20 times, and the contexts of its emergence and use suggest a link, somewhere in its indexical valence, with issues of power. The class first encountered the words 'sonar bangla' during their Humanities class, where they were studying slavery and imperialism, and where they were very active and interested participants, particularly in oral discussion. 'Sonar Bangla' appeared in written form on the front of a booklet about the colonial relationship between England and Bengal in the eighteenth and nineteenth centuries, and to begin with they could not see what Bengali word it was that 'sonar' was intended to represent. Mr Alcott's pronunciation of it varied between 'sauna' and 'sonner', and the boys found this very amusing, revoicing it among themselves at least eleven times before Hanif asked what it was actually supposed to mean. On being told by Mr Alcott that the phrase meant 'Golden Bengal', Masud and Hanif – the two English–Bengali bilinguals – agreed that 'sonar' should be [ʃənɑɑ] ('shenaa'), but they and their friends continued to play with the word, 'Londonising' its vowels[15] and joking, for example, about 'Captain Shooner'. Knowing that the mispronunciation of a minority language by teachers can be politically sensitive, I later asked whether they minded the mispronunciation when I played parts of the recording back to them, but the response from Hanif was:

NO! ... no we don't mind. We laugh it off cos we ... if there's anything to be made out of a joke, if there's anything that can be made into a joke, then we'll do that ... we're not a very serious bunch us lot. (PB2:190)

There are strong grounds, then, for saying that the catchphrase 'sonar bangla' was relatively well-established as a source of peer group humour; there is circumstantial evidence that they linked it with imperial domination (albeit in a spirit that was none too solemn); and in fact this combination of politics and levity gets reproduced in the sequence here. Rafiq's first 'sonar bangla' comes in the phase where Mr Newton's negative characterisation of the class is approaching its climax – ``so unfortunately, because you're all from ...'' – and indeed, this is a moment of double shaming, with the derogatory perspective relayed by Mr Newton being supplemented by Hanif's conspicuous failure to predict the teacher's words. But far from trying to "cover" and "restrict the display of those failings most centrally identified with the stigma" being attributed to them (Goffman 1963:126), 'sonar bangla' rolls both of the explanations on offer – being a Bangladeshi and a Londoner – into one, and the switch to a Cockney accent *underscores* the dimension of social class.[16] In all, stylised Cockney 'sonar bangla' achieves a much sharper image of the boys' structural position at the intersection of class and 'race' hierarchy than anything else said up to this point. At the same time, it carries on being entertaining, and the wit and aptness of its use evidently make it a minor source of aesthetic pleasure.

It is worth now reviewing the data and discussion in this chapter, first focusing on the dynamics in Class 9A, and then turning to broader educational implications.

8.7   Local educational trajectories in the symbolisation of social class

The cultural, political, material and discursive processes that bring Hanif, Joanne and Ninnette to ``eand'', ``stars and galaxies'' and ``sonar bangla'' stretch a long way back and beyond the extracts considered in this chapter, and these processes have obviously been addressed in a huge body of rather different political and academic discourses about class, ethnicity, race and other types of stratification. Here, though, my concern is with class as active local concept in these youngsters' reflexive sensitivity to their circumstances, and in many of the episodes in this chapter, stylised posh and Cockney coincided with the drawing of educational lines implying 'higher' and 'lower'. These episodes have shown my informants

- doing parodic posh when they were placed 'on the lower side' by a teacher who failed to display routine respect for their status or knowledge – retaliating to degradation in Extracts 8.3 and 8.4, as well perhaps as 8.5;
- doing exaggerated Cockney to hold their peers' attention during periods when they had either been publicly placed in a higher position by the teacher, or were quite fully involved in schoolwork – code-switching to incorporate easily distracted peers in officially ratified activity in Extracts 8.2 and 8.11; and
- doing Cockney and playful posh at moments of intensified attention to work, which friends-on-hand might have construed as placing themselves on the higher side – mitigating self-elevation in Extracts 8.6, 8.7 and 8.9.

At the same time, the accents that they used to respond to these moments of educational line-drawing were not restricted to those traditionally linked to British social class. They also used accents that indexed other groups who have been stereotyped as either unsuccessful or unenthusiastic in recent British educational history. During Mr Newton's syllogistic exposition of the causes of disadvantage, 'Bangladesh' was Hanif's initial analysis and Rafiq et al. mixed Cockney and quasi-Bengali, while the other voice that Hanif used to vernacularise the science task was Caribbean (Extract 8.10).

How do these findings relate back to Vološinov's discussion of 'established' and 'behavioural ideologies'? As Chapter 6.3 reported, Vološinov distinguishes between 'established' and 'behavioural ideology'. The former finds expression in "systems of social ethics, science, art and religion" (1973:92) and the latter is a "social orientation" that is often "haphazard and ephemeral and characteristic only for some adventitious and loose coalition of a small number of persons". Behavioural ideologies involve sets of "experiences born of a momentary or accidental state of affairs ... vague and undeveloped experiences, thoughts and idle accidental words that flash across our minds", although at the same time, "[t]he *upper strata* of behavioural ideology, the ones directly linked with [established] ideological systems, are more vital, they are a great deal more mobile and sensitive: they convey changes in the socio-economic basis more quickly and more vividly" (1973:92 [emphasis added]).

In the previous chapter, I suggested that class did not figure with any assurance or systematicity in *established* ideologies among these youngsters, and that they had not mastered any "politicising [propositional and lexico-grammatical] scripts of class oppression to counter the prevalence of views that it is all their own fault" (Reay 1998:267; my parenthesis). But in this chapter, the stylisation data shows that something like class was actively and critically apprehended in *behavioural* ideology, and indeed in the synthesis of class and ethnicity in 'sonar bangla', behavioural ideology can be seen picking up on ethnicity in the newer demographics of the British working class, responding to "changes in the socioeconomic basis", reflecting the "complex experiential chemistry of class [and] 'race'" (Gilroy 1987:19). To clarify how intuitions of class could be displayed in fleeting responses to the circumstances on hand, Ochs' pragmatic model was outlined in Chapter 8.5, and this can in fact be taken as a model of 'behavioural ideologies' pushing towards the "upper strata", a theory of "experiences born of a momentary ... state of affairs" finding communicative expression which makes them more than just "vague and undeveloped ... thoughts and idle accidental words that flash across our minds" (Vološinov 1973).

But how far into the "upper strata" did they reach? Vološinov argues that it is in the upper strata of behavioural ideology that

> those creative energies build up through whose agency partial or radical restructuring of ideological systems comes about. Newly emerging social forces find ideological expression and take shape first in these upper strata of behavioural ideology before they succeed in dominating the arena of some organised, official ideology.   (1973:92; cited in Chapter 6.3 above)

What can the data tell us about this?

There can be little doubt that even though it is still often heterodox and contested in Britain, the syncretic consciousness intimated in 'sonar bangla' has found expression in propositional discourses and in a range of other relatively stable media in urban areas, in the arts and in the academic literature on 'new ethnicities', (e.g. Gilroy 1987; Hall 1988; Mercer 1994; Brah 1996; Back 1996; Harris 2004; Chapter 1.1). Indeed, it can be quite plausibly proposed that

processes like the ones associated with 'sonar bangla' occur elsewhere, and that they do feed these much more established articulations. But unfortunately, I do not have any data on the subsequent
development of class consciousness specifically among Hanif et al.,
Ninnette and Joanne, and I cannot say what happened when, for
example, a number of them took sociology courses the following
year. Indeed, it would be foolish to speculate. Williams warns:

new meaning and values, new practices, new relationships and kinds of
relationship are continually being created ... but it is exceptionally difficult
to distinguish between those which are really elements of some new phase of
the dominant culture.. and those which are substantially alternative or
oppositional to it: emergent ... rather than merely novel.   (1977:123)[17]

But although I cannot say where these youngsters' class awareness
leads – how far it travels along the road from behavioural to established ideology – it is possible to say a little more about the ways in
which the particular expressions seen in the data were shaped and
constrained by their school profiles and trajectories as individuals.
This emerges if their stylisations are compared, setting up a contrast
that may simplify some of the intricacy and indeterminacy in these
performances, but that generates a quite suggestive characterisation
of how their critical class awareness was actually influenced by their
positions at Central High.

In Extracts 8.6, 8.7 and 8.8 (``eand'', ``the date of today''
and ``fienieshed''), Ninnette and Joanne linked school writing
to very stylised posh (or literate) speech, and in this respect they
appeared to follow the conventional sociolinguistic link between
literacy and standard English. But the shift to more formal language
did not actually usher in any serious task-focused concentration,
and instead the exaggeration in their speech pointed to an interest in
peer group sociability. So on the one hand, they were doing what
they were supposed to, attending to their work and speaking in
educated voices, while on the other, they were simultaneously making space for activities more to their liking. This brings de Certeau's
discussion of 'tactics' to mind, typified in his account of *la perruque*
in France:

La perruque is the worker's own work disguised as work for his employer. It
differs from pilfering in that nothing of material value is stolen. It differs
from absenteeism in that the worker is still officially on the job. *La perruque*

may be as simple a matter as a secretary's writing a love letter on 'company time' or as complex as a cabinet-maker's 'borrowing' a lathe to make a piece of furniture for his living room ... With the complicity of other workers (who thus defeat the competition the factory tries to instill among them), [the worker] succeeds in 'putting one over' on the established order on its home ground. (1984:25–26)

In fact this fits with what we have seen of Ninnette and Joanne's conduct much more generally (e.g. Chapters 2.4, 3.5, 7.1). They sat in the class and they handed in their work as they were expected to, but they spent huge amounts of their time quietly talking together, eating sweets and so forth. And indeed all of their posh and Cockney stylisations were relatively private, either confined to relatively hushed peer–peer talk in class, or performed more noisily elsewhere outside teachers' earshot.

Hanif was very different, and out of about fifteen episodes in which he used an exaggerated posh or Cockney accent in school-related business, eight were either loudly performed on the classroom floor, or directly addressed to teachers themselves. In addition, when he used Cockney in reading and engaging with school knowledge (Extracts 8.9, 8.10, 8.11), his stylisation ran against the grain of the conventional sociolinguistic equation of literacy with standard speech. If this is now set within a wider picture of his conduct in class, it is clear that just like Joanne and Emma's, these patterns in Hanif's stylisation were actually *symptomatic* of his more general orientation to schooling. He was the ringleader in the group of boys who were often interested in lessons and attended very closely to teacher-talk, but who nevertheless (a) transgressed the traditional IRE structure of classroom talk more or less as a matter of routine, and who (b) continuously sought to liven things up with the importation of all sorts of extraneous, non-curriculum materials (see Chapters 2.2 and 2.3). Indeed, I suggested that these boys' conduct pointed to an at least partial separation of respect-for-knowledge-and-learning from a respect-for-the-institutions-of-schooling (Chapter 2.7). Against such a background, there should be little to surprise us in the vernacularisation of school knowledge that I attributed to Hanif's Cockney performance of 'stars and galaxies'.

When their stylisations of posh and Cockney are contextualised like this and then compared, there are some quite striking differences in the reflexive class awareness displayed in Hanif, Joanne and Ninnette's performances. Hanif seems to be much more confident in his assumptions about how tractable mainstream conventions might be, as well as in his approach to establishing a congenial space for himself in the schooling-and-stratification process. But this cannot be attributed to his being somehow more of a radical free-spirit than Joanne and Ninnette. On the contrary, the relative power and assertiveness displayed in his class-inflected stylisations owes a lot to the habits and prestige he had developed at the top of the educational hierarchy in Class 9A. Teachers gave him a lot of discursive space in the lessons, listening to what he had to say, and largely accepted his stylisations of Cockney. In these conditions, he had good cause for thinking of school as a generally hospitable institution, receptive to the interest and energy that he and his friends brought to the curriculum, and open to his sociolinguistic innovations and transgressions. For Ninnette and Joanne, the class-room was obviously experienced as a much less welcoming place, made up of a set of rules and expectations that had to be followed but were hard to respect. In all, there were some quite striking differences in the sense of social possibility carried in these young-sters' stylisations, and these differences were neither independent of, nor ran counter to, the interactional 'settlement' that prevailed in Class 9A. Instead, it looks as though they were one of its systemic elements/products.

8.8   Language attitudes at school: an update

Following the discussion of sociolinguistics and schooling at the start of the present chapter (Chapter 8.1), there are three educa-tional questions to which I can now respond, drawing on the data from London in late 1990s:

a)   how relevant to contemporary conditions are the assump-tions about schooling that Trudgill and others made in the 1970s when they formulated their injunctions about the edu-cational importance of showing respect for non-standard speech? How far do the conditions in which they wrote still apply, providing continued relevance and urgency to these exhortations?

b) If conditions *have* changed, have posh and vernacular speech stopped being associated with class hierarchy, making efforts to de-stigmatise non-standard speech redundant?

c) And how far can we still speak of 'linguistic insecurity' being a central systemic product in the schooling process?

a) In their injunctions about dialect tolerance/respect in the 1970s, sociolinguists appeared to assume that classrooms were arenas where middle-class teachers dominated, and where pupils were very vulnerable to the stigmatisation of non-standard speech. But the data and discussion in Chapters 2 and 3 demonstrate that nowadays anyway, it would be a serious mistake to assume that teachers are always assured in the control and command of their classrooms. At Central High, the IRE structure of classroom discourse ('teacher initiation', 'pupil response', 'teacher evaluation') certainly did not operate as it is traditionally supposed to, and there are good reasons for thinking that this is actually part of quite a wide-spread shift in the communicative order, both in schools and in society at large (Chapter 2.7). This shift has been accompanied by quite a substantial challenge to the rigid prescription of standard English, and sociolinguists have played a significant public role articulating it. With the introduction of the National Curriculum, the 1990s certainly saw a resurgence of linguistic prescriptivism, to the extent that child-centred progressivism can now be regarded as a 'residual' rather than 'dominant' formation within education. Even so, vestiges of dialect tolerance can still be found in the curriculum texts produced by government, and there are schools and teachers who continue to hold on to the values that sociolinguists started to advocate in the 1970s. Indeed, teachers' commitment to hearing the voices of their students forms one part of a wider trend that Fairclough calls the "conversationalisation" of public discourse, and although it is very hard to say how this educational commitment might mutate at the intersection of different cultural forces in late modernity, it seems rather unlikely that urban classrooms are on the threshold of a massive return to deferential silence.

There are good grounds for saying, then, that there are significant areas where the educational and cultural conditions implied in the 1970s sociolinguistic defence of dialect no longer apply. What about the second question?

b) Trudgill's defence of non-standard speech was founded in a critique of class prejudice. Has this defence lost its edge because in the cultural conditions associated with late modernity, class no longer matters?

Material inequalities certainly have not diminished since the 1970s, the education system remains highly stratified, and Central High occupied a relatively lowly position in hierarchies of wealth, status and conventional achievement (Chapter 2.1). The staff at Central High tended to accept the pupils' non-standard speech, but if they felt slighted by their teachers, pupils could invoke posh in scathing parodies of class snobbery. When they style-shifted in their routine talk, my informants tacitly accepted the class-related stratification of speech situations that Labov, Trudgill and other quantitative sociolinguists have been documenting for at least a quarter of a century, and in transition between formal and informal frames of activity, they displayed a critical reflexive awareness of this in their fleeting stylisations. Compared with what they had to say about racism, ethnicity, gender and sexuality, the 13 and 14 year olds in my study were rather inarticulate about social class in explicit discussion, but in their symbolic stylisations, they repeatedly foregrounded the 'drawing of lines' that can be analytically tied to class. And rather than allowing ethnicity to *replace* class as an axis of social differentiation in everyday activity, in their stylisations these youngsters could either fuse the two in combinations of lexis and phonology ('sonar bangla'), or display their equivalence by alternating between classed and ethnic voices in similar speech acts ('stars and galaxies' in Cockney and Caribbean).

So the answer to Questions (a) and (b) is that on the one hand, cultural and educational circumstances have changed, but that on the other, class still counts. What, then, of 'linguistic insecurity'? On the evidence here, is Hymes still right that "[i]t is the latent function of the educational system to instil linguistic insecurity" (1996:84; Chapter 8.1 above)?

c) I have tried to look for evidence of 'damage getting done' in the way teachers spoke about non-standard language, but instead of seeing students being cowed into linguistic self-hatred, the data in this chapter shows them getting quite a lot of pleasure from the posh-Cockney nexus in whole-class role-play (Chapter 8.2), in peer-talk working on written tasks (Chapter 8.4), even when they were being warned of their own vernacular handicaps (Extract 8.12). Indeed, at least in Hanif's case, it seemed to be more a matter of linguistic over-confidence than insecurity, and so overall, the analysis of metalinguistic episodes suggests that responses to accent status are far more active and differentiated than one might infer from a totalising notion like 'linguistic insecurity'.

Even so, both Hanif and Ninnette had fairly clear images of the kinds of disadvantaged lives they wanted to avoid (Chapter 7.1). As a form of artful and sometimes quite flam-boyant performance, stylisation is a practice in which one is rather unlikely to find any very obvious displays of linguistic insecurity, and more generally, interaction analysis normally lacks both the inclination and tools for identifying deeper feelings beneath the surfaces of talk. And so although varia-tionist assertions about linguistic insecurity look rather over-blown, as well as rather narrow in their empirical grounding,[18] I cannot claim to have exhausted this issue in the interactional analyses so far, arriving at a position where links between class, language and feelings of insecurity can be dismissed as an analytic delusion or a relic of the past.[19] Working-class pupils might not be quite as fragile as sociolinguistics has sometimes implied, but everyday experience and a huge non-linguistic literature on class provides ample reason for taking class-related insecurities very seriously. In the next chapter, I shall take analysis of the affective dimensions of language and social class further, and in doing so, it will be necessary to look a little beyond the conceptual apparatus of interactional socio-linguistics, turning instead to cultural theory for a richer frame-work for empirical exploration of the links between language and felt experiences of social class.

Notes

1. Researchers' early first-hand personal experience of dialect stigmatisa-tion as school-children themselves may also have provided some impetus

for the defence of non-standard speech, but the possibility of cultural change always makes this unreliable as evidence for the present.

2. 'No' involves a fronted, half-open vowel at the onset of the diphthong which according to Wells (1982:294), is 'now widely considered to be affected'.

3. 'Oh I can fly' probably refers to R. Kelly's 'I believe I can fly', which had just been released.

4. In fact, they had encountered Mr Alcott several times that morning, first in their tutor-group period and then in a Humanities class. But there was nothing in either of these two sessions that resembled the direct exchange between Mr Alcott and the girls which had occurred in the playground shortly before Extract 8.3. Also, given the lapse of time since the last lesson contact (about an hour), as well as the intervening exchange, one would expect some extra contextualising work from Ninnette if she had an episode that occurred in the early part of the day in mind – for example, 'this is Mr Alcott in the Tutor Period'.

5. The mid-central onset of "oh" in line 16 contrasts with the more open, more London, realisation of the first elements of the GOAT vowel in his "oh right okay" a few moments earlier – [ʌʊ ɹaɪʔ ʌʊkeɪ]

6. Cf. Clark 1998:239 for an example of a student sarcastically flagging up their teacher's patronising 'hyper-explanation' with "Yes, we understand. We are very intelligent. We gotcha"

7. When she refocused on her writing after some chat a little later, she retuned to her text so far by reading out "and it would change her whole life completely and she".

8. The reading passage that she is working on comes from E. Hautzig's *Endless Steppe*, and it describes a tragic scene in which a girl is taken away from her house when Poland was invaded by Russia.

9. The mid-central starting point for the diphthong in the last syllable ([ə])

    a) was highly untypical of Hanif's pronunciation of the *happ*Y vowel elsewhere,

    b) he associated it with the accent of a cousin who lived in London's East End when the sequence was replayed to him, and

    c) Wells describes it as broad Cockney (1982:319).

10. This, for example, was how Hanif had greeted his friend Hari a few minutes earlier when he was doing the rounds handing out science books:

| 1 | HANIF | ((c. 7 seconds without speaking. Then, in broad Cockney:)) |
| 2 | | >ˌawight< ˌari [ɔʷᴵʔ ʔæ‿ɪʔ] |

3   `ow are \you
                                     [æʊ ɑː juː]
4 HARI *((loudly, with*   \\WHEEYY
   *long falling
   intonation))*

11. He certainly showed a sensitivity to the different pulls of school and
    peer group in interview:

    "Some of us have been together from nursery ... I was with Masud
    since (we were) 4 years old – 3 years old. We used to go to a play-
    school ... we hope, right, our friendship's going to go on to
    university, because we know that once we're older ... you lose
    [your friends] after you come to a certain time ... that's what
    we're dreading to happen" *((simple transcription. See also
    Chapter 7.1))*

12. At the end of the lesson, Hanif read out what he had written to the rest
    of the class, but he did not use any stylised Cockney when he did so.
13. In Extract 8.3, Ninnette explicitly flags that some meta-level represen-
    tation of a person is coming up ('oh this is ___ ') and that this will be a
    characterisation of Mr Alcott ('oh this is Mr Alcott, look this is Mr
    Alcott' (lines 2 to 7). In line 8, the phonological styling of 'oh no' marks
    poshness as a characteristic she wants to draw attention to, and within
    the indexical valence of posh, the word and particle in her depiction
    ('oh no') identify disdain as being relevant to the world she is conjuring.
    Joanne still has to identify what aspect of Mr Alcott's conduct could be
    construed as posh disdainfulness; she displays her inference that it was
    his intended tease in Extract 8.4 in the posh mocking laugh she attri-
    butes to him ('hehe haw haw' lines 12 and 17); and Ninnette does
    nothing to contradict this. Overall, this is a rather well-packaged
    piece of stylisation, and the connotations activated between the two
    girls are fairly stereotypic (posh people are often protrayed as looking
    down and scoffing at ordinary folk). But the situation is very different
    with "eand" in line 21 of Extract 8.6. Here, Ninnette's switch into an
    exaggerated accent invites us to break with the assumption that she is
    engaged in routine business-as-usual, and the particular phonological
    codings she chooses once again alert us to poshness as an additional
    realm of meaning that is relevant to what she's doing. But there are no
    other guides in her vocal performance to indicate what aspects of the
    indexical valence of posh might be relevant, and as interpreters, we are
    left just with the feeling that somehow or other this voice must be
    connected to her writing at this moment. The most confident inference
    we can draw from this stylisation is, as already indicated, that
    Ninnette's stance in this activity is non-serious – she's doing the work,
    but she's not completely dedicated to it – and this is an interpretation
    that is ratified in her subsequent sound-play. It also chimes with our

wider understanding of how Ninnette and Joanne like to pass their time together, and more generally, our sense that this is an intentional practice is confirmed when she and Joanne engage in other posh(-ish) stylisations at the point where they are either entering or exiting written schoolwork (Extracts 8.7 and 8.8). Much the same commentary could be repeated with Hanif in Extract 8.9 ('Stars and Galaxies'), only there it is Cockney that he stylises.

14. It is impossible to say how far Hanif would himself accept 'Bangladesh' as an adequate account of the alleged language handicap, since here he is anticipating the explanation that Mr Newton is about to offer. At the same time, though, there is nothing in the way that he says 'Bangladesh' in lines 24 and 26 to suggest that he is sardonically identifying a racist explanation that he wishes to challenge. On both occasions, the word is spoken rapidly and with a rising intonation that matches Mr Newton's, and these features make it sound much more like convergent support than obtrusive disruption. Furthermore, although it differs from the regimented turn exchange patterns that are most often described in classroom discourse analysis, there is nothing particularly threatening here in the fact that Hanif tries to complete the teacher's turn for him – as we saw in Chapter 2, this was a common pupil practice, and teachers often accepted it.

15. In addition to heavy nasalisation, the first vowel in 'sonar', [əʊ] (as in RP 'GOAT') sometimes became [ʌʊ] (as in 'MOUTH') (cf. Wells 1982:308–309).

16. After all, on its own, London-ness does not necessarily entail being working class – there are plenty of very posh people who live in London.

17. In order to claim that an apparently dissonant social practice really is counter-hegemonic, and that it is not part of the incorporation, accommodation and negotiation that hegemony always entails (Williams 1977; Anderson 1977; Fairclough 1992a:92), one needs a historical, or at least longitudinal, perspective. Without such a perspective, it is impossible to know "whether, for example, a particular argumentative sequence constitutes routine dispute or counter-hegemonic resistance, whether it instantiates business-as-usual or points to incipient social change[. W]ithout recourse to knowledge of longer-term eventuations situated in a much wider social field, there is a considerable risk of over-reading, with analysts opting for romantic optimism and gloomy determinism according to personal preference." (Blommaert et al. 2003:6)

18. The structured elicitations generally used in studies of linguistic insecurity may be much better than ethnographic micro-analysis for getting a sense of how attitudes are distributed across a large group of people, but because they look for language attitudes *outside* the situated everyday interactional activity where people continuously cope with the pressures and possibilities of ordinary life, it is hard for these techniques to pick up on the creative agency with which individuals and groups respond to the prospect of symbolic domination. In

contrast, if people are studied in their own cultural habitats, where they have had time and space to develop a range of (more and less) subtle, enduring and/or collective responses to their socio-structural positioning, then they can be seen exploring, exploiting and contesting accent stratification in range of different ways. Coupland makes this point in his call for a 'dialect stylistics' (1995), and Macaulay provides extensive discussion of accent as a focus and resource in aesthetic performance (1987, 1997). More generally, for a very thorough critique of the theoretical and methodological underpinnings of 'linguistic insecurity' as a sociolinguistic concept, see Macaulay 1987, 1997: Chapters 5, 6, 7 and 11.

19. Methodological differences make it hard to use my data for historical assessment of whether or not schools are nowadays more or less effective instilling (or indeed freeing) their students with/from a sense of linguistic insecurity than they were 25 years ago (cf. Chapter 2.7). When Trudgill, Hymes and Labov began discussing linguistic insecurity at school in the early 1970s, interactional discourse analysis had hardly been invented and instead, researchers relied on a range of attitude elicitation experiments, often playing recordings of different accents to their informants/subjects, asking them to evaluate these voices and compare them with their own (see Hudson 1996: Chapter 6.2.3). What might Trudgill and Labov have found if they had based their accounts of linguistic insecurity in the detailed investigation of metalinguistic episodes in naturally occurring interaction? Equally, what would I conclude about the linguistic security of Hanif, Joanne and Ninnette if they had participated in a 'subjective reaction test'?

9

Classed subjectivities in interaction

In the last Chapter, I looked at the way in which, in one way or another, exaggerated performances of posh and Cockney coincided with the drawing of educational lines, and I suggested that these stylisations are best interpreted as small pieces of class analysis that speakers produce *in media res* in an effort to clarify their institutional positioning. In this Chapter, the focus turns to stylisation in peer interaction and it is based on a set of about twenty episodes where no one sought to exercise institutional control, but where something more than just the sound properties of posh and Cockney seemed to be involved. In the course of the analysis, it will become clear that class sensitivities were not confined to the work relationships associated with school, but that they were much more pervasive, manifesting themselves in quite personal aspects of these young people's social lives. And to do justice to this, it will be necessary to look beyond the traditional vocabularies of interactional sociolinguistics to wider discussions of subjectivity.

The chapter begins by comparing sociolinguistic conceptions of identity as a local interactional projection with the interest in more pervasive and enduring sensibilities that one finds in cultural studies and in other work on discourse, power and inequality in sociology, anthropology and literary theory (indeed henceforth, I shall use the term 'cultural studies' as a short-hand to stand for these as well). The interactionist perspective risks trivialising social class; it has little to say about the way in which the fears, hopes and subjectivities of individuals are influenced by class structure; and most important, as I shall try to show over the chapter as a whole, on its own it cannot do justice to the class processes evidenced in the stylisation data (Chapter 9.1). I then turn to quite detailed discussion of five cases of exaggerated posh and Cockney being used among peers (Chapter 9.2), and when these are drawn together, the influence of a high–low/mind–body/reason–emotion binary with a long history in English class society can be discerned. Raymond Williams' notion of 'structures of feeling' provides one way of seeing how this cultural schema works, avoiding reification and recognising the binary's fluid integration into situated inter-actional experience, although in the discussion of data so far, relatively little has been said either about the affective dimensions of this class binary, or about the distorted forms in which it is sometimes articulated (Chapter 9.3). But this changes when the stylisation of hyper-correct speech in a performance of the grotesque is considered. Here the potential physicality of the connotations of the posh-Cockney nexus gets underlined, as well as its involvement in processes where "fantasy and ideology conjoin" (Chapter 9.4). After that, the boys' Cockney stylisation of one of the girls in their class reveals a complicated intermingling of social class and sexuality, which appears to emerge from the challenge that some of the girls presented to the boys' sense of sexual, gender and educational hierarchy (Chapter 9.5). Overall, posh and Cockney were very fecund in their symbolism and in their capacity to infuse speech with extra meaning in different situations, and Bakhtin's notion of 'internally persuasive discourse' provides a good characterisation. In the last two sections of the chapter (9.6 and 9.7) I use a combination of Bakhtin and Williams both to summarise the relationship between stylisation and style-shifting, and to clarify some of the ways in which interactional socio-linguistics can – and should – engage with debates about class and subjectivity in cultural studies. The terms for analysis of the psycho-social interiority of language are inevitably looser than the preferred vocabularies of discourse and linguistic analysis, but combined with interactional data, they can still lead to empirical claims that are both substantial and discriminating, and this becomes apparent when posh and Cockney are compared with German/*Deutsch*. Interaction analysis reveals a lot about class consciousness in late modernity, but to apprehend its depth and to realise the potential contribution to wider debates, scholars of language, culture and society like Bakhtin and Williams provide sociolinguistics with a useful lead.

9.1 Sociolinguistics, cultural studies and classed subjectivities[1]

The analytic tools of interactional and discourse-oriented sociolinguistics are potentially very sensitive to the ways in which social class can operate on-line as an locally activated, emic category. Studies of language and ethnicity often show, for example, how a switch of speech variety can communicate a change of stance (e.g. Blom and Gumperz 1972, Gumperz 1982a), and in the previous chapter, I used this perspective to look at classed speech styles, studying how, as a loosely defined cluster of associations, social class formed a part of the interactional meaning, proposing affiliative or oppositional relations in episodes that involved some of the hierarchisation endemic to schooling – class, one might say, as practical consciousness on-line in dialectical moments of social differentiation and conflict.[2] There is a sense, though, in which this kind of analysis still only skims the surface of the lived experience of social class, and this becomes clearer if interactional discourse analysis is compared with some of the perspectives provided in cultural studies and related disciplines.

Discourse analyses of interactional self-positioning generally

a) focus on the situated use of specific linguistic structures,
b) look beyond the encounter on hand for the larger images/ categories that these structures appear to invoke (= 'indexical valence'), and then
c) attend to the pragmatic and sequential impact that the emerging index has in interaction (see e.g. Antaki and Widdicombe 1998:3; Chapter 8.5 above).

The second element in this set of concerns – the wider set of images/ representations/identities that an item evokes – are often of less interest than their pragmatic relevance and effect, and indeed in some cases, such extrinsically-derived 'social meanings' are regarded as irrelevant to the local interaction, being treated as little more than unwarranted analytic attributions (e.g. Antaki 1998).[3] The time-frame is interactional, and effects, conflicts and change are studied within the moment-to-moment unfolding of interpersonal encounters.

In contrast in cultural studies, rather than the agent's interactional self-positioning *per se*, there is much more of an interest in the manner and extent to which agents reproduce, recognise and/or resist the social principles that structure their consciousness, and analysis often moves from

(a) a focal interest in expressive texts, artefacts and genres, to
(b) an engagement with the wider cultural conventions and socio-political relations that they are embedded in, to
(c) an interpretation of the more general sensibilities and 'structures of feeling' that are articulated in these texts, artefacts and genres (Geertz 1973; Williams 1977:128–135; Eagleton 1984:110).

Whereas interactional analysis tends to treat (b) as (mere) 'resources', cultural studies pays extensive attention to the circum-ambient relations, conventions and imageries that specific expressive works are set within/against. Its time-frame is historical, and it attends to the emergence, ascendance and decline of the social formations and cultural movements that give shape to particular forms of consciousness.

Writing about his own research on language, interaction and ageing, Nik Coupland offers the following comments on the limitations of the interactionist perspective:

When sociolinguists write about identity, they often interpret the term in a rather anodyne way, as if 'having an identity' or 'negotiating an identity' were selecting and displaying options from a repertoire of equally plausible alternatives ... But in the context of ageing, identity work assumes a more profound personal importance than this model proposes. The word 'essentialist' is commonly used in disparagement of theoretical orientations which fix social identities too rigidly and which are unresponsive to the social contextual process (see for example, Rampton 1995[a]), and ... this is an important insight. But age-identities *are*, in another sense, 'essential'. They are the products of the evaluative component of our life narratives ... the cumulative assessment of where we stand, developmentally – as individuals and in relation to our social environments. This isn't to say that ... talk directly exposes our essential understandings of our ageing selves. But ... identity in ageing ultimately connects to morale and well-being. (Coupland 2001c:203[4])

Coupland is concerned that interaction analysis trivialises age-identity, but his concerns could equal well apply to class identities, and in my discussion of Jameson's critique of post-modernism in Chapter 6.6, I have already noted that discourse analyses of the projection of 'multiple identities' might end up exaggerating the power of individuals, succumbing to market ideologies which treat class position as a matter of individual will, effort and enterprise. But hitherto anyway, I have not gone as far as my data permit with broader questions about class and subjectivity.

In sociology and cultural studies, for example, Skeggs stresses the role that "everyday negotiations of the mundane" play in the formation of classed subjectivities, but she insists on the complexity of the relationship between subjectivity and routine practice:

> Representations [of class] ... are not straightforwardly reproduced but are resisted and transfigured in their daily enactment. Categories of class operate not only as an organising principle which enable access to and limitations on social movement and interaction but are also reproduced at the intimate level of 'structures of feeling' (cf. Williams 1961, 1977) in which doubt, anxiety and fear inform the production of subjectivity.   (1997:6)

Ortner goes further in her attempt to understand the "phenomenology of class cultures", proposing that individuals and groups 'internalise' class stratification, and that all of us live with 'fears, anxieties' and an insistent sense that people in higher and lower class positions mirror our "pasts and possible futures" (1991:177):

> While we normally think of class relations as taking place *between* classes, in fact each class contains the other(s) within itself, though in distorted and ambivalent forms ... [E]ach class views the others not only, or even primarily, as antagonistic groups but as images of their hopes and fears for their own lives and futures ... If much of working-class culture can be understood as a set of discourses and practices embodying the ambivalence of upward mobility, much of middle-class culture can be seen as a set of discourses and practices embodying the terror of downward mobility. In both cases, the complex attitudes held about adjacent classes derive from the classes functioning as mirrors of these possibilities.   (1991:172, 175, 176)

These perspectives connect with Coupland's interest in developing a deeper analysis of identity processes, and up to a point at least, they can actually also speak to sociolinguistics on its home ground.

Ortner's view of the "introjection" of class stratification provides a much better base for understanding the relationship between class and Labovian style-shifting than the traditional sociolinguistic view of class as group membership or a fixed parental inheritance (Chapter 8.1). Her emphasis on "objective" class hierarchy being internalised as a "mirror" of our hopes and fears can be matched with Allan Bell's celebrated assertion that "variation on the style dimension within the speech of a single speaker derives from and echoes the variation which exists between speakers on the 'social' dimension" (1984:151; 2001:145), and indeed, if individuals both live and speak with an ingrained sense of social hierarchy, then contrast and relationality should be basic to accounts of style:

> Whatever 'styles' are, in language or elsewhere, they are part of a *system of distinction*, in which a style contrasts with other possible styles, and the social meaning signified by the style contrasts with other social meanings ... The characteristics of a particular style cannot be explained independently of others. Instead, attention must be directed to relationships among styles – to their contrasts, boundaries and commonalities. (Irvine 2001:22; also Parkin 1977)

Irvine's insistence on the 'relationality' of styles can be connected with Ortner's class mirroring, and they can both be can be taken as a justification for the decision to analyse stylised posh and Cockney together.[5] More generally, these points of contact between sociolinguistics and broader discussions of classed subjectivity provide initial grounds for delving further into the meaning of stylisation, looking a little beyond pragmatic effects and the social divisions (re)produced in schooling, towards more pervasive and enduring psycho-social states and processes.

At the same time, these connections suggest a need to be sensitive to the limits of coherence and system as properties of the empirical relationship between class-marked styles. Skeggs (1997:5) insists that as "as a discursive, historically specific construction ... [class] includes elements of fantasy and projection" (in a loosely psycho-analytic sense), and as already noted, Ortner emphasises the "distorted and ambivalent forms" generated by the tensions around class. In a discussion of language and sexuality – which becomes directly relevant to language and class in Chapter 9.5 below – Kulick prefers the notion of *identifications* to identity, and he insists that these are only ever likely to be incomplete, held in check by an inescapable involvement with their opposites. Like Coupland, he criticises the view that "identity ... is either revealed or concealed by fully intentional subjects" and makes the case for identifications that "are animated by fantasy, desire, repression and power". "[I]n sociolinguistic and linguistic anthropological work", he says, identity is conventionally presented as a more or less conscious claim-staking of a particular sociological position, [whereas ...] identifications are just as much structured by rejections, refusals and disavowals as they are structured by affirmations ... A psycho-analytic truism about identifications is that they do not constitute a coherent relational system. (2003:149; Cameron and Kulick 2003)

Following Ortner and Skeggs, the same might be said of class, and so it is also important to be alert to the points where, *contra* the Irvine quotation above, the relationship between posh and Cockney starts to lose its contrastive coherence.

In sum, then, there is a risk that if the notions of 'identity' prevailing in sociolinguistic analyses of interaction are allowed to dominate interpretation, a rather shallow view of social class will emerge, neglecting the complicated ways in which the fears, hopes and subjectivities of individuals are shaped by class structure. And crucially, as I hope to show over the course of this chapter, it will not be possible to do justice to the empirical data on posh and Cockney stylisation. Against this background of issues for consideration, I should now move to the first subset of stylised interactions between peers.

9.2   Stylised posh and Cockney in peer-centred interaction

Here are two relatively simple instances of stylised posh

Extract 9.1
Humanities lesson. Rafiq is sitting at the same table as Mansur (and some other boys), and he has been getting on Mansur's nerves. (Blex 4 3:265)

```
1  MANSUR    if that goes on
2            I'm gonna kill you
3  RAFIQ     ((loud, with a long high-fall on the second
             word: ))
             ˈoh ˋno::=
             [ɔ nəʊ]
4  ANON      ((chuckles))
5  RAFIQ     ((quieter, in his ordinary voice))
             is that a threat
             [ɪz ð æʔ ə]
6  MANSUR    yeh
7  RAFIQ     ((with slow delivery: ))
             ˋoh: ˋno:
             [əʊ   nəʊ]
```

```
 8            Mansur
 9            ˈdoːnˈt ˋspaːnner me
              [dəʊnt spæːnəː miː]
10            like (you done) with ˈSa/ˌtesh
11  MANSUR    (cut it out)
12            (cut it out)
13            (2.5)
14  RAFIQ     ((fast, normal pitch:))
              >(should've) beat him up with your hands<
                           [biː? ɪm ʌp wɪᶿ jə hænz]
15            not with a spanner
              [nɒ? wɪᶿ ə spænʌ]
16  BOY       ((referring to his work:)) I'm on three
17  RAFIQ     why did you have to hit him with a spanner
18            you should hit ˈim with your hands
19            (.)
20            it'd prove that you're more of a man
```

Rafiq's utterance "oh no, oh no, don't spanner me like Satesh" (lines 3, 7–10) expresses mock trepidation and seeks to remind Mansur of his unmanly behaviour at some earlier point (lines 18 and 20). Although it is not an extreme example of posh, and although the overall effect may be either mitigated or made more comically anomalous by the non-standard use of 'spanner' as a (transitive) verb (as well, perhaps, as by the partly inaudible syntax in line 10), the mock plea is expressed in much more standard pronunciation than usual. The delivery is slow, the pitch movement is exaggerated, and in terms of segmental phonetics, there is a clustering of standard rather than vernacular variants. The GOAT vowel in 'no' and 'oh no' in lines 3 and 7 is realised with RP [əʊ], rather than with the more open [ʌʊ] that Rafiq had used in 'no' a little earlier and that is characteristic of Cockney more generally (Wells 1982:308–309). Although it cannot be seen due to the pseudonymisation, the final syllable in Mansur's real name finishes with a velarised rather than vocalic L (Wells 1982:313–317), and there is no T glottalling in "don't" and "Satesh" in lines 9 and 10. A moment later in lines 14 and 15, the distinctiveness of these features is further flagged when Rafiq expresses his own moral view, speaking much more rapidly, glottalling his T's and articulating the final -ER in spanner with a more open, non-standard [ʌ] (cf. Wells 1982:305). The overall effect is to cast Mansur's "if that goes on I'm gonna kill you" as the kind of feeble threat that could only frighten posh softies.

In Extract 9.2 below, Ninnette has just been given the radio-microphone (by me) outside in the playground, and conscious that they are being tape-recorded, she and Joanne are playing with *risqué* sexual topics, incriminating each other, and pretending to censor key words by inserting 'beep' into their utterances, a device used in broadcasting to eliminate words deemed improper. Joanne has just said

as I know from previous experience, Ninnette is very strong (.) she likes to catch boys' (2) beeps ((*laughs*))

Ninnette responds:

Extract 9.2
(Blex 59 33:77)

```
 1   N    and YOU:
 2        (.)
 3        .hh
 4        ((half-laughing and then very high pitched at the
          end:))
 5        and (        )
 6        (1.5)
 7        and as for (Br    )
 8   JO   and as for`ME::
 9        ˆwell
          [weɫ]
10        ((half-laughing, and with an element of
          constriction:))
11        ＼I ⌐don't get ⌐up
          [aɪ dəʊn get ʌp]
12        to this ⌐sort of ⌐thing=
          [tə ðɪs sɔ: tʰ əv θɪŋ]
13        =((laughing:)) ahh hah hah
14        .huh
15        this
          [ðɪs:]
16        ＼ru::de thi⌐ng
          [ɹəʊːd    θɪŋə]
17   N    ((high pitched shriek:)) AAGH
```

Within this playful sequence of incrimination and denial, Joanne's claims to proper conduct in lines 9–12 and 15 are 'carefully' enunciated with standard rather than Cockney consonantal variants.[6]

This style can be designated 'literate speech', and it follows in a tradition that Mugglestone dates back to Dr Johnson's dictum: "For pronunciation the best rule is, to consider those as the most elegant speakers who deviate least from the written words" (Mugglestone 1995:208; see also Chapter 8.4 above). And in this instance, it suggests a rather commonplace association between standard speech features and restrained/refined sexual conduct, counterposed to the vulgarity that Joanne jokingly attributes to her friend. But exploitation of this social imagery was not always so straightforward, and Joanne invoked it in less blatant, more piquant ways elsewhere:

Extract 9.3

A week later, Joanne, Ninnette and others are in the playground during break (Blex 78: 49/260). Ninnette and Joanne have been talking about a party Ninnette says she's arranging, joking about booze, sex and the boys they could invite. Ninnette then notices Ricky, a boy that she fancies but doesn't go out with:

```
 1  N    oh oh oh
 2       my boyfriend's here
 3       (2)
 4  JO   ((?short kissing noise:)) mwa
 5       (3)
 6  N    ((audibly moving away from Joanne and the mic:))
         my little scooby do thing
 7       (2)
 8  JO   ((posh, at a higher than normal pitch level:))
         oh you ′are: ˋhere
         [əʊ jʊ ʷɑ::  hɛ̃ə̃]
 9       ˎRi｜cky
10       (.)
11       ˈRi｜cky
12       ((quietly, with half-laugh at the end:))
         Niˈnnette′sˇhere
                   [hiɑ̃]
13       (1)
14  BOY  ((a little way away:)) (   coming to your party)
15  N    (        )
16  JO   ((short, quite loud high pitched laugh:)) hh hh (.)
17       ((loudly, in a vernacular accent:)) Ninnette
18       I bet you′re gonna invite him
19  N    (             )
20  JO   no
21       you′re too shy:
```

```
22      (1)
23      cos if he asked you out
24      ((high-pitched:)) OOH:: NO::
```

In this episode, there is quite a lot of moving around in a relatively crowded outdoor space, and it is hard to hear or follow everything that is going on in it. But in line 6, Ninnette moves away from Joanne, leaving her silent for about 2 seconds. From the lack of an audible response to her utterances in lines 8–9 and 11–12, from the inaudibility of the talk later on in lines 14 and 15, and from the increased loudness with which she uses Ninnette's name to regain her attention in line 17, it sounds as though in line 7, Joanne temporarily becomes a solo bystander, somewhat at the edge of whatever's going on. Then, left to the side like this, in lines 8–12, she performs what sounds like a small piece of dramatic commentary on the scene she is observing, beginning with "oh you are here", the change-of-state token ('oh') and the stress on 'are' both suggesting that up until now, she had not taken Ninnette's earlier claim seriously (line 8). She also appears to address Ricky himself (lines 9 and 11), though once again, the circumstantial details mentioned above lay it open to question whether or not she actually expects to be heard.

It seems even more likely that she's engaged in self-talk in her next utterance in line 12, where she also formulates the sentence as if it was addressed to Ricky, but actually *drops* her voice and speaks more quietly – "Ricky, Ninnette's here". Even though they are co-present, Ricky evidently is not talking to Ninnette, and in this utterance, Joanne pretends to draw his attention to her. There are good reasons, though, why she should keep this relatively quiet.

Joanne knows that Ninnette fancies Ricky, but she has no reason to suppose that Ricky reciprocates. Because of this, it would be very presumptuous if she really did single Ninnette out for Ricky's attention. It would betray Ninnette's confidence, make her interest in Ricky obvious to him, and also force him to a declaration in the order of either "Hi Ninnette!" or "So? Fuck off!" Her friend might not feel quite ready for that, as Joanne herself subsequently acknowledges in lines 18–24. On the other hand, as is often the case among adolescents (e.g. Foley 1990:33, 70, 95; Rampton 1995a:187–189), such disclosures were the focus of a great deal of peer group activity, and even only in anticipation, they seemed replete with risk and promise for one or both of the named parties, and an endless source of entertainment for their friends. It is this rich vein of excitement, ambivalence and potential embarrassment that Joanne is playing with in her apostrophe to Ricky, and she animates it with a switch to much posher than normal speech.

In line 8, Joanne's 'here' sounds like 'hair' ([hɛə]). The first part of the centring diphthong is much more open than is typical either in 'ordinary' RP [ɪə] or in Cockney [iə], and to me anyway, this makes it sound very upper class. Her second 'here' in line 12 contains an open second element – [iɑ] – that Wells associates with "the duchess, officer and don stereotypes" (1982:281), and neither involves any Cockney H-dropping. Though the need for pseudonyms prevents me giving details, Joanne's pronunciation of Ninnette's name in line 12 is also noticeably standard, containing 'literate' elements that are then dropped when she repeats it a moment later in her normal accent in 17, and there is also no Cockney glottalisation of the intervocalic /k/ in Ricky in lines 9 and 11 (Wells 1982:324). It would be foolish to try to be too specific about the aesthetic effect that these phonetic selections produce within her performance overall, but assuming that posh is associated with politeness, putting-your-best-foot-forward and/or sexual restraint, it introduces a note of formal propriety into Joanne's mock mediation, and when this is laid over the subterranean abundance of sexual, amatory and/or embarrassing consequences that the encounter might unleash, it gels in something like an oxymoron, a knowing encapsulation of both inhibition and desire.

So far, I have focused on the stylisation of posh. We can now turn to Cockney, and begin with an episode involving Simon.

Extract 9.4

Simon (wearing the radio-microphone) and Ameena are sitting at a table together chatting during a Humanities lesson in the library. They've just been agreeing on how embarrassing it would be to fart when your parents had guests in the house, or when you were out on a date (Blex 44b 24:294):

```
1   SIMON     oh my word (.)
2             that would be just too depressing (.)
3   AMEENA    that is dumb ((half-laugh))
4             (2)
5             or pretend (.)
6             (as soon as) you ate your dinner
7             right
```

```
 8              you (really had to)-
                you had to burp
 9              ((softly:)) oh go::d (.)
10   SIMON      sometimes girls don't mind that
11              they go
                    [gɛʊ]
12              ((breathy:)) oh ˋgo on
                            [ɒʊ gɒ° ɒn]
13              ˈled id ˋout ((= 'let it out'))
                [lẹd ɪd æʊʔ]
14              ˈyou're a ˈma:n
                [jɒ ʷə mæn]
15              ((laughs:)) hhhh (1)
16              you're like
17              er-
18              er I raader not
                    [ɹɑːdə]
19              and then they get
20              ((makes funny noise trilling his lips.
                Approximately:)) brbrbr
21              and you go
22              em
23              ((sniffs, then tuts))
24              neyeugh!
25              ((light laugh)) (.)
26   AMEENA     (they go)
27              go on
28              go on ˈen
29   SIMON      goˋo:n
                [gəwʊn]
30              ˈled id ˋout
                [lẹd ɪd æʊ:ʔ]
31              (.)
32              / biks-
33   TEACHER    there's only about
34              three minutes of your favourite lesson left
35              so you'd better get a move on
```

Having come to an agreement on the horror of farting on a date, Ameena introduces another embarrassing scenario – "pretend ... you had to burp, oh god". Simon runs with this, but argues that this can be more acceptable – indeed, more than being merely indifferent, girls sometimes positively encourage it as proper manly conduct. In proposing this view, Simon offers a characterisation of what they say, signalling clearly that this is a dramatised enactment rather than a straighter piece of direct reported speech by switching (again) into a breathy voice (lines 12–14). At the same time, the performed voice is clearly also a London vernacular one, involving a glottal stop, a broad London realisation MOUTH vowel ([æʊʔ]) in 'out', and an intervocalic voiced [d] for T in the phrase 'led id out').

Simon then goes on to offer a characterisation of how ordinary people like him and Ameena respond to such encouragement ("you're like er ..." [line 16–17]), their polite reluctance at the start ("er I raader not" line 18) leading (under the pressure of non-word actions that it is rather hard to interpret without a visual record – lines 19, 20) up to what sounds like an emphatic refusal (line 24). In representing this position – the position taken by people like Ameena and himself – he drops the breathiness from his speech and avoids traditional Cockney TH fronting in 'rather' in line 18, which would have been [ɹɑːvə] (Wells 1982:328–330). At the same time, the articulation of this refusal to belch avoids the impression of priggish propriety, most obviously through the non-word 'neyeugh', an energetic revulsion sound that appears to blend 'no' and 'eugh', but also through the production of a stopped TH in 'rather' – [ɹɑːdə] – a variant characteristic of black London vernacular speech rather than posh or standard, where the voiced fricative [ð] would be normal. After the climactic refusal in line 24, Ameena appreciatively recycles the most surprising part of the scene – the girls' enthusiasm for manly burping – and Simon repeats his stylisation of 'let it out'. Evidently, the fit between burping and a broad London accent feels sufficiently euphonious to merit an *encore*.

Lastly, it is worth looking at an episode where posh and Cockney are juxtaposed, set within a shift of footing where there is quite a sharp contrast in the cultural values and communicative forms that they are each associated with:

Extract 9.5

During the tutor period while Mr Alcott is talking to the class about a racist incident the previous day, Joanne (wearing the radio-microphone) has been telling Ninnette a bit about her parents and grandparents, and has just been talking about her mum's difficult pregnancy (Blex 68 42:244):

```
1   JOANNE    (.)
2             ((quietly: )) she could have lost me ((light
                  laugh))
```

```
3                (3)
4                ((with a hint of tearfulness in her voice: ))
                 n you'd all be sitting here today without me
                                 [sɪtʔɪn hɪə]
                 ((laughs))
5   TANNOY       ((eleven pips, followed by the din of chairs
                 moving))
6   JO           ((louder, and in literate speech: ))
                 but you 'wouldn't 'care
                 [bt jə wʊdʰntʰ kɛə]
7                cos you 'wouldn't ` know ((laughs))
                 [kəz jə wʊdʰnt⁻ næu]
8   ?N           (                    )
9   JO           nothing I'm just jok-    )
10               I'm being st-
11               ((high-pitched)) ᐟ˅oooh::
                                  [u::  ]
12               ᐟ˅Ninne::tte
13               you've got eᵢnough with you to˅day
                 [ju  gɒt enʌf  wɪθ ju: tədēī]
14               and ᵢthen you ᵢgo and ` chee::k ˅me::
                 [æn  en jə gəʊn  tʃi:k  mi:]
15               ᵢyou ˅little:: ᵢbuggᵢayeᵢayeᵢayeᵢaye
                 [ju  lɪtʔʊ::ʔ  bʌg  āī  jāī jāī jāī]
16               (15) ((the teacher is giving clearing up
                 instructions))
17               ((Joanne leaves the classroom and then hums
                 quietly to herself))
```

At the start of the extract, Joanne finishes her story with quite a momentous conclusion: she could have died before birth (line 2). But there is no audible response (line 3) (understandably, perhaps, in view of the fact that the teacher is talking to the whole class and Joanne and Ninnette are having to chat *sotto voce* anyway). Joanne doesn't leave it at that, though, and with a suggestion of mock tearfulness in her voice, she draws out the immediate consequences of her mother's loss – ''you'd all be sitting here today without me'' (line 4). Before there is any uptake, the Tannoy interrupts, announcing the end of the lesson with a series of loud pips, and when the pips have finished, Joanne resumes with a dramatic change of footing. The picture of a school class saddened by her absence is logically contradictory – ''but you wouldn't care cos you wouldn't know'' (lines 6 and 7) – and in the deflation of such sentimentality, Joanne combines 'literate speech' with epi-grammatic style. There is no elision (or glottalisation) of the alveolar consonants in either of the two ''wouldn't's'', and instead, the plosives [d] and [t] are aspirated in three of the four occasions where they occur. At the same time, the sentence breaks into two lines characterised by rhythmic, grammatical and lexical parallelism

```
bt you would n't care
cz you would n't know
```

and the formulation of a sardonic analytic point in this succinct poetic structure warrants comparison with the classical epigram: "a short, polished poem ending with some graceful, ingenious, pointed, weighty, witty or satirical turn of thought; more personal and specific than a proverb" (Shipley (ed.) 1970:103).

Ninnette's reaction to this is not audible (line 8), but from what follows, it must have involved some kind of challenge (something such as 'what are you up to?'). Joanne begins to formulate a retraction, minimising what she has just been saying and explaining that it wasn't serious in lines 9 and 10 (''nothing, I'm just jok- ((=> joking)), I'm being st- ((=> stupid?))'') but before she has finished, she interrupts herself with an emphatic change-of-state token and redirects the focus from herself to her friend, using a stretched rise-fall in both of these actions – ''/\ooh /\Ninnette'' (lines 11 and 12). According to Cruttenden, rise-fall tones tends to express attitudinal stances of either 'being impressed' or 'being challenging' (1986:101–102), and both could fit the data here, ''/\ooh'' expressing 'impressed' and ''/\Ninnette'' articulating 'challenge'. These are then blended in lines 13 and 14 in an indignant reprimand, in which she accuses Ninnette of already being at the limits of tolerable conduct (''you've got enough with you today'' line 13), and of then exceeding these limits with impertinence (''and then you go and cheek me''). After that, the sequence closes with a damning summary of Ninnette's character: ''you little buggaye aye aye aye''. Of course Joanne is not being serious here – you can only be cheeky to someone who is older or in a superior position, and since Joanne and Ninnette are actually peers of the same age, it would be a fatuous accusation if she really meant it. Instead, in claiming to be the recipient of Ninnette's cheek, Joanne is playing a part, and she articulates this in the London vernacular, using L vocalisation and T glottaling in Ninnette's name and in "little" in line 15, as well as (what sounds to me like) a non-standard idiom in line 13 ("you've got enough with you today").

Overall, Joanne's performance in this extract constructs a quite sharp contrast between the footings associated with standard and vernacular speech. With the shift to careful 'literate' speech, she uses logic to *undermine* sentiment, and symetrical patterns of rhythm and grammar provide her propositional argument with elegant poetic structuring. In contrast, when she pretends to *intensify* the emotion in her speech – when she abandons her apology, cancelling the effort to restore equanimity to her relationship with Ninnette, and issues an indignant reprimand – her speech becomes markedly Cockney, and the relationship between sound and semantic meaning loses its balance. As a non-lexical response cry, the "ooh" that Joanne uses to initiate her reprimand makes a "show of [being a] 'natural emotional expression'" (Goffman 1981:108), and in cutting mid-word into the apology that immediately preceded it, it makes the reprimand look like a spontaneous outburst. And then at the end, sound disrupts lexis once again when a word that initially looks like it is maybe going to be 'bugger' is carried off half-way through into a repetitive non-word sequence of "aye aye aye aye".

At this point, it is worth turning to consider these five episodes together, also referring as necessary to the larger subset of posh and Cockney stylisations of which they form a part.

9.3   The 'high–low' cultural semantic

In the episodes I have been considering, stylised posh was used to express mock trepidation at a threat that is judged unmanly (Extract 9.1 "oh no, Mansur, don't..."), and it was associated both with sexual restraint/inhibition ("I don't get up to this sort of thing" in Extract 9.2 and "Ricky, Ninnette's here" in 9.3) and with being gay ("I'm not going down there with them gay people" in Extract 8.3, lines 28 and 29). In another episode, it was linked to inanity in sport ("oh helloo", addressed to an arriving football by someone who says their new glasses stop them seeing it properly), although we have also seen it articulate elegant wit (Extract 9.5: "you wouldn't care ..."). Meanwhile, stylised Cockney was associated with bodily relaxation/freedom ("led it out" in Extract 9.4), passionate indignation (Extract 9.5: "buggaye"), and with territorial assertiveness ("gid out", "gid out of London" in an episode I have not presented). Reframing this, it looks as though a relatively *standard accent* is used to articulate an incompetent or uneasy relationship with both the body and with feelings and emotions (e.g. Extracts 9.1, 9.2 and 9.3), that the words selected express an apparent regard for social decorum (e.g. Joanne's feigned mediation between Ninnette and Ricky in Extract 9.3), and that there is an association with literate cultivation rather than oral spontaneity, both in the use of 'spelling' pronunciation (Extract 9.2) and in the approximation to a classical genre (the epigram in Extract 9.5). A *Cockney accent*, in contrast, is associated with bodily activity, with the expression of feeling unconstrained by social manners (e.g. Extract 9.4), with profane language that emphasises sexual activity ("eff off" in another episode), and with a disruption of conventional (written) word structure ("buggaye" [9.5]; elsewhere "gid out" becomes "gidyoo").

A pattern emerges, then, in which vigour, passion and bodily laxity appear to be associated with Cockney, while physical weakness, distance, constraint and sexual inhibition are linked to posh. In fact, at a more abstract level, this can be easily accommodated within a more general set of contrasts between mind and body, reason and emotion, high and low. According to Bourdieu, the notion of 'popular speech' is itself "one of the products of the application of dualistic taxonomies which structure the social world according to the categories of high and low ..., refined and coarse ... distinguished and vulgar, rare and common, well-mannered and sloppy" (1991:93), and in Phil Cohen's analysis (1988), the emergence of 'class racism' from the seventeenth to the nineteenth centuries in England was built around a contrast between on the one hand, elevated reason and "bourgeois virtues of industriousness and thrift", and on the other, sexual promiscuity and "the body ..., the heart of unreason, the site of 'base pleasures' and vulgar instincts as against the higher and more refined faculties" (1988:66, 67). This dualistic idiom, argues Cohen, was generated "from within certain strategic discourses in British class society, [and] from the very outset [it was] applied across a range of sites of domination, both to the indigenous lower orders and ethnic minority settlers as well as to colonial populations overseas" (1988:63), and Stallybrass and White propose that this 'high-low' dichotomy is fundamental to bourgeois subjectivity: "[b]ourgeois democracy emerged with a class which, whilst indeed progressive in its best political aspirations, had encoded in its manners, morals and imaginative writings, in its body, bearing and taste, a subliminal [high vs low] elitism which was constitutive of its historical being." (1996:202). Mugglestone's historical account of self-improving efforts to 'talk proper' documents some of the linguistic consequences of these dualisms, and within sociolinguistics, variations on this dualistic idiom have been repeatedly reported in matched guise studies of speech evaluation.[7]

So across the range of stylised performances of posh and Cockney, it looks as though these youngsters were reproducing a 'cultural semantic' (Stallybrass and White) that is very well-established both in Britain and in class-stratified western societies more generally. Cultural analysts associate class with the dualities of mind–body, reason–emotion etc.; historical and variationist sociolinguists associate class with posh and Cockney; and my informants introduced posh and Cockney into stylised performances in which they engaged with elements in these dualities. Indeed, if there were any need for it, these data might themselves be taken as corroboration of the cultural analysts' claims about the class significance of such dualism.

In terms of the map of stylised meaning-making in Chapter 8.5 (Figure 8.1, drawn from Ochs 1996), we are here identifying the historical provenance and more of the 'contents' of posh and Cockney's 'indexical valence' (or connotational potential). That map, though, has more general significance. In starting and basing the analysis in *speech practice*, in *acts* which evoke rather than in *conventions, structures and schema* which merely find articulation in speech, it stops the account prioritising structure and insists that activity is just as important. As a model, it emphasises the crucial part that the local contingencies of situated interaction play in the production of indexical meaning, guiding participants (with varying degrees of clarity) towards particular aspects of posh and Cockney's indexical potential, and in consequence, it also underlines the cumulative capacity of interactional acts to *change* the associative meaning potential of a particular language form or variety. And so although we may say in our analytic short-hand that posh and Cockney are tied to the high–low cultural semantic identified by cultural theorists, the key point is that this general schema *lives* in the kinds of quotidian practice seen in Extracts 9.1 to 9.5, and here it may also slowly change.

This account is consistent in sociolinguistics with Hanks' practice-oriented view of how collective socio-historical schemas are continuously reconstituted within the flows and contingencies of situated activity (1996:257–258), and the dynamic relationship between schema/indexical valence and interaction points to one aspect of the processes involved when Skeggs claims that "[r]epresentations [of class] ... are not straightforwardly reproduced but are ... transfigured in their daily enactment" (1997:6). Indeed, up to a point at least, this bridges the two views of identity polarised in my initial comparison of cultural studies and interaction analysis in Chapter 9.1 – the 'high–low' schema constitutes a relatively stable element in these youngsters' classed subjectivity, but rather than just being a predefined mental template available for the interpretation of experience, it is always being animated, respecified and inflected in practical action tuned to the circumstances on hand. Skeggs invoked Williams' notion of 'structures of feeling' to characterise the intimate level at which class categorisation functioned (1997; Chapter 9.1 above), and in fact this notion itself does a good deal to erase the polarisation of subjectivity and interaction that I posited at the outset.

In Williams' account of them, 'structures of feeling' are socially and historically shaped, and they are trans-situational, drawing on experiences prior to the communicative present, to the extent that one can speak of the structures of feeling characteristic of a person, a set of people, a collection of texts, or indeed a period. The 'structure' part of 'structures of feeling' involves "a set [of affective elements of consciousness and relationships] with specific internal relations, at once interlocking and in tension" (1977:132), and in the data considered so far, the historically grounded, high–low/mind–body/reason–emotion binary might be identified as one such structure. In terms of their relationship with interaction, structures of feeling "exert pressures and set effective limits on experience and action" (1977:132), but they are much more indeterminate than 'ideology', and "cannot without loss be reduced to belief-systems, institutions, or explicit general relationships" (1977:133). Instead, structures of feeling are "practical consciousness of a present kind, in a living and interrelating continuity", and "can be defined as social experience *in solution*, as distinct from other social semantic formations which have been *precipitated* and are more evidently and more immediately available" (1977:133). We can get a sense of the high–low binary as "social experience in solution", capable of infusing very different preoccupations and immediate concerns, if we think back, for example, to Ninnette and Joanne's angry parody of Mr Alcott (Extract 8.3), to Hanif's Cockney as he turned to science (Extract 8.9), or to Rafiq's Cockneyfication of 'sonar bangla' (Extract 8.12), or to the posh voice that Joanne used in the pretended introduction of Ninnette to Ricky (Extract 9.3). Williams' 'structure of feeling' offers an account of more stable dimensions of subjectivity, related to particular aspects of socio-historical experience,[8] but this is nevertheless incessantly recoloured, and at least potentially open to reshaping, amidst the pressures and contingencies of everyday practice.

This is, though, only the first step in analysis of the relationship between stylisation, subjectivity and social class. There are still important elements missing, and little has been said to link stylisation to the 'feeling' side of 'structures of feeling', "the *specifically affective* elements of consciousness and relationships: not feeling against thought, but thought as felt and feeling as thought" (Williams, 1977; emphases added). Both Ortner and Skeggs linked social class to hopes, fears and anxieties capable of troubling the 'fully intentional subject', but hitherto, my discussion has not dwelt on these in any empirical detail. Indeed, of itself the fact that these youngsters were playing on culturally rooted dualities of high–low, mind–body, reason–emotion, does little to question theoretical models that presuppose a separation between symbols and the controlling subject who deploys them, or that see speech as involving the flexible strategic selection of social images from a mental repertoire of stereotypes (Le Page and Tabouret-Keller 1985:181–186; Hudson 1996:237–243; Lippi-Green 1997:30, 63). All it illuminates, one could say, is something of the ideological structuring of the multi-dimensional socio-symbolic space that speakers allude to in their linguistic acts of identity. But this changes if we now turn to posh, Cockney and the grotesque.

9.4   Posh and Cockney in the grotesque

Here are Ninnette and Joanne in the playground once again:

Extract 9.6: 'funny eyes'
Ninnette (wearing the radio-microphone), Joanne and Linda are outside in the playground, and they're started to talk about their faces. (Blex 62: 36:260)

```
 1  N    Linda's face gets hurt more easily than mine
 2       (.)
 3  JO   because yours is looser
 4  N    no
 5       (.)
 6       because she::
 7       (.)
 8       feels pain more than I do
 9       (.)
10  JO   no
11       cos yours is looser
12  N    ((loud brief laugh))
13       (.)
14       loo:: ((='look'))
15       ((?Does something funny with her eyes for the
         first time))
16       ((laughs:)) hah hah /haah
17  JO   it's a lot more (      /   )
18  N    loo(k) loo(k) loo(k)
         [lʊʔ  lʊʔ   lʊʔ]
19       look loo(k)
         [lʊk   lʊʔ]
20  JO   Linda's skin's str/aighter
21  N    loo(k)
         [lʊʔ]
22       (2) ((Second performance of 'funny eyes'))
23  JO   what're you loo- hhh ((:starts short breathy
         laugh))
24       (.)
25       >(look a' 'er)< eyes
26       watch her eyes again
27       (2.5)
28  N    ((Third performance of 'funny eyes',
         accompanied by quieter speech:)) and `whaT
                                      [ænd wɒt ˢʰ]
29       ((Suddenly breaks into laughter for 2.5))=
```

```
30              =loo:k
                [lʊʔ]
31              l- l-
32              /loo(k) loo(k)=
                [lʊʔ    lʊʔ]
33    LINDA     cow's eyes
34    N         =watch 'is
                [wɒtʃ  ⌐ɪs]
35              (.)
36              ((Fourth performance of 'funny eyes', with
                quieter speech:))
                ˈwhaT
                [wɒtʰ]
37              are you ˋlooKing /aT
                [ɑː ju lʊkɪŋ ætsʰ]
38    JO        ((slowly, and quite quiet:)) your fu/nny:
39              hea(d)
40    LINDA     (                              )
41    N         ((laughing:)) loo(k) loo(k) hah hah hah
42              ((fifth performance, with speech that ends with
                exaggerated lip-rounding:))
                ˈWHAT ˈhare ˈyou ˋlooking /at
                [wɒtʰ hɑː juː lʊkɪŋ æɵʔ]
43              (.)
44    LINDA     lookin' at your funny eyes
45              (.)
46    N         I cn s-
47    JO        ((laughing:)) they no
48              (but look                     )
49    GIRL      ((high pitched, mock laugh:)) a hah
50    N         I can see TWO:
51              (.)
52              I can see FOUR big things
53              pokin out your jacket
                   [ɪn]
54              (.)
55              er
56              wonder what they (hhh)ar/e
57    JO        ((laughs))
58              (2.5)
```

The extract begins with a short dispute between Ninnette and
Joanne about the reason why Linda's face is more sensitive to pain
than Ninnette's (lines 1–11). The argument has not developed very
far when Ninnette laughs abruptly after Joanne's second reference

to her 'loose' face and tells them all to 'look'. There is no visual record, but it is clear from the dialogue that follows that she is asking them to attend to her face, and that the spectacle they are to attend to involves her doing something funny with her eyes:

```
line 26: Joanne:     watch her eyes again
line 33: Linda:      cows' eyes
line 42: Ninnette:   what hare you looking at
line 44: Linda:      lookin' at your funny eyes
```

From the stretched vowel of 'loo(k)' in line 14 and the laugh that follows immediately after (line 16), it sounds as though she pulls the face there and then, but Joanne does not notice, carrying on instead with her discussion of Linda's face (lines 17 and 20). Ninnette evidently decides that it is worth another performance, and so she now intensifies her efforts to get their attention, asking them to 'look' six times in quick succession (lines 18, 19, 21). In line 22, she evidently judges that the audience is sufficiently settled, and performs the eyes act a second time. Joanne apparently tunes in a little late, but laughs when she catches on and suggests they see it again (lines 23–26). After an attentive pause (line 27), Ninnette starts her third performance, this time providing a verbal accompaniment (line 28), but she cracks up in laughter very soon after the start (line 29) and has to reassemble the audience (and recompose herself) (lines 30, 31, 32, 34). During the fourth and fifth performances in lines 36–37 and 42, the verbal accompaniment is fully articulated in the sentence ``what are you looking at'', and it turns out that this involves a hybrid mixture of both posh *and* Cockney.[9] This is combined with a stilted, effortful style of delivery, and together they bring hyper-correct, 'adoptive RP' to mind, what Wells calls the "the variety of RP spoken by adults who did not speak RP as children' (1982:283).[10]

Certainly there *are* social types and real social groups who do use 'adoptive RP', but real groups and individuals are not the focus of the girls' attention in this episode, they are not engaged in poking fun at particular people, and I personally cannot think of any real or fictional precedent that warrants an association between (a) upward-aspiring-people-with-limited-linguistic-capital (the variationists' hyper-correcting Lower Middle Class) and (b) 'funny (cows) eyes'. Instead, it looks as though Ninnette is engaged in some kind of grotesque, and to get more purchase on this, and to move closer to cultural analysts' concern with subjectivity, it is worth referring in more detail to the work of Stallybrass and White (1996).

Like other cultural analysts, Stallybrass and White argue that the differentiation of social groups on a hierarchy of high and low is a central cultural process in class societies, and that this has a profound impact on the way in which individuals make sense of the world. But very much influenced by Bakhtin (1968), they go on to propose that in the course of defining outgroups and marking the boundaries between 'us' and 'them', social groups develop a history with the Other and internalise an imagery that becomes dangerously unstable in the group's 'political unconscious', a mixture not just of fear and disgust but also of fascination and desire (1996:194). One of the most powerful cultural expressions of this group process, they claim, can be found in the grotesque, and in one of its forms, the grotesque involves hybridisation and inmixing, transgressing the boundaries that separate high from low. I think it is this that we are seeing in Extract 9.6.[11] Ninnette is performing peculiar physiognomical contortions, which she evidently feels highly compelling (``look look look look look look look look look'' – lines 18–32), and to accompany them, she draws on a speech style which is widely recognised as a(n often comically anomalous) mixture of Cockney and posh. As a discursive and historical construction, says Skeggs, class includes "elements of fantasy and projection" (1997:5), and, argues Ortner, "each class contains the other(s) within itself, though in distorted and ambivalent forms" (1991:172). Fantasy, distortion *and* class are all evident in Ninnette's performance, and if we are willing to accept the orientation offered by Stallybrass and White, then these data encourage us to locate posh and Cockney somewhere in these youngsters' 'Imaginary', in a zone where 'ideology and fantasy conjoin' (Stallybrass and White 1996:25).

This evidence of an extravagant grotesque is the first element in Extract 9.6 that helps to deepen the sense of what social class might mean for these youngsters, looking beyond speech act notions of 'meaning', potentially destabilising the idea of a rational, tactical actor in control, pointing to processes where posh and Cockney "identifications [cease to] constitute a coherent relational system" (Kulick 2003:149; Chapter 9.1 above). The second aspect worth emphasising is the pre-eminence of corporeality in Ninnette's performance. As already noted, many cultural analysts point to the way in which classed notions of high–low extend to representations of the body. Indeed in

Extracts 9.1 to 9.4, it was the fact that sexuality and bodily matters were thematically at issue in posh and Cockney stylisations that made it possible to speak of the high–low cultural semantic. Left like that, though, the relationship might be construed as just that – as a semantic correlation, a cognitive pattern linking linguistic, cultural and social stereotypes. What Extract 9.6 attests is that beyond its verbal articulation, class-marked semiotic stylisation could also involve the vigorous physical enactment of different face and body images.

This is hardly a startling discovery, and the intimate enactive relationship between social class and the body is spelt out in Bourdieu's notion of hexis (1977:660–663; 1991).[12] Even so, there is quite a deep-seated logo-centric bias in linguistics and discourse analysis (Finnegan 2001), and within this, accent is often viewed as just a surface-level phonological resource. In contrast, the evidence on stylisation fits more closely with the view that

most knowledge … is organised into highly complex and integrated networks or mental models … which are not language-like precisely because of the simultaneous multiplicity of ways in which information is integrated in them. These mental models are, what is more, only partly linguistic; they also integrate visual imagery, other sensory cognition, the cognitive aspects of learned practices, evaluations, memories of sensations, and memories of typical examples. (Bloch 1998:24–25)

Even in episodes where bodily articulations of dialect remain obscure due to my reliance on audio-recordings, moments of heightened performance involved fluent, spontaneous compositions in which a mix of vocal, generic, linguistic and cultural cues and images were clustered (cf. Bauman [1975] 2001). So rather than simply being phonological or linguistic entities, the posh–Cockney nexus comprised distinctive clusterings of dialect, mode of speech, preoccupation, and interpersonal and physical demeanour – stylings, in other words, that "crosscut … communicative and behavioural modalities and integrate[d] … them thematically" (Irvine 2001:23; see also Coupland 2001a:348; Agha 2003:232–233).

Summing up its overall significance, Extract 9.6 can be regarded as an extreme case forcing us towards an interpretive idiom that is actually relevant to a great many of the episodes in my dataset. With other episodes, we might just be able to scrape by with notions like strategy, appropriateness and calculable impacts, but these signally fail with Extract 9.6, which insists instead that we engage with the *aesthetic*, a convenient umbrella term to stand, among other things, for the processes discussed in this section. Exactly how the aesthetic should best be theorised can be left open, although fantasy, emotion, psychic interiority, physical activity, body imagery, and sensory atunement to the material setting all now become potentially relevant (Downes 2000; Finnegan 2001; Knoblauch and Kotthoff 2001; Irvine 2001). Overall, an orientation to the aesthetic helps to thicken the apprehension of what is entailed in the stylisation of posh and Cockney, and the resonance and penetration of class-marked language gains depth – Extract 9.6 demands that we stretch our descriptive vocabulary, forcing a recognition of processes that bring linguistic analysis closer to the cultural analysts' discussions of class and subjectivity.

That said, Extract 9.6 is of course only one episode, and if it was the only empirical warrant for the shift of analytic idiom that is being suggested, we would be hanging a great deal on it. But it isn't and we're not, and this will become clear if we now move to the last subset of stylisation data. This subset involves episodes in which boys use exaggerated Cockney in their depictions of Marilyn, one of the girls in their tutor group, and though the context is London rather than the US, here there is a good deal of relevance in Ortner's observation that

gender relations for both middle-class and working-class Americans ... carry an enormous burden of quite antagonistic class meaning. To turn the point around, class discourse is submerged within, and spoken through, sexual discourse, taking 'sex' here in the double English sense of pertaining to both gender and the erotic. (1991:171–172)

9.5   Stylised Cockney, gender and sexuality

During a double science lesson, the teacher sent Marilyn, one of the five white girls in the class, out of the room, but when the lesson ended, she came back to collect her books. One of the boys called out a very loud, Cockney greeting, which Simon echoed straightaway.[13] And then a minute and a half later, he developed this into an impersonation of Marilyn:

Extract 9.7

The end of a double science lesson, and Hanif (wearing the radio-microphone) is taking in the textbooks. About 40 minutes earlier, Marilyn was sent out of the class but by line 17, she has evidently reappeared (to collect her things). (Blex 14)

```
 1   HANIF        TEXTBOOKS
 2                (.)
 3                bloody textbooks (.)
 4       TEACHER      Gopal come on (        )
 5   HANIF        textbooks (.) textbooks
 6                (2)
 7                alright Zainab (.)
 8                textboo:ks
 9                (.)
10   BOY          ((funny voice counting: )) o::ne tw:o
11   HANIF        ((quieter: )) textbooks
12                (.)
13                ((louder: )) are you ready or not
14                alright
15                (.)
16   BOY          ((shouting out in an exaggerated Cockney
                  accent¹⁴ and a very loud, deep, gruff voice
                  from somewhere else in the class))
17                \ELLO /MARILYN
                  [ʔælʌʊ]
18   SIMON        ((echoing the other boy's accent, pitch and
                  intonation: ))
                  \ELLO /MARILYN
                  [ʔæl ]
19   BOY          \AWRIGH /MARILYN
20                ((pips signalling the end of the lesson))
21   HANIF        Gopal (.) Gopal (my      )
22                (.)
23                please
24                (.)
25                tuna sandwich yeh
```

Extract 9.8

A minute and a half after Extract 9.7, at the end of a double science lesson,
Simon starts impersonating Marilyn. (Blex 16)

```
 1   SHAHID       (how about me Sir)
 2                look
 3   ANON         ((very high pitched: )) perdum prdm
                  prdm prdm perdum
 4   ANON         ello
 5   SIMON        ((loud, low-pitched, slow, nasalised and
                  broad Cockney: ))
                  a:/llo
                  [ʌl:ʌʊ]
```

```
 6               (.)
 7               a/llo
                 [ə̄lʌ̄ū]
 8               (.)
 9               e/llo
                 [ē̩lʌ̄ū]
10               (.)
11               e/llo
                 [ē̩lʌ̄ū]
12               ₁my   ₁name's   \Marily::n
                 [mɔ̃ĩ  nə̄ĩmz]
13               e/llo
                 [ə̄lʌ̄ū]
14   BOY         ((slow and Cockney as well:))
                 he/ll:o
                 [həlʌu]
15   SIMON       ((at the same slow pace and low pitch-level as
                 line 12:))
                 ₁bler ₁bler \bler
                 [bʰlə̄  bʰlə̄  bʰlə̄]
16   ANON        e\llo  /(mate)
                 [əlou  meɪ?]
17   SIMON       ((as before:))
                 e/llo
18               ₁bler ₁bler \ble::r
                 [ə̄bʰlə̄  bʰlə̄  bʰlə̄::]
19   TEACHER     ((trying to get everyone to be quiet:))
                 Joanne
20               (.)
21               Ninnette
22               can I have a quick word at the
                 end of the lesson
23               (4)
24               er
25               (.)
26               Simon
27               I want a quick word at the
                 end of the lesson
```

A few days later in the playground, I asked Hanif about this way of addressing Marilyn:

Extract 9.9

During breaktime, I'm asking Hanif (wearing a radio-microphone) a few questions about the recordings I have listened to (Blex 22)

```
 1  BEN    Marilyn
 2         (.)
 3  HANIF  oh right
 4         yeh yeh
 5  BEN    kind of (.) a lot of jokes with Marilyn
 6  HANIF  oh yeh (.) ye:h
 7         ((several seconds getting the ball for someone,
           and comes back))
 8         yeh
 9  BEN    yeh
10  HANIF  ((with half-laugh in his voice:))
           eh (.)
11         crack a few jokes with Marilyn
12         yeh
13  BEN    yep yep yep yep okay okay (.)
14         anything- anything- any reason for that
15         or
16  HANIF  YEH:
17         y see everyone does
18         you know
19         just a (.)
20         thing
21         I guess
22  BEN    lots of instances of- of- of- allo Marilyn
                                           [ʔæləʊ]
23  HANIF  ((in a broad Cockney accent:)) alright Marilyn
                                           [ʔɔ:ˈaɪʔ]
24         yeh
25         I do that
26         I try to act drunk
27         (.)
28         she likes that though
29         she likes that when I do that
30         I crack-
31 ·       she- I crack her up when she does that
32         I make her laugh
33         (.)
34         yeh it's (like tha )
35         awrigh Ma:rilyn
           [ɔˈaɪʔ]
36         or
37         allo Marilyn
           [ʔæləʊ]
38         something (like this)
39  BEN    so how do you act how do you act
40  HANIF  er > (now and then) <
```

```
41          the way I speak to her
42          that really- tha- 'at makes her laugh
43          and I like it when she laughs
44          (.)
45          I like it when she laughs (.)
46          so:
47    BEN   so acting drunk
48   HANIF  yeh
49          I like to-
50          er the way I sound
51          right
52          she says she says
53          that I act drunk
54          (anyway)
55    BEN   right
56          ((light laugh)) that's what she says
57   HANIF  yeh
58          that's what she says
59    BEN   yeh
```

The association between Marilyn and a broad London accent was evidently quite well established among the boys, and the stylisation extended to a relaxed mode of speech delivery – in Extract 9.8, Simon's impersonation of Marilyn moved from "my name's Marilyn" to "abler bler ble::r" and if alcohol produces a slurring of words, this overlaps with Hanif's gloss on "the way I speak to her" as 'acting drunk'. In all three episodes, the Marilyn–Cockney connection is articulated in sociable greetings and introductions, and in Hanif's account, these performances are acceptable to Marilyn as a source of shared amusement.

In fact, Marilyn was quite widely talked about among members of the tutor group. I didn't hear any of the girls using broad London to characterise Marilyn, but she seemed to have a reputation among them for energy, forcefulness and daring.[15] In interview with Joanne and Linda, Michelle explained:

```
'cos she's big so-
no one gets on the wrong side of her ((laughter))
but if you get on the wrong side of her, she'll like,
fight you
that's how we work things out now
It's like- like- saying,
someone calls you a slag or something
Marilyn would go up to them and chin them or something
```

In interview with Simon, Satesh and Guy, the boys did not say anything about physical retaliation from Marilyn, but they made it clear on two occasions that you'd get a reaction worth witnessing if you used particular nick-names to address her ("say it to her and see what she does"; "I wanna see her (and call her it) and see what happens"). They twice singled her out as someone with unusual skills in slang (slang words and backslang), and Simon also linked her a couple of times with Luke, a much admired friend who had now left the school.

But the big difference in how girls and boys talked about Marilyn lay in the emphasis that the latter gave to her sexuality. Marilyn was not tall but she was physically well-developed, and according to Simon, Satesh and Guy, her breasts had been nicknamed 'Pinky' and 'the Brain' (after two cartoon mice, white with pink noses, one large and one small). Indeed, Marilyn's sexuality figured in their talk in other ways:

Extract 9.10

Simon and others at the end of Maths, just after the pips have gone. (Blex 46)

```
 1   SIMON    ((to someone:)) still got that splitting
              headache?
 2   GIRL     (     )
 3   SIMON    is it a migraine
 4            or is it just a headache
 5            (3)
 6   BOY      (is it okay if I wear a polo neck
 7            (.)
 8   MAN?     Why is this (   )
 9   SIMON    ((rhythmically chanting, quite high-pitched
              with a strong Cockney accent in the last word:))
              |Marilyn |for a |paund
                              [pæ̃ᵊn]
10            ((to the same rhythm, at higher pitch:))
              ‖Marilyn ‖for a ‖pa- ((breaks off in laughter))
11   JOHN     (     for a cigarette)
12   SIMON    ((repeating the chant down the corridor:))
13            |Marilyn |for a ((laughing:)) |paund
                                            [pæ̃hə̄n]
14            ((laughs for c. a second))
15            it's true
16   HANIF    (      )
17            I know
```

```
18              I know
19              (.)
20   SIMON      she showed her tits
21              for a pound
                    [pɑʊnd]
22              (.)
23              I'd never do that
24              (.)
25              that is just-
26              I d/on't- I I woul-
```

In this episode, Simon holds to the Cockney he had used in his Marilyn impersonation at the end of the science lesson in Extracts 9.7 and 9.8,[16] but now he adds a vulgar, disreputable sexuality (on sale at a knock-down price in what sound like the market cries of a street hawker), and he backs this up by claiming it has its basis in fact.

What can be seen here is gendered representation at the 'low' end of the cultural semantic discussed in Chapter 9.3. In Ortner's account, "the working class is cast as the bearer of an exaggerated sexuality, against which middle-class respectability is defined … [M]iddle class kids, both male and female, define working-class kids as promiscuous, highly experienced, and sexually unconstrained" (1991:177–178), and Skeggs claims that

the White female working-class body is often represented as out of control, in excess, such as that of *Roseanne* … [W]orking-class women have often been associated with the lower unruly order of bodily functions such as that of expulsion and leakage (and reproduction) which signified lack of discipline and vulgarity … Working-class women's relationship to femininity has always been produced through recourse to vulgarity.   (1997:100)

The historical emergence of these gendered representations is located in the same period as the high–low binary more generally, and Skeggs refers, for example, to the way in which in the nineteenth Century, "middle- and upper-class women … would visit the houses of the poor in an attempt to redeem them from themselves, that is from themselves as a sign of dangerous, disruptive, sexual women" (1997:99). Against this background, a number of the other elements in these youngsters' portrayal of Marilyn come together in a conventional iconography: the deep, gruff (non-feminine) voice in Extracts 9.7, 9.8; the descent into non-words in Extract 9.8 (lines 15 and 18); the reputation for retaliation; the excessive consumption of alcohol ("drunk" in Extract 9.9); the cigarette in Extract 9.10; and elsewhere, "Jabber the Hut" as a nickname cited by both boys and girls.[17] At the same time, the data show that these visions of working-class female excess do not simply feature in the efforts of one social class group to differentiate itself from another, but that much more locally and much more intimately, they can also be very active within the classroom micro-culture of a largely working-class school.

As we have seen, Stallybrass and White 1996 propose that the grotesque plays an important part in processes of social differentiation. The previous section considered 'the grotesque of hybridisation and inmixing', whereas here, the focus is on the other form that Stallybrass and White consider, an initially more straightforward "grotesque [of] the Other of the defining group or self"(p 193). Stallybrass and White insist, though, that the boundary between the grotesque Other and the self remains permeable, and that simple repulsion gives way to more complex feelings. I cannot say how far and in what ways Marilyn operated as a symbolic figure among the girls, referred to in the definition of their own feminities.[18] But the grotesque figured prominently in the boys' Cockney representations of Marilyn, and their feelings appeared to be quite ambivalent.

As fourteen year olds, these boys were quite early on in their adolescence, and it would be hardly surprisingly if their feelings about girls and sex were complicated. 'Showing your tits' might be something that Simon said he would never do (Extract 9.10, lines 20–26), but he still had a fair go at replaying the scene (lines 9–14) and more generally, anyone who associated with Luke seemed worth attending to. Similarly, while Hanif (who was Muslim) could tell Lara and others that "my religion comes first in everything", he could still "try to act drunk" with Marilyn because "I like it when she laughs" (Extract 9.9). At least according to Lara (in a *sub rosa* conversation during science), quite a few of the boys were "scared of girls, ennit... they can't talk to girls". And when she singled out Simon as someone who "can have a conversation with a boy AND a girl", Hanif's immediate response was "well Simon's bio" (meaning bi-sexual), foregrounding sexuality as the issue *and* constructing Simon's hetero-sociability as *sexually* deviant. About a week later, I saw these relations in action: Lara was with Marilyn, and as people were going into assembly, she took hold of Arun's hand and tried to pinch his bum while the poor boy struggled to break free in embarrassment. Beyond that, it is possible that during the previous year, conflicting views on hetero-sociability had played some part in a lasting rupture in the male friendship group: Rafiq, I was told, used to hang around with Hanif, Masud, John et al., but now he spent his free time elsewhere, and in class, he often sat next to Lara and Marilyn, leaning sometimes with an arm on one of their shoulders.[19]

In fact, the challenge that Marilyn and Lara presented to the boys was particularly visible when whole-class discourse turned to questions of sexuality itself. In Mr Newton's favourable account of her, Marilyn held her own in class debate quite generally, refusing to allow the boys shut her up, and in the two sustained discussions of unwanted pregnancy and homophobia in my c. 37 hours of radio-microphone recordings, Marilyn and/or Lara came out better than boys. We saw in some detail in Chapters 2 and 3 that Hanif, John and company were accustomed to dominating classroom discussion, monopolising the attention and approval of their teachers. But when everyone's attention turned to sexuality, a sensitive topic where there were serious ethno-religious differences and where feelings sometimes ran high, these boys lost their supremacy and gained some experience of being on the *wrong* side of an institutional line, lower down the classroom hierarchy. Space constraints prohibit detailed illustration,[20] but in these episodes Marilyn and Lara produced assessments that actually came much closer to their teachers'. Using a confident but low-key, vernacular style that formed a marked contrast to the conspicuously aspirational postures projected by Hanif and friends, they articulated worldly knowledge of family life on a low income, and in the process, they showed they could split the usual alliance between these boys, winning plaudits from peers and teachers as well.

Overall, there is little point in trying to specify exactly what axis of social differentiation mattered most in the boys' deep-voiced, Cockney caricatures of Marilyn – her discursive power, her sexuality and gender, her working-classness, her whiteness – since to do so would be forcing a secondary analytic category onto an aspect of 'behavioural ideology' where symbolic resonance was much more polyvalent (Chapter 6.3). But it is clear that there were a number of occasions when Marilyn said and did things that challenged the sexual, gender and educational relations and identities that these boys either liked, took-for-granted or believed in, and it now seems really quite likely that there were complicated psycho-social processes involved when they choose to represent her in a Cockney voice.

We should now move to some conclusions, using Chapters 6, 7 and 8 as well as this one to formulate a position on the relationship between subjectivity and interaction, as well as a more general overview of language, stylisation and social class in late modernity. I will begin by characterising the perspective on language and speech that has emerged in this account of posh and Cockney, also drawing on the German/*Deutsch* analysis by way of comparison.

9.6   The dynamics of classed speech

In the analysis in this part of the book, posh and Cockney appear to be rather more than just 'accents' or 'dialects' as they are usually described by linguists.

First, everyone's speech combined both standard *and* vernacular elements, and although there were other speech varieties that the informants could switch into, for the most part at school, becoming posher in one's speech meant being less Cockney, and vice versa. This could be seen in the quantitative analysis of style-shifting (Chapter 7.3), and three of the four informants stylised *both* varieties, not just one or the other. This interdependence of the two varieties accords with Irvine's notion of a 'system of distinction', in which "a style contrasts with other possible styles, and the social meaning ... contrasts with other social meanings" (2001:22).

In line with this, second, my account is in broad agreement with Agha when in a study of the social history of Received Pronunciation, he notes that

the folk term 'accent' does not just name a sound pattern alone, but a sound pattern linked to a framework of social identities ... The identifying descriptions associated with its forms consist mainly of characterological labels and discourses that identify speakers in terms of the mental, aesthetic and class attributes ... [A]ccent does not name a sound pattern as such but a system of social personae stereotypically linked to contrasts of sound. (2003:232–233, 241–242)

Although there were episodes of sound play where it was analytically very hard to identify the connotations of exaggerated Cockney (Chapter 7.5), overall in my corpus, posh and Cockney pronunciation was linked to a high–low 'cultural semantic' with deep roots in British history. This constituted much of their indexical valence (or what Bakhtin would call their 'socio-ideological horizons'), and it was an important part of their stylisation. At the same time, to the extent that it implies a purely cognitive frame operating at one level of language, 'semantic' (in 'cultural semantic') is probably the wrong term – the stylisation of posh and Cockney often entailed bodily performance and carried an emotional charge, it involved a varied combination of linguistic, vocal, generic and cultural cues, and it often took the kinds of artful or imaginary form associated with the aesthetic (Chapter 9.4 *et passim*). Indeed, Agha's argument that accents evoke 'identities', 'personae' and 'characters' overstates the clarity/definiteness of the symbolic resonance of posh and Cockney. It was certainly true in some instances in the data – for example, Ninnette and Joanne's vigorous depiction of Mr Alcott in Extract 8.3 – but in many other cases (e.g. the transitions between work and sociability in Chapter 8.4), the effect seemed more subtle and indeterminate, and it would be more accurate to speak of posh and Cockney introducing a particular 'taste' to the proceedings, "imparting [their] own specific tones" (Bakhtin 1981:293, 347; Chapter 8.5), invoking a psycho-social schema that certainly includes different social types but extends much further to more pervasive contrasts (high–low, mind–body, reason–emotion).

So our understanding of 'accent', 'dialect' or 'linguistic variety' should encompass much more than just a set of co-occurring pho-nological and grammatical forms. Instead, the operative sense in this study comes much closer to the view articulated by Coupland and others when they argue that "there is a wide range of semantic and pragmatic phenomena on the fringe of dialect which sociolinguistics has not systematically addressed, having to do with rhetorical style, stance and implicature" (Garrett, Coupland and Williams 1999:323; Silverstein 1976:51–52; Bakhtin 1981:293; Tannen 1989:Chapter 2; Becker 1995:15; also Coupland 1995). How far, though, is this view of posh and Cockney's semiotic fullness con-fined to their production in *stylised performance*? Stylisation pushes particular speech varieties into the foreground in interaction, and spotlighted like this, they demand a lot more metalinguistically focused interpretive work from the recipients than they normally do in routine talk. In such contexts, the extra inferencing that goes on around standard and vernacular speech is likely to increase their symbolic resonance, and so the question emerges: just how relevant to *non*-stylised, routine speech is this talk of aesthetics, socio-ideological horizons and high–low psycho-social schema?

The high–low schema was in fact intrinsic to a great deal of school routine. High–low ranking and stratification are intrinsic to the schooling process (Foucault 1977, Varenne and McDermott 1998, Chapter 2); physical activity is tightly constrained ($\approx$ mind over body); the curriculum prioritises the production of lexico-grammatical propositions in thematically connected strings and for the most part, school learning is treated as different from humming, singing and the modalities of popular culture (Chapters 2.3, 3) ($\approx$ reason over 'emotion'). Against this background, Agha makes a lot of sense when he emphasises that "[i]n speaking of 'cultural values' [associated with RP], I wish to invite no metaphysics of shared belief. To say that pragmatic behaviours ... have cultural *values* associated with them is simply to say that certain regularities of *evaluative behaviour* can be observed and documented as data" (2003:242. Original emphases). The same can be said of the high–low, mind–body, reason–emotion schema drawn out from the analyses of posh and Cockney stylisation. This was very far from being a transcendent cultural essence or "some predefined mental structure" (cf. Hanks 1996:257), and instead, these binaries were (re)produced and legitimated in every-day activity at school.

Beyond that, this binary scheme was continuously ratified in my informants' routine speech production. Taking the terms used in variationist sociolinguistics, this educational emphasis on 'high'/'mind'/'reason' can be equated with 'formal', while 'low'/'body'/'emotion' can be linked to the 'informal', and from the findings of the quantitative analysis of style-shifting (Chapter 7.3), it was clear that these youngsters accepted this conventional differentiation when they moved up and down between Cockney and posh in their routine activity, sometimes becoming more vernacular and sometimes more standard, in line with the formality of the situation. Admittedly, I have not analysed more ethnically-marked speech variants and so I cannot claim that posh and Cockney were the *only* axis of social differentiation inscribed in their routine speech (Chapter 7.3). But from the data I did quantify, the informants seemed to be breathing and swimming in this high–low

schematisation. Tacit apprehension of this framing guided the interpretation and production of speech in these young Londoners' practical consciousness as they navigated their everyday experience at
school. They lived the intimate tension between posh and Cockney
in their everyday talk, and variationist sociolinguistics can be
applauded for its capacity to reveal the routinisation achieved in
hegemony, "the saturation of the whole process of living ... [by]
the ... dominance and subordination of particular classes" (Williams
1977:109; Bourdieu 1991).

So the high–low binary's institutional embodiment in schooling
was broadly ratified in routine style-shifting. In fact, this tacit but
continuous reiteration of high–low structuring processes provided
performative stylisation with a lot of the material it worked with
and much of the pertinence it sought. In performative stylisation,
youngsters made the social structuring of everyday life more conspicuous, exaggerating and elaborating evaluative differentiations
that were otherwise normally treated as non-problematic in practical activity, and we can clarify this by referring to both Williams and
Bakhtin.

Drawing on Bakhtin, posh and Cockney can be regarded as
'internally persuasive' discourse. Bakhtin sees all utterances as
intrinsically dialogical, shaped in the encounter with other people,
but there are a range of different ways in which we can orient our
own ways of speaking to the language and speech of others.
Sometimes we hold their discourse at a distance, but at other times
in 'internally persuasive discourse', the boundary between them and
us is much harder to maintain, and their discourse starts to permeate
into our talk and thinking. "[I]n the everyday rounds of our consciousness", says Bakhtin,

the internally persuasive word is half-ours and half-someone else's. Its
creativity and productiveness consist in the fact that ... it organises masses
of our words from within, and does not remain in an isolated and static
condition. It is not so much interpreted by us as it is further, that is, freely
developed, applied to new material, new conditions; it enters into inter-
animating relationships with new contexts ... The semantic structure of an
internally persuasive discourse is *not finite*, it is open.   (1981:345–346)

Internally persuasive discourse is "supple and dynamic to such an
extent that [it is] literally ... *omnipresent* in the context, imparting
to everything its own specific tones" (Bakhtin 1981:347), and this

accords with the portrait of the posh–Cockney nexus produced in the quantitative variationist analysis. But from time to time, says Bakhtin, supple, dynamic, internally persuasive discourse "break[s] through to become a completely materialised thing" (1981:347), and these were the moments of stylisation – spontaneous moments when these youngsters were artfully reflexive about the dichotomous values that they tacitly reproduced in the variability of their routine speech, moments when they crystallised the high–low structuring principles that were influential but normally much more obscure in their everyday variability (see also Vološinov 1973: 90–92; Bauman and Briggs 1990:60). Stylisation entailed an objectification of speech practices and highlighted the symbolic loadings of posh and Cockney. It denaturalised a pervasive cultural hierarchy and disrupted its authority as "doxa", as an interpretive frame that that was "accepted undiscussed, unnamed, admitted without scrutiny" (Bourdieu 1977:169–170; Eckert 2000:14, 43; Coupland 2001a:370–372; Rampton 1995b:508, 2001b). Performative stylisations were moments of what Bakhtin calls 'ideological becoming',[21] or what Williams calls 'creative practice': moments when tensions "at the very edge of semantic availability … active, pressing but not yet fully articulated" find "specific articulations – new semantic figures … in material practice" (1977:130, 134). Indeed, the analysis has been very specific about the particular fields of power and domination in which this 'ideological becoming' emerged.

Schooling is an institutional process designed for the shaping of young people, and most of its activities are consequential for their future positioning, most immediately (and perhaps most weakly) in the evaluative phase of the IRE, more forcefully after that in the marks they are given, after that in the classes they get assigned to, the exams they take, and ultimately their opportunities on the job market and positioning in hierarchies of cultural distinction. Secondary pupils and teachers all know this, and as small meta-social commentaries symbolically inserted into the flow of practical activity, these youngsters' acts of stylisation have been construed as micro-political interventions, agentive efforts to problematise, clarify or alter the reproduction of social structure as it seemed to be unfolding before them. During Mr Newton's warning about London linguistic handicaps, Rafiq's Cockney 'sonar bangla' spontaneously synthesised the conjunction of class and ethnic identities that they'd only struggled with hitherto, and other boys immediately endorsed it (Extract 8.12, Chapter 8.6). As they turned towards written text, Ninnette and Hanif used stylisations of posh and Cockney to refuse the role of 'submissive student' entailed in serious/straight engagement in curriculum tasks (Chapter 8.4). In the boys' grotesque Cockney portraits of Marilyn, they battled to reassert their status and sense of the rightful communicative order in their classroom (Chapter 9.5).

Beyond immediate contexts of hierarchisation such as these, my informants' stylisations have also been located in longer and broader trajectories of 'ideological becoming', relating both to the kinds of educated person that these youngsters were becoming and to historical movements in education. There were a number of quite striking differences in the way that Hanif and Ninnette stylised posh and Cockney, and these were symptomatic of rather contrasting individual paths. Hanif's stylisations were often loud and public, they sometimes sought to reverse the conventional sociolinguistic equation of literacy and standard language, and this coincided with his wider position as the leading 'contrapuntalist' in whole class discussion (Chapters 2.3 and 8.7). In contrast, Ninnette and Joanne habitually kept a much lower profile in class, and rather than seeking to rewrite the literacy-standard language rule, it was their exaggerated observance that subverted it (Chapters 2.4, 8.7). And both tactics and trajectories were influenced by the position that their teachers took in a much larger and longer cultural dispute over diversity and standardisation in language and the curriculum (Chapters 2.1, 7.2, 8.2, 8.7, 8.8).

In the list of questions in Chapter 6.4 that provided the direction for this analysis, the last one asked:

Do these voices seem to be politically engaged, and if so, what kinds of politics do they involve? What are the (micro-)political interests and identities at issue, and where do they seem to lead?

The extent of my answers has varied. There has been extensive documentation of the way that stylisation often crystallised a reflexive apprehension of power and status, in a wide range of social and educational relations and activities, and I have also been quite specific about some of the ongoing change and contestation – both biographical and historical – in which these processes of 'ideological becoming' were situated. But what about the political 'complexion' of the stylisations of posh and Cockney that we've seen? Was the stylisation of posh and Cockney a progressive – a liberal or radical – strategy, as one might infer in Williams' phrase 'creative practice', or was it actually reactionary?

The answer to this depends, of course, on one's politics and vantage point, but in terms of the short-term reproduction of hierarchic social relations, at different times it was both and neither. Sometimes when stylisation denaturalised the high–low psychosocial schema that youngsters observed in their routine styleshifting, it seemed to be 'heterodox', resisting social differentiation. This appeared to be the case when Hanif, Ninnette and Joanne found themselves being placed on the wrong side of an educational line by a teacher (Chapter 8.2), or were putting themselves on the higher side in the company of peers (Chapter 8.4). But there were also times when stylisation involved a very reactionary reassertion of local 'orthodoxy', and this was clearest in the boys' depiction of Marilyn (Chapter 9.5). Indeed, in Hanif's use of Cockney in *both* these cases, it is clear that the same variety could be used by the same person to very different effect. At the same time, though, there were episodes elsewhere where it was hard finding any social meaning – let alone any politics – in stylisation.

This variation in political 'colouring' is entirely consistent with the identity of posh and Cockney as internally persuasive discourses, flexibly lending themselves to a range of different situations. Bakhtin argues that the internally persuasive word is "half-ours" and "half someone else's", and even when they were being exaggerated in stylisation (rather than just being left as unnoticed but constitutive elements in routine speech), *neither* variety held steady across the corpus as a political emblem, whether of solidarity ('ours') or of otherness ('someone else'). Instead, *both* could be used to typify objects of disdain: Ninnette and Joanne used *posh* to 'other' Mr Alcott (Extract 8.3), as did Rafiq in his contempt for Mansur (Extract 9.1), while Simon used *Cockney* to distance himself from post-prandial belchings (Extract 9.4) and from the image he had of Marilyn's sexual availability (Extract 9.10). At least on occasions like these, it was clear in the surrounding talk that the speaker's own self-positioning as 'principal' was quite distinct from the 'figure' they were portraying (Goffman 1974:Chapter 13), but the permeation of stylised posh and Cockney went further, and it was often very hard to say *where* the speakers positioned their 'real' selves in relation to the voices they were using (cf. Johnstone 1999). In the transition between school work and peer sociability, stylisation seemed designed to articulate a likeably non-serious stance that could let Ninnette and Hanif have it *both* ways, and surely what mattered in Joanne's ``Ninnette, Ricky's here'' (Extract 9.3) was the piquancy of the conjunction of posh with sexual possibility – whether or not she endorsed or objected to social types associated with posh seems beside the point. Similarly, in Extract 9.5 ("buggaye"), it makes little sense to say that Joanne identified with posh, dis-identified with Cockney, or vice-versa – what counted were the aesthetics of performance. With this kind of pervasiveness and flexibility in the everyday rounds of these adolescents' consciousness, it is hardly surprising that stylised posh and Cockney varied both in the kinds of political angle on dominant social conventions that they articulated, and the extent to which they did so at all.

The identity of posh and Cockney as "internally persuasive" discourses stands out particularly clearly when compared with the way these youngsters engaged with *Deutsch* / German. The pupils' primary access to German was through the modern language class, and after an analysis of its use both in MFL lessons and in my informants' informal improvisations, I aligned the language with Bakhtin's account of "the authoritative word", which "binds us, quite independent of any power it might have to persuade us internally … It demands our unconditional allegiance … It enters our verbal consciousness as a compact and indivisible mass" (1981:342–343; Chapter 5.5). The German lessons, I proposed, provided Hanif and his friends with a series of unenjoyable experiences where their normal style of classroom participation was seriously inhibited, and in the knock-about *Deutsch* that they used in other lessons, they returned to this and reworked it to their own ends. But these reworkings were generally very restricted. On the whole, they were expressively limited to sound play and rather formulaic speech acts involving thanks, apologies, commands and expression of disapproval, and youngsters tended to insert these foreign elements into moments of collective interactional uncertainty, in liminal phases outside any consensus of attention focused on curriculum tasks.

Like *Deutsch*, posh and Cockney were often stylised during periods where there were problems establishing a work frame, but posh and Cockney were part of these young people's everyday speech and in contrast to German where their linguistic proficiency was very rudimentary, stylisations generally carried propositional meaning, formulated with full command of the requisite lexico-grammar. On the one hand, this allowed stylisation to work much more subtly, and youngsters could announce the local relevance of the 'high–low' psycho-social frame by simply exaggerating one or two sub-elements of speech that might otherwise pass unnoticed as ordinary contributions to the business under way. In this way, acts of stylisation drew critical reflexivity closely into the routine flow of all sorts of school activity, and constituted a series of very fine-tuned interruptions to the hegemonic reproduction of social structure. On the other, posh and Cockney's capacity to combine with large parts of these youngsters' knowledge of lexico-grammar meant that when stylisation aimed for more spectacular effects, the images portrayed could be fuller, more detailed and more aesthetically complex. Beyond issues of propositional and lexicogrammatical flexibility, the contrast with German also extended to their indexical valence. Whereas the posh–Cockney nexus was bound into a system of values and practices that has been fundamental to English culture for more than two hundred years, the indexical significance of German seemed restricted to the German lessons, to (funny) Ms Wilson, and to other lads messing around. The logical possibility that Germans and Germany were also a symbolic resonance could not be eliminated, but there was very little evidence of this in the spontaneous improvisations. In sum, German "had entered [these youngsters'] verbal consciousness as a compact and indivisible mass", but internally persuasive posh and Cockney were "open", "freely developed, applied to new material, new conditions", and as such the latter were stylised both much more frequently and in a much wider range of contexts: in the negotiation of interpersonal and curriculum-focused relationships with teachers, managing the boundaries between work and sociability with peers, addressing gender-relations and issues of sexuality, attending to physical capacities, demeanour and deportment.

That is probably sufficient as a general characterisation of the speech and language dynamics revealed in posh and Cockney stylisation and style-shifting. What can we conclude about the relationship between interaction and subjectivity in the analysis of social class, and in what ways can investigation of this relationship benefit from dialogue between sociolinguistics and cultural studies?

9.7   Interaction, subjectivity and social class: sociolinguistics and cultural studies

Like other sociological commentators cited in Chapter 6, Skeggs notes that there has been a "retreat from class ... across a range of academic sites" (1997:6), but she sets out to "re-nuance it to show how it is a major feature of subjectivity, a historical specificity and part of a struggle over access to resources and ways of being" (p 7). She investigates this among a group of white working-class women through interviewing and long-term participant observation, and finds that

[t]alking about class ... is somewhat different from living it. Class connotations may be ubiquitous but they are rarely directly spoken by those who do not want to be reminded of their social positioning in relation to it.   (1997:77)

And she concludes that for the classed subjectivities of her informants,

it is ... the everyday negotiations of the mundane that ... matter, that are formative, that ... count and ... these mundane experiences are a product of systematic inequality. They are not free-floating emotional experiences. They are profoundly located in structural organisation ... This means that ... we need to rework [the study of experience] to explore how subjects are produced and produce themselves through their different experiences, exploring how different processes produce experience, which ones matter, which are authorised and how interpretation is central to production.   (1997:167)

How do the interactional sociolinguistic analyses in this book connect with the kind of research that Skeggs conducts?

My findings generally concur with Skeggs and many others when they say that for most people, talking about class is difficult. My study also agrees that "class connotations [are] ubiquitous", but in doing so, it goes further than researchers can manage if they are not using the tools of interactional sociolinguistic discourse analysis. In their everyday negotiations of the mundane, my informants did not actually say 'this is a class issue', but in putting on posh and Cockney voices, they did the next best thing. In these acts of stylisation, they momentarily stepped back from the flux of activity and suggested that more general qualities and/or categories associated with posh and Cockney were relevant to the proceedings on hand. For the analyst reviewing the dataset of recordings as a whole, these instances of exaggerated posh and Cockney functioned as 'book-marks', identifying a sub-set of episodes to scrutinise more closely for whatever posh and Cockney might signify. From this, it then emerges that these two voices correlate with (non-phonological) processes and classifications that are frequently tied to social class in cultural theory – school stratification, the line-drawing associated with political agency, cultural semantics shaped in bourgeois society, and varieties of class-marked grotesque. Fully formed, lexico-grammatical specifications of what is involved in social class might be hard to find in the discourse of ordinary people, but if one looks closely at the fine details of speech, there is a lot of more symbolically articulated reflexivity about class – much higher levels of active class consciousness – than one might infer from the propositions formulated in interviews, or the accounts of activity recollected and recorded in a field diary.

Linguistic stylisations of social class certainly aren't news for sociology and cultural theory (see e.g. Gilroy 1987:194–7; Back 1996; Hey 1997; Mahony and Zmroczek 1997:3), but radio-microphone recordings of natural interaction that can be repeatedly replayed and intensively analysed can pick up on their pervasiveness and subtlety. "Sociolinguistic analysis", says Gumperz, "can yield of new insights into the workings of social process" (1982a:7), and among other things, we have seen something of the intricacy with which people manage the flexibilities of speech in the negotiation of their social positions and relationships. In its more formal dimensions, language combines pronunciation, vocabulary, grammar and speech acts (like commands and requests), and in my data, youngsters played on the capacity of these 'levels' to contribute different symbolic elements to the production of meaning, achieving, to give just two examples, the synthesis of ethnicity and class that could be seen in 'sonar bangla', where Bengali words were pronounced in a Cockney accent, and the vernacularisation of school literacy when Hanif read out science words in Cockney and Caribbean.

Micro-analysis of moment-to-moment interaction also generates a good deal of contextual data on ordinary conduct oriented to routine regulative norms, and so when these stylised acts occur, it is possible to scrutinise the circumambient scene in which they are inserted, situating them in the flow of events and actions before, during and afterwards. In this way, these acts can be read as micro-political interventions in specific social relations there-and-then, and the outcome is a detailed and differentiated account of class processes in face-to-face activity, revealing the activation of class sensitivities in modes, moments and relationships that it would otherwise be very hard to anticipate. I have summarised some of this plurality in the previous section on posh and Cockney as internally persuasive discourse, but the data on stylised posh and Cockney in interaction between teachers and pupils provides a good illustration of the importance of not taking "everyday negotiations of the mundane" for granted. One might expect to find pupils invoking class images to separate themselves from teachers, and sometimes they did, but there were also a number of other occasions when the lines were far from clearly drawn and broad Cockney was well-received in class (Chapter 8).

Micro-analysis tries to reach down into the details of interaction, to the point where participants can be seen trying to make some kind of intersubjective sense of their worlds from one moment to the next. In doing so, it can serve as quite a useful validity check on what theorists might want to say about class, getting as close as possible to participants' sense-making procedures in action. In their stylisations of posh and Cockney, young people themselves flagged up the relevance of the issues and processes that analysts gloss as 'class', and so these are very strong grounds for saying that class consciousness is more than just an analyst's attribution.

According to Skeggs,

[t]he way class was experienced [among my informants] was through affectivity, as a 'structure of feeling' (cf. Williams 1961, 1977). This is the emotional politics of class fuelled by insecurity, doubt, indignation and resentment (but also lived with pleasure and irreverence) ... These are not free-floating emotional experiences. They are profoundly located in structural organisation.   (Skeggs 1997:162, 167)

My data confirm some of the detail of what Skeggs says here, and set within forms of structural organisation that could be said to stretch from the economic through the institutional down into the local dynamics of face-to-face encounters, we have seen insecurity, indignation, resentment, pleasure and irreverence situated in mini-dramas of communication that might be described as a practical everyday aesthetics (see e.g. Extracts 8.3, 8.9, 8.12). Transcripts of interaction often involve a vividness and detail that surpass most of what informants can report in interview, and they are capable of pointing to subtleties of contextualised feeling that it can be hard to capture in a list of emotions such as Skeggs', to the extent indeed that meta-analytic terms like 'insecurity' look crude and reductive (Chapter 8).

Those then are some of the ways in which interactional discourse analysis might enhance discussions of classed subjectivity in sociology and cultural studies. But in the course of this Chapter, I have also referred to subjectivity in my analyses of interaction.

In Chapter 8, there was quite extensive reference to Ochs' notion of "indexical valence" (Chapter 8.5), and following Ochs and others, this was generally treated as a semiotic resource for communication, an array of potential connotations that speakers and listeners referred to in their attempts to make sense of linguistic (and other) forms in the here-and-now of situated communication. From this vantage point, indexical valence could be construed as 'encyclopedic knowledge' available for communicative problem-solving, but in the course of the present chapter, this formulation has begun to look like a convenient/functional analytic simplification. Considered more broadly, indexical valence can be said to cover consciousness, memory and all the hugely complicated and uncharted interactions between language, "visual imagery, other sensory cognition, ... learned practices, memories of sensations, and memories of typical examples" that Bloch refers to (1998:24–25; Chapter 9.4). The data on stylisation in the grotesque have pressed us to expand 'indexical valence' so that it encompasses a rather unruly psycho-social 'stew' where "fantasy and ideology", repulsion, fascination and desire co-mingle, and at this point, cultural analysis rather than sociolinguistics provided the analytic vocabulary. Stallybrass and White provided terms for interpreting Ninnette's hyper-correct performance of funny-eyes as the grotesque of in-mixing, produced from the "dangerously unstable mixture" of high and low in these youngsters' "political unconscious" (Chapter 9.4), and Ortner's account of the interpenetration of class and sexuality helped to make sense of the boys' caricatures of Marilyn (Chapter 9.5).

This kind of subjectivity is often avoided in sociolinguistics. Where it is influenced by 'rational action' theories (Coupland 2001b:10–12), interactional discourse analysis generally confines its horizons to situated agents, acts and resources, thinking in terms of a controlling subject who selects items from the linguistic repertoire according to his/her rhetorical purpose (see Chapter 9.1 above), and when it works within a 'praxis' perspective (Coupland, 2001b), there is often an anti-Romantic rejection of the idea that "'human consciousness' has a 'deep interior'" (Silverman 1999:416 in a sympathetic overview of conversation analysis). Indeed, in Chapter 5.8, I also noted that sociolinguistics rarely attends to the psychic and emotional intensity of the ritual experience, or seeks to develop explicit theories of ritual as a psycho-social process. Although there has been quite a lot of recent interest in language and affect in linguistic anthropology, the intra-psychological dimensions of discourse and cultural process are somewhat excluded. Rather than the energies of feeling, it is either the cultural constitution and outward display of emotion that holds centre stage, or attention centres on the meta-level, folk psychology of emotions in the groups being examined (Schieffelin and Ochs 1986:178–190; Ochs and Schieffelin 1989; Besnier 1990; Irvine 1990:155; Lutz and Abu-Lughod 1990; contrast Eckert and McConnell-Ginet 1992:485, 486 and Hewitt 1992:38–40).[22]

Certainly in much of this work, there is an important challenge to the tendency in traditional mainstream psychology to reduce the social and cultural to the psychic and individual and to codify experience in single measures and group types. There are also strong ethnographic reasons for caution in any attempt to describe "the rich communication within a mind that is not possible between minds" (Hutchins 1993:62). Anthropologists routinely define themselves by their wariness of high-inference, *a priori* and potentially ethno-centric theory (Geertz 1973:20, 25; Bauman and Briggs 1990:61), and the risk of this increases whenever one looks towards processes that are not transparent in empirical data. If one speaks of psycho-social interiority, the individual becomes more than the part that they are playing either in the interaction on hand or in the cultural fields described in ethnography, and this can slide into a psychological essentialism that sometimes mystifies the social and cultural reproduction of inequality. According to Varenne and McDermott in their reflexive discussions of politics and interaction at school, we must struggle against the ideological underpinning of th[e US education] system when it tells us to center our gaze on the person as self-constituted individual. As one focuses on the learner, the focusing mechanism – America – disappears. Worse, the 'individual' that appears alone, standing in isolation, thereby overwhelms the landscape and is yet subverted. The more attention paid to the individual, the more 'determined' and the more restricted the person. To respect the individual, politically and morally, one must analytically cast one's eyes away ... The greater our concern with individuals, the greater must be our efforts to document carefully the social conditions in which they must always express themselves.   (1998:161, 145)

McDermott and his collaborators certainly acknowledge the gap between individuals and the expressive resources at their disposal – and the tension between what's felt and what's said – but they concentrate their analytic energies on the cultural and interactional conditions that produce this (McDermott 1988; McDermott and Tylbor 1986).

Against this weight of scholarly scepticism about psycho-social interiority in research on language and society, how can the move in this study from interaction analysis to 'subjectivity' be warranted? My justifications for this move are (a) ethnographic, (b) political and (c) disciplinary:

a) *Ethnographic*: To downplay the interior and emotional in favour of the established sociolinguistic definitions of language, studied within the accepted parameters of sociolinguistic research, it would have been necessary to refuse the notions of language and dialect offered in acts of stylisation themselves. Once I had resolved that the stylisation of posh and Cockney was a topic worth investigating, the decision about which strips of language and discourse to focus on was not taken by myself as analyst alone. I followed the performance and images of exaggerated posh and vernacular London speech that these teenagers themselves produced in their everyday interaction, and so in that sense it was them, not me, that articulated – with passion, physical involvement and aesthetic effect – the link between dialect-styles, grotesque bodies and unsettling sexualities. In ethnography, noted Hymes, "problems lead where they will and ... relevance commonly leads across disciplinary boundaries" ([1969]1999:44–45), and in this research, stylised posh and

Cockney have drawn an analysis that started in sociolinguistics into the explorations of class and subjectivity in cultural studies.

b) *Political*: Varenne and McDermott do actually recognise the interiority of the individual (1998:214), but they take a principled political decision not to dwell on it based on their analysis of hegemonic ethno-cultural essentialism (and psychological reductionism) in US education. The topic and context in the present study are different. Social class now plays a relatively insignificant part in prevailing educational discourses about UK schooling, and if students have browner skins, the assumption is that it is ethnicity and race that we should be talking about, not class. In a setting like this, if it turns out that in a multi-ethnic school, social class actually 'cuts quite deep' – if it emerges that class is rather extensively ingrained in young people's practical consciousness, that they show quite high levels of sensitivity to class in everyday interaction, and that at times the sociolinguistic indexicalities of class become a little unruly – then it is important to say so (and potentially counter-hegemonic).

c) *Disciplinary*: Linguistic anthropology and micro-interaction analysis provide important critiques of mainstream psychology, but there is a danger of this spilling into a denial of psyche, and there is a case for suggesting that as the 'children of their times', they have been influenced by the repudiation of 'depth models' of social, cultural and psychic life that Jameson attributes to post-modernism (1984; Chapter 6.6). For psychosocial interiorities of feeling certainly have not always been off-limits in research on language and society. As already extensively indicated, there are invitations to look beyond the relatively well-formed, conventionalised, cognitively accountable outer surfaces of speech in Vološinov's discussion of the 'lower strata' of 'behavioural ideology' (1973:90–92), in Bakhtin's theorisation of 'internally persuasive discourse' and 'the authoritative word' (1981), in Sapir's interest in personality (1949, 2002), and, much more recently, in Billig, Cameron and Kulick's concern for the repressed (Chapter 5.6). *None* of this work leaves language and discourse out, and *un*like Freud and indeed most of modernist sociolinguistics

(Chapters 1.2, 4.1; Rampton 1998), it argues that psycho-social interiority, the unconscious, etc., are produced not in early childhood but in the reiterations of hegemonic practice (Chapters 5.6, 9.6). All of these approaches can be seen as arguments for the relevance of language and discourse analysis to 'depth' processes (see also Williams 1977:40–41), although at the same time, there is recognition that there will be points in analysis where the elegance, precision and/or falsifiability of linguistic and pragmatic models become reductive and misleading.

Analysing the stylisation of posh and Cockney – and German/ *Deutsch* as well – I have ventured beyond the most conventional territorities of linguistic and interactional description, and I hope to have shown that in the process, empirical analysis need not become vacuous or unprincipled. The theoretical frameworks provided by Vološinov, Bakhtin and Williams invite sociolinguistics to consider the dynamic relationship between socio-historical constitution of language and its psycho-social interiority, and there is further evidence of the progress that can be made charting this territory if the empirical distribution and use of Cockney/posh is compared with German/ *Deutsch*. When I have stood back from the pragmatics of particular episodes and asked more general questions about language and subjectivity, trying to identify a more pervasive consciousness of language in play across a range of episodes, it has become clear that at a 'personal', or 'emotional', or 'psycho-social' level, German/*Deutsch* and Cockney/posh had very different kinds of significance. I have already pointed to part of this in the previous section (9.6) where I compared posh-Cockney as 'internally persuasive' with German as an 'authoritative word'. But to bring out the difference in their historical origins and developmental dynamics, it is worth restating that the stylisation of *Deutsch* was a very limited process and seemed to be event-generated, emerging from the students' experience of foreign language lessons. These language lessons provided informants with a rather intense but unpleasant experience of highly ritualised education, and searching for a psycho-social explanation, I suggested that this turned German into something of a condensation symbol, so that when the boys improvised *Deutsch*, this was in part "the ready release of emotional tension in conscious or unconscious form" (Sapir

1949:565). Dominance and subordination clearly mattered a lot in the origins and recycling of *Deutsch*/German but this was not hegemonic power or "a saturation of the whole process of living", and since its indexical valence seemed rather straightforward, there is much less of a warrant for linking *Deutsch*/German to a pervasive 'structure of feeling'. In contrast, posh and Cockney were integral to these youngsters' lives as Londoners, taking shape within and reproducing an evaluative schema that has historic roots in English class society and that points towards the more enduring dimensions of socio-historically-shaped sensibility that interest cultural analysts. In sum, the psycho-social terms I have used may be much less detailed or precise than those normally used in linguistic and discourse analysis, but they are not meaningless and if their relative imprecision served as a deterrent, we would miss the chance to bring detailed and varied interactional data to bear on cultural theory, constructing some potentially consequential claims about the infusion of language by class consciousness.

Such, then, are the justifications and frameworks that I have used to venture into territories of language that contemporary sociolinguistics tends to avoid, treating speakers as more than rational-calculating-actors, virtuosos and card-sharps (Moerman 1988:56). Posh and Cockney are more than just surface-level phonological resources differentially available in the later stages of utterance production to people in specific socio-geographic locales, and instead, these two class varieties have an interior career in 'rich communication' with desires, anxieties, imagery, evaluations, memories of sensations, etc. Indeed, though the emerging portrait is very different, the scope of my analysis of *Deutsch*/German has been broadly similar.

9.8   Language and class in late modernity

Stepping back from this discussion of the scope of sociolinguistics to the issues announced at the start of Chapter 6, the most consequential point to emerge is of course, that it is a mistake to assume that social-class identities have lost their significance in recent years. Instead, we have seen first of all that:

i)   the tension between posh and Cockney was pervasive in these youngsters' routine style-shifting;

ii)   they dramatised this in a wide range of performative stylisa-
      tions, on average about once or twice an hour;
iii) these performances took place in relatively symmetrical inter-
      actions between peers, not just in pupil–teacher exchanges
      where at a micro-political level, one might most expect to
      find a clash of class interests;
iv)   they inserted classed voices into performances of the gro-
      tesque, which suggests that class penetrated quite 'deep' into
      their psycho-social imaginations.

It is true that there was not much evidence of explicit, proposition-
ally elaborate class consciousness among my informants, but this
lexico-grammatical inarticulateness cannot be construed either as
the effect of some kind of all-encompassing 'linguistic insecurity'
(Chapter 8), or as an indication that class was now a non-issue for
these youngsters. Instead, class was repeatedly drawn into the
'upper strata of behavioural ideology' in the small-scale acts of
political 'crystallisation' achieved in stylisation (Vološinov
1973:90–92).

Second, these youngsters' parents often came from other countries, using English as very much a second language, and so it cannot
be claimed that these youngsters were implicated in the inter-
generational reproduction of an English working-class family culture
(Willis 1976:191). Even so, their stylisations of posh and Cockney
amounted to far more than a superficial engagement with the class
dynamics of English society, to far more than ironic impersonations
performed by peripheral spectators. Of course the more specific
meanings of class varied interactionally and biographically, and in
their intersections with ethnicity, they also took historically new
forms. But within this, these youngsters appeared to be very full
participants in the "emotive intimacies of class" (Reay 1998:265).

Lastly, it is often said that class has been undermined by key
processes associated with globalisation and late-modernity – by
the fracturing and pluralisation of identities, by the pre-eminence
of the individual as consumer, and by a loss of faith in the 'grand
narratives' and totalising theories of modernism (Bradley 1996;
introduction to Chapter 6). It would be difficult to claim that either
the data or the analysis in this study have been shielded from these
processes. The informants in the research were young people, who

according to sociologists "are especially responsive to ... the cultural changes discerned by post-modernists" and who, as a result, are most likely to be affected by "the decline of class awareness" (Bradley 1996:77). The fieldsite was also very far from being a traditional cultural enclave: youngsters came to the school from many different parts of London, approximately a third of them were from refugee and asylum-seeking families, and in Hanif and Ninnette's class of 30, they spoke about a dozen different languages. Furthermore, methodologically, much of my research has been micro-analytic, attentive to unpredictable contingencies of situated activity, and sympathetic to many of the ontological assumptions of post-modernism (Chapters 1.2, 1.3, 4.1). But despite these notionally inauspicious conditions, adolescent stylisations repeatedly foregrounded social class as a frame relevant to the flux of experience, and when these occasions are taken together, it would be very hard indeed to ignore the complex influence of a polarising cultural binary that has been long and intimately linked to class systems both in Britain and elsewhere.

Notes

1. See Gal [1991] 2001 for a broadly comparable discussion of the relationship between sociolinguistics and cultural studies in analyses of gender.
2. See Clark 2003 for further exemplification in a US context.
3. Admittedly, this characterisation is more relevant to, say, conversation analysis than to linguistic anthropology. One of the linguistic anthropologist's first instincts is to contextualise specific strips of activity within larger social formations, and an interaction-based study of class would seem distinctly 'thin' if it was not supplemented with historical and/or ethnographic analysis.
4. See also Gal [1994] 2001:424, Holland et al. 1998:13–15, and Pendle 2002 for broadly compatible accounts of competing views of identity.
5. In fact, this chimes with standard *methodological* practice in variationist research, where the measurement of linguistic variables involves a calculation of the extent to which both vernacular *and* prestige variants emerge in the speech of representative individuals (in particular contexts – see e.g. Hudson 1996:Chapter 5). But this methodological procedure has not necessarily worked its way through into a theoretical acceptance of the indelible relationality of styles, of the central part that contrast and difference play in defining a style's symbolic significance. Since the 'vernacular' has traditionally been prized as the most valuable, most authentic data, it is easy for the variationist to see the relationality of

styles as an impurity potentially contaminating the data, and as Irvine goes on to observe, "[l]inguists' conception of dialects … has not necessarily implied user-awareness of a system of alternative varieties. Classically, a dialect has been seen as a variety formed independently of others under conditions of communicative isolation" (2001:28).

6. Joanne selects standard rather than Cockney variants for

- the L in 'well' in line 9, which is velarised rather than vocalic (Wells 1982:313–317)
- the Ts in 'get' and 'sort' in lines 11 and 12, which are alveolar rather than glottal (Wells 1982: 324–325)
- the THs in 'this' and 'thing' in lines 12, 15 and 16, which are alveolar rather than labio-dental (Wells 1982: 328–329)

7. "RP speakers were perceived as relatively more ambitious, intelligent, self-confident, determined and industrious than the regional accented speakers … Nevertheless, non-standard accented speakers were found to be more favourably evaluated than standard accented speakers with respect to personal integrity and social attractiveness … the non-standard speakers were perceived as less serious and more talkative, good natured and humorous than the RP speakers" (Giles and Powesland 1975:68; see also Hudson 1980:201; Trudgill 1983:211).

8. In this case class, but e.g. gender or profession for other structures of feeling (see McElhinny 2003).

9. The standard, careful and 'literate' speech features include:

- aspirated and also sometimes affricated Ts (in 'whaT' in lines 28, 36, 42 and in 'aT' in line 37);
- non-contraction of the auxiliary 'ARE' (lines 37 and 42);
- 'AND' realised with a non-schwa vowel and non-elided alveolar consonants (line 28);
- velar plosives in 'looKing', instead of the glottals used in the build-up (compare lines 37 and 42 with 18, 19, 21, 32);
- velar nasal realisations of 'lookING' in lines 37 and 42 (in contrast to the alveolar in 'pokIN' in line 53).

At the same time, in the climactic fifth time round in line 42,

- a hyper-correct H is inserted into the auxiliary 'are', producing non-standard [hɑː], and
- in the effortful, lip-rounded final 'AT', there is a vernacular glottal rather than a standard alveolar stop.

(With regard to the H-insertion, it is perhaps worth noting that Ninnette's family had roots in the Francophone Caribbean, and so there are no *prima facie* grounds for assuming that it derives from an English lexicalised creole, thereby indexing a Caribbean identity).

10. Wells notes that "one crucial characteristic of most speakers of adoptive RP is their lack of control of the informal and allegro characteristics of RP. Native speakers of RP make extensive use of Elision, Assimilation,

Smoothing and other special-context variants, particularly of course in informal contexts; adoptive RP speakers tend to avoid them" (1982:284). "Informal and allegro" features are conspicuously absent from the voice that Ninnette puts on when she pulls her funny face.

11. Indeed, when Ninnette goes on to point to ``four things pokin' out'' of Joanne's jacket (lines 50–53), there is a further striking parallel with Stallybrass and White's claim that "grotesque realism images the body as multiple, bulging, over- or under-sized, protuberant and incomplete" (1996:9).

12. There are obviously substantial traditions describing visual, physical and material semiosis in (micro-) ethnography and video-based interaction analysis (e.g. McDermott et al. 1978), and some of this explicitly addresses emotion (e.g. Goodwin and Goodwin 2001).

13. In fact, I observed a broadly comparable episode early on in fieldwork: Towards the end of the lesson, Mr Newton sent a white girl, Marilyn, outside. She went outside straightaway, rather noisily but not noticeably bothered, peered back through the glass and put her head round the door once or twice. There was quite a bit of joking and jibing with and about her from the other kids, to which Mr N again acted oblivious. At the end of the class when she came back in, there were more jokes, with Luke calling out to another girl ``Becky's cuter, and podgier!'' (fieldnotes)

14. In Extracts 9.7 and 9.8, the broad London features in Simon's impersonation include H-dropping (which was quite rare in his routine speech – see Table 7.3), half-open onset of the diphthong in the GOAT vowel in 'ell_o_' (Wells 1982:308, 312), nasalisation (Wells 1982:318), an open variant of the DRESS vowel in '_e_llo', and other elements that are lost in pseudonymisation.

15. In a couple of tales of adventure told to Joanne, Ninnette named Marilyn first among the allies who rescued a boy locked in a shop by an angry shopkeeper and who, on another occasion, got apprehended by the police for climbing on private property. ``I went in and bust the door open and pulled him out and ran. And Marilyn and everyone did''; ``me, Marilyn, Marcia and everyone got arrested''

16. This is conspicuous in the fronting of the onset of the vowel in 'paund' in lines 9 and 13, where there is a sharp contrast with the posher, back variant he uses in his non-performative production of the word in line 21 (see Wells 1982:309).

17. Jabber the Hut is a kind of giant slug – fat, shapeless, lascivious and cruel – in one of the *Star Wars* films.

18. Although Ninnette obviously liked Marilyn's energy, and Michelle described her being emphatic in the defence of her sexual respectability.

19. Looked at from another angle, the boys' exaggerated depiction of Marilyn – their portrait of her sexuality and habits of consumption

(boozing and smoking) – positioned her at a stage closer to white working-class adulthood than they themselves had reached. If the school's inner urban location and the socio-economic profile of its student population are considered, if the distortions that the boys introduced are removed and it is accepted that attitudes towards it might vary from hope to fear, then something like this version of maturity was a prospect for quite a few of the students, and as such, 'uncertainties about the future' can perhaps be added to 'uncertainties about sex' as the ingredients in the Cockney stylisation of Marilyn.

20. Detailed illustration and discussion can be found at http://www.cambridge.org/0521812631.

21. "This process – experimenting by turning persuasive discourse into speaking persons – becomes especially important in those cases where a struggle against such images has already begun, where someone is striving to liberate himself from the influence of such an image and its discourse by means of objectification, or is striving to expose the limitations of both image and discourse" (Bakhtin 1981:348).

22. Hymes recognises intra-psychological processes when he welcomes Bauman's performance as an improvement on the "collection and analysis of texts" but sees performance as only the second moment of three (1996:118): "Continuous with the first [moment – the collection and analysis of texts –] and the second [– the analysis of performance –], this third is the process in which performance and text live, the inner substance to which performance is the cambium, as it were, and the crystallised text the bark" (1996:118). As I read it, these 'third moment' processes connect with Williams' structures of feeling, but Hymes goes on to say that this kind of process constitutes "something a bit beyond our current concerns" (1996).

PART V

Methodological Reflections

10

Reflections on generalisation, theory and knowledge construction

Parts I, II and III of the book all carry conclusions of their own, and so I would like to end with some methodological reflections. The research that I have reported can be described as 'linguistic ethnography', and as such, by taking a close look at situated language use, it has tried to provide insights into everyday social and cultural production that are both fundamental and – methodologically – relatively distinctive. But exactly what *kinds* of 'insight' are these, and how were they actually put together? If books such as this want to be seen as a contribution to social science, if students are to learn how to do it themselves, and if researchers in other disciplines are to weigh up the potential value of the procedures at work in analyses like mine, it is important to be clear about (a) the ways in which this book makes claims to wider relevance, and (b) the steps and elements involved in the production of these knowledge claims. So in this final chapter, I shall try to formulate an explicit account of the analytic procedures, focusing in particular on the interplay between data and theory.

It has often been said that, in ethnography, researchers allow their data to speak for itself, and that once the researcher has come to understand a local culture from within, the meanings of activity can be captured in its own terms (Hammersley 1992:19–20,22; Hammersley and Atkinson 1995:Chapter 1). Indeed, in certain respects, it is true that in ethnography, data and description aren't forcefully dominated by theory. In contrast to experiments, for example, fully elaborated theory isn't required before ethnographic data collection and analysis can begin; theory isn't used to structure and control the contexts of data elicitation in ways that makes the data maximally relevant to the testing of specific hypotheses; and it is quite common for a substantial part of the analysis and discussion to be conducted in ordinary language. Even so, data cannot speak for itself, and descriptions are never inference- and interpretation-free. The ideas, models and assumptions that inform ethnographic data interpretation may vary very substantially in their elaboration, cohesiveness and grounding in evidence elsewhere (and they may be woven seamlessly into the description of everyday worlds in ways that make them very hard to spot). But whether we class them as scientific or 'folk' theories, the very act of reporting itself introduces a set of rationales, values and assumptions that are extrinsic to the site being described. This can be seen right at the start, in the issues and arguments that provide research with its initial impetus, and in Chapter 10.1 I comment on these points of departure. At the same time, research also gets configured by axiomatic beliefs about the social world being described, by the interpretive dispositions insti-tutionalised in different disciplines, and by the tools and procedures that these disciplines make available – the ontological, epistemolo-gical and technical underpinnings for this book are summarised in Chapter 10.2. Lastly, ethnographic claims about the world take a range of different forms, produced by a number of different analytic strategies, and in Chapter 10.3, I identify four that have played a part in the book: descriptive generalisation about particular types of practice, structural modelling, ecological description, and general interpretation motivated by a theoretical literature.

Overall, this chapter offers a *functional* account of theory in its attempt to explain how the book tries to generalise beyond the handful of youngsters that it actually focuses on, and it is worth beginning the account by addressing the relationship between gen-eralisation and case study research.

10.1   Case studies, contextualisation and relevance

The analyses in Parts I, II and III seek the kind of generality tradi-tionally associated with anthropological case studies, and not the type of generalisation produced in surveys. In surveys, researchers often take great care to select a sample that is representative of a larger population, so that they can then extrapolate from their findings to make precise statements about the wider distribution of the processes and phenomena they are interested in. This kind of 'enumerative' generalisation is not much of an option in case studies. Instead, case studies seek generality by speaking more directly to existing theories and ideas, and they use their detailed analyses of particular circumstances to probe at the general principles, processes and relationships that these theories and ideas normally see at work in the worlds they refer to.

Admittedly, Chapter 3.2 contained a quantitative survey of the ways in which students engaged with popular media culture, and the findings were then connected with wider trends in the youth population in Britain through the comparison with Livingstone and Bovill 1999. But there was no systematic calculation of exactly how representative West Park and Central High were of any wider population, and the survey did not lead into statistical statements about trends in media consumption across schools in, say, London. Instead, the survey was used ethnographically in two ways. First, the broad similarity with research findings elsewhere was used to show that there was no *prima facie* case for *eliminating* my analyses from wider consideration as the account of a group of youngsters who happened to be very unusual. Second, the comparison with West Park enabled the reader to tune in more closely to the specificity of Central High, with the figures on, for example, the pupils' informal music-making pointing to more general differences in the texture of every classroom discourse in the two schools. In both instances, the account glanced outwards to a larger context beyond the empirical case where most of my energies were concentrated (Central High), and this is consistent with Mitchell's assertion that in case study research, "the particularity of the circumstances surrounding any case or situation ... must always be located within some wider setting or context" (1984:239). Comparably, Hymes insists ethnography should always "entail ... [a] comparative perspective", and he goes on to suggest that "'feet on the ground, one eye on the horizon' might be [the] motto" for ethnography (1999:xxxiii,xl). In fact, there were a lot of other contexts and processes that I invoked or referred to, "on the horizon" beyond the central problem-spaces where my own analyses were focused. Globalisation was probably the most general, associated on the one hand with the shifts in policy that introduced both marketisation and a back-to-basics cultural authoritarianism into education, and on the other, with demographic movements and new populations in English schools. Popular media culture was obviously another important backdrop, and so too were circumambient (and often conflicting) academic and professional discourses about multiculturalism and non-standard dialects.

But although different forms of contextualisation like these can contribute to a case-study's potential relevance to a wider set of processes, they are not enough on their own to give it any argumentative direction, and for this, it is necessary to take issue with a range of more specific claims about such processes, using them both as a point of departure and as a 'foil' to return to a different stages of the analysis.

The general claims that served as the 'launching' platform for the arguments in the book have varied a great deal in their elaborateness and tone,[1] in their origins and networks of circulation, and in the parts and amounts of the real world that they purport to describe. Educational policy nostrums have served as one target, and here I addressed government prescriptions about whole-class pedagogy centred on the teacher, as well as the common assumption that if minority-language speakers are the focus of attention, discussions of language and identity should focus on ethnic languages and on English as a second language. Sociolinguistic orthodoxies have been another critical target, manifest in the neglect of instructed foreign languages, in the doctrine about working-class students being threatened by linguistic insecurity, and in a general commitment to the idea that identities are discursive, flexible and plural, itself a view that recurs in certain forms of post-modernism. Sociological discussions of contemporary conditions have served as a third source, contending that teachers and other authority figures are undermined by popular culture, and that social class isn't what it used to be.

These views are, though, still only a starting point for the main enterprise, and indeed if my only objective had been to controvert them, it might have been sufficient simply to have set these views next to strategic selections from my data in a series of juxtapositions, shaping it all into a readable argument by adding some commentary and a few polemical conclusions.[2] In fact, though, rather than just refuting these influential arguments and ideas, my aim has been to produce a *better* account of the processes they address. The goal, in other words, has been *theoretical reconstruction*, not only recognising the significance of these concerns identified in educational policy, sociolinguistics and sociology, but also reconfiguring them within more encompassing empirical accounts and analytic frameworks (Burawoy et al. 1991). So, for example, rather than just being dismissed as misleading political dogma, the government's prioritisation of teacher-led whole-class instruction was treated as an ideological current that participants themselves were well aware of, even though it didn't adequately represent the totality of their own experience and they resisted it in different ways. But it still mattered, and it was central, for example, to my characterisation of whole-class discussion at Central High as an 'interdiscursive genre'. Similarly, sociolinguistic and educational debates about linguistic insecurity actually seemed to have impacted on the general language ideological climate at the school, and this background contributed to the licence that Hanif experienced in his stylisations of Cockney. The details of this reconstruction are contained, of course, in the preceding chapters,[3] but staying with the task of reflexive methodological explication set for this conclusion, it is worth saying more about the range of ways in which theory has figured in this reconstruction process, as well as a little more about differences in the kinds of theory involved.

The general educational, sociolinguistic and sociological claims identified so far may have varied in their elaboration, cohesiveness and evidential base, but functionally, they were similar in the role they played as initial 'challenges' for my analyses. Another assortment of relatively well-established theories and perspectives have served as *underpinnings*, and these have shaped

i)   my basic assumptions about the social world,
ii) my understanding of how knowledge of the world is influenced by different (sub-)disciplinary perspectives, and
iii) the tools and procedures that I use to produce and examine my data.

It is worth taking each of these in turn, not only outlining the particular ontologies, epistemologies and technical apparatus that have shaped the book, but also acknowledging the points where the solidity of these foundations has itself been opened to question.

10.2   Underpinnings

10.2.1   Ontological assumptions about social reality

Ira Cohen (1987) draws a useful distinction between 'substantive theory', comprising a set of claims that are open to empirical refutation, and 'ontology', which consists of very general ideas specifying the kinds of fundamental entity occurring in a given domain, together with the ways in which these entities interact. Ontologies involve non-refutable, metaphysical presuppositions about the qualities and forces thought to underlie the phenomena being addressed, and this takes several forms in my analysis.

Ideas about reality being partially reproduced, constructed and sometimes revised in social interaction form part of my ontological base. So within the territory I try to engage with, I assume axiomatically:

a) that there are individual agents who interact with one another;
b) that there are conventional structures that both configure and constrain their actions together;
c) that these actions can also reshape some of the conventions, often fleetingly but sometimes in more lasting ways (particularly if these revisions catch on and are endorsed collectively); and
d) that it is in the interplay between agency, structure, constraint and change that we can see the operation of relations of power.

All of these claims could be debated philosophically, but there is no real attempt to do so in the book, and instead, they are used to justify and promote discursive interaction as a focus for social analysis. Indeed, there is also support for the consequentiality of social interaction in the post-structuralist view that 'communities' and 'languages' are ideological constructs rather than natural phenomena with an objective reality of their own. If communities and languages – and indeed social classes – are regarded as ideas that are discursively produced rather than as facts that are given, then we should be able to see them being defined and negotiated in the evaluations, self-differentiations, metalinguistic censures, etc., that recur in everyday talk.

At the same time, however, I make the additional assumption that although they may impinge on social interaction in ways that are centrally at issue in my own research, there are a great many phenomena and processes – ranging from global economies, nation-states, class hierarchies and school systems to traumas and desires – that also operate far beyond locally-situated discourse, in ways that are unintelligible to interaction analysis (cf. Burawoy 1991:272–279; Carter and Sealey 2000). In fact, when the data led me into discussion of depth-psychological processes in Chapters 6 and 9, the idea of social-reality-being-interactionally-constructed actually moved from being an ontological premise to becoming an issue in 'substantive theory', and empirical analysis probed at the limits of the claims and frameworks produced in linguistic and interactionist research. Indeed, this is just one instance of the kind of licence for data to disturb 'theory' that ethnography provides, and further clarification of this emerges if we turn to my study's epistemological framing in both ethnography and linguistics.

10.2.2   *Ethnographic and linguistic epistemologies*[4]

Although the differences are much sharper in some cases than in others, there are a number of significant points where linguistics and ethnography diverge in their conceptions of knowledge and discovery, and their conjunction in 'linguistic ethnography' produces an interesting tension. This becomes clear if each is taken in turn.

There is in fact quite a lot of disagreement about the nature of ethnography (cf. Hymes 1996:3), but it can be generally attributed the following (connected) characteristics:[5]

(a)   *Regard for local rationalities in an interplay between 'strange-ness' and 'familiarity'*: Ethnography typically looks for the meaning and rationality in practices that may seem strange at first/from the outside, and it tries both to enter the informants' life-world and to abstract (some of) its structuring features in a process that entails continuing alternation between involvement in local activity and orientation to exogenous audiences and frameworks (Todorov 1988). Ethnography tries to comprehend the tacit and articulated understandings of the participants in whatever processes and activities are being studied, and it tries to do justice to these understandings in its reports to outsiders.

(b)   *Cultural ecologies*: Ethnography focuses on a number of different levels/dimensions of socio-cultural organisation/process at the same time, and assumes that the meaning and significance of a form or practice involves an interaction between these (and other) levels/dimensions.

(c)   *Systems and particularity*: Ethnography looks for patterns and systematicity in situated everyday practice, but recognises that hasty comparison across cases can blind one to the contingent moments and the complex cultural and semiotic ecologies that give any phenomenon its meaning (see (b)).

(d) *Sensitising concepts, openness to data, and worries about idealisation*: Ethnographic analysis works with 'sensitising' concepts "suggest[ing] directions along which to look" rather than with 'definitive' constructs "provid[ing] prescriptions of what to see" (Blumer 1969:148). Questions may change during the course of an enquiry, and the dialectic between theory, interpretation and data is sustained throughout (Hymes 1996:10ff.). Although it recognises that selectivity and idealisation are intrinsic to data, analysis tries to stay alert to the potential consequentiality of what gets left out.

(e) *Reflexivity and participation*: Ethnography recognises the ineradicable role that the researcher's personal subjectivity plays throughout the research process. It looks to systematic field strategies and to accountable analytic procedures to constrain self-indulgent idiosyncrasy, and expects researchers to face up to the partiality of their interpretations (Hymes 1996:13). But the researcher's own cultural and interpretive capacities are crucial in making sense of the complex intricacies of situated everyday activity among the people being studied, and tuning into these takes time and close involvement.

(f) *The irreducibility of experience*: Ethnography's commitment to particularity and participation ((c) and (e)) combines with its concerns about idealisation (d) to produce a strong sense of what is unique and 'once-only' in situated acts and interactions (see Willis and Trondman 2001 on 'this-ness'). Ethnographic writing is often tempered by a sense of the limitations of available forms of representation, and it recognises that there is an important element in actions and events that eludes analysis and can only be intimated or aesthetically evoked (Hymes 1996:12, 118).

Linguistics is a massively contested field. There are a number of very robust linguistic sub-disciplines which treat language as an autonomous system (separating it from the contexts in which it is used), but there are also varied, large and long traditions of research which have addressed language and culture together, using both linguistics and ethnography. But whatever their views on what aspects of language are worth studying how, most people affiliating with linguistics would accept:

- that language is almost universal among humans, at the same time as changing over time and varying across social groups (of different sizes, durations and sitings)
- that it is possible to isolate and abstract structural patterns in the ways in which people communicate, and that many of these patterns are relatively stable, recurrent and socially shared (to different degrees)
- that there is a wide range of quite well-established procedures for isolating and identifying these structures
- that the description and analysis of these patterns benefits from the use of relatively technical vocabularies, and
- that although there is certainly much more involved in human communication, these technical vocabularies can make a valuable contribution to our understanding of the highly intricate processes involved when people talk, sign, read, write or otherwise communicate.

Ideas like these are basic to linguistics in all or most of its guises, and its combination with ethnography produces a tension. Linguistics and ethnography generally differ in their sense of the extent to which their objects of study can be codified, and the formulation of rules is normally regarded as more problematic in ethnography than in linguistics:

i)   Ethnography's traditional object of study, 'culture', is a more encompassing concept than 'language' (Hymes 1996:6; Duranti 1997:97), and for all sorts of reasons,[6] 'culture' appears to be generally less determinate as a focal entity.[7]

ii) In linguistics, empirical procedures – elicitation techniques, data-regularisation, and rules of evidence – are relatively standardised and can often be taken more or less for granted, at least within particular schools/paradigms. The social and personal processes that have brought the researcher to the level of understanding where s/he could start to formulate linguistic rules are seen as relatively insignificant. In contrast in ethnography, participant-observation plays a major role and the processes involved in learning and adjusting to different cultural practices are regarded as themselves instructive and potentially consequential for the analysis. The researcher's presence/prominence in the field setting defies standardisation and it introduces a range of contingencies and partialities that really need to be addressed/reported.

iii) Linguistics seeks to generalise about language structure and use, and typically only looks beyond what is actually said/signed/written when implied meaning is highly conventionalised (e.g. as in presupposition and implicature). Ethnography dwells longer in situated particularities, and this difference between them shows up in their finished products. Ethnographies involve rhetorical forms, such as vignettes and narratives (Hymes 1996:12–13), that are designed to provide the reader with some apprehension of the fullness and irreducibility of the 'lived stuff' from which the analyst has abstracted (cultural) structures. Grammars, on the other hand, normally don't.

Admittedly, the differences between linguistics and ethnography are often more a matter of degree than of kind, but the overall effect of their combination can be characterised as, first:

- *'opening linguistics up'*, inviting reflexive sensitivity to the processes involved in the production of linguistic claims, pointing to the potential importance of what gets left out, and encouraging a willingness to accept (and run with) the fact that beyond the reach of standardised falsification procedures, "[e]xperience ... has ways of *boiling over*, and making us correct our present formulas" (James 1978:106, cited in Willis and Trondman 2001:2).

In Chapter 9, my discussions of 'depth-processes' and psycho-social 'interiority' stepped somewhat outside the bounds of contemporary linguistic anthropology, and ethnography was one of the perspectives that I cited in my efforts to justify this.

Second, the combination with linguistics has the effect of

- *'tying ethnography down'*, pushing ethnography towards the analysis of clearly delimitable processes, increasing the amount of reported data that is open to falsification, looking to impregnate local description with analytical frameworks drawn from outside. Rather than presenting focal data in their own words, language and discourse analysts tend to work with transcripts, and although transcription is of course itself a selective process guided by the researcher's interests and assumptions (Ochs 1979), the shift from perception to textual representation is generally less vulnerable to researcher's idiosyncratic interpretation than it is in, say, the composition of descriptive vignettes. For the reader, having access to data that hasn't been quite so heavily processed by the researcher makes it easier to challenge the analysis, while for researchers, the element of standardisation in the representation of data facilitates comparison with other analyses, making it easier to check whether the use of an analytic term is consistent with other people's.

The capacity of sociolinguistic discourse analysis to 'tie ethnography down' formed part of my argument about the potential relevance of sociolinguistics to cultural studies, and it points to the third way in which my analyses rely on established theory.

10.2.3   Tools and procedures for data analysis

Because descriptive linguistics and discourse analysis have substantial histories and are extensively developed and tested with empirical data, they offer a lot of relatively trustworthy procedures and frameworks that analysts can draw into the pursuit of non-linguistic issues, fairly free from anxiety about the need to check, justify or elaborate the descriptive terms being used. In line with this, this book draws quite a lot of phonetics and phonology into its account of social class (especially in Part III), without ever seeking to contribute to the analysis of speech sound as an autonomous field of enquiry, and much the same instrumentality characterises my engagements with conversation analysis, Goffmanian interaction analysis, and theories of indexicality in linguistic anthropology.

The application of these frameworks was itself often embedded in a particular procedural discipline, involving long, slow immersion in the recordings of specific episodes, repeatedly replaying a given sequence, carefully following its turn-by-turn development as the participants tried to build a common understanding. In fact, this process can be broadly aligned with the discovery-procedures formalised in conversation analysis. CA begins the investigation of any particular sequence with a sustained period of relatively "unmotivated observation", rather than with strongly preconceived ideas (Schegloff 1999:577–578; ten Have 1999:102–104); it is very sensitive to the uniqueness and particularity of each episode and to the fact that the regularities of conduct emerge from the participants' 'artful practice', with rules always being applied for 'another first time' (Garfinkel 1967; Heritage 1984a:120ff.); and the analysis holds to an "aesthetic of smallness ... and slowness" (Silverman 1999).[8] Admittedly, my appropriation of this methodology was rather impure: the selection of episodes to analyse had already been motivated by my interest in e.g. the humming or the Cockney they contained; I had normally sorted them into broad categories like 'interaction with teachers' vs 'interaction with peers'; and I had usually begun to formulate rather general arguments about the ways in which each of the varieties seemed to be used in these settings. But once potentially relevant transcripts had been selected, I would go over them in more transcriptional detail, and then try to 'inhabit' each of them, putting my sense of a developing argument to one side, taking instead a slow, close look at the moment-by-moment unfolding of each episode, bringing in different concepts from linguistics and discourse analysis in provisional ways, exploring whether they could help illuminate what was going on. For this immersion process, I tried to work with a rule that I would never put pen to paper about a conceptual link between one fragment and another, or incorporate an extract into a prose commentary or argument, until I had spent at least one hour on it. Almost invariably, the hour turned into two or four, and sometimes days not hours, and even though I sometimes found myself sitting for ten minutes wondering what on earth else I could say to fill up the time, when I did eventually finish on a sequence, the propositions I had started out with usually looked either crude or just plain wrong. Instead, I had a clearer idea of which aspects of the interaction I really could start to make plausible claims about, as well as a much sharper sense of the dimensions that I either couldn't understand or couldn't properly comment on (even though they might seem intriguing).

So the application of relatively technical linguistic and discourse analytic concepts certainly wasn't mechanical, and instead remained broadly in line with some of the tenets of ethnography (e.g. (d), (e) and (f) in Chapter 10.2.2). In fact, the notion of 'applying' established models to specific pieces of empirical data is itself an oversimplification. In the process of providing particular concepts for characterising strips of interactional meaning-making, linguistics and discourse analysis help to constitute the very data to which they are then applied as descriptive resources. All data involve selection and analytic preparation, guided by their relevance to particular issues and by their tractability within different methods, and a single lesson, for example, can be examined from a huge variety of different angles, concentrating on learning processes, curriculum sequencing, the distribution of speaking rights, etc., focusing on whichever aspects of classroom life seem most pertinent and practicable. At the level of data-description, my own perspective was particularly strongly influenced by Goffman's frameworks for exploring the interactional dynamics of physical co-presence and for analysing the configurations of activity in, around and 'under' any dominant line of communication, and with these at the front of my 'tool-box', I experienced those parts of my dataset where the commitments of teachers and students were potentially disjunctive as particularly rich sites for investigation.

These empirical predilections were, of course, supported by the opportunities for observation provided by the radio-mic, and in fact cases like this illustrate the way in which ontology, epistemology and 'tools' come together, enriching one's sense of the intricacy of social and cultural processes. Social constructionism flags up to the potential consequentiality of interactional activity; ethnography and CA (in its discovery phase) insist that analysts take time to observe and that they shouldn't expect to button everything up 'in the first pass'; and then linguistics and interactional discourse analysis provide descriptive equipment that helps analysts to articulate their perceptions of the data, resulting in sets of statements and claims which show that indeed this is a 'seam' of social life that really is quite workable.

None of this, though, says very much about the general significance of the statements and claims that are eventually constructed on foundations like these. In the first part of the chapter, I referred to influential discourses that seemed worth contesting, and in focusing on underpinnings in the last three sections, I have only outlined what I 'brought along' to the debate. What about the 'brought about'? If the activity that these broadly theoretical ingredients contribute to is to count as research, the claims emerging also need to say something *new*, and they should not only speak to wider interests but also rest on procedures that make them relatively trustworthy.

As with the underpinnings on which it rests, the production of claims to new knowledge takes a number of different forms, and it is convenient to start with the most basic.

10.3   Knowledge production

10.3.1   *Descriptive generalisations about particular types of practice*

My book contains a number of general statements about the way that youngsters hummed and sang in my corpus, how they switched into *Deutsch*, and how they put on exaggerated posh and Cockney accents. These represent some of the most basic general findings in my research, and there were at least four analytic activities involved in their production.

The first involved assembling topic-focused datasets – picking out and putting together all the recordings of episodes where *Deutsch* was used, repeating this with posh and Cockney, etc. (see Chapter 1.5). The second involved the fairly protracted immersion in particular episodes described in the previous section, and the attempt to work out what was going on in particular utterances entailed constant movement between my own subjective intuitions, the prompts and refinements on offer in linguistics and interactional discourse analysis, and the focal utterances themselves, together with preceding and contiguous parts of the same episode. In the end, this produced characterisations of a given instance of singing/*Deutsch*/posh/ Cockney that addressed its timing, its responsiveness to what had just gone before, and its impact on subsequent conduct (including its uptake-by-others within the unfolding of interaction); its positioning within – and orientation towards – the micro-interactional frames and priorities in play, as well as within larger institutional genres and activity types; and its identity as semiotic resource – its interactional affordances and its indexical connotations, often compared, hypothetically, with other semiotic resources that might have been used just then. This process of episode-by-episode analysis was preceded by, interspersed with, and then followed by, a third activity – inter-episode comparison in which my sense of similarities and differences gradually became more refined, starting, for example, with a broad distinction between posh and Cockney stylisations oriented to teachers *versus* peers, and developing subsequently into more subtle differentiations between, for example, stylisations that ran with *versus* against the grain of dominant patterns of stratification, or between the kinds of stylisation, humming and singing that Hanif engaged in, as opposed to Ninnette and Joanne.

All this immersion, analysis and sorting eventually led to the fourth activity – descriptive generalisation itself. This involved distinguishing general features of *Deutsch*, posh-and-Cockney and humming-and-singing that held across all (or most) of the instances, from those aspects which were specific to particular episodes and subsets, and the output of this process is illustrated in, for example, my claims about humming-and-singing's differences from talk (Chapter 3.4), and my comments on peer group *Deutsch*'s relative propositional opacity (e.g. 4.4). Indeed, I also drew in theories from outside to support and clarify general patterns of this kind – for example, I used Bauman's ideas about performance to enhance my general assertions about *Deutsch*, and the writings of Bourdieu and Cohen brought historical depth to my account of the high–low cultural semantic pervading the stylisations of posh and Cockney (Chapter 9.3).

Close attention to differences in the data clearly played an important part in the production of these descriptive generalisations, and the process of trying to work out whether and how 'discrepant cases' fitted in with wider patterns made a crucial contribution to the formulation and sharpening of these general claims. Nevertheless, in the end, these descriptive generalisations prioritise *similarities* across subsets of the data, and the differences rather drop from view. There are, though, at least three other types of knowledge claim which make these differences more focal, and the first of these involves the development of structural models which position such differences as the variable 'surface' output of an underlying system.

10.3.2   *Modelling structural systems*

At its simplest, in the study of grammar the modelling of systems involves the identification of underlying categories in a collection of phrases or sentences, and a demonstration of how different actualisations and arrangements of these abstract categories produce predictably different meanings. In this way, for example, the position of an auxiliary verb like 'is' systematically affects whether the sentence is declarative or interrogative ('It is green.' vs 'Is it green?'). Similarly, in interaction, conversation analysts have shown that turns in an exchange are often organised in 'adjacency pairs', where the current turn sets up only a limited range of possible responses and where there is a ranking among these responses, 'preferred' responses being structurally simpler than those that are 'dispreferred'. So questions set up answer or disclaimers, invitations initiate acceptances or declinations, complaints apologies or justifications; and in each case, the formulation of the response is likely to be more elaborate if the speaker goes for the second ('dispreferred') option rather than the first.

Research on these kinds of linguistic and interactional system has been enormously valuable as input to my analyses (Chapter 10.2.3), but I have not generally treated the production of formal models as a central objective of my own (contrast Goodwin 1990). In Chapter 2.6, however, there is one point in my discussion of classroom discourse where the analysis looks towards what might, at a pinch, be called a 'grammar' of classroom participation. There, assessment, audienceship and platform performance were proposed as the constitutive elements shaping classroom conduct, and I suggested that very different results emerged when the expectations associated with each of these elements were altered.

This 'system' was formulated inductively through a comparison of the ways students behaved during whole-class discussion, during writing exercises and in role-play. The comparison process helped to eliminate a number of possible explanations for the students' conduct during teacher-talk – total disaffection, inability to act collectively, inability to focus on semiotically-reduced communication – and instead of looking for extrinsic factors to explain the patterns of activity during teacher-fronted discourse, attention turned to dimensions that seemed more fundamental to classroom life, warranting this with a mixture of Foucault, Goffman, McDermott and Bauman. The pressures and expectations associated with assessment, audienceship and performance certainly did vary in these three classroom contexts, and using assessment, audienceship and performance as basic dimensions that needed to be addressed in any characterisation of classroom interactional experience, I went on to offer a 'respecification' of teacher-talk, tuning this to the empirical data on pupil participation rather than to educational policy ideals. In this way, teacher-talk became "a jostling but expressively depleted genre which marginalises students' judgement but threatens to drag them onto the platform with curriculum-scripted performances that in the end don't actually count for very much" (see Chapter 2.6 above), and this subsequently fed into discussion of how the forms of assessment, performance and audienceship required at school co-existed in an uneasy tension with popular music.

Compared with many of the structural systems described in linguistics and conversation analysis, this model still has an extremely long way to go in terms of empirical testing and elaboration, and rather than claiming that it identifies real organisational principles underpinning the ways pupils talk and interact together, it would be much wiser just to class it as an analytic heuristic. Even so, it illustrates one way of responding to differences in the data. The idea that differences in classroom conduct might be explained as variation produced by the different 'values' attached to each element in its 'deep structure' amounts to a rudimentary theory, and this can be subsequently tested, elaborated or refuted in a range of different classroom settings.

As a particular form of knowledge production, the theorisation of structural systems often tends to be relatively agonistic. Researchers write for robustly sceptical readers, and once presented, vigorous processes of refutation and defence are expected to play a major part establishing the theory's validity. The second strategy for dealing with differences in the data is generally less combative, and it is more closely associated with ethnography than linguistics (Chapter 10.2.2). In this second strategy, there is a stronger sense of the limitations of theory,[9] and researchers and their readers are often drawn together in their respect for the awesome complexity of the scenes being described. This second strategy produces knowledge claims which I would call 'ecological descriptions'.

10.3.3   Ecological descriptions

'Ecological descriptions' take subsets of practices and emphasise their relationship with other kinds of practice, process and phenomenon in the field setting, many of them occupying different levels of social and cultural organisation. Ideas about 'cross-level' relationships certainly play a part in the production of 'descriptive generalisations', forming much of the substance of the third (sorting and sifting) activity described in Chapter 10.3.1. But rather than being just a means towards generalisation about stable similarities, as 'ecological descriptions', cross-type and cross-level relationships are drawn from the backroom, promoted centre-stage, and elaborated in the spotlight. In this way in my own analyses, the differences between Hanif and Joanne's humming-and-singing were, for example, seen as both reflecting and contributing to the different kinds of friendship they participated in; the fact that Joanne's quiet humming was vulnerable to censorship while Hanif's noisy singing was acceptable was tied to the particular interactional settlement in Class 9A; Hanif and Ninnette's different uses of Cockney were linked to their contrasting school trajectories, with Hanif's confidence itself being linked to the school's tradition of respect for non-standard dialect; and the use of *Deutsch* at moments of heightened classroom surveillance was connected to German's status as an official language at school and to Hanif's ambivalent commitment to prestige both in school learning and his friendship group.

My assumption here was that these links were contingent, emerging within the particular group and situations that I studied but not necessarily obtaining in other settings that researchers might study. Of course other studies might turn up broadly similar links between semiotic practice, peer group dynamics and classroom culture, but the governing assumption is that there are huge and fundamental qualitative differences in the phenomena and processes that fall within the ambit of semiosis, friendship and institutional organisation, so that it would be pointless trying to unite all these connections in a system of tight interdependencies of the kind that one finds in structures of English syntax or conversational turn exchange. Instead, by spelling out the ways in which different interactional practices seem to be nested within larger patterns of social organisation, these cross-level connections are most appropriately seen as increasing the ease with which other researchers can compare my findings with their own. Rather than taking sole responsibility for a general claim which stands or falls in subsequent argument (Chapter 10.3.2), the objective is to build towards cumulative, comparative generalisations, sharing the responsibility for doing so with critical but cooperative readers (Hymes 1980:119 ff.). By specifying as many of the conditioning factors as can be reasonably identified, there is an attempt to enhance the comparability and translatability of the account, saying in effect: "these are the practices I found, and this was the situation. Look at it in detail. How does it compare with the practices and situations you're studying? Are there processes and conditions that compare with things you've observed? Are your processes a bit different? What is it in our two situations that could account for these similarities and differences?" (cf. LeCompte and Goetz 1982:34; also Chapter 10.2.2(b) and (c)).

In fact, in this book, the cumulative comparative analysis that ecological descriptions aim for has been both actual and potential. In Chapter 2.7, the description of classroom discourse in Class 9A in the 1990s was compared with the ethnographies of interaction in broadly similar working-class schools produced by British sociologists in the 1970s and 80s. There were a lot of similar practices, and this resemblance reinforced the sense that like was being compared with like. But at the same time, in the 1990s there was evidence of a commitment to learning dissociated from respect for the teacher which was unreported in the earlier work, and this prompted historical speculation about the causes of this apparent difference, linking in, among other things, more general sociolinguistic claims about shifts in the order of public discourse. Elsewhere, cross-study comparisons have demonstrated that my dataset isn't particularly eccentric and that the prospects for setting it next to others look good,[10] but because I have focused on interactional practices that haven't yet been widely documented, I am unable myself to undertake broader comparative analysis of the processes I am most interested in, and here the most I can hope is that my findings can provide a base-line for comparison for studies in the future.

The last strategy that I have used to propose a relationship between pieces, subsets and types of data that initially seem different is more assertive than ecological description in its claims to generality, and here I look for authorisation in a theoretical literature.

10.3.4   General interpretations sanctioned by a theoretical literature

In seeking similarities and connections between processes and phenomena that appear very different on the surface, 'general interpretations sanctioned by a theoretical literature' differ from 'descriptive generalisations', which, I have suggested, concentrate on data where the similarities seem fairly clear. At the same time, they diverge from 'ecological descriptions' and 'structural models' in the strategies they use to make sense of empirical differences. Rather than focusing on contextual correlations within the dataset, or trying to isolate the constitutive ingredients in a set of practices, these general interpretations pull different practices together by going outside the data to conceptual frameworks produced elsewhere.

General interpretations motivated by a theoretical literature were crucial to the coherence of Parts II and III of the book, and they also played a role creating coherence in Part I. In Part II, I looked outside the data and found that the literature on ritual suggested some plausible connections between improvised *Deutsch* and instructed German. Among other ideas, Raymond Williams' theory of hegemony, 'practical consciousness' and 'creative practice' served to integrate style-shifting and stylisation in Part III. And in Part I, when I tried to draw together the patterns of classroom interaction in Class 9A – deviation from the IRE, over-exuberant boys, and excluded and resistant girls – the literature on 'genre' became indispensable, also facilitating their integration with the data on humming and singing.

Cross-referring to theoretical literatures might lack the parsimony of structural modelling, and disturb the impression of uncontaminated naturalism that ecological descriptions sometimes convey, but there is no reason why it should entail a retreat from the disciplines of empirical data. I tried, for example, to be as careful as I could tying the theories of institutional and interactional ritual offered by Du Bois, Bernstein, Goffman into the patterns of activity in the German lessons and the peer-group improvisations, and comparable efforts accompanied my appropriations of 'hegemony' and 'genre'.[11] And then, once the empirical connection with a body of theoretical work was established, new avenues of empirical analysis and interpretation opened up, drawing other parts of the dataset into the reckoning in ways that couldn't otherwise have been anticipated. Taking for example the analysis of German/*Deutsch*, Du Bois' sketch of the ritual speech could be mapped quite closely onto the discourse of the foreign language class, but other scholars, including Durkheim and Turner, pointed to the emotional intensity and 'flow' that rituals often aspire to, and this opened the door to a consideration of the psycho-social dimensions of my informants' experience of instructed German. I then looked for data relevant to this psycho-social interpretation in my corpus, and to elaborate it, I focused both on the stark empirical contrasts between German and other lessons, and on some of the particularities of Hanif's involvement with the language.[12]

Admittedly, theoretical literatures featured in other types of analysis and knowledge claim, but they did not play such a prominent role. Theories of language and discourse certainly contributed to the apparatus used to interrogate specific episodes (Chapters 10.2.3 and 10.3.1), but if a particular theoretical lens was removed from the intensive investigation of a given extract, the outcome would merely be an analysis that was slightly duller/more blunt. In contrast, if it was subtracted from these general interpretations, a whole argument would fall apart and the data would regress to a set of separate piles. Cross-reference to theories in the literature also played a part in the process I have called 'descriptive generalisation' – to take the examples cited in Chapter 10.3.1, Bauman's theory of performance was invoked in the general characterisation of improvised *Deutsch*, and Cohen and Bourdieu were brought in to clarify the high–low cultural semantic. Indeed, since perceptions of similarity and difference themselves shift depending on the criterion being used in the comparison – and since there were in fact lots of differences in the improvisations and stylisations themselves – it might be argued that there was actually no essential difference between the role Bauman, Cohen and Bourdieu played in pointing to common features of Deutsch and posh-and-Cockney on the one hand, and on the other, the part that ritual played in establishing connections between improvisations and lessons, or that Williams played linking stylisation and style-shifting. But this would be wrong. The *Deutsch* improvisations, for example, intuitively form a much tighter class of similar phenomena than the improvisations and the lessons together, and eliminating Bauman from the account wouldn't substantially detract from this. Instead, the references to Bauman, Cohen and Bourdieu merely help to summarise commonalities in improvised *Deutsch* and posh-and-Cockney extracts, pointing to broad similarities in the keying and the indexical connotations of the activity presented in each. In contrast, the discussions of ritual, hegemony and genre drew different types of data together by positing deeper or more general processes beneath or beyond the utterances presented. With both ritual and hegemony, different practices evidenced in my data were variously construed as 'inputs' and 'outputs' connected to the complex and partly unmappable workings of language in human consciousness, while with genre, a range of diverse actions were framed together as on-line socio-communicative efforts to give tolerable shape to the dynamics of situated co-presence.

Making use of theoretical literatures to draw my data together within an account of more encompassing processes, I have referred to quite a wide range of different authors, and these include Turner, Durkheim, Goffman, Sapir, Billig, Cameron and Kulick in the discussions of ritual, Williams, Thompson, Ortner, Skeggs, Stallybrass and White in the investigation of hegemony, Bauman, Hanks and Fairclough on genre. But underpinning the variety of ways in which this plurality of scholarship has been tied into my data, I would argue that there is a more or less unified theory of consciousness, language, and communication-situated-both-in-interaction-and-in-history, and that this emerges from a general orientation to the thinking of Bakhtin and Vološinov, both within the book and in the humanities and social sciences more generally.

The book itself refers to Bakhtin and Vološinov in different ways throughout, and they provide direction for the analysis as well as quite detailed resources for the description of particular practices and processes.[13] Indeed, Bakhtin also plays a crucial part pulling the whole of Parts II and III together when *Deutsch*/German and posh-and-Cockney are characterised as inner languages with very different kinds of psycho-social resonance (Chapters 9.6, 9.7). But just as important, the writings of Bakhtin and Vološinov are explicitly acknowledged by a number of the other authors I lean on. There are very strong links with Vološinov and Bakhtin in Williams' thinking, and they are also important for Hanks, Bauman, Stallybrass and White, and Fairclough. Bakhtin and Vološinov often do provide analyses that can be mapped quite precisely into empirical data, but they have also played an prominent part outlining an agenda of issues that, with varying degrees of conscious awareness, other scholars have subsequently elaborated in quite a lot more detail. Hanks, for example, develops Bakhtin's ideas about genre (1987), Goffman elaborates Vološinov/Bakhtin's ideas about voicing (1981), and Hymes has even suggested that Bakhtin 'scooped' the ethnography of communication itself (Cazden 1989:117; also Duranti 1988:225, 1997:10). Bakhtin and Vološinov have a track-record identifying dimensions of language that other researchers have subsequently drawn more fully into the mainstream of empirical sociolinguistics, and in my own efforts to justify involvement with a topic that contemporary linguistic and discourse analysis might not feel entirely comfortable with – the psycho-social interiority of language – it has been helpful invoking a Bakhtinian pedigree. But beyond intra-disciplinary self-justification of this kind, very widespread scholarly interest in Bakhtin/Vološinov means that if sociolinguists and discourse analysts can elaborate descriptive frameworks capable of linking broadly Bakhtinian ideas more closely into empirical data, then their potential *inter*-disciplinary value is increased.

10.3.5   *Claiming cross-disciplinary relevance*

Synthesising topics, concepts, authors and/or methods from different (sub-)disciplinary areas is another way in which research can claim to extend knowledge. In this book, I have used interactional sociolinguistic analysis to address problems identified in public discourse, education and/or sociology and cultural studies (Chapter 10.1), and I have suggested that the benefits of this cross-disciplinarity can flow both ways. But if such mixings are to be more than polemical or merely eccentric – if the goal is 'theoretical reconstruction', repositioning prevailing concerns in more robust conceptual and empirical frameworks – then the work producing these syntheses needs to look beyond novelty to the wider range of criteria by which the quality of research is normally judged. As well as being novel/original, such work needs to be careful, logical, accurate, accountable/explicit, sceptical, comparative and generally well-informed, resting on combinations of data, analysis, inferencing and theorisation that seem solid and properly constructed. Of course final judgement of the adequacy of these foundations falls to the reader, as does the assessment of the value of the project overall. Indeed, disciplinary discourse communities themselves often differ in their ideas of exactly how 'care', 'logic', 'accuracy' etc. are constituted, and so in a relatively cross-disciplinary enterprise like mine, methodological reflections are probably even more limited in the kinds of validation they can hope to achieve than in projects where the affiliations are more clear cut. Even so, descriptions of method can still help to orient the task of critical assessment, and that is what I have tried to do in this conclusion.

Notes

1. Some aimed to describe the world as it is (e.g. claims about the nature of social class), while others aimed to characterise the world as it should be (e.g. government advocacy of teacher-centred pedagogy).
2. Such juxtapositions could have involved, for example: the emphasis on IRE discourse in education policy set next to the data on interaction in Class 9A; the essentialism of sociolinguists' traditional interest in identity-at-the-intersection-of-home-and-school contrasted with the examples of *Deutsch*; and so forth.
3. As far as the other dominant ideas listed in the previous paragraph are concerned, the 'reconfigurations' have been as follows: (i) *Deutsch*'s ethno-linguistic neutrality might make it look dull to sociolinguists, but for children, this may well have been a significant factor facilitating its use in a highly multilingual class (Chapter 4.5). At a more theoretical level, (ii) the orthodox sociolinguistic view of identity as a motile interactional projection was integrated with notions of subjectivity from cultural studies under the aegis of Bakhtin (Chapter 9.8), and (iii) the 'demise of class' was not only partially attested in the analysis of my informants' explicit, lexico-grammatical discourse (Chapter 7.2), but also combined with the data on stylisation and style-shifting in Williams' theory of hegemony and creative practice (Chapter 9.7).
4. A number of these ideas were developed in dialogue with the Coordinating Committee of the UK Linguistic Ethnography Forum (www.ling-ethnog.org.uk), and I would like to thank Janet Maybin, Karin Tusting, Angela Creese, Richard Barwell and Vally Lytra.
5. There is another point to add, though I have omitted it from the list in the main text because much of it is covered in Section 10.1 above:

   - *Anti-ethnocentricity and relevance*: Ethnography normally questions the oversimplifications in influential discourse, and interrogates prevailing definitions. It often seeks to produce 'telling' (rather than typical) cases (Mitchell 1984:237–240), and it demands our attention for the "delicacy of its distinctions [rather than] the sweep of its abstractions" (Geertz 1973:25). In ethnography, "small facts . . . get in the way of large issues" (Hannerz 1987:556).

6. Including the representation of language in writing, and the success of linguists (from ancient times) in isolating structural elements from the communicative flow, modelling them in formal systems and testing these models empirically.
7. Admittedly, a sense of the 'codifiability' of culture has varied at different times and with different topics in anthropology.

8. For another approach which holds to a broadly similar approach to analysis, see e.g. the 'modern philology' of Becker (1995) and Johnstone (1997).

9. According to Geertz, "cultural systems must have a minimal degree of coherence, but tight, elegant, formal theories are disreputable ... The first need is for theory to stay rather closer to the ground than tends to be the case in sciences more able to give themselves over to abstraction ... What generality [cultural theory] contrives to achieve grows out of the delicacy of its distinction, not the sweep of its abstractions" (1973:20,25).

10. See the cross-references to Livingston and Bovill in Chapter 3.2; to Mitchell 2003, Mitchell and Martin 1997, Boaks 1998 and DfES 2002 in Chapter 5; and to Reay and others in Chapter 6.1.

11. Rather than being fast and loose, the introduction of 'hegemony' was fitted quite closely both to the posh–Cockney style-shifting and to my informants' relative inarticulateness about social class (Chapters 7.2, 7.3, 9.7), and the introduction of 'genre' as an encompassing frame first made way for the comparison of teacher-talk with role-play and writing (which resulted in the rudimentary structural modelling described in Chapter 10.3.2), and after that, provided a general frame for the historical comparison with classroom ethnographies from the 1970s and 80s (Chapter 10.3.3).

12. Similarly, once the relevance of Williams' notions of hegemony and practical consciousness was established, the associated 'structures of feeling' idea presented itself (Chapter 9.3), and this then prompted more focused investigation of how ideology came together with fantasy and sexual desire in posh and Cockney stylisation – lines of investigation which, once again, drew in new subsets of empirical data. With genre, Fairclough's theoretical discussion of 'interdiscursivity' provided a way of understanding how classroom activity took shape at the intersection of both educational and popular cultural commitments (Chapter 3.7), and Bauman's view of how genres can become the focus of intense ideological contestation helped explicate the relevance of my analyses to wider public discussion.

13. The relationship between Vološinov's behavioural and established ideologies is a central problem in Part III (cf. Chapter 6.4), and elsewhere I draw on Bakhtin's ideas about genre (Chapters 2.6, 3.8), stylisation (Chapter 6.3), indexicality (Chapter 8.5), the 'authoritative word' (Chapter 5.5), 'internally persuasive' discourse and 'ideological becoming' (Chapter 9.6).

References

Abercrombie, N. & A. Warde, with R. Deem, S. Penna, K. Soothill, J. Urry, A. Sayer & S. Walby. 2000. *Contemporary British Society. 3rd Edition.* Cambridge: Polity Press.

Abrahams, R. 1976. *Talking Black.* Rowley, MA: Newbury House.

1984. Goffman reconsidered: pros and players. *Raritan: A Quarterly Review.* 3(4): 76–94.

Agha, A. 2003. The social life of cultural value. *Language and Communication.* 23: 231–273.

Alexander, J. (ed.) 1988. *Durkheimian Sociology: Cultural Studies.* Cambridge: Cambridge University Press.

Andersen, E. 1990. *Speaking with Style: The Sociolinguistic Skills of Children.* London: Routledge.

Anderson, B. 1983. *Imagined Communities: Reflections on the Origin and Spread of Nationalism.* London: Verso.

Anderson, P. 1977. The antimonies of Antonio Gramsci. *New Left Review.* 100: 1–78.

Androutsopoulos, J, & A. Scholz. 2003. Spaghetti Funk: appropriations of hip-hop culture and rap music in Europe. *Popular Music and Society.* 26(4): 489–505.

Antaki, C. 1998. Identity ascriptions in their time and place: 'Fagin' and 'the terminally dim'. In C. Antaki and S. Widdicombe (eds.) *Identities in Talk.* London: Sage. 71–86.

Antaki, C. & S. Widdicombe. 1998. Identity as an achievement and as a tool. In C. Antaki and S. Widdicombe (eds.) *Identities in Talk.* London: Sage. 1–14.

Appadurai, A. 1990 Disjuncture and difference in the global cultural economy. In M. Featherstone, (ed.) *Theory, Culture and Society.* London: Sage 295–310.

Appadurai, A. & C. Breckenridge. 1988. Why public culture. *Public Culture Bulletin.* 1: 5–9.

Arthur, J. 2001. Codeswitching and collusion: classroom interaction in Botswana primary schools. In M. Heller and M. Martin-Jones (eds.) *Voices of Authority.* Westport, CT: Ablex 57–76.

Atkinson, P. 1985. *Language, Structure and Reproduction: An Introduction to the Sociology of Basil Bernstein*. London: Methuen.

Audit Commission. 2000. *Money Matters: School Funding and Resource Management*. London: Audit Office. http://www.audit-commission. gov.uk.

Auer, J. 1990. A discussion paper on code-alternation. *ESF Network on Code-switching and Language Contact: Papers for the Workshop on Concepts, Methodology and Data*. Strasbourg: European Science Foundation. 69–91.

Auer, P. (ed.) 1998. *Codeswitching in Conversation*. London: Routledge.

Auer, P. & Ý. Dirim. 2003. Socio-cultural orientation, urban youth styles and the spontaneous acquisition of Turkish by non-Turkish adolescents in Germany. In J. Androutsopoulos and A. Georgakopoulou (eds.) *Discourse Constructions of Youth Identities*. Amsterdam: John Benjamins. 223–246.

Back, L. 1996. *New Ethnicities and Urban Culture*. London: University College London Press.

Baker, P. & J. Eversley. 2000. *Multilingual Capital*. London: Battlebridge Publications.

Bakhtin, M. 1968. *Rabelais and his World*. Cambridge, MA: Massachusetts Institute of Technology Press.

1981. *The Dialogic Imagination*. Austin, TX: University of Texas Press.

1986. The problem of speech genres. In *Speech Genres and Other Late Essays*. Austin, TX: University of Texas Press. 60–102.

Barber, M. 1997. *A Reading Revolution: How We can Teach Every Child to Read Well*. London: Institute of Education.

Barnes, D., J. Britten & H. Rosen. 1969. *Language, the Learner and the School*. Harmondsworth: Penguin.

Basso, K. 1979. *Portraits of 'the White Man': Linguistic Play and Cultural Symbols among the Western Apache*. Cambridge: Cambridge University Press.

Bauman, R. [1975] 2001. Verbal art as performance. American Anthropologist. 77: 290–311. (Also in A. Duranti (ed.) 2001 *Linguistic Anthropology: A Reader*. Oxford: Blackwell 165–188.)

1986. *Story, Performance and Event: Contextual Studies of Oral Narrative*. Cambridge: Cambridge University Press.

1987. The role of performance in the Ethnography of Speaking. *Working Papers and Proceedings of the Center for Psycho-social Studies* 11. University of Chicago.

1989. Performance. In E. Barnouw (ed.) *International Encyclopedia of Communications Volume 3*. New York, NY: Oxford University Press. 262–266.

1996. Transformations of the Word in the production of Mexican festival drama. In M. Silverstein and G. Urban (eds.) *Natural Histories of Discourse*. Cambridge: Cambridge University Press. 301–328.

2001. Genre. In A. Duranti (ed.) *Key Terms in Language and Culture*. Oxford: Blackwell. 79–82.

Bauman, R. & C. Briggs. 1990. Poetics and performance as critical perspectives on language and social life. *Annual Review of Anthropology*. 19: 59–88.

Bauman, R. & J. Sherzer. 1989. Introduction to the second edition. In R. Bauman and J. Sherzer (eds.) *Explorations in the Ethnography of Speaking: Second Edition*. Cambridge: Cambridge University Press. ix–xxvii.

Bauman, R. & J. Sherzer (eds.). 1974. *Explorations in the Ethnography of Speaking: Second Edition*. Cambridge: Cambridge University Press.

Bauman, Z. 1992. *Intimations of Post-modernity*. London: Routledge.

1998. *Globalisation: The Human Consequences*. Cambridge: Polity Press.

Bausinger, H. 1984. Media, technology and daily life. *Media, Culture and Society* 6: 343–351.

Baxter, J. 2002. A juggling act: a feminist post-structuralist analysis of girls' and boys' talk in the secondary classroom. *Gender and Education* 14(1): 5–19.

Becker, A. 1995. *Beyond Translation: Essays towards a Modern Philology*. Ann Arbor, MI: University of Michigan Press.

Becker, H. S. 1971. Footnote. In M. Wax, S. Diamond and F. Gearing (eds.). *Anthropological Perspectives on Education*. New York, NY: Basic Books. 3–27.

Bell, A. 1984. Language style as audience design. *Language in Society*. 13(2): 145–204.

2001. Back in style: Reworking audience design. In P. Eckert and J. Rickford (eds.) *Style and Sociolinguistic Variation*. Cambridge: Cambridge University Press. 139–169.

Berger, P. & T. Luckman. 1966. *The Social Construction of Reality*. Harmondsworth: Penguin.

Bernstein, B. 1975. Ritual in education. In *Class, Codes and Control Volume 3: Towards a Theory of Educational Transmissions*. London: Routledge and Kegan Paul. 54–66.

1971a. *Class, Codes and Control Volume 1*. London: Routledge and Kegan Paul.

1971b. On the classification and framing of educational knowledge. In M. F. D. Young (ed.) *Knowledge and Control*. London: Collier-Macmillan. 47–69.

1996. *Pedagogy, Symbolic Control and Identity*. London: Taylor and Francis.

1999. Official knowledge and pedagogic identities. In F. Christie (ed.) *Pedagogy and the Shaping of Consciousness*. London: Continuum. 246–261.

Besnier, N. 1990. Language and affect. *Annual Review of Anthropology*. 19: 419–451.

Beynon, J. 1985. *Initial Encounters in the Secondary School*. Lewes: Falmer Press.

Billig, M. 1995. *Banal Nationalism*. London: Sage.

  1999. *Freudian Repression: Conversation Creating the Unconscious*. Cambridge: Cambridge University Press.

Blair, T. 1999. *E-Commerce*: (Speech by the Prime Minister, Tony Blair, 13.9.99).

Blakemore, D. 1992. *Understanding Utterances*. Oxford: Blackwell.

Bloch, M. 1975. Introduction. In M. Bloch (ed.) *Political Language and Oratory in Traditional Society*. New York, NY: Academic Press. 1–28.

  1998. *How We Think They Think: Anthropological Approaches to Cognition, Memory, and Literacy*. Colorado, CO: Westview Press.

Blom, J. P. & J. Gumperz. 1972. Social meaning in linguistic structure: Codeswitching in Norway. In J. Gumperz and D. Hymes (eds.) *Directions in Sociolinguistics*. Oxford: Blackwell. 407–434.

Blommaert, J. 2004. *Discourse: A Critical Introduction*. Cambridge: Cambridge University Press.

Blommaert, J., J. Collins, M. Heller, B. Rampton, S. Slembrouck & J. Verschueren (eds.). 2003. *Ethnography, Discourse and Hegemony*. Special issue of *Pragmatics* 13(1).

Blumer, H. 1969. *Symbolic Interaction*. Berkeley CA: University of California Press.

Boaks, P. 1998. Languages in schools. In A. Moys (ed.) *Where Are We Going with Languages?* London: Nuffield Foundation. 34–43.

Bourdieu, P. 1977. *Outline of a Theory of Practice*. Cambridge: Cambridge University Press.

  1991. *Language and Symbolic Power*. Cambridge: Polity Press.

Bourdieu, P. & J.-C. Passeron. 1977. *Reproduction in Education, Society and Culture: 2nd Edition*. London: Sage.

Bourne, J. 1988. 'Natural acquisition' and a 'masked pedagogy'. *Applied Linguistics*. 9(1). 83–99.

Bradley, H. 1996. *Fractured Identities: Changing Patterns of Inequality*. Cambridge: Polity Press.

Brah, A. 1996. *Cartographies of Diaspora*. London: Routledge.

Branaman, L. & N. Rhodes. 1998. *A National Survey of Foreign Language Instruction in Elementary and Secondary Schools*. Washington, DC: Centre for Applied Linguistics.

Brandt, G. 1986. *The Realisation of Anti-racist Teaching*. Lewes: Falmer Press.

Briggs, C. 1993. Personal sentiments and polyphonic voices in Warao women's ritual wailing. *American Anthropologist*. 95(4): 929–957.

Brown, P. & S. Levinson. 1987. *Politeness*. Cambridge: Cambridge University Press.

Bucholtz, M. 1999. You da man: narrating the racial other in the production of white masculinity. *Journal of Sociolinguistics*. 3(4): 443–460.

Burawoy, M. 1990. The limits of Wright's analytic Marxism and an alternative. In E. Wright (ed.) *The Debate on Classes*. London: Verso. 78–99.

Burawoy, M. et al. 1991. *Ethnography Unbound*. Berkeley CA: University of California Press.

Cameron, D. 1990. Demythologising sociolinguistics: Why language does not reflect society. In J. Joseph and T. Taylor (eds.) *Ideologies of Language*. London: Routledge. 79–96.

1995. *Verbal Hygiene*. London: Routledge.

1996. The language–gender interface: challenging co-optation. V. Bergvall, J. Bing and A. Freed (eds.) *Rethinking Language and Gender Research*. London: Longman. 31–53.

Cameron, D., E. Frazer, P. Harvey, B. Rampton & K. Richardson. 1992. *Researching Language: Issues of Power and Method*. London: Routledge.

Cameron, D. & D. Kulick. 2003. *Language and Sexuality*. Cambridge: Cambridge University Press.

Candela, A. 1999. Students' power in classroom discourse. *Linguistics and Education* 10(2): 139–163.

Carter, B. & A. Sealey. 2000. Language, structure and agency: what can realist social theory offer to sociolinguistics? *Journal of Sociolinguistics*. 4(1): 3–20.

Carter, R. 1992. LINC: The final chapter? *BAAL Newsletter*. 42: 16–19.

1999. Standard grammars, spoken grammars: some educational implications. In T. Bex and R. Watts (eds.) *Standard English: The Widening Debate*. London: Routledge. 149–168.

Castells, M. 1996. *The Rise of the Network Society*. Oxford: Blackwell.

Cazden, C. 1985. Classroom discourse. In M. Wittrock (ed.) *Handbook of Research on Teaching*. 3rd Edition. London: Macmillan. 432–463.

1989. Contributions of the Bakhtin circle to 'communicative competence'. *Applied Linguistics* 10(2): 116–127.

Cazden, C., V. John & D. Hymes (eds.). 1972. *Functions of Language in the Classroom*. Columbia, MO: Teachers College Press.

Chick, K. & N. Hornberger. 2001. Co-constructing school safetime: safetalk practices in Peruvian and South African classrooms. In M. Heller and M. Martin-Jones (eds.) *Voices of Authority*. Westport, CT: Ablex. 31–56.

Clark, H. 1996. *Using Language*. Cambridge: Cambridge University Press.

Clark, J.T. 1998. *'Can Anyone Say what is Reasonable?': Promoting, Accommodating to, and Resisting Elite Rhetorical Inquiry in a High-School Classroom*. Unpublished PhD Dissertation, Graduate School of Arts and Sciences, Georgetown University, Washington, DC.

2003. Abstract inquiry and the patrolling of black/white borders through linguistic stylisation. In R. Harris and B. Rampton (eds.) *Language, Ethnicity and Race: A Reader*. London: Routledge. 303–313.

Coggle, P. 1993. *Do You Speak Estuary English?* London: Bloomsbury.

Cohen, I. 1987. Structuration theory. In A. Giddens and J. Turner (eds.) *Social Theory Today*. Cambridge: Polity Press. 273–308.

Cohen, P. 1988. The perversions of inheritance: studies in the making of multi-racist Britain. In P. Cohen and H. S. Bains, (eds.) *Multi-Racist Britain*. Basingstoke: Macmillan. 9–120.

Cohen, R. 1997. Diasporas in the age of globalization. Chapter 7. in *Global Diasporas: An Introduction*. London: University College London Press. 155–176.

Collins, J. 1987. Conversation and knowledge in bureaucratic settings. *Discourse Processes* 10: 303–319.

   1996. Socialisation to text: structure and contradiction in schooled literacy. In M. Silverstein and G. Urban (eds.) *Natural Histories of Discourse*. Cambridge: Cambridge University Press. 203–228.

Comaroff, J. & J. Comaroff. 1992. *Ethnography and the Historical Imagination*. Colorado, CO: Westview Press.

Cook, G. 2000. *Language Play, Language Learning*. Oxford: Oxford University Press.

Corfield, P. (ed.) 1991. *Language, History and Class*. Oxford: Blackwell.

Coulmas, F. (ed.) 1997. *The Handbook of Sociolinguistics*. Oxford: Blackwell.

Coupland, J., N. Coupland and J. Robinson 1992. 'How are you?': Negotiating phatic communion. *Language in Society* 21(2): 207–230.

Coupland, N. 1995. Pronunciation and the rich points of culture. In J. Windsor-Lewis (ed.) *Studies in English and General Phonetics: In Honour of J. D. O'Connor*. London: Routledge. 310–319.

   1997. Language, ageing and ageism: a project for applied linguistics? *International Journal of Applied Linguistics*. 7(1): 26–48.

   1998. What is sociolinguistic theory? *Journal of Sociolinguistics* 2(1): 110–117.

   2001a. Dialect stylisation in radio talk. *Language in Society* 30(3): 345–376.

   2001b. Introduction: sociolinguistic theory and social theory. In N. Coupland, S. Sarangi and C. Candlin (eds.) *Sociolinguistics and Social Theory*. London: Longman. 1–26.

   2001c. Age in social and sociolinguistic theory. In N. Coupland, S. Sarangi and C. Candlin (eds.) *Sociolinguistics and Social Theory*. London: Longman. 185–211.

Coupland, N., S. Sarangi and C. Candlin (eds.). 2001. *Sociolinguistics and Social Theory*. London: Longman.

Crapanzo, V. 1993. Text, transference and indexicality. In J. Lucy (ed.) *Reflexive Language*. Cambridge: Cambridge University Press. 293–314.

Crowley, T. 1989. *The Politics of Discourse*. London: Routledge.

Cruttenden, A. 1986. *Intonation*. Cambridge: Cambridge University Press.

Cutler, C. 1999. Yorkville crossing: white teens, hip hop and African American English. *Journal of Sociolinguistics*. 3(4): 428–442.

Czerniewska, P. 1992. *Learning about Writing*. Oxford: Blackwell.

Davies, N. 2000. *The School Report: Why Britain's Schools are Failing*. London: Vintage.

de Certeau, M. 1984. *The Practice of Everyday Life*. Berkeley CA: University of California Press.

Delamont, S. 1983. *Interaction in the Classroom* 2nd edition. London: Methuen.

Delamont, S. & P. Atkinson. 1995. *Fighting Familiarity: Essays on Education and Ethnography*. Kresskill, NJ: Hampton Press.

DFE (Department for Education). 1995a. *English in the National Curriculum*. London: HMSO.

DfEE (Department for Education and Employment). 1998. *The National Literacy Strategy: Framework for Teaching*. London: DfEE.

  1999. *Minority Ethnic Pupils in Maintained Schools by Local Education Authority Area in England* – January 1999 (Provisional). DfEE Statistical First Release (SFR 15/1999). Government Statistical Service. http://www.dfee.gov.uk.

DES (Department for Education and Science) 1985. *Education for All: The Report of the Committee of Inquiry into the Education of Children from Ethnic Minority Groups* (Chair: Lord Swann). London: HMSO.

  1988. *Report of the Committee of Inquiry into the Teaching of English Language*. (Chair: Sir John Kingman). London: HMSO.

  1989. *English for Ages 5 to 16*. London: HMSO. (Also in B. Cox 1991. *Cox on Cox: An English Curriculum for the 1990s*. London: Hodder and Stoughton.)

DfES (Department for Education and Skills). 2002. *Languages for All: Languages for Life: A Strategy for England*. London: DfES Publications.

  2003. *14–19 Opportunity and Excellence*. http://www.dfes.gov.uk/14–19/index.shtml.

Dobson, A. 2002. *MFL Inspected: Reflections on Inspection Findings 1996/97*. London: CILT.

Douglas, M. 1966. *Purity and Danger*. London: Routledge and Kegan Paul.

Downes, W. 1984. *Language and Society*. London: Fontana.

  2000. The language of felt experience: emotional, evaluative, intuitive. *Language and Literature*. 9(2): 99–121.

Drew, P. 1987. Po-faced receipts of teases. *Linguistics* 25: 219–253.

Drew, P. & E. Holt. 1988. Complainable matters: the use of idiomatic expressions in making complaints. *Social Problems* 35(4): 398–417.

Du Bois, J. 1986. Self-evidence and ritual speech. In W. Chafe and J. Nichols (eds.) *Evidentiality*. New Jersey, NJ: Ablex. 313–336.

Duranti, A. 1988. Ethnography of speaking: toward a linguistics of the praxis. In F. Newmeyer (ed.) *Linguistics: The Cambridge Survey*.

Volume 4. Language: The Sociocultural Context. Cambridge: Cambridge University Press. 210–228.

1997. *Linguistic Anthropology.* Cambridge: Cambridge University Press.

2001. Linguistic anthropology: History, ideas, and issues. In A. Duranti (ed.) *Linguistic Anthropology: A Reader.* Oxford: Blackwell. 1–38

2003. Language as culture in US anthropology. *Current Anthropology.* 44(3): 323–335.

Durkheim, E. 1912. The elementary forms of religious life. In W. Pickering, *Durkheim on Religion* London: Routledge and Kegan Paul, 1975.

1972. *Selected Writings* (edited by A. Giddens). Cambridge: Cambridge University Press.

Eagleton, T. 1984. *The Function of Criticism.* London: Verso.

Eckert, P. 2000. *Linguistic Variation as Social Practice.* Oxford: Blackwell.

Eckert, P. & S. McConnell-Ginet. 1992. Think practically and look locally: language and gender as community-based practice. *Annual Review of Anthropology.* 21: 461–490.

Eco, U. 1992. A guide to the neo-television of the 1980s. In Z. Baranski and R. Lumley (eds.) *Culture and Conflict in Post-War Italy.* London: Macmillan. 245–255.

Edwards, A. & D. Westgate. 1994 *Investigating Classroom Talk (2nd edition).* Lewes: Falmer Press.

Edwards, D. & N. Mercer. 1987. *Common Knowledge.* London: Methuen.

Erickson, F. 2001. Co-membership and wiggle room: some implications of the study of talk for the development of social theory. In N. Coupland, S. Sarangi and C. Candlin (eds.) *Sociolinguistics and Social Theory.* London: Longman. 152–182.

Erickson, F. & J. Shultz. 1982. *The Counsellor as Gatekeeper.* New York, NY: Academic Press.

Erikson, E. 1969. The development of ritualisation. In D. Cutler (ed.) *The World Year Book of Religion: The Religious Situation.* Volume 1. London: Evans. 711–733.

Esarte-Sarries, V. & M. Byram. 1989. The perception of French people by English students. *Language, Culture and Curriculum.* 2: 153–165.

Fairclough, N. 1989. *Language and Power.* London: Longman.

Fairclough, N. (ed.) 1992a. *Critical Language Awareness.* London: Longman. 1992b. *Discourse and Social Change.* Cambridge: Polity Press.

1995. *Critical Discourse Analysis.* London: Longman.

Fasold, R. 1990. *The Sociolinguistics of Language.* Oxford: Blackwell.

Ferguson, C. 1976. 'The Collect as a form of discourse' and 'The structure and use of politeness formulas'. In C. Ferguson 1996. *Sociolinguistic Perspectives* (edited by T. Huebner). Oxford: Oxford University Press. 124–132 and 133–147.

Fiddick, J. 1999. *Immigration and Asylum.* Research Paper 99/16. London: House of Commons Library.

Finnegan, E. & D. Biber. 2001. Register variation and social dialect variation: the Register Axiom. In P. Eckert and J. Rickford (eds.) *Style and*

Sociolinguistic Variation. Cambridge: Cambridge University Press. 235–267.

Finnegan, R. 2001. 'Not the message': media, meanings and magicality. In H. Knoblauch and H. Kotthoff (eds.) *Verbal Art across Cultures*. Tübingen: Gunter Narr Verlag. 33–62.

Fischer, C. 1985. Studying technology and social life. *Urban Affairs Annual Review* 28: 284–300.

Foley, D. 1990. *Learning Capitalist Culture*. Philadelphia, PA: University of Pennsylvania Press.

Foley, W. 1997. *Anthropological Linguistics*. Oxford: Blackwell.

Foucault, M. 1962. *The Archaeology of Knowledge*. London: Tavistock.

  1977. *Discipline and Punish*. Harmondsworth: Penguin.

  1980. *Power/Knowledge: Selected Interviews and Other Writings 1972–1977 by Michel Foucault*. (edited by C. Gordon). Brighton: Harvester Press.

  1982. The subject and power. In H. Dreyfus and P. Rabinow (eds.) *Michel Foucault: Beyond Structuralism and Hermaneutics*. New York, NY: Harvester Wheatsheaf. 208–226.

Foulkes, P. & G. Docherty (eds.). 1999. *Urban Voices: Accent Studies in the British Isles*. London: Edward Arnold.

Fowler, R. 1988. Notes on critical linguistics. In R. Steele and T. Threadgold (eds.) *Language Topics Volume 2*. Amsterdam: Benjamins.

Frazer, E. & N. Lacey. 1993. *The Politics of Community*. Hemel Hempstead: Harvester Wheatsheaf.

French, P. & M. MacLure. 1983. Teachers' questions, pupils' answers: an investigation of questions and answers in the infant classroom. In M. Stubbs and W. Hillier (eds.) *Readings on Language, Schools and Classrooms*. London: Methuen. 193–211.

Frith, S. 1996a. Music and identity. In S. Hall and P. du Gay (eds.) *Questions of Cultural Identity*. London: Sage. 108–128.

  1996b. *Performing Rites: Evaluating Popular Music*. Oxford: Oxford University Press.

Fuller, M. 1984. Black girls in a London comprehensive school. In M. Hammersley and P. Woods (eds.) *Life in School: The Sociology of Pupil Culture*. Milton Keynes: Open University Press. 77–88.

Furlong, V. 1976. Interaction sets in the classroom: towards a study of pupil knowledge. In M. Hammersley and P. Woods (eds.) *The Process of Schooling*. London: Routledge and Kegan Paul. 160–169.

Furlong, V. 1985. *The Deviant Pupil*. Open University Press.

Gal, S. & J. Irvine. 1995. The boundaries of languages and disciplines: how ideologies construct difference. *Social Research* 62(4): 967–1001.

Gal, S. 1989. Language and political economy. *Annual Review of Anthropology*. 18: 345–367.

  [1991] 2001. Language, gender and power: An anthropological review. In A. Duranti (ed.) *Linguistic Anthropology: A Reader*. Oxford: Blackwell. 420–430.

Gal, S. & K. Woolard (eds.). 2001. *Languages and Publics*. Manchester: St Jerome Press.

Gardiner, M. 1992. *The Dialogics of Critique*. London: Routledge.

Garfinkel, H. 1967. *Studies in Ethnomethodology*. Cambridge: Polity Press.

Garrett, P., N. Coupland, & A. Williams. (1999). Evaluating dialect in discourse: teachers' and teenagers' responses to young English speakers in Wales. *Language in Society* 28(3): 321–354.

Gee, J., G. Hull and C. Lankshear. 1996. *The New Work Order*. London: Allen and Unwin.

Geertz, C. 1973. *The Interpretation of Cultures*. London: Hutchinson.

Giddens, A. 1976. *New Rules of Sociological Method*. London: Hutchinson.

   1984. *The Constitution of Society*. Cambridge: Polity Press.

   1990. *Social Theory and Modern Sociology*. Cambridge: Polity Press.

   1991. *Modernity and Self-Identity: Self and Society in the Late Modern Age*. Cambridge: Polity Press.

Gilbert, P. 1988. Authorship in the writing classroom. In S. De Castell, A. Luke and C. Luke (eds.) *Language, Authority and Criticism*. Lewes: Falmer Press.

Giles, H. & P. Powesland. 1975. *Speech Style and Social Evaluation*. New York, NY: Academic Press.

Gillborn, D. 1997. Ethnicity and educational performance in the United Kingdom: racism, ethnicity, and variability in achievement. *Anthropology and Education Quarterly*. 28(3): 375–393.

Gillborn, D. & C. Gipps. 1996. *Recent Research on the Achievement of Ethnic Minority Pupils*. London: OFSTED.

Gillborn, D. & H. Mirza. 2000. *Educational Inequality. Mapping Race, Class and Gender: a Synthesis of Research Evidence*. London: OFSTED.

Gillespie, M. 1995. *Television, Ethnicity and Cultural Change*. London: Routledge.

Gilroy, P. 1987. *There Ain't no Black in the Union Jack*. London: Hutchinson.

   1993. *The Black Atlantic: Modernity and Double Consciousness*. London: Verso.

Gimson, A. 1970. *An Introduction to the Pronunciation of English (2nd Edition)*. London: Edward Arnold.

Goffman, E. 1959. *The Presentation of Self in Everyday Life*. Harmondsworth: Penguin.

   1963. *Stigma*. Harmondsworth: Penguin.

   1967. *Interaction Ritual*. Harmondsworth: Penguin.

   1971. *Relations in Public*. London: Allen Lane.

   1974. *Frame Analysis*. Harmondsworth: Penguin.

   1981. *Forms of Talk*. Oxford: Blackwell.

   1983. The interaction order. *American Sociological Review*. 48: 1–17.

Goodwin, C. & M. Goodwin. 1987. Children's arguing. In A. Grimshaw (ed.) *Conflict Talk*. Cambridge: Cambridge University Press. 200–248.

Goodwin, M. 1990. *He-Said-She-Said*. Bloomington, IN: Indiana University Press.

Goodwin, M. & C. Goodwin. [2000] 2001. Emotion within situated activity. In A. Duranti (ed.) *Linguistic Anthropology: A Reader*. Oxford: Blackwell. 239–257.

Goulbourne, H. 1998. *Race Relations in Britain Since 1945*. London: Macmillan.

Grabiner, Lord. 2000. *The Informal Economy*. London: HMSO.

Grahame, P. & Jardine, D. 1990. Deviance, resistance, and play: a study in the communicative organization of trouble in class. *Curriculum Inquiry*. 20(3): 283–304.

Grimes, R. 1985. *Research in Ritual Studies*. Metuchen, NJ: Scarecrow Press.

Gumperz, J. 1982. *Discourse Strategies*. Cambridge: Cambridge University Press.

    1986. Interactional sociolinguistics in the study of schooling. In J. Cook-Gumperz (ed.) *The Social Construction of Literacy*. Cambridge: Cambridge University Press. 45–68.

    1999. On interactional sociolinguistic method. In S. Sarangi and C. Roberts (eds.) *Talk, Work and Institutional Order*. Berlin: Mouton de Gruyter. 453–472.

Gumperz, J. & J. Cook-Gumperz. 1982. Introduction: language and the communication of social identity. In J. Gumperz (ed.) *Language and Social Identity*. Cambridge: Cambridge University Press. 1–21.

Gumperz, J., T. Jupp & C. Roberts. 1979. *Crosstalk: A Study of Cross-cultural Communication*. Southall, Middlesex: National Centre for Industrial Language Training.

Günthner, S. & H. Knoblauch. 1995. Culturally patterned speaking practices – The analysis of communicative genres. *Pragmatics* 5(1): 1–32.

Gutierrez, K., B. Rymes & J. Larson. 1995. Script, counterscript and under-life in the classroom. *Harvard Educational Review*. 65(3).

Hall, S. 1988. New ethnicities. In A. Rattansi and J. Donald, (eds.), 1992. *'Race', Culture and Difference*. London: Sage/The Open University. 252–259.

    1990. Cultural identity and diaspora. In J. Rutherford (ed.) *Identity: Community, Culture, Difference*. London: Lawrence and Wishart. 222–237.

    1996. Introduction: who needs identity? In S. Hall and P. du Gay (eds.) *Questions of Cultural Identity*. London: Sage. 1–17.

Halliday, M. 1978. *Language as a Social Semiotic*. London: Arnold.

Hammersley, M. 1974. The organisation of pupils' participation. *Sociological Review*. August 359–368.

    1976. The mobilisation of pupil attention. In M. Hammersley and P. Woods. (eds.) *The process of Schooling*. London: Routledge and Kegan Paul 104–115.

    1992. *What's Wrong with Ethnography?* London: Routledge.

Hammersley, M. & P. Atkinson. 1995. *Ethnography: Principles in Practice (Second Edition)*. London: Routledge.

Hammersley, M. & G. Turner. 1984. Conformist pupils? In Hammersley and P. Woods (eds.) *Life in School: The Sociology of Pupil Culture*. Milton Keynes: Open University Press 161–175.

Hammersley, M. & P. Woods. (eds.). 1984. *Life in School*. Milton Keynes: Open University Press.

Handelman, D. 1977. Play and ritual: complementary forms of metacommunication. In A. Chapman and H. Foot (eds.) *It's a Funny Thing, Humour*. Oxford: Pergamon. 185–192.

Hanks, W. 1987. Discourse genres as a theory of practice. *American Ethnologist*. 14(4): 668–692.

   1996. *Language and Communicative Practices*. Colorado, CO: Westview Press.

Hannerz, U. 1987. The world in creolisation. *Africa* 57(5): 546–559.

   1992a. *Cultural Complexity*. New York, NY: Columbia University Press.

   1992b. The global ecumene as a network of networks. In A. Kuper (ed.) *Conceptualising Society*. London: Routledge and Kegan Paul. 34–56.

   1996. *Transnational Connections*. London: Routledge.

Harris, R. 1997. Romantic bilingualism: time for a change? In C. Leung and C. Cable. (eds.) *English as an Additional Language: Changing Perspectives*. Watford: National Association for Language Development in the Curriculum (NALDIC). 14–27.

   2002. *Notes on classroom data analysis*. Manuscript King's College London.

   2004. *New Ethnicities and Language Use*. Unpublished Ph.D. Dissertation, Dept. of Sociology, Goldsmiths' College, London University.

Harris, R., C. Leung & B. Rampton. 2001. Globalisation, diaspora and language education in England. In D. Block and D. Cameron *Globalisation and Language Teaching*. London: Routledge. 29–46.

Harris, R. & B. Rampton (eds.). 2003. *The Language, Ethnicity and Race Reader*. London: Routledge.

Hartley, D. 1997. *Re-schooling society*. London: Falmer Press.

Heap, J. 1985. Discourse in the production of classroom knowledge: reading lessons. *Curriculum Inquiry* 15(3): 245–279.

Heath, S. 1982. What no bedtime story means: narrative skills at home and school. *Language in Society* 11(1): 49–76.

   1983. *Ways with Words*. Cambridge: Cambridge University Press.

Heller, M. 1989. Speech economy and social selection in educational contexts. *Discourse Processes*. 12: 377–390.

   1995. Language choice, social institutions and symbolic domination. *Language in Society*. 24(3): 373–405.

   1999. *Linguistic Minorities and Modernity: A Sociolinguistic Ethnography*. London: Longman.

Henry, M., B. Lingard, F. Rizvi & S. Taylor. 1999. Working with/against globalization in education. *Journal of Education Policy*. 14(1): 85–97.

Heritage, J. 1984a. *Garfinkel and Ethnomethodology.* Oxford: Blackwell.

   1984b. A change-of-state token and aspects of its sequential placement. In
      M. Atkinson and J. Heritage (eds.) *Structures of Social Action.*
      Cambridge: Cambridge University Press. 299–345.

   1997. Conversation analysis and institutional talk: analysing data. In
      D. Silverman (ed.) *Qualitative Research: Theory, Method, Practice.*
      London: Sage. 161–182.

Hesmondhalgh, D. 2002. Popular music audiences and everyday life. In
   D. Hesmondhalgh and K. Negus (eds.) *Popular Music Studies.*
   London: Edward Arnold. 117–130.

Hewitt, R. 1986. *White Talk Black Talk.* Cambridge: Cambridge University
   Press.

   1992. Language, youth, and the destabilisation of ethnicity. In
      C. Palmgren, K. Lovgren and G. Bolin (eds.) *Ethnicity in Youth
      Culture.* Stockholm: Youth Culture at Stockholm University. 27–41.

Hey, V. 1997. Northern accent and Southern comfort: subjectivity and
   social class. In P. Mahony and C. Zmroczek (eds.) *Class Matters:
   'Working Class' Women's Perspectives on Social Class.* London:
   Taylor and Francis. 140–151.

Hill, J. 1993. Hasta la vista, baby: Anglo Spanish in the American
   Southwest. *Critique of Anthropology.* 13: 145–176.

   1995. Junk Spanish, covert racism, and the (leaky) boundary between
      public and private spheres. *Pragmatics* 5(2): 197–212.

Hoechsman, M. 1997. Benetton culture: marketing difference to the new
   global consumer. In H. Riggins (ed.) *The Language and Politics of
   Exclusion.* London: Sage. 183–202.

Holland, D., D. Skinner, W. Lachicotte & C. Cain. 1998. *Identity and Agency
   in Cultural Worlds.* Massachusetts MA: Harvard University Press.

Holmes, D. & G. Russell. 1999. Adolescent CIT use: Paradigm shifts for
   educational and cultural practices? *British Journal of the Sociology of
   Education* 20(1): 69–78.

Holmes, J. 1992. *An Introduction to Sociolinguistics.* London: Longman.

Honey, J. 1989. *Does Accent Matter?* London: Faber and Faber.

   1997. *Language is Power: The Story of Standard English and its Enemies.*
   London: Faber and Faber.

Hudson, R. 1980. *Sociolinguistics.* Cambridge: Cambridge University Press.

   1996. *Sociolinguistics: Second Edition.* Cambridge: Cambridge
   University Press.

Hudson, R. & A. Holloway. 1977. *Variation in London English.*
   Unpublished manuscript. Dept. of Phonetics and Linguistics,
   University College London.

Humphries, S. 1981. *Hooligans or Rebels? An Oral History of Working-
   Class Childhood and Youth 1889–1939.* Oxford: Blackwell.

Hutchins, E. 1993. Learning to navigate. In S. Chaiklin and J. Lave (eds.)
   Understanding Practice. Cambridge: Cambridge University Press.
   35–63.

Hymes, D. [1969] 1999. The use of anthropology: critical, political, personal. In D. Hymes (ed.) *Rethinking Anthropology*. Ann Arbor, MI:
University of Michigan Press. 3–79.

1972. On communicative competence. In J. Pride and J. Holmes (eds.)
Sociolinguistics. Harmondsworth: Penguin. 269–293.

1975. Breakthrough into performance. In D. Ben-Amos and K. Goldstein
(eds.) *Folklore: Performance and Communication*. The Hague:
Mouton. 11–74.

1980. *Language in Education: Ethnolinguistic Essays*. Washington, DC:
Centre for Applied Linguistics.

1996. *Ethnography, Linguistics, Narrative Inequality*. London: Taylor
and Francis.

1999. Introduction to the Ann Arbor Paperbacks edition. In D. Hymes
(ed.) *Reinventing Anthropology*. Ann Arbor, MI: Ann Arbor
Paperbacks. v–xlix.

Irvine, J. 1989. When talk isn't cheap: language and political economy.
American Ethnologist 16(2): 248–267.

1990. Registering affect: heteroglossia in the linguistic expression of
emotion. In C. Lutz and L. Abu-Lughod (eds.) *Language and the
Politics of Emotion*. Cambridge: Cambridge University Press.
126–161.

2001. 'Style' as distinctiveness: The culture and ideology of linguistic
differentiation. In P. Eckert and J. Rickford (eds.) *Style and
Sociolinguistic Variation*. Cambridge: Cambridge University Press.
21–43.

Jakobson, R. 1960. Concluding statement: linguistics and poetics.
In T. Sebeok (ed.) *Style in Language*. Massachusetts NY:
Massachusetts Institute of Technology Press.

James, W. 1978. *Pragmatism and the Meaning of Truth*. Massachusetts,
MA. Harvard University Press.

Jameson, F. 1984. Post-modernism, or the cultural logic of late capitalism.
New Left Review 146: 53–92.

Jernudd, B. 1993. Planning English language acquisition in ESL and EFL
societies: development and maintenance of languages and cultures.
Journal of Multilingual and Multicultural Development. 14:
135–150.

Ji, F. Y. K. & S. Shu. 1990. Language and revolution: Formulae of the
Cultural Revolution. *Language in Society* 19(1): 61–79.

Johnstone, B. 1997. *The Linguistic Individual*. Oxford: Oxford University
Press.

1999. Uses of Southern-sounding speech by contemporary Texas women.
Journal of Sociolinguistics. 3(4): 505–522.

Joseph, J. & T. Taylor (eds.). 1990. *Ideologies of Language*. London:
Routledge.

Kachru, B. 1982. Introduction: the other side of English. In B. Kachru (ed.)
The Other Tongue: English across Cultures. Oxford: Pergamon. 1–12.

Kamberellis, G. 2000. Hybrid discourse practices and the production of classroom (multi)cultures. In R. Mahalingam and C. McCarthy (eds.) *Multicultural Curriculum: New Directions for Social Theory, Practice and Policy*. London: Routledge. 261–285.

2001. Producing heteroglossic classroom (micro)cultures through hybrid discourse practice. *Linguistics and Education*. 12(1): 85–125.

Kamberellis, G. & L. de la Luna. 1996. Constructing multiculturally relevant pedagogy: Signifying the basal. In D. Leu, C. Kinzer and K. Hinchman (eds.) *Forty-Fifth yearbook of the National Reading Conference*. Chicago: National Reading Conference. 329–344.

Kapferer, J. 1981. Socialisation and the symbolic order of the school. *Anthropology and Education Quarterly*. 12(4): 258–274.

Katriel, T. 1985. *Brogez*: Ritual and strategy in Israeli children's conflicts. *Language in Society*. 14(4): 467–490.

1987. *Bexibùdim!:* Ritualised sharing among Israeli children. *Language in Society*. 16(3): 305–320.

Kelly, A. 1987. *Science for Girls*. Milton Keynes: Open University Press.

Kerswill, P. 1987. Levels of linguistic variation in Durham. *Journal of Linguistics*. 23: 25–49.

Knoblauch, H. & H. Kotthoff. 2001. The aesthetics and proto-aesthetics of communication. In H. Knoblauch and H. Kotthoff (eds.) *Verbal Art across Cultures*. Tübingen: Gunter Narr Verlag. 7–32.

Kramsch, C. 1993. *Context and Culture in Language Teaching*. Oxford: Oxford University Press.

2000. Social discursive constructions of self in L2 learning. In J. Lantolf (ed.) *Sociocultural Theory and Second Language Learning*. Oxford: Oxford University Press. 133–153.

Kress, G. [1982] 1994. *Learning to Write*. London: Routledge.

1986. Language in the media: The construction of the domains of public and private. *Media, Culture and Society*. 8: 395–419.

Kroskrity, P. 2004. Language ideologies. In A. Duranti (ed.) *A Companion to Linguistic Anthropology*. Oxford: Blackwell. 496–517.

Kroskrity, P, B. Schieffelin & K. Woolard (eds.). 1992. Special Issue on Language Ideologies. *Pragmatics*. 2(3): 235–456.

Kuipers, J. 1984. Place, names, and authority in Weyéwa ritual speech. *Language in Society*. 13(4): 455–466.

1990. *Power in Performance*. Philadelphia, PA: University of Pennsylvannia Press.

Kulick, D. & B. Schieffelin 2004. Language socialisation. In A. Duranti (ed.) *A Companion to Linguistic Anthropology*. Oxford: Blackwell. 349–368.

Kulick, D. 2003. No. *Language and Communication*. 23: 139–151.

Labov, W. 1969. The logic of non-standard English. In J. Alatis (ed.) *Georgetown Monographs on Language and Linguistics 22*. Washington, DC: Georgetown Press. 1–22, 26–31.

1972a. *Sociolinguistic Patterns*. Oxford, Blackwell.

1972b. Rules for ritual insults. In *Language in the Inner City*. Oxford: Blackwell.

1982. Objectivity and commitment in linguistic science: the case of the Black English trial in Ann Arbor. *Language in Society*. 11: 161–201.

Lambert, W. 1972. A social psychology of bilingualism. In J. Pride and J. Holmes (eds.) *Sociolinguistics*. Harmondsworth: Penguin. 336–349.

Lave, J. & E. Wenger. 1991. *Situated Learning: Legitimate Peripheral Participation*. Cambridge: Cambridge University Press.

Laver, J. 1975. Communicative functions of phatic communion. In A. Kendon, R. Harris and M. Key (eds.) *Organisation of Behaviour in Face-to-face Interaction*. The Hague: Mouton 215–238.

Lawton, D. 1994. *The Tory Mind on Education 1979–94*. London: The Falmer Press.

Layder, D. 1993. *New Strategies in Social Research*. Oxford: Polity Press.

LeCompte, M. & J. Goetz. 1982. Problems of reliability and validity in ethnographic research. *Review of Educational Research*. 52(1): 31–60.

Lee, A. 1996. *Gender, Literacy, Curriculum*. London: Taylor and Francis.

LePage, R. 1988. Some premises concerning the standardisation of languages, with special reference to Caribbean Creole English. *International Journal of the Sociology of Language*. 71: 25–36.

LePage, R. & A. Tabouret-Keller. 1985. *Acts of Identity*. Cambridge: Cambridge University Press.

Levinson, S. 1979. Activity types and language. *Linguistics*. 17(5/6): 356–399.

1983. *Pragmatics*. Cambridge: Cambridge University Press.

Lightbown, P. & N. Spada. 1993. *How Languages are Learned*. Oxford: Oxford University Press.

Lippi-Green, R. 1997. *English With An Accent*. London: Routledge.

Livingstone, S. & M. Bovill. 1999. *Young People, New Media*. London: London School of Economics.

Lo, A. 1999. Codeswitching, speech community membership, and the construction of ethnic identity. *Journal of Sociolinguistics*. 3(4): 461–479.

Lucy, J. 1993. *Reflexive Language*. Cambridge: Cambridge University Press.

Ludwig, J. 1983. Attitudes and expectations: a profile of female and male students of college French, German and Spanish. *Modern Language Journal*. 67: 216–227.

Lüger, H.-H. 1983. Some aspects of ritual communication. *Journal of Pragmatics*. 7: 695–711.

Lukes, S. 1975. Political ritual and social integration. *Sociology*. 9: 289–308.

Lutz, C. & L. Abu-Lughod (eds.). 1990. *Language and the Politics of Emotion*. Cambridge: Cambridge University Press.

Mac An Ghaill, M. 1988. *Young, Gifted and Black*. Milton Keynes: Open University Press.

Macaulay, R. 1987. The social significance of Scottish dialect humour. *International Journal of the Sociology of Language.* 65: 53–63.

1997. *Standards and Variation in Urban Speech.* Amsterdam: John Benjamins.

Mahony, P. & C. Zmroczek. 1997. Why class matters. In P. Mahony and C. Zmroczek (eds.) *Class Matters: 'Working-Class' Women's Perspectives on Social Class.* London: Taylor and Francis. 1–7.

Marginson, S. 1999. After globalization: emerging politics of education. *Journal of Education Policy.* 14(1): 19–31.

Marx, K. & F. Engels 1970. *The German Ideology.* (edited by C. J. Arthur). London: Lawrence and Wishart.

McDermott, R. 1988. Inarticulateness. In D. Tannen (ed.) *Linguistics in Context: Connecting Observation and Understanding.* New Jersey, NJ: Ablex. 37–68.

1993. The acquisition of a child by a learning disability. In S. Chaiklin and J. Lave (eds.) *Understanding Practice.* Cambridge: Cambridge University Press. 269–305.

McDermott, R. & K. Gospodinoff. 1981. Social contexts for ethnic borders and school failure. In H. Trueba, G. Guthrie and G. Au (eds.) *Culture and the Bilingual Classroom.* Rowley: Newbury House. 212–236. (also in R. Harris and B. Rampton (eds.) 2003. *The Language, Ethnicity and Race Reader.* London: Routledge. 276–290.)

McDermott, R., K. Gospodinoff & J. Aron. 1978. Criteria for an ethnographically adequate description of concerted activities and their contexts. *Semiotica* 24(3/4): 245–275.

McDermott, R. & H. Tylbor. 1986. On the necessity of collusion in conversation. In S. Fisher and A. Dundas-Todd (eds.) *Discourse and Institutional Authority: Medicine, Education and Law.* New York, NY: Ablex. 123–139.

McDermott, R. & H. Varenne. 1996. Culture, development, disability. In R. Jessor, A. Colby and R. Shweder (eds.) *Ethnography and Human Development.* Chicago, IL: Chicago University Press. 101–126.

McDowell, J. 1983. The semiotic constitution of Kamsà ritual language. *Language in Society.* 12(1): 23–46.

McElhinny, B. 2003. Fearful, forceful agents of the law: ideologies about language and gender in police officers' narratives about the use of physical force. *Pragmatics* 13(2): 254–284.

Measor, L. & P. Woods. 1984. *Changing Schools: Pupil Perspectives on Transfer to a Comprehensive.* Milton Keynes: Open University Press.

Mehan, H. 1979. *Learning Lessons.* Cambridge, MA: Harvard University Press.

1985. The structure of classroom discourse. In T. van Dijk (ed.) *Handbook of Discourse Analysis Volume 3.* New York, NY: Academic Press.

Mercer, K. 1994. *Welcome to the Jungle.* London: Routledge.

Mertz, E. 1985. Beyond symbolic anthropology: introducing semiotic mediation. In E. Mertz and R. Parmentier (eds.) *Semiotic Mediation: Sociocultural and Psychological Perspectives*. New York, NY: Academic Press.

1996. Recontextualisation as socialisation: text and pragmatics in the law school classroom. In M. Silverstein and G. Urban (eds.) *Natural Histories of Discourse*. Cambridge: Cambridge University Press. 229–252.

Mey, J. 1993. *Pragmatics: An Introduction*. Oxford: Blackwell.

Milroy, J. 1999. The consequences of standardisation in descriptive linguistics. In T. Bex and R. Watts (eds.) *Standard English: The Widening Debate*. London: Routledge. 16–39.

Milroy, J. & L. Milroy. 1985. *Authority in Language*. London: Routledge.

Milroy, L. 1999. Standard English and language ideology in Britain and the United States. In T. Bex & R. Watts (eds.) *Standard English: The Widening Debate*. London: Routledge. 173–206.

2000. Conversation, spoken language and social identity. In P. Eckert and J. Rickford (eds.) *Style and Sociolinguistic Variation*. Cambridge: Cambridge University Press. 268–278.

Mitchell, J. C. 1984. Case studies. In R. Ellen (ed.) *Ethnographic Research: A Guide to General Conduct*. London: Academic Press. 237–241.

Mitchell, R. 2000. Applied linguistics and evidence-based classroom practice: the case of foreign language grammar pedagogy. *Applied Linguistics*. 21(3): 281–303.

2003. Rethinking the concept of progression in the National Curriculum for Modern Foreign Languages: a research perspective. *Language Learning Journal* 27: 15–23.

Mitchell, R. & C. Martin. 1997. Rote learning, creativity and 'understanding' in classroom foreign language teaching. *Language Teaching Research*. 1(1): 1–27.

Mitchell-Kernan, C. 1971. *Language Behaviour in a Black Urban Community*. Language Behaviour Research Laboratory Monograph 2. Berkeley CA: University of California Press.

Moerman, M. 1988. *Talking Culture*. Philadelphia PA: University of Pennsylvania Press.

Moores, S. 2000. *Media and Everyday Life in Modern Society*. Edinburgh: Edinburgh University Press.

Mugglestone, L. 1995. *Talking Proper*. Oxford: Clarendon Press.

Myers, F. & D. Brenneis. 1984. Introduction: language and politics in the Pacific. In D. Brenneis and F. Myers (eds.) *Dangerous Words*. New York, NY:

Ochs, E. 1979. Transcription as theory. In E. Ochs and B. Schieffelin (eds.) *Developmental Pragmatics*. New York, NY: Academic Press. 43–72.

1996. Linguistic resources for socialising humanity. In J. Gumperz and S. Levinson (eds.) *Rethinking Linguistic Relativity*. Cambridge: Cambridge University Press. 438–469.

Ochs, E. & B. Schieffelin. 1989. Language has a heart. *Text.* 9(1): 7–25.

Opie, I. & P. Opie. 1959. *The Language and Lore of Schoolchildren.* Oxford: Oxford University Press.

Ortner, S. 1991. Reading America: preliminary notes on class and culture. In R. Fox (ed.) *Recapturing Anthropology: Working in the Present.* Santa Fe: School of American Research Press. 164–189.

O'Sullivan, T. 1998. Nostalgia, revelation and intimacy: tendencies in the flow of modern, popular television. In D. Lusted and C. Geraghty (eds.) *The Television Studies Book.* London: Edward Arnold. 175–209.

Papastergiadis, N. 2000. *The Turbulence of Migration: Globalization, Deterritorialization and Hybridity.* Cambridge: Polity Press.

Parkin, D. 1977. Emergent and stabilised multilingualism: polyethnic peer groups in urban Kenya. In H. Giles (ed.) *Language, Ethnicity and Intergroup Relations.* New York, NY: Academic Press. 185–210.

1984. Political language. *Annual Review of Anthropology.* 13: 345–365.

Pendle, M. 2002. The crisis of 'identity' in high modernity. *British Journal of Sociology.* 53(1): 1–18.

Pennycook, A. 1994. *The Cultural Politics of English as an International Language.* London: Longman.

Philips, S. U. 1972. Participant structures and communicative competence: Warm Springs Indian children in community and classroom. In C. Cazden, D. Hymes and V. John (eds.) *Functions of Language in the Classroom.* New York, NY: Teachers College Press. 370–394.

Phillipson, R. 1992. *Linguistic Imperialism.* Oxford: Oxford University Press.

Pilkington, A. 2000. *Poetic Effects.* Amsterdam: John Benjamins.

Pollard, A. 1979. Negotiating deviance and 'getting done' in primary classrooms. In L. Barton and R. Meighan (eds.) *Schools, Pupils and Deviance.* Driffield: Nafferton Books.

1985. *The Social World of the Primary School.* London: Holt, Rhinehard, Winston.

Pomerantz, A. 1986. Extreme case formulations: a way of legitimising claims. *Human Studies.* 9: 219–330.

Portes, A. 1997. *Globalization from Below: The Rise of Transnational Communities.* Oxford: ESRC Transnational Communities Working Paper WPTC-98–01. http://www.transcomm.oxford.ac.uk.

Potter, R. 1995. *Spectacular Vernaculars: Hip-Hop and the Politics of Postmodernism.* New York, NY: State University of New York Press.

Pratt, M. L. 1987. Linguistic Utopias. In N. Fabb, D. Attridge, A. Duranti & C. McCabe (eds.) *The Linguistics of Writing.* Manchester: Manchester University Press. 48–66.

Preston, D. 1982. Lusty language learning: confessions on acquiring Polish. *Maledicta.* 6: 117–120.

1989. *Sociolinguistics and Second Language Acquisition.* Oxford: Blackwell.

Pujolar, J. 2001 *Gender, Heteroglossia and Power: A Sociolinguistic Study of Youth Culture*. Berlin: Mouton de Gruyter.

Quirk, R. 1990. Language varieties and standard language. *English Today*. 21: 3–10.

Quirk, R. & S. Greenbaum. 1973. *A University Grammar of English*. London: Longman.

Qureshi, K. & Moores, S. 1999. Identity remix: tradition and translation in the lives of young Pakistani Scots. *European Journal of Cultural Studies*. 2(3): 311–330.

Ramdin, R. 1987. *The Making of the Black Working Class in Britain*. Aldershot: Gower.

Rampton, B. 1990. Displacing the 'native speaker': expertise, affiliation and inheritance. *ELT Journal*. 44(2): 97–101.

1991. Second language learners in a stratified multilingual setting. *Applied Linguistics*. 12(3): 229–248.

1995a. *Crossing: Language and Ethnicity among Adolescents*. London: Longman. (2004: Second edition. Manchester: St Jerome Press).

1995b. Language crossing and the problematisation of ethnicity and socialisation. *Pragmatics*. 5(4): 485–514.

1997. Retuning in applied linguistics? *International Journal of Applied Linguistics*. 7(1): 3–25.

1998a. Language crossing and the redefinition of reality. In P. Auer (ed.) *Code-switching in Conversation*. London: Routledge. 290–320.

1998b. Speech community. In J. Verschueren, J.-O. Östman, J. Blommaert and C. Bulcaen (eds.) *Handbook of Pragmatics*. Amsterdam: Benjamins. 1–34. (Also available as *WPULL* 15 at http://www.kcl. ac.uk/depsta/education/ULL/wpull.html)

1999. Sociolinguistics and cultural studies: new ethnicities, liminality and interaction. *Social Semiotics*. 9(3): 355–373.

2000a. Continuity and change in views of society in Applied Linguistics. In H. Trappes-Lomax (ed.) *Change and Continuity in Applied Linguistics*. Clevedon: Multilingual Matters.

2000b. Multilingualism and heteroglossia in and out of school: end of project report. *Working Papers in Urban Language and Literacies* 12. London: King's College. http://www.kcl.ac.uk/depsta/education/ULL/wpull.html.

2001a. Language crossing, 'Crosstalk' and cross-disciplinarity in sociolinguistics. In N. Coupland, S. Sarangi and C. Candlin (eds.) *Sociolinguistics and Social Theory*. London: Longman. 261–296.

2001b. Critique in interaction. *Critique of Anthropology*. 21(1): 83–107.

Rampton, B., R. Harris & C. Dover. 2002. Interaction, media culture and adolescents at school: end of project report. *Working Papers in Urban Language and Literacies* 20. http://www.kcl.ac.uk/education/wpull.html.

Rampton, B., R. Harris & C. Leung. 2002. Education and speakers of languages other than English. *Working Papers in Urban Language and Literacies 18*. King's College London. http://www.kcl.ac.uk/education/wpull.html.

Rampton, B., C. Leung & R. Harris. 1997. Multilingualism in England. *Annual Review of Applied Linguistics*. 17: 224–241.

Rappoport, R. 1999. *Ritual and Religion in the Making of Humanity*. Cambridge: Cambridge University Press.

Reay, D. 1998. Rethinking social class: qualitative perspectives on class and gender. *Sociology*. 32(2): 259–275.

Richards, C. 1998. *Teen Spirits: Music and Identity in Media Education*. London: University College London Press.

Rivers, W. 1964. *The Psychologist and the Foreign Language Teacher*. Chicago, IL: University of Chicago Press.

Roberts, C., M. Byram, A. Barro, S. Jordan & B. Street. 2001. *Language Learners as Ethnographers*. Clevedon: Multilingual Matters.

Romaine, S. 1984. *The Language of Children and Adolescents*. Oxford: Blackwell.

Rose, E. & associates. 1969. *Colour and Citizenship: A Report on British Race Relations*. Oxford: Oxford University Press.

Rothenbuhler, E. 1998. *Ritual Communication*. London: Sage.

Ryan, E. & H. Giles (eds.). 1982. *Attitudes to Language Variation*. London: Edward Arnold.

Sansone, L. 1995. The making of black youth culture: lower-class young men of Surinamese origin in Amsterdam. In V. Amit-Talai and H. Wulff (eds.) *Youth Cultures: A Cross-cultural Perspective*. London: Routledge. 114–143.

Sapir, E. 1931. Communication. In *Encyclopedia of the Social Sciences*. New York, NY: Macmillan. 4: 78–81. (Reproduced in D. Mandelbaum. (ed.) 1949 *Selected Writings of Edward Sapir in Language, Culture and Personality*. Berkeley, CA: University of California Press. 104–109.)

   1949. *Edward Sapir: Selected Writings in Language, Culture and Personality*. (edited by D. Mandelbaum) Berkeley, CA: University of California Press.

   2002. *The Psychology of Culture: A Course of Lectures*. (edited by J. Irvine.) Berlin: Mouton de Gruyter.

Sarangi, S. & C. Roberts (eds.). 1999. *Talk, Work and Institutional Order*. Berlin: Mouton de Gruyter.

Sarangi, S. & S. Slembrouck. 1996. *Language, Bureaucracy and Social Control*. London: Longman.

Schegloff, E. 1988. Goffman and the analysis of conversation. In P. Drew and A. Wootton (eds.) *Erving Goffman: Exploring the Interaction Order*. Oxford: Polity Press. 89–135.

   1999. Naivete vs sophistication or discipline vs self-indulgence: a rejoinder to Billig. *Discourse and Society*. 10(4): 577–582.

Schieffelin, B. & E. Ochs. 1986. Language socialisation. *Annual Review of Anthropology*. 15: 163–191.

Schiffrin, D. 1994. *Approaches to Discourse*. Oxford: Blackwell.

Schulz, R. 1998. Foreign language education in the United States: trends and challenges. *ERIC Review*. 6(1): 6–13.

Scott, J. 1990. *Domination and the Arts of Resistance*. New Haven: Yale University Press.

Sebba, M. 1993. *London Jamaican*. London: Longman.

Sefton-Green, J. (ed.). 1998a. *Digital Diversions: Youth Culture in the Age of Multimedia*. London: University College London Press.

1998b. Introduction: Being young in the digital age. In J. Sefton-Green (ed.) *Digital Diversions: Youth Culture in the Age of Multimedia*. London: University College London Press. 1–20.

Shils, E. 1969. Ritual and crisis. In D. Cutler (ed.) *The World Year Book of Religion: The Religious Situation*. Volume 1. London: Evans. 733–749.

Shipley, J. T. (ed.). 1970. *Dictionary of World Literary Terms*. London: George Allen and Unwin.

Silverman, D. 1998, *Harvey Sacks: Social Science and Conversation Analysis*. Oxford: Polity Press.

1999. Warrior or collaborators: reworking methodological controversies in the study of institutional interaction. In S. Sarangi and C. Roberts (eds.) *Talk, Work and Institutional Order*. Berlin: Mouton de Gruyter. 401–425.

Silverstein, M. 1976. Shifters, linguistic categories, and cultural description. In K. Basso and H. Selby (eds.) *Meaning in Anthropology*. Albuquerque, NM: University of New Mexico. 11–55.

1979. Language structure and linguistic ideology. In P. Clyne, W. Hanks and C. Hofbauer (eds.) *The Elements*. Chicago, IL: Chicago Linguistic Society. 193–248.

1981. The limits of awareness. *Sociolinguistic Working Paper No 84*. Austin, TX: Southwest Educational Development Laboratory.

1985. Language and the culture of gender. In E. Mertz and R. Parmentier (eds.) *Semiotic Mediation*. New York, NY: Academic Press. 219–259.

1996. Monoglot 'Standard' in America: standardisation and metaphors of linguistic hegemony. In D. Brenneis and R. Macaulay (eds.) *The Matrix of Language: Contemporary Linguistic Anthropology*. Colorado, CO: Westview Press. 284–306.

1999. NIMBY goes linguistics: conflicted 'voicings' from the culture of local language communities. In S. Billings, J. Boyle and A. Griffith (eds.) *Proceedings from the Panels of the Chicago Linguistic Society's Thirty-fifth Meeting*. Chicago, IL: Chicago Linguistic Society. Volume 35(2): 101–123.

Silverstein, M. & G. Urban (eds.). 1996. *Natural Histories of Discourse*. Cambridge: Cambridge University Press.

Silverstone, R. & E. Hirsch (eds.). 1992. *Consuming Technologies*. London: Routledge.

Skeggs, B. 1997. *Formations of Class and Gender*. London: Sage.

Sontag, S. 1967. *Against Interpretation*. London: Eyre and Spottiswoode.

Sperber, D. & D. Wilson. 1986. *Relevance*. Oxford: Blackwell.

1975. *Rethinking Symbolism*. Cambridge: Cambridge University Press.

Spitulnik, D. 1997. The social circulation of media discourse and the mediation of communities. *Journal of Linguistic Anthropology*. 6(2): 161–187.

2001. Media. In A. Duranti (ed.) *Key Terms in Language and Culture*. Oxford: Blackwell. 143–146.

Stallybrass, P. & A. White. 1996. *The Politics and Poetics of Transgression*. London: Methuen.

Stanworth, M. 1981. *Gender and Schooling: A Study of the Sexual Divisions in the Classroom*. London: Hutchinson.

Stanworth, M. 1984. Girls on the margins: a study of gender divisions in the classroom. In A. Hargreaves and P. Woods (eds.) *Classrooms and Staffrooms*. Milton Keynes: Open University Press. 95–128.

Stedman-Jones, G. 1983. *Languages of Class: Studies in English Working Class History 1832–1982*. Cambridge: Cambridge University Press.

Stern, H. 1983. *Fundamental Concepts of Language Teaching*. Oxford: Oxford University Press.

Strecker, I. 1988. *The Social Practice of Symbolisation: An Anthropological Analysis*. London: Athlone Press.

Street, B. 1984. *Literacy in Theory and Practice*. Cambridge: Cambridge University Press.

Stubbs, M. 1976. *Language, Schools and Classrooms*. London: Methuen.

1986. *Educational Linguistics*. London: Blackwell.

Stubbs, M. & W. Hillier (eds.). 1983. *Readings on Language, Schools and Classroom*. London: Methuen.

Szuchewycz, B. 1994. Evidentiality in ritual discourse: the social construction of religious meaning. *Language in Society*. 23(3): 389–410.

Tannen, D. 1989. *Talking Voices*. Cambridge: Cambridge University Press.

Tate, N. (Chief Executive, School Curriculum and Assessment Authority) 1996. *Cultural Values and Identity*. Speech made at SCAA Conference on Curriculum, Culture and Society Conference 7.2.96.

ten Have, P. 1999. *Doing Conversation Analysis*. London: Sage.

Thompson, E. P. 1978. *The Poverty of Theory and Other Essays*. London: Merlin.

Thompson, J. 1984. *Studies in the Theory of Ideology*. Cambridge: Polity Press.

Tiffin, J. & L. Rajasingham. 1995. *In Search of the Virtual Class: Education in an Information Society*. London: Routledge.

Todorov, T. 1988. Knowledge in social anthropology. *Anthropology Today*. 4(2): 2–5.

Trudgill, P. 1974. *The Social Differentiation of English in Norwich*. Cambridge: Cambridge University Press.

1975. *Accent, Dialect and the School*. London: Edward Arnold.

1983. *On Dialect*. Oxford: Blackwell.

1986. *Dialects in Contact*. Oxford: Blackwell.

1999. Standard English: what it isn't. In T. Bex and R. Watts (eds.) *Standard English: The Widening Debate*. London: Routledge. 117–128.

Trudgill, P. & H. Giles. 1983. Sociolinguistics and linguistic value judgements: correctness, adequacy and aesthetics. In P. Trudgill. *On Dialect*. Oxford: Blackwell. 201–225.

Turner, G. 1983. *The Social World of the Comprehensive*. London: Croom Helm.

Turner, V. 1969. *The Ritual Process*. London: Routledge and Kegan Paul.

1978. Encounter with Freud: The making of a comparative symbologist. In G. Spindler (ed.) *The Making of Psychological Anthropology*. Berkeley, CA: University of California Press. 558–583.

1982. *From Ritual to Theatre: The Human Seriousness of Play*. New York, NY: PAJ.

1987. *The Anthropology of Performance*. New York, NY: PAJ.

Urciuoli, B. 1996. *Exposing Prejudice: Puerto Rican Experiences of Language, Race and Class*. New York, NY: Westview Press.

van Leeuwen, T. 1999. *Speech, Music, Sound*. Basingstoke: Macmillan.

van Lier, L. 1996. *Interaction in the Language Curriculum: Awareness, Autonomy, and Authenticity*. London: Longman.

2000. From input to affordance: social-interactive learning from an ecological perspective. In J. Lantolf (ed.) *Sociocultural Theory and Second Language Learning*. Oxford: Oxford University Press. 245–260.

Varenne, H. & R. McDermott. 1998. *Successful Failure*. Colorado, CO: Westview Press.

Verschueren, J. 1999. *Understanding Pragmatics*. London: Edward Arnold.

Vološinov, V. [1927] 1976. *Freudianism: A Marxist Critique*. New York, NY: Academic Press.

1973. *Marxism and the Philosophy of Language*. Seminar Press.

Wardhaugh, R. 1998. *An Introduction to Sociolinguistics: 3rd Edition*. Oxford: Blackwell.

Watson, M. & R. McGregor. 1999. *Asylum Statistics United Kingdom 1998*. Home Office Statistical Bulletin. 10/99.

Wells, G. 1981. *Learning through Interaction*. Cambridge: Cambridge University Press.

Wells, J. C. 1982. *Accents of English. Volumes 1–3*. Cambridge: Cambridge University Press.

Williams, R. 1958. *Culture and Society*. Harmondsworth: Penguin.

1961. *The Long Revolution*. Harmondsworth: Penguin.

1977. *Marxism and Literature*. Oxford: Oxford University Press.

Willis, P. 1976. The class significance of school counter-culture. In M. Hammersley and P. Woods, (eds.) *The Process of Schooling*. London: Routledge and Kegan Paul. 188–200.

1977. *Learning to Labour: How Working Class Kids Get Working Class Jobs*. Farnborough: Saxon House.

Willis, P. & M. Trondman. 2000. Manifesto. *Ethnography* 1(1): 5–16.

Wolpe, A-M. 1988. *Within School Walls: The Role of Discipline, Sexuality and the Curriculum*. London: Routledge.

Woods, P. 1990. *The Happiest Days? How Pupils Cope with School*. London: Falmer.

Woolard, K. 1985. Language variation and cultural hegemony: Toward an integration of sociolinguistic and social theory. *American Ethnologist*. 12: 738–748.

1992. Language ideology: issues and approaches. *Pragmatics*. 2(3): 235–250.

2004. Codeswitching. In A. Duranti (ed.) *A Companion to Linguistic Anthropology*. Oxford: Blackwell. 73–94.

Woolard, K. & B. Schieffelin. 1994. Language ideology. *Annual Review of Anthropology*. 23: 55–82.

Zimmerman, D. 1998. Discourse identities and social identities. In C. Antaki and S. Widdicombe (eds.) *Identities in Talk*. London: Sage. 87–106.

Index of names

Subject index

Central High 44–47, 216
class
  & agency 219–220
  as an analytic concept 215,
    219–221, 236
  articulated views of 241, 243–252,
    319, 369
  & education ritual 206–207
  & ethnicity and race 231, 243–244,
    308–312, 314
  & high–low cultural semantic
    342–343
  & informant profiles 228, 240–241,
    242–243
  & interaction analysis 27, 28, 221, 325
  new forms of working-class
    Englishness 308–312, 314
  & race, ethnicity, gender and sexuality
    221–224, 227, 236,
    243–244, 319
  retreat from class analysis 10–11,
    215–216, 235, 238, 319, 369,
    377–379
  & schooling 43–44, 269, 375
  in sociolinguistics 228–233, 275–276
    risks of trivialising class 27, 235,
    260, 325, 328, 375–376
  & standard language 257
  & subjectivity 329, 346–349
  see also linguistic insecurity, posh &
    Cockney, sociolinguistics,
    stylisation, style-shifting
classroom discourse
  contrapuntal aesthetic 58–62, 164,
    184, 197
  exclusion of girls 63–69
  girls' assertiveness 359–360
  & historical change 81–88
  IRE and deviation from it 48–57, 56,
    70–74, 85–86

IRE in the German lessons 198,
  207–208
new classroom settlement 70–75,
  118–119
  & singing 117–120, 133
research in the 1970s and 1980s
  81–85
whole class pedagogy 29–30,
  31, 41–42, 57–58, 90, 207–208
  as a distinctive genre 75–81,
    399–401
  vs singing 109, 120–123

depth psychologies 28, 29, 234,
  329, 330–331, 349,
  373–377
condensation symbolism 198–201,
  202–203, 205, 211, 376
see also sexuality, sociolinguistics,
  stylisation
Deutsch (improvised peer group
  German) 137
acceptability to teachers 166–167
& classroom management 160–162
connotations of 195
& Creole and Panjabi crossing 160
ethnic neutrality of 167
frequency of 144, 145
in interaction 148–163
as an inversion of instructed German
  191–195, 202, 203–204
origins of 144–148
as performance 163–164
& posh & Cockney stylisation 160,
  367–368, 376
as ritual 165–166, 190–191
& singing 155–160, 164–165, 200
& sound play 153, 165
see also German as an instructed
  language